W9-BLQ-441

ANIMISM, MAGIC, AND THE DIVINE KING

By the same author
Australian Totemism

ANIMISM, MAGIC,
AND
THE DIVINE KING

GÉZA RÓHEIM

INTERNATIONAL UNIVERSITIES PRESS, INC.

New York

First published 1930
Published in the United States of America, 1972,
by International Universities Press, Inc.
New York

ISBN 0–8236–0150–1

Library of Congress Catalog Card No. 78–190281

Printed in Great Britain

FOREWORD

ANIMISM AND MAGIC

TYLOR'S *magnum opus* on *Primitive Culture* is the beginning of anthropology and primitive culture and is essentially a study of animism. " Animism characterizes tribes very low in the scale of humanity and thence ascends, deeply modified in its transmission, but from first to last preserving an unbroken continuity, into the midst of high, modern culture." " Animism is, in fact, the ground of Religion, from that of savages, up to that of civilized men." [1] It is hardly an exaggeration to say that for some decades the leading feature in anthropology was the study of animism and that the term became a catchword which explained all the secrets of primitive psychology. We have also had excellent studies on animism in European folklore, Greek, Hebrew, and all other religions. Later on it was discovered by Marett and Preuss that besides the concept of the soul and of personal entities as the leading actors in the drama of life, mankind has the idea or feeling of a force, a power, a mysterious something dubbed by anthropologists *mana* (Melanesian) or *wakan* (Sioux) or *orenda* (Iroquois). Whether this pre-animistic religion " represents a phase of human thought " prior to animism is a matter of opinion.[2] As a type of human behaviour it is equivalent to magic. But then again, considering matters from a purely empirical point of view, we find a constant and intimate relation between magic and animism.

" *La magie est la stratégie de l'animisme,*" as Reinach puts it. It is by magic that mankind takes the offensive against the world at

---

[1] E. B. Tylor, *Primitive Culture*, 1903, i, p. 426.
[2] R. R. Marett, " Pre-animistic religion," *Folk-Lore*, 1900, pp. 162–82. *Idem*, *The Threshold of Religion*, 1909, p. 115. K. Th. Preuss, " Der Ursprung der Religion und Kunst," *Globus*, lxxxvi, 1904. For a summary of these views see Róheim, " A varázserő fogalmának eredete " (*The Origin of the Mana Concept*), 1914.

large, begins to command the " spirits ", and believes that they will obey. Science is born when this illusion begins to be a reality and though the beginning of science is the end of the magical art, science itself could never have been born without this ancestry.[1]

We shall commence our investigation of these questions with the widespread mode of action called sympathetic magic, not because of the elementary processes of thought implied in these practices[2] but rather because here we actually find that the theory of animism and the practice of magic are nearly co-extensive.

From Tylor's dream-theory to Freud, who regards animism as the narcissistic and therefore natural original attitude of mankind, many views have been put forward on the origins of animism. I hope that a renewed investigation of the subject will carry me a step beyond my predecessors—the list of previous works includes my own contributions to the subject—though at the same time I recognize that the views put forward by many authors are completely justified by our data.[3] Animism means our mental past[4] ; it must therefore mean many things superimposed on each other. Future studies may attempt to determine the relative importance of these factors.

[1] S. Reinach, *Cultes, Mythes et Religions*, 1909, ii, p. xv.

[2] J. G. Frazer, *The Magic Art*, 1911, i, p. 52.

[3] The dream-theory : Tylor, op. cit. The soul as memory-image, A. E. Crawley, *The Idea of the Soul*, 1909. An individualization of the totemic principle " the latter being the same thing as society ", E. Durkheim, *Les formes élémentaires de la vie religieuse*, 1912, p. 342. As for the views put forward by psycho-analysts on the subject, see Freud, *Totem und Tabu* (Gesammelte Schriften, x), pp. 109, 112 ; S. Ferenczi, " Entwicklungs-stufen des Wirklichkeitssinnes," *Zeitschrift für Psychoanalyse*, i, p. 124 ; O. Rank, " Der Doppelgänger," *Imago*, iii, p. 97 ; Róheim, *Spiegelzauber* (Internationale Psa. Bibliothek.), 1919 ; Róheim, " Das Selbst," *Imago*, vii ; L. Kaplan, *Das Problem der Magie*, 1927.

[4] Cf. " Whereas nations have hitherto submitted to, and enforced law, and order, and undertaken costly works of utility or splendour, in large measure under the influence of animistic illusions, it is now everywhere noticeable in the more civilized countries, that these illusions are being dissipated and it is very difficult to judge how people will behave when they are gone." Carveth Read, *The Origin of Man and his Superstitions*, 1920, p. 342.

CONTENTS

vii

II THE PSYCHOLOGY OF MAGIC

symptoms.   The Gros Ventre keeper of the pipe ; it is
taboo for him to have his hair cut.   Myth of the Father
and the Pipe.   Ceremonial coitus connected with the Sun
Dance ; " The root of Man " ; homosexual identification
with the father on basis of the penis as ego-ideal.
Identification of the mother's nipple and the father's penis.
Friendship established on basis of the pipe.   The pipe of
the Omaha produces life and numerous issue, it represents
both the masculine and the feminine forces.   Male and
female pipe in the *Hako* representing the father and the
mother.   The Son and the Father are united by the Mother.
The importance of identification with the Father.

The power of the magician is derived from beings who
represent the Father-Imago.   Mana always connected with
ghosts and spirits.   Ghosts, spirits, chiefs, and medicines
are mana in Fiji.   Mana belongs to the immigrant " kava-
people " or Polynesians rather than to the Melanesians.
Identification with the gods as the source of mana.
Indecision is fatal to mana.   Complete submersion of the
ego in the ego-ideal.   Ambivalency is the attitude of the
mass ; he who has mana, i.e. the superman, is " beyond
good and evil ".   The picture tallies with Freud's view of
the Leader in the Primal Horde.   Father-Son conflict and
mana.   The beginning of morality is the end of mana in the
old sense of the word.   The mana-bearers of to-day are actors
playing a part, identifying themselves with the Leaders of the
Primal Horde.   Analogy between mana and hypnosis.   The
King as father-substitute and hypnotizer.   Prestige derived
from *præstigiæ*, i.e. from the deceitful art of the magician.
In the case of hypnosis reality is modified till it agrees with the
ego-ideal, but in Polynesia it is mana that must be in
harmony with reality.   Mana and libido.   Supernatural
influence in paranoia and the sperm.   Mana or deflected
sexual striving as the basis of society.   Ora and mana are
synonymous expressions. Ora is vitality and its chief seat is the
penis.   Another term for the same thing is *hau*, meaning
fertility.   Mana emanating from the penis.   Sadism is the
differential feature in the mental make-up of the medicine-
man and this sadism is carried over from the oral to the
anal and from the anal to the genital phase of organization.
Penis and nipple, father and mother.

By the descent of the dove the Saviour is recognized in
his capacity of Messiah, the Anointed King of Israel.   The
bird that alights on the new king bears the soul of the dead
king who must have been killed by his successor.   Thus the
Holy Ghost is really a holy ghost, the ghost of the father who

has been murdered by his son. The voice from heaven is a voice from Egypt; the pharaoh as the "beloved" or "chosen" of Ra. Parricide and castration in the myth of Osiris. The passage of the divine spirit from the body is the act of procreation. Gods die after begetting a son in their own likeness. The Easter candle which symbolizes the Holy Ghost is dipped into the water of baptism or uterus and fertilizes the water. The Holy Ghost as *digitus dexteræ patris*. Phallic meaning of the finger. The dove in Egypt represents a son who kills his father and has intercourse with the mother. Prophetic ecstasy as supernatural pregnancy. Union with the divinity; the mystic quality of this union is due to repression. The dove as mother-goddess, Ishtar. The "doves" are prostitutes. The King of Sumer and Babylon as husband of the mother-goddess. Libido displaced from the nipple to the penis, from the mother to the father. Condensation of father and mother in the medicine-man. In his ecstatic state he is over-come by the father. Apollo enters the body of Pythia through the vagina. The shaman's inspiration and his drum. The drum-stick as penis. The Yakut shaman is dressed in a woman's cloak and inspired by a spirit whom he calls "mighty bull". Homosexual shamans of the Chukchee. Ecstasy, prophecy, and pregnancy. The medium is the wife of the god. Professional activity of the medicine-man; substitute-formations of the oral, anal, and genital functions. He plays the rôle of father, mother, and child. His initiation period is oral-sadistic and melancholiac; his medical activity, obsessional and anal, while his attitude to the supernatural world is hysteric and genital.

Sadism and sublimation. The idea of projecting substances into the body of another human being derived from coitus. The False Cure and other stories. Big-Light marries the woman whom he first "shoots" (magically) and then heals. The magic fish-hook and the myth of the wife-angler. Identification with the patient. Acting the disease and the recovery. The patient as a pregnant woman, the relief obtained by disease as delivery. Patient and medicine-man; the calling of the latter is disease made permanent and sublimated into a vocation. Cure and initiation. The snout projected into the victim's mouth by the *Subach* is the mother's nipple and behind the regression to the female attitude we find the regression to the impressions received by the sucking child. Relief as castration. Pathoneurosis is the displacement of the genital function to some other part of the body. The treatment offered by the primitive medicine-man is adapted not to the organic but to the libidinal aspect of the process.

sperm. The soul and the seminal fluid. The super-ego derived from the object cathexis of the negative Oedipus complex. Father and mother, penis and nipple. The difference between the super-ego and the ego-ideal.

IV THE DIVINE KING

The original rulers carry through the unconscious desires
of their subjects and suffer the talion punishment for
them. African kings marry their sisters and daughters, they
represent a divinity, and they are regarded as sources of
fecundity or life. Apis and the phallic nature of Osiris.
Some pharaohs represent Osiris, others the Sun God. The
Sun as "Bull" or husband of his mother. Phallic
nature of Egyptian royalty and the regalia. The crown and
the secondary sex characters. The sceptre projects "life".
Conveying power and ejaculation. The Sed festival, rebirth a
mitigated form of sacrifice, death as castration. The same
elements in Baganda royalty. The Kauzumu in Uganda
acts as a scapegoat for the king and his functions are closely
connected with the sexual sphere. Other substitutes. The
king's Mother and taboo. The king stands for the infantile
period of unbroken wish-fulfilment. The boy-substitute
and castration anxiety. The phallic bull as scapegoat for
the king. Royal spears. Regicide and substitute formations.
The "Kawanauo", i.e. "he who escaped", in charge of
the king's wives. Shilluk royalty. Egyptian influence
reaches as far as the Ewe. African and ancient
Oriental royalty. The king and the Primal Sire as phallus
of the social organism. Regicide and puberty rites ; cock and
goat as substitutes for the king. Hausa king-killing and
totemism. As death appears under the guise of coitus,
kings fertilize the earth by their death. The corpse in the
bull's hide means identification with the bull, that is, the
penis. Incest, parricide, castration as outstanding features
of royalty.

Cecrops, the Serpent King, and his wife, Athena Kekropeia.
Athena as foster-mother of Erichtonios, the king of Athens.
The king represented by a wooden phallus. Serpent kings
followed by bull-kings. Theseus, fourth king of Athens, son
of the bull-god, Poseidon, kills the bull. Oriental influence and the Minotauros. Death of this second bull,
followed by the death of Aigeus, the father of Theseus.
Oschophoria and initiation. The Sacred Marriage.

The Hymn of the Kouretes. Leaping and dancing to
make the flax grow. Jumping over the Midsummer fire.
Naked couples rolling on the cornfield. Dancing. Coitus as
principal activity of the gods in Mexico. Phallic element
in *eniautos* ritual. Good wishes, fertility, and initiation in
European folklore. The Megistos Kouros as "first foot".
The *Du-thor-ambos* is the song to make Zeus "leap", i.e.

V THE SCAPEGOAT

ANIMISM, MAGIC, AND THE DIVINE KING

I ANIMISM AND THE OTHER WORLD

1 SYMPATHETIC MAGIC

AMONG the Tharumba and neighbouring tribes, if a sorcerer obtains some of the excreta, hair, nails, or other parts of the enemy's body, he takes it to a " squeaking tree " and places it between the touching surfaces of the two branches causing the " squeak ". When the wind blows, this fragment is squeezed and ground to atoms, and the owner is believed to suffer in the same way.[1] The Koko-minni blacks of the Palmer River employ an instrument known as Ti or Eti for injuring one another at a distance. It is formed of a piece of human shinbone or a slip of bamboo, the free end being covered with cement, and the whole is enclosed in a bark covering. When the magician has put some of the intended victim's hair, urine, or excrement into the bone or bamboo, he burns it and so makes his victim sick. A cure can be effected by taking the patient's spear and dilly-bag to the waterside. A supernatural serpent, visible only to the medicine man, devours these objects, and the patient is saved. The Proserpine River black makes an enemy sick by sticking a bone pin into the place where he has been defecating or micturating.[2] Among the Kabi and Wakka, to obtain possession of a man's hair or ordure was to ensure his death. He declined as these decayed. It was dangerous to pass under a leaning tree or fence. The reason alleged for caution in this respect was that a woman might have been under the tree or fence and that blood from her might have fallen upon it.

[1] R. H. Mathews, *Ethnological Notes on the Aboriginal Tribes of New South Wales and Victoria*, 1905.

[2] W. E. Roth, " Superstition, Magic, and Medicine," *North Queensland Ethnography*, Bull. 5, 1920, pp. 31, 32.

Akin to this dread of passing under an elevated object, and due no doubt to the same cause, is the fear of another person's stepping over one's body.[1]

This kind of sorcery is called *ngadhungi* by the Narrinyeri. It is practised in the following manner : every adult blackfellow is constantly on the look-out for bones of ducks, swans, or other birds, or of the fish called ponde, the flesh of which has been eaten by a human being. Of these he constructs his charms. All the natives, therefore, are careful to burn the bones of the animals which they eat, so as to prevent their enemies from getting hold of them ; but in spite of this precaution, such bones are commonly obtained by disease-makers who want them. When a man has obtained a bone—for instance, the leg bone of a duck—he imagines that he possesses the power of life and death over the man, woman, or child who ate its flesh. The bone is prepared by being scraped into something like a skewer ; a small round lump is then made by mixing a little fish oil and red ochre into a paste, and enclosing in it the eye of a Murray cod and a small piece of the flesh of a dead human body. This lump is stuck on the top of the bone and a covering tied over it, and it is put in the bosom of a corpse in order that it may derive deadly potency by contact with corruption. After it has remained there for some time it is considered fit for use, and is put away until its assistance is required. Should circumstances arise calculated to excite the resentment of the disease-maker towards the person who ate the flesh of the animal from which the bone was taken, he immediately sticks the bone in the ground near the fire so that the lump aforesaid may melt away gradually, firmly believing that as it dissolves it will produce disease in the person for whom it was designed, however distant he may be. The entire melting and dropping off of the lump is supposed to cause death.[2]

This form of magic is well known to anthropologists, and is usually, but loosely, called sympathetic magic, on account of the sympathy which is still supposed to connect the original owner with the severed part of his body. Sir James Frazer lays stress on the former connection of the severed part with the whole and speaks therefore of contagious magic.[3] It is remarkable that this well-nigh universal form of magic is conspicuous by its absence in Central Australia. We quote Spencer and Gillen.

[1] J. Mathews, *Eaglehawk and Crow*, 1899, p. 144. Id. *Two Representative Tribes of Queensland*, 1910, p. 177.
[2] Taplin, *The Narrinyeri Tribe*, 1879, p. 24.
[3] Frazer, *The Magic Art*, 1911, 1, § 3.

" In connection with the question of magic, it may be noticed, in conclusion, that a special form which is widely met with in other Australian tribes is not practised amongst these. We refer to the attempt to injure an enemy by means of securing and then practising some form of charm upon some part of his person such as hair or nail clippings." [1]

We can guess the reason of this difference. The Central Australian native dreads something else ; the loss of his churinga. If this is the real reason, we should say that the displacement of a phobia has taken place and then there must be an identical meaning underlying these two losses. Be that as it may, at any rate, we find sympathetic magic again among the Kakadu who have only the rudiments of the churinga concept. [2] On account of this magic, called *korno* (excrement), they are very careful to hide from view all excremental matter, so that their camps are more cleanly than those of other tribes. But a medicine man, of course, can find the desired *korno*. They put it in little wax spheres, dig a pit, and when the fire is hot enough the real performance begins. The men bend forward each of them with his hand between his legs, and the women do the same, because the spirit must not, on any account, see their private parts. If it were to do so they would swell enormously.

Now some feathers that have been prepared are knocked into the sphere, one by·one, the natives saying : " Keep quiet, keep quiet," the idea being that the birds they represent will thereby be persuaded not to give notice to the victim that any danger such as a snake or crocodile threatens him. Then the men sway about, looking as fierce as they possibly can, while they place the wax spheres in the peindi. Away in the distance they can hear the spirit cursing and swearing, saying : " *Mulyarinyu koiyu*," [3] and using other opprobrious expressions. The men say : " *Nerk, nerk, nerk*," and beckon it onwards. It is under a spell and comes on cursing more and more loudly. When it is near, the natives crouch down silently, the front man ready for action. On it comes like a whirlwind, rushes along the trench, scraping against the sharp Pandanus leaves. Suddenly, when it reaches the brink of the peindi, the front man knocks the stick representing it into the fire on the top of the *korno*. All of them shout : " Ah, Ah, Ah, Ach, Ach, Brng, Brng ! " at the top of their voices. Without a moment's pause, stones and earth are piled on the *Yalmuru* (soul), one specially large stone being placed on top, the men

---

[1] Spencer and Gillen, *Native Tribes*, p. 553.
[2] Cf. Róheim, *Australian Totemism*, 1925, 313, 184.
[3] Curse directed against the mother.

pressing down hard with all their might to keep it in. The spirit underneath can be heard sizzling and swearing. It tries to lift the stone, but cannot. At length it is heard to say : " Grr, Grr, u-u." Then it is quiet and all is over. The Pandanus leaves are rubbed on the top stone, while the names of different snakes, Ngabadaua, Yidaburabara, and Numberanerji, are hissed out. One or other of them is supposed to be sure to bite the victim before long. Finally a log of wood that is supposed to represent a crocodile, which it is hoped will seize him some day when he is bathing, is placed on top, and then, when the performers have smeared their bodies over with burnt cork-wood and grass, the ceremony is at an end, and they go back to camp. Anyone coming across the remains of the trench, and seeing the stones and log piled up above the small mound, knows that evil magic has been performed. It is supposed that, by the capture of the *Yalmuru*, the man is left without his protector. If, for example, he be out in the bush, there will be no spirit to warn him of approaching danger, or guide him to where he can secure his food.[1]

After having thus given a few facts from the Australian continent, we must call the reader's attention to some prominent features of this form of magic. It seems that the fundamental fear of savages is connected with the idea of a *part being separated from the whole*. This part is inserted between two branches put into a bamboo, or burnt. From the case of the Kakadu we gather the idea that the whole ceremony must have something to do with the genital act ; otherwise why do they cover the private parts and why does the bad language used by the spirit refer to the mother ?

If we make use of explanations arrived at elsewhere our work will be made easy indeed. We have shown the frequent use of the tree as a mother-symbol in Australia ; between the two branches would therefore mean between the two legs, in the vagina. The churinga is a penis-symbol, and therefore the loss of the churinga would be castration. This is curiously confirmed by the fact that Mathew, after describing sympathetic magic, passes on to the phobia of the aboriginals with regard to women's blood, a phobia that develops into a dread of passing under a tree, thus confirming our view of the symbolic equation woman (mother) = tree, and at the same time revealing the real dread as that of passing under a woman, i.e. into her vagina. The next analogy again confirms this ; they are afraid of somebody stepping over them. We have already found sufficient reason for explaining " stepping over " as a symbol of

[1] B. Spencer, *Native Tribes of the Northern Territory of Australia*, 1914, dp. 259, 260.

coitus,[1] and in point of fact, it is in coitus that a *part is separated from the whole*. This is what the whole body feels in a hallucinatory fashion, the penis itself gets nearer to this danger and finally the seminal fluid really suffers this separation.[2] From the wish-fulfilment point of view, all this refers to uterine regression, and it is also from this point of view that we may, following Ferenczi, call the penis the wish-object or ego-ideal of the body and the seminal fluid a still more "ideal" representative of the same tendency. The fundamental dread of primitive man, therefore, seems to be the dread of castration, or, what amounts to the same thing from the unconscious point of view, the dreaded expenditure of the semen.

It is very probable that the peculiar Australian punishment for breaking certain taboos, the abnormal swelling of the genitalia, is only a cover for the opposite dread (castration) and that those who are castrating their enemy in the Kakadu ceremony dread the talion punishment of their nefarious wishes.

The Kai, in New Guinea, have this phobia in a very prominent degree. They believe that anything done to their " soul-substance " is done to their whole person. As the " soul-substance " is believed to be present in every particle of his body, and in anything that may come into contact with his body, a member of these tribes is in perpetual danger of being killed by means of any careless deed of his own. Hence the great anxiety in the behaviour of these tribes. If a thread of his girdle or a lock of his hair gets entangled in the bush and torn off, he does not pass on before having annihilated every trace of its presence. He does not throw anything away, and the leavings of his meals he carefully hides or throws into the fire. Soul-substance also remains where he sat ; therefore, when he rises he makes it disappear by stamping with his leg or poking the place with a stick. Or he may sprinkle water on the place, or use " cool " leaves to cool it down, i.e. to drive the soul-substance away.[3] The black art itself is called *hafe*, i.e. to bind. The first thing is to procure a *ga*, a medium containing the soul-substance of the victim. As the soul-substance is contained in the smallest particle of the body, and in anything that comes into contact with a person, some hair, a drop of perspiration, the excrements, or anything else can be used. But it must be quite

---

[1] Cf. Róheim, "The Significance of Stepping Over," *International Journal of Psycho-analysis*, iii, p. 320. See also on the churinga *Australian Totemism*, 1925, p. 183.

[2] Ferenczi, *Genitaltheorie*, 1923.

[3] Ch. Keysser, *Aus dem Leben der Kaileute*. Neuhauss, *Deutsch Neu Guinea*, iii, p. 117.

fresh, otherwise it is possible that the soul-substance has already evaporated. As the chief thing seems to be not to let it cool down, it is therefore quickly put into a little tube of bamboo and this is hidden under the arm-pit. The object must not come into contact with water or fire. Sharp or pointed objects are also prohibited as they might frighten the soul out of the parcel. Trees from a " ghost-place " must be used for making the parcel. The first bamboo tube is put into a second, and this again into a third of correspondingly larger size. During the preparation they sing : " Cockatoo, cockatoo, come and tear his body open, and hack his bowels into pieces till he dies." The spirits are expected to come from a mythical cave and take the victim's soul with them into the other world. After various other incantations the magician finishes with the following spell :—

> " Fall off and rot like cucumbers.
> X. wind himself in pain.
> His arms and leg shall wind themselves in pain.
> His whole body shall wind itself in pain.
> His head shall wind itself in pain.
> His bowels shall wind themselves in pain.
> His genital organ shall wind itself in pain."

Now comes the application of fire to the parcel. The medicine-man is identified with the man whose soul is in the parcel and he strictly avoids water or anything that has come into contact with water. Water would cool him, and hence cool the soul he has caught. By cooling it, it would stop the " roasting ", and hence the burning pain the patient suffers from the fire would be alleviated. The other great taboo of our practitioner in the black arts is woman, presumably for the same reason. Intercourse would certainly cool him, by relieving him of sexual tension, and it seems that his tension is some-how identical with the feverish state of disease. The whole thing comes to an end at a village festival where all the parcels are finally burnt. At the moment when the bark envelope is cut through the little tubes fall to the ground, and the magicians " act " the agony of their victims.[1] At the King William Cape they call this " binding the soul ". The chief thing is that the parcel containing the hair or nail-parings should not come into contact with water.[2]

A Bukaua lives in perpetual fear of these devices, and it is therefore very difficult to get the substance needed. But they have their cunning methods. The magician offers some betel-fruit to the intended victim in a friendly manner. Before doing so, however, he pinches a small piece off the fruit and this is sufficient for magic to work on.

[1] Keysser, loc. cit., pp. 135–8.
[2] Stolz, *Die Umgebung von Kap König Wilhelm*, p. 248.

When they have made the victim ill there are two possibilities. Either " he comes back to himself " (*eng king tau*), that is, gets better, or the reverse takes place. What is meant by coming back to himself? The Bukaua tell us that a slimy excretion proceeds from people who are dangerously ill. This slime is a continuous sticky sort of jelly : it hangs down through the clefts of the floor and sparkles at night. If the victim gets better the slimy mass returns into his body, that is " he comes to himself ". But if the " undefinable mass " is torn off, loses connection with the body, then " *eng king tau tom* " (" he does not come to himself "), and the victim dies.[1]

Among the Mafulu the use of the inedible remnants of recently consumed vegetable food as a medium for causing illness and death is confined to the case of a victim who has passed the stage of very young childhood. A man or woman never carelessly throws aside his own food remnants of this character ; and his reason for this is fear of sorcery. He carefully keeps them under his control until he can take them to a river, into which he throws them, after which they are harmless as a medium against him. The fear concerning these remains is that a sorcerer will use them for a ceremony somewhat similar to that described in connection with the death of a chief, but in a hostile way. No such precautions are taken with reference to similar food eaten by very young children.

Secondly, there are the discharged excrements and urine. This, for some reason, only applies to the case of an infant or quite young child. Here again it is not possible to learn the reason for the limitation ; but it is confirmed by the fact that grown-up persons take no pains whatever to prevent the passing of these things into the possession of other people, whereas, as regards little children, the mothers or other persons having charge of them always take careful precautions. The mother picks up her little child's excrement and wraps it in a leaf, and then either carefully hides it in a hole in the ground, or throws it into the river, or places it in a little raised-up, nest-like receptacle, which is sometimes erected near the house for this purpose, and where also it is regarded as being safe. As regards the urine, she pours upon it, as it lies on the ground or on the house floor or platform, a little clean water, which she obtains from any handy source, or sometimes from a little store which, when away from other water supply, she often carries about with her for the purpose.[2]

---

[1] St Lehner, *Bukaua*. Neuhauss, loc. cit., iii, p. 464.
[2] Williamson, *The Mafulu, Mountain People of British New Guinea*, 1912, pp. 280–1.

According to Romilly the hair-cutting and the refuse of a man's meals are the chief objects for a sorcerer to work on.[1] The Marindanim call the particle of the body they obtain for a sorcery a *papahi*. Hair, excrement, the remains of food, may all serve as a *papahi*, as they all contain the soul-substance of their owner. If they put this *papahi* into a bamboo and then throw the bamboo into a swamp the person concerned will become ill, and if the *papahi* is burnt the victim will die. The idea is that while the patient is being tortured by the disease, it is really the *papahi-nakari* who are playing with the *papahi* and throwing it about. By *nakari* the Marind mean certain mythical girls who, according to their ideas, are connected with nearly everything in nature.[2]

In reconsidering this small collection of facts from New Guinea, the point we must lay stress on seems first to be that the body particle operated on seems to be identified with the soul. True, this was the case among the most northern of the Australian tribes we took into consideration, the Kakadu, but it was certainly not so prominent in Australia as in New Guinea. What the soul really is seems evident enough if we consider the belief of the Bukaua that a slimy jelly proceeds from the patient and when it falls off, he dies. The jelly is the seminal fluid and its loss in the act of cohabitation seems to be an experience fraught with such anxiety that the idea of death is modelled on it. If this explanation is valid, we can also understand why the spell of the Kai leads up to the pains in the genitalia as to a sort of climax, the other pains serving merely as an introduction to this one. Water being a very frequent symbol of woman, the two taboos of our sorcerer seem to mean the same thing ; and as he identifies himself with his victim who is to be castrated, it is both easy to see why woman should be taboo to him and why with the Marind the disease arises from the circumstance that mythical females are trifling with the tiny part that has been segregated from the whole.

In Melanesia the wizards who cure the diseases are very often the same men who cause them, the mana derived from spirits and ghosts being in both cases the agent employed ; but it often happens that the darker secrets of the magic art are possessed and practised only by those whose power lies in doing harm, and who are resorted to when it is desired to bring evil upon an enemy. Their secrets, like others connected with mana, are passed down from one generation to

---

[1] H. H. Romilly, *From my Verandah in New Guinea*, 1889, p. 83.
[2] P. Wirz, *Die Marind-anim von Holländisch-Süd-Neu-Guinea* (Hamburgische Universität), 1925, pp. 72–3.

another, and may be bought. The most common working of this malignant witchcraft is that, so common among savages, in which a fragment of food, bit of hair or nail, or anything closely connected with the person to be injured, is the medium through which the power of the ghost or spirit is brought to bear. Some relic such as a bone of the dead person whose ghost is set to work is, if not necessary, very desirable for bringing his power into the charm ; and a stone may have its mana for doing mischief. What is needed is the bringing together of the man who is to be injured and the spirit or ghost that is to injure him ; this can be done when something which pertains to the man's person can be used, such as a hair, a nail, a leaf with which he has wiped the perspiration from his face, and with equal effect when a fragment of the food which has passed into the man forms the link of union. Hence in Florida when a scrap from a man's meal could be secreted and thrown into the *vunuha* haunted by the *tindalo* ghost, the man would certainly be ill ; and in the New Hebrides, when the mae snake carried away a fragment of food into the place sacred to spirits, the man who had eaten of the food would sicken as the fragment decayed. It was for this reason that a constant care was exercised to prevent anything that might be used in witchcraft from falling into the hands of ill-wishers ; it was the regular practice to hide hair and nail-pairings and to give the remains of food most carefully to the pigs. There is little doubt that the common practice of retiring into the sea or a river has its origin in the belief that water is a bar to the use of excrement in charms. It is remarkable that at Mota where clefts in rocks are used (no doubt also for security) the word used is *tas*, which means sea. In the Banks' Islands the fragment of food, or whatever it may be, by which a man is charmed is called *garata* ; this is made up by the wizard with a bit of human bone, and smeared with a magic decoction in which it would rot away. Or the *garata* would be burnt, and while it was burning the wizard sang his charm ; as the *garata* was consumed, the wizard burning it by degrees day after day, the man from whom it came sickened, and would die, and the ghost of the man whose bone was burning would take away his life. In Aurora the fragment of food is made up with certain leaves ; as these rot and stink the man dies. In Lepers' Island the *garata* is boiled together with certain magical substances in a clam shell with charms which call on Tagaro. It is evident that no one who intends to bring mischief to a man by means of a fragment of his food will partake of that food himself, because by doing so he would bring the mischief on himself also. Hence a native offering even a single banana to a visitor will bite the end of it before he gives it, and a European giving medicine to a sick native gives confidence by himself taking a little first.[1]

It is interesting to note the ambivalency underlying these customs, for, whereas in New Guinea this pinching off is a dark practice of the magician, in fact, castration itself, here it occurs as the indication of a sort of covenant between the two parties. On the Gazelle Peninsula black magic will only take effect if the medium contains a particle of the intended victim ; for instance, his hair, a shred of his clothes, his saliva or footprints.[2] The central tribe of New Ireland call this method *mumut*. Here the magician makes two little parcels ; one of them he puts near the fire and the other he dangles over a swamp by means of a rod and a string. Now he goes to the swamp, and lo there the poor soul is sitting staring into the water ; now to the fire, there again he sees the soul warming itself.[3]

At Limbo, Vellalavella, and Rubiana all personal refuse is usually burnt from fear of wizards. Their method here is to make a parcel of leaves and dig the object into the earth. Then they tread on it and put three hot stones above—this kills the victim.[4]

In Fiji if a man desired the death of a rival he procured something that had belonged to his person—a lock of hair, the parings of his nails, a scrap of food, or, best of all, his excreta, for witchcraft produced incurable dysentery through these. The wizard then prepared the charm by wrapping the object in certain leaves of magical properties and burying the parcel in a bamboo case either in the victim's plantation or in the thatch of his house.[5] A man will take the remains of the food, clothing, or tobacco left by his enemy. With these he mixes certain leaves and slugs from the sea. He carries the mixture into the woods, puts it in empty coconuts, pieces of bamboo, or native jars. Then he buries the vessel and believes that his enemy sickens as the mixture ferments.[6]

One mode of operating is to bury a coconut, with the eye upward, beneath the temple-hearth, on which a fire is kept constantly burning ; and as the life of the nut is destroyed so the health of the person it represents will fail, till death ensues. At Matuku there is a grove

[1] R. H. Codrington, *The Melanesians*, 1891, pp. 202–4.
[2] Parkinson, *Dreissig Jahre in der Südsee*, 1907, p. 118.
[3] Parkinson, loc. cit., p. 192.
[4] R. Thurnwald, *Forschungen auf den Salomo Inseln und dem Bismarck Archipel*, i, pp. 443–4.
[5] B. Thomson, *The Fijians*, 1908, p. 164.
[6] W. Deane, *Fijian Society*, 1921, p. 162.

sacred to the god Tokalau—the wind. The priest promises the destruction of any hated person in four days if those who wish his death bring a portion of his hair, dress, or food which he has left. This priest keeps a fire burning, and approaches the place on his hands and knees. If the victim bathe before the fourth day, the spell is broken. The most common method, however, is the *Vakadranikau,* or compounding of certain leaves supposed to possess a magical power, and which are wrapped in other leaves, or put into a small bamboo case, and buried in the garden of the person to be bewitched, or hidden in the thatch of his house. Processes of this kind are the most dreaded, and the people about Mbua are reputed to prepare the most potent compounds. The native imagination is so absolutely under the control of fear of these charms that persons, hearing that they were the objects of such spells, have lain down on their mats and died through fear.

Those who have reason to suspect others of plotting against them avoid eating in their presence, or are careful to leave no fragment of food behind ; they also dispose their garment so that no part can be removed. Most natives, on cutting their hair, hide what is cut off in the thatch of their homes. Some build themselves a small house and surround it with a moat, believing that a little water will neutralize the charms which are directed against them.[1]

In New Britain the general plan is for someone who wishes to injure another man to secure something that he has touched with his mouth, and to guard against this the natives very carefully destroy the peelings of yams, the refuse of food, skins of bananas, and such-like articles. They are careful not to expectorate except by blowing the spittle out in spray, and the smallest quantity of blood falling on the ground or on a leaf would be at once carefully gathered up and destroyed. The principal ways in which these are destroyed are by burning or by throwing into the sea. Natives used to defecate in the sea, and would take great precautions to ensure that the matter was dissolved in the water.[2]

Just as the slimy substance trickles through the clefts of the floor when somebody is ill among the Bukaua, the witches of the Siauw Islands crawl under the houses, which are raised above the ground on posts, and gather up the spittle of the inmates to make them ill.[3]

[1] Thomas Williams, *Fiji and the Fijians,* 1858, i, pp. 248–9.
[2] George Brown, *Melanesians and Polynesians,* 1910, p. 233.
[3] B. C. A. I. van Dinter, " Eenige geographische en ethnographische aanteekeningen betreffende het eiland Siaoe," *Tijdschrift voor Indische Taal, Land-en Volkenkunde,* xli, 1899, p. 381. Frazer, *Taboo,* p. 288.

Among the Klemantans of Borneo an image of the victim called *tegulun* is made (literally *tegulun kalingai usa* = the reflected image of the body). The operator makes a fire beside the *tegulun*, digs a small hole in the ground and fills it with water coloured with ferruginous earth. This pool is called *Bawang Daar*, " the lake of blood." He immerses the image in the pool of reddened water and taking it out again, he thrusts a little spear into it. After this he buries the *tegulun* in the ground, covering it with earth, this being the normal burial for people who die by violence. *Bawang Daar*, the lake of blood, is the dwelling-place of the souls of those who died a violent death and here they are married to the souls of women who died in childbirth.[1]

Are we, however, justified in connecting this case with sympathetic magic ? Instead of hair or excreta we find here an image. Fortunately, we know that Malay magicians take the parings of nails, hair, eyebrows, saliva, etc., of the intended victim and they form it into a likeness of his person with beeswax.[2]

Moreover, the whole proceeding is exactly like what takes place in the case of sympathetic magic. There the parcel containing the parings is submerged in a swamp, here we have a pool of red water for the same purpose. This appears to be a symbolic representation of the Lake of Blood of the Hereafter, and it is at this lake of blood that men who die a violent death are united to the souls of women who die in childbirth. At childbirth the vagina of a woman might well be called a lake of blood, and we suspect that this meaning underlies both the symbolism of Klemantan and the various waters into which the parings are put by sorcerers.

Among the Iban, if a man finds that somebody has deposited dirt about his premises he takes a few burning sticks and thrusting them into the dirt, says : " Now let them suffer the pains of dysentery." [3] The Sea Dayak do not throw their hair into the fire, for if they did they would get headache.[4]

There is a considerable degree of uniformity in all these cases, and we shall conclude our survey of savage instances by a few cases chosen at random from Africa. The Thonga tribes are very careful to cover up their own blood should any have dripped from a wound,

---

[1] Hose and McDougall, *Pagan Tribes*, ii, 1912, pp. 40, 118.
[2] Skeat, *Malay Magic*, p. 570.
[3] Hose and McDougall, loc. cit., ii, p. 120.
[4] H. Ling Roth, *The Natives of Sarawak and British North Borneo*, 1896, i, p. 28.

because it is by means of this blood that evil magic can be worked on a man.[1]

Among the Baganda, a blade of grass which a man put into his mouth and then threw aside or a little spittle could also be used to work a spell with. Hair that had been cut or nail-parings that fell into the hands of the enemy were enough to compass a man's death. Such objects would be taken to the medicine-man, who would give the necessary advice as to how they were to be destroyed. For this reason cut or loose hairs and nail-parings were concealed in the garden of a female relative and spittle was carefully covered over so as to leave no trace of it behind.[2] Among the Kpelle the surest method of practising black magic on a person is to carry out the intended action, whether it be simply touching, cutting into pieces, or anything else, on a particle of his body such as nail-parings, hair, saliva, excrements, shadow, footprints, or anything that may have been in contact with his person. Therefore they are very careful not to let these fall into the hands of malicious sorcerers. They usually do not expectorate at all, and if unavoidable the saliva is carefully covered with earth. Hair and nail-parings are burnt ; as for defecation, it is performed into flowing, running water, and if only stagnant water is available they defecate where one of the holy totem-fish will devour the excrements. Special dogs are kept for doing the same with the excrements of children.[3]

We shall return to these data later on and find the answer to the obvious question why the excrements are safe inside the totem-fish and the hair in the garden of a female relative. For the moment, however, we intend to end our small collection of cases by some references to European folklore. In European folklore the idea of an object coming into hands that might use it for malicious purposes, the fear of a part being separated from the whole, is closely connected with witchcraft.

In Herefordshire it is regarded as extremely unlucky to borrow fire during the twelve days from 25th December to 6th January. Ill-luck can be averted by giving some trifle in return.[4] In Holderness it is very unlucky if a woman enters the house first thing on Christmas morning, and nobody would permit a light to be taken out of the house on any pretence whatever between New and Old Christmas.[5]

[1] H. A. Junod, *The Life of a South African Tribe*, 1913, ii, p. 467.
[2] Roscoe, *The Baganda*, 1911, pp. 344, 345.
[3] Westerman, *Die Kpelle*, 1921, p. 206.
[4] E. M. Leather, *Folk Lore of Herefordshire*, 1912, p. 108.
[5] Gutch, *County Folk Lore*, vi, 1912, p. 115.

Among the Wends, the taboo lasts from the 25th December to the New Year ; they believe that some damage will follow if anything is lent to anybody.[1] It is the witches that borrow things on these days.   They will have anything connected with cattle, a bucket, fork, or the like, and when they have it they use it to injure the cattle. It is taboo to borrow anything during the critical period, especially salt and fire.[2]

In Brandenburg no butter will be given out of the house at Christmas, because it is the witches who are after it.[3] The reason for all this is that sympathetic magic is practised by witches and anything they get into their hands gives them the desired object to work on.   On the 30th July, Russian witches milk cows to death at a great distance away, frequently dying themselves of a surfeit. In order to milk a cow, a witch sticks a knife into a plough, a post, or a tree ; the milk trickles along the edge of the knife and continues to do so until the cow's udder is emptied. On the eve of St George's Day, Whit-Sunday, and Midsummer Day witches go out at night without clothing, and cut chips from the doors and gates of farmyards. These they boil in a milk-pail and so charm away the milk from those farms.[4] Wend witches will milk the rope by which the cow wa bound or they cut the cow's tail off and milk that.   Sympathet magic is frequently employed against the witch herself, as she 1 become identified with the medium she works through or with 1 victim. This is what happened to a witch in Cambridgeshire.

"There was a witch there, Miss. Well, they put the chilu illness down to her. So my brother he got a bottle and filled it with water and put in some of the child's hair and a lot of other things as I can't remember, then they corked it up and put it on the fire to boil. Then when the bottle burst that would hurt the witch." And on the other hand, if you gave or lent anything to a witch then she had a hold over you.[5] The regular charm against witchcraft is to attack the witch by sympathetic magic and a part of the victim is as efficacious in this case as the excreta of the witch herself. For example, a Somerset farmer cut off the ears of his bewitched cattle and burned them " that the witch should be in misery, and could not rest till

[1] Veckenstedt, *Wendische Sagen, Märchen und abergläubische Gebräuche*, 1880, p. 436.

[2] Schulenberg, *Wendische Volkssagen und Gebräuche*, 1880, pp. 159, 246.

[3] Brandenburg, *Z. d. V. f. Vk.*, 1891, p. 178.

[4] Ralston, *The Songs of the Russian People*, 1872, p. 391.

[5] H. L. F. Lenning, " A Cambridgeshire Witch," *Folk-Lore*, xvi, pp. 189, 190.

they were plucked out ".[1] In the Western Highlands, if an evilly disposed person who possesses an evil eye gets a little milk from another he or she will be able to operate through that to injure all the milk that remains and even the cows.[2] In Silesia, if a witch manages to procure milk from a house after sunset, she will put a bag on a pole and milk the pole till the cow gives bloody milk. The counter charm is to prick needles into a blanket used in milking and the witch will appear.[3]

What is the difference between primitive and European folklore ? For the savage, everything separated from the body brings danger, and behind the danger we find, mostly though not exclusively, male beings. In Europe these ideas are rather more specified, it is concerned with dew,[4] giving away milk, fire, salt, and footprints, chips of wood, etc. We shall consider the meaning conveyed by these objects below, in the chapter on magic ; for the present it will suffice to point out that the mischief-doers are women, witches, and that as I have pointed out before, the whole fear of witchcraft seems to be centred round the dread of castration by the mother. The social atmosphere of the Middle Ages as shown many years ago by Dr Jones [5] seems to have been a particularly unhealthy one and to have favoured neurotic regression. The original anxiety is that something becomes separated from the body in the act of coitus, and this is made particularly clear by the idea of the fire and salt-stealing witch who with fire and salt steals the very pith of life.

2 The Moment of Death and the Soul

According to the Akamba, death is due to the *Aiimu* (souls) leaving the human frame and when a person dies his *Aiimu* goes and lives in a wild fig-tree. For two days after death the men of the village may not cohabit with their wives, and for about seven days they may not cut their hair.[6] When death is approaching, the Nandi say : " The soul has become very small," and just before death milk is poured into a dying person's mouth.[7] According to the Suk, a man's

[1] W. R. Halliday, " Force of Initiative in Magical Conflict," *Folk-Lore*, 1910, p. 150.

[2] R. C. Maclagan, *The Evil Eye in the Western Highlands*, 1902, p. 91.

[3] P. Drechsler, *Sitte etc. in Schlesien*, 1906, ii, pp. 247, 254.

[4] Cf. Róheim, *Magyar Néphit és Népszokások* (Hungarian Folk-Belief and Custom), 1928, pp. 45–53.

[5] Jones, *Der Alptraum*, 1912.

[6] C. W. Hobley, *Ethnology of the A-kamba*, 1910, pp. 67, 85.

[7] Hollis, *The Nandi*, 1909, p. 70.

spirit at death passes into a snake.[1] The Masai believe that the soul of a rich man or medicine-man turns into a snake as soon as the body rots.[2] According to some tribes in Madagascar, at death a worm or lizard or serpent called *fanany* emerges from the putrefying body. The *fanany* contains the soul of the deceased.[3]

According to the Ho, a man has two souls, a life-soul and a death-soul. The life-soul leaves the body at the moment of death, whereas the death-soul remains with the corpse to the grave and then goes to the other world.[4] When a man dies his breath or soul leaves him.[5] The beliefs of the Tami are remarkably like these of West Africa. Here also we have a " long " and a " short " soul, the long one leaving man at the moment of death and the other remaining close to the corpse.[6] In Buin we have an elaborate myth about the banyan-tree on the path to the other world. The tree is a sort of world-tree, for on its branches live the soul-birds of people. As often as a man is born a leaf sprouts on the tree. There is a branch for each village, and of course the leaf appears on the branch that belongs to its own village. As long as the leaf is on its branch the man to whom it belongs continues to live. If he is sick the leaf withers. If the leaf is plucked from the branch and falls to the ground, it is a human being who is dead. But just as a man or woman does not die of his own accord but by the magical intervention of somebody else, so the leaf only drops from the tree when plucked by the soul-bird.[7]

In Europe the general idea is that at death the soul leaves the body in the shape of breath, a cloud, or a bird and the windows must be opened to let it out. " During the blessing or saining of a corpse in Scotland all the windows are open to give the soul free egress. In Fuhkien they carry out a similar idea by making a hole in the roof." [8] In Tyrol the souls of the virtuous appear as white clouds coming from the mouths of the dying,[9] and among the Slovaks in Northern Hungary as white doves.[10] In Voigtland they open the window at the moment when the dying person breathes his last, so that the soul

[1] Beech, *The Suk*, 1911, p. 20.

[2] Hollis, *The Masai*, 1905, p. 307.

[3] L. Frobenius, *Die Weltanschauung der Naturvölker*, 1898, p. 52.

[4] J. Spieth, *Die Ewe Stämme*, 1906, p. 503.

[5] Spieth, loc. cit., pp. 810, 864.

[6] Neuhauss, *Deutsch Neu Guinea*, 1911, iii, p. 518.

[7] R. Thurnwald, *Forschungen auf den Salomo Inseln und dem Bismarck Archipel*, 1912, i, pp. 316, 317.

[8] *Notes and Queries*, iv, p. 350.

[9] Wuttke, *Der deutsche Volksaberglaube*, 1901, p. 458.

[10] *Ethnologische Mitteilungen aus Ungarn*, v, p. 96.

should have free egress.[1] In Silesia a case is mentioned where this was omitted and next day a cloud of smoke was hovering in the room ; it was the dead man's soul.[2] The Slovaks fumigate a dying person with burning grass, believing that his soul will fly away with the smoke. The custom of making a hole in the roof over the sufferer's head reappears in Ruthenia.[3]

A soul seems to be a being for which holes possess a remarkable attraction. According to what people believe in Dorset, it can vanish through a small hole in the window no bigger than the glasses of a pair of spectacles.[4] This side of the question we shall consider later : what we should like to know at present is what this separation from the body, this fission, can mean.

We have sufficient data in clinical analysis to believe in the ubiquitous nature of the symbol serpent-penis. This would mean that death is a second castration, for what becomes separated from the body is a serpent or a bird, a flying being, all these amounting to very much the same thing.

The external soul of the Meithei Raya appears as a serpent. This serpent is called Pakung-ba and is regarded as the ancestor of the royal family. A priestess is in attendance and she receives the serpent with certain ceremonies calculated to please it.[5] A Baya chief calls his serpent his grandfather and one of the chief blessings it can confer on him are children. The serpent's death means the death of the chief, but if the chief dies the serpent, as representative of the libido of the species, lives on.[6] But most convincing of all is the belief of the Romans in a genius. The genius is a serpent. Every man had a genius and every woman a juno. Genius and Juno were in the same relation to each other as procreation and conception. Later on, through an extension of the original meaning, the genius means also strength, energy, capacity for pleasure, the whole personality of a man, but originally it is simply the procreative faculty.[7]

Genialis lectus is the marriage bed above which the genius presides and never permits the family to lack offspring. *Geniales homines*

---

[1] I. A. E. Köhler, *Volksbrauch, Aberglauben, Sagen und andre alte Über-lieferungen im Voigtlande*, 1867, p. 251.

[2] Drechsler, *Sitte, Brauch*, ii, p. 291.

[3] W. R. S. Ralston, *The Songs of the Russian People*, 1872, p. 314.

[4] Hy. C. March, " Dorset Folklore," *Folk-Lore*, xi, p. 110.

[5] Hodson, *The Meitheis*, 1908, pp. 100, 101.

[6] Frobenius, *Und Afrika sprach*, 1913, iii, p. 182. Cf. Róheim, " Das Selbst," *Imago*, viii, p. 436.

[7] G. Wissowa, *Religion und Kultus der Römer*, 1902, p. 154.

are hospitable, friendly, genial people.[1] Undoubtedly it means the
libido, but also a second personality, connected more with pleasure
and less with reality. If a man enjoys something pleasant he says :
" *Nunc et amico meo prosperabo et genio meo multa bona faciam.*" [2]
And again the worst that could be said of a curmudgeon was " *genium
festo vix suum aestimat* ".[3] Lovers call upon him,[4] and the genius
of the husband is invoked on the wedding night.[5] The birthday is
the festival of the *genius natalis.* It seems that bloody sacrifices were
avoided on this day, just as it was taboo to kill an animal at the altar
of the Delian Apollo γενετως.[6] Naturally enough, for if the
genius is the serpent, the penis, spilling blood on this day would mean
castration. Substantially we suppose Varro was quite right when he
explained the genius as the soul.[7]

The relation between the Roman and his genius was exactly the
same as that of the Egyptian to his Ka. It is used as a pleonasm for
the individual. " Your Ka, beloved by Re," means " you ".[8] The
Ka of the King = the King. " I drink to your Ka," i.e. to your
health.[9] According to the ideas of the Egyptians, the difference
between the living and lifeless lies in the circumstance that the former
category is in possession of a Ka. " He is healthy and happy with his
Ka," means that he is alive. The hieroglyph for the Ka is a
representation of two extended arms, and it is by this movement that
the Ka is transmitted from one person to another. When the Sun God
created the first divine beings he spread his arms and endowed them
with a Ka. At death the Ka leaves the body, but yet there is hope
that it returns to re-animate the corpse from time to time.[10] According
to Steindorff, the Ka is the protecting genius of the individual.[11]

The king has a living Ka that appears behind the king as a small
juvenile human figure.[12] The Ka never gets old, it is always
youthful and appears in the guise of a child or a dwarf. Guimet

---

[1] L. Preller, *Römische Mythologie*, 1858, p. 69.
[2] Plautus, *Persai*, ii, 3.   [3] *Rheinisches Museum*, xxxiv, p. 539.
[4] Tibull., 2, 2, 4, 5.   [5] Arnobius, *Adversus nationes*, ii, 67.
[6] H. Usener, *Götternamen*, 1896, p. 297. W. Schmidt, *Geburtstag im
Altertum*, 1908, p. 23. Wissowa, loc. cit., 1902, p. 155. Tibull., ii, 2, iv, 5.
Censorinus, *De die natali*, 2. O. Jahn, *ad Pers.*, 119. Ovid, *Trist*, iii,
13, 18.
[7] Augustine, *De Civitate Dei*, vii, 1323.
[8] Erman, *Die ägyptische Religion*, 1913, p. 103.
[9] Erman, loc. cit., p. 103.   [10] Erman, loc. cit., p. 102.
[11] Steindorff, " Ka und die Grabstatuen," *Zeitschr. für aegypt. Sprache*,
xlviii, 1910, p. 152.
[12] Steindorff, loc. cit., pp. 157–9.

believes that the dwarfs who were held at the courts of Egyptian royalty were regarded as incarnations of the divine Ka.[1] Under the name of Khnumu certain dwarfs with big heads, crooked legs, and long moustaches play a conspicuous part in Egyptian mythology. Earthenware images of them are found in the tombs, for they were supposed to help in reconstituting the bodies of the dead.[2] Khnumu or Khnemu is one of the great original gods ; indeed, his name signifies " the builder ". The root *khnem* signifies " to join, to unite " : astronomically it means " conjunction ".[3] Perhaps also conjunction in the human sense, not only conjunction of the sun and moon, but also of the male and female. In this case we should be justified in regarding the dwarfs reviving the corpse as phallic demons and the dwarf representation of the Ka as an embodiment of the same concept. Now, Lefebure who translates Ka by genius, points out that the root *ka* with the bull or the phallus as determinative means a bull.[4] Loret derives the word from a root meaning " to procreate ",[5] so that we should have an exact equivalent of the Roman genius.

Instead of explaining the meaning of the moment of death, we here have regarded it as necessary to lay more stress on souls and doubles. In a paper on this subject that was published in the *Imago* we have already discussed these and some other beliefs and our conclusion was that the soul is the narcissistic double of the ego. Self-love, searching for an object, splits the individual into two beings, the active and the passive part, the one who loves and the one who is beloved, the human being and his god, the Ka. But since then analytic research has proceeded to show that the personification of the penis is the root of this second or pleasure-ego, that the primacy of the genital zone is the basis of the unity of personality. Just as the diverse non-genital erotic trends are finally melted into the genital striving, the magic qualities of every particle of the body are united in the anxiety of losing the soul. It is this anxiety that explains why the soul or soul-substance is not more frequently localized in the seminal fluid. Usually such an idea can only be shown to exist in a displaced form (soul in hair, etc.), for should this be otherwise, each coitus would be a conscious equivalent to a loss of the soul, e.g. to death.

[1] Guimet, " Les Âmes Egyptiennes," *Rev. Hist. de Relief*, (g) lxviii, 1913, p. 18.

[2] W. J. Perry, *The Children of the Sun*, 1923, p. 203. Wiedemann, *Religion*, p. 133.

[3] E. A. Wallis Budge, *The Gods of the Egyptians*, 1904, ii, p. 50.

[4] *Sphinx*, i, p. 108.

[5] Loret, *Revue Egyptologique*, 1904, xi, p. 87.

This equivalence of coitus and death is certainly the unconscious concept that is at the bottom of animism and magic. Thus, among the Kiwai Papuans a man before going to war may not cohabit with his wife as this might cause his death.[1] Going to war seems to be regarded as another form of coitus, or coitus as another shape of death or murder. On leaving for war a man is sometimes given a medicine by his wife consisting of a piece of ginger which she has kept for some time in her vulva. In the fight he will chew a little of it, spit the juice on to himself, saying : " My wife, like lightning straight where vulva I go." [2] Or an old man will chew a little ginger and squirt the juice out in the direction of the enemy, saying : " All same I go for wife, straight for thing belonging wife all same I go for that fighting place." [3] Here we have coitus, that is the expenditure of the semen, as the prototype of war, and on the next page we are told that some men send off their spirits beforehand to conquer the spirits of the enemy. It seems there is something in common between the egress of the soul from the body and of the semen from the penis.[4] In the excitement of the fight the soul of a man may jump out of his body. He forgets women, children and house, and the soul plays about like a bird.[5] In order to foretell the result of a fighting expedition an old man and woman may withdraw into the bush, where she lies down on the ground. If the man then does not feel " strong along women " he advises his companions to return home for there will be a defeat.[6] If the discharge of semen and the egress of the soul are the same thing, naturally the phallus and the semen, or urine as its substitute, contain soul-stuff. The penis of a slain foe is cut off and dried. Before a fight a small piece of it mixed with banana is given to the young warriors. One of the Mawatta leaders used to let men drink his urine from a coconut bowl in order to make them strong, " all the same fire inside," for the fighting spirit is like fire,[7] and fire is a very frequent symbol of urethral eroticism. Among the Marind-anim sperm is a very important medicine, that is according to the New Guinea view, an object containing soul-substance. It is applied to wounds or taken as a medicine and in both cases a quick healing is expected. In the Majo ceremonies it is mixed into the food administered to the novices. This is explained by saying that it makes it easier for them to digest the food, but the original idea seems to be

---

[1] G. Landtmann, "The Magic of the Kiwai Papuans in Warfare," *Journ. Roy. Anthr. In.*, 1916, p. 323.

[2] Landtmann, loc. cit., p. 355.

[3] *Idem*, loc. cit., p. 325.

[4] Loc. cit., p. 325, 326.

[5] Loc. cit., p. 330.

[6] Landtmann, loc. cit., p. 328.

[7] *Idem*, loc. cit., p. 325.

the vivifying power of the sperm. Another property of the semen is that it makes everything it comes into contact with more durable. It is also an amulet against ghosts, that is against death, for if a Marind has to leave camp in the evening alone without a firebrand, the best thing he can do is to smear sperm on his forehead. Thus he is enabled to resist the ghost.[1] In Australia we find the custom of using seminal fluid as a medicine on the Riverina.[2] In the Birripi initiation ritual the old men form a ring and commit mutual onanism, making the emission go on the boy.[3]

The idea that the male member contains life while the loss of sperm means death appears with a peculiar distinctness in the beliefs of the Maori. To begin with, we are told that the spirit (*wairua*) of a child which is frequently identical with that of an ancestor is implanted during coitus. Notwithstanding the fact that this seems to imply a definite belief and not an unconscious concept with regard to the identity of the soul and the seminal fluid, yet at the same time we find a sort of incorporation of the soul into the mantis. For if a mantis is seen upon a woman it is a sign that she has conceived and the sex of the child depends upon the sex of the insect.[4] The *wairra* or soul appears also as a butterfly. According to Maori belief, the *hau* and *wairua* of a child are implanted during coition by the father.[5] The *hau* of man seems to be the vital essence or life principle.[6] The *hau* of land is its vitality, fertility.[7] In the mind of the Maori and the Polynesian in general there is a close connection between procreative ability and great courage. The peculiar state of the virile organ of a warrior when engaged in mortal combat is a matter well recognized in Maori superstition.[8] The idea that the male organ is life, the female death, is uppermost in the mind of the Maori. " Natural death originated in the time of Tane. Tane said to his parent Rangi on the day that he forced him apart from Papa : ' Where is the *uha* ' (female organ) ? And Rangi said : ' The *whare* or *aitua* (cause

---

[1] P. Wirz, *Die Marind- anim von Holländisch Süd Neu Guinea*, 1915, ii, pp. 89, 90.

[2] P. Beveridge, *The Aborigines of Victoria and Riverina*, 1889, p. 53.

[3] G. R. Brown, " Birripi Language of the Hastings and Wilson Rivers," *Science of Man*, 1898, i, p. 89.

[4] Elsdon Best, " The Lore of the Whare Kohanga," *Journ. of the Polynesian Society*, xv, 1906, p. 2.

[5] Elsdon Best, " Spiritual Concepts of the Maori," *Journ. P.S.*, ix, p. 181.

[6] *Id.*, loc. cit. 189.   [7] *Id.*, loc. cit., 193.

[8] W. G. Gudgeon, " Phallic Emblem from Atiu Island," *Journal P.S.*, xiii, p. 193.

of death) yawns below, the abode of life is above. Even so we see the *whare* or *aitua* the passage by which man enters the world to be assailed by misfortune, by disease, by death, it is seen in woman.' " [1] " That which destroys man is the mana of the female organ." [2] An old Maori remarked to Elsdon Best : " Friend ! it seems to me that the *ora* (health, vigour, vitality) of the white men and their exemption from disease is caused by their never forgetting the *koutu mimi* (urine) at night time.   It is ever in the room to protect them. For urine represents the *tawhito* (membrum virile) and will avert witchcraft. For that organ was the life and salvation of my ancestors, and saved them from trouble and death." [3] A man will recite a spell against witchcraft, holding the membrum virile in his hands. [4] The usual explanation of death is the well-known myth of how Maui met with death in the vagina of his ancestress Hine-nui-te-po. The female organ is the *whare* or *aitua*, the cause of death. The term might also be applied to Papa the Earth-Mother, for she said to Rangi : " Our offspring shall return to me in death." The organs of generation were always deeply imbued with *tapu* and *mana*. When a person repeated a magic spell, for instance to ward off the witchcraft of others or cause their death, he would place his hands on his genital organs in order to give *mana* to the spell. [5]   " The salvation of my ancestors was the *tawhito*" [6] (sacerdotal name for the penis) a Maori said.   " By its aid were the shafts of magic warded off and life retained." *Tawhito* means the ancient one or perhaps cause, origin. Another mystical expression for the male organ is *tangata matua*. *Matua* means parent and also to quicken, [7] therefore *tangata matua* = the procreating man. The idea of the penis being a minute human being is well known in dream-symbolism and folklore [8] and the soul itself is usually conceived as a duplicate of the body, as a mannikin.

The key to the general attitude of the Maori seems to lie in the myth of Maui and Hine-nui-te-po. The female organ is the cause of death because it killed Maui. This happened when Maui entered the vagina of his ancestress Hine-nui-te-po, that is, during coition. The contrast between life and death in cohabitation seems

[1] Elsdon Best, " Maori Medical Lore," *Journal P.S.*, xiii, 215.
[2] Ibid.   [3] Loc. cit., 220.
[4] Elsdon Best, " Maori Medical Lore," *Journ. P.S.*, xiv, p. 3.
[5] Elsdon Best, "The Lore of the Whare Kohanga," *Journal P.S.*, xiv, p. 207.
[6] Loc. cit., p. 208.   [7] Tregear, loc. cit., p. 231.
[8] Cf. *Imago*, vii, p. 168.

to be between the male member standing erect (life) and its subsequent " death " after ejaculation. Therefore we might say that the soul is really the seminal fluid and it is only because the penis in the act of cohabition is in danger of being separated from the body (castration) that it enters into the unconscious concept of the soul. The Yayurveda, a collection of Indian spells and magical proceedings, has a spell for taking back the semen and with it the radiance and luck that have become lost in the act of pollution,[1] and the Aitareya Upanishad tells us that the Atman, the self or the soul of man, is contained in his semen.[2] The climax of the Yogi's art is not to let the " drop " (the semen) leave him and to compel it to return from the female organ if it is on its way ; by doing this he vanquishes death, for the drop he retains means life and the drop that falls from him is death.[3]

Further argument for our point of view might be derived by a sort of logical inversion from the beliefs found in Central Australia and New Guinea with regard to conception. Having shown in my book on Australian totemism that the ancestral ghost or his materialization, the churinga, is really the penis, we might now refer to the part played by the soul in making children, to prove its general identity with the member and substance of procreation. In fact I believe this to be a perfectly legitimate conclusion ; after having shown that " mystic " theories of procreation arise from the repression of natural knowledge it seems evident that the active agents in this supernatural procreation must be symbols of the real ones.

The natives of the Morehead and Wassi kussa rivers in Western Papua believe that an invisible something which they call *Birumbir* is the animating principle of human beings. Now this *Birumbir* is actually the embryo from which the body develops in the uterus. It comes into the uterus by way of the vulva in the form of semen.[4] But here we have to do with repression of facts that seem quite evident to us. It seems too plain for anybody to deny that the semen passes from the penis into the vulva and yet we are told that this animating principle is inserted into the woman " by an eel-like creature called Tombabwir ". Tombabwir's haunts are rivers,

---

[1] P. Deussen, *Sechzig Upanishads des Veda*, 1905, p. 514.

[2] Deussen, loc. cit., p. 19.

[3] Schmidt, *Fakire und Fakirtum im alten und modernen Indien*, 1908, p. 228.

[4] A. P. Lyons, " Animistic and other spiritualistic beliefs of the Bina Tribe," *Journ. R.A.I.*, 1921, p. 432.

creeks, and waterholes. If a married woman enters one of these while Tombabwir is there she will become pregnant but this can only occur when the physical act has opened the passage for Birumbir to enter the uterus.[1]

I have attempted to prove that the churinga which to the conscious mind of the native is a symbol of his second-ego, a sort of ego-ideal, and is active in the work of procreation, really means the penis.[2]

Some interesting evidence on this topic is contained in a recent publication on the Wonkonguru. After relating how circumcision was established by the Mura-Mura (in a version of the myth discussed on p. 112 of my book), we are told that when the Mura-Mura and his assistant were getting weak they got two stones and on one of them carved the mark of circumcision and subincision. The other stone they shaped like a penis and for every boy they had circumcised they set up a conical sandstone on a small hill.[3] Then they died and two trees rose up to mark the spot ; the stones are visible to this very day. Any one acquainted with the general style of Central Australian legends must feel a slight discrepancy at this point. Stones, of course, always crop up towards the end of a myth but they are usually the petrified ancestors themselves, and it is also these petrified ancestors who reappear in the stone churinga. In another version of the myth we are told that the conical stones are the petrified *wuntu* (penis) of somebody who died as the result of having been circumcised by a fire-stick.[4] Just like other churinga, the petrified phalli are used in the ceremonies for producing a better supply of vegetable food or snakes and it seems that they have something to do with the hereafter as they are used to mark the graves.[5]

Therefore we must say that this penis-shaped object, the representative of a second body or soul which springs up at the moment when one of the Alcheringa ancestors dies and is derived from a mitigated ceremonial castration (subincision), seems not only to mark the grave but to indicate the passage from and to the Land beyond the Grave. The penis appearing at the moment of death is merely a compensation for something widely different : for the loss of the penis. Our sources call the something that is separated from the body at the moment of death a soul. But various features of world-wide beliefs, such as the serpent-shaped soul and other phallic symbols

---

[1] A. R. Lyons, *Paternity Beliefs and Customs in Western Papuan Man*, 1924, p. 44.

[2] Cf. *Australian Totemism*, pp. 100, 172, 200.

[3] Horne and Aiston, *Savage Life in Central Australia*, 1924, p. 163.

[4] Horne and Aiston, loc. cit., p. 168.   [5] *Idem*, ibid., p. 167.

for the soul, the analogy felt in many places between cohabitation, that is, the egress of semen and extasis, that is, the egress of the soul, together with the procreative faculty attributed to the latter— all these show that the eternal idea of the soul is but the sublimation of a male member pure and simple.[1]

After all, this is not a very surprising conclusion to arrive at, since research shows with increasing certainty that supernatural ideas are but the symbolic representation of biological facts. Whence could mankind derive the idea of immortality if not from the power of propagation which ensures, if not the immortality of the individual, at least the duration of the species ? And since, onto-genetically, nobody has experienced death, where could a more natural prototype be found for the final scene of life than in the loss of vitality which unavoidably attends life's first pulsations ?

Whether we explain the part that is split off as the seminal fluid or as the penis makes no essential difference, and depends mainly on the point of view taken. Actually it is the seminal fluid which leaves the body, but there is an unconscious tendency to dread the total cutting off of the penis, i.e. castration, as the inevitable consequence of coitus. Following the recent researches of Dr Ferenczi, we may regard this as the survival of the archaic multiplication by fission, the phase of development in which the propagation of the species was also the death of the individual. In the case of the Kakadu, Sir Baldwin Spencer observes : " It is really like a very crude forerunner of the theory of the continuity of the germ-plasm. The old Yalmuru splits as it were into two, one half, the Yvaiyu, persists, and the other finally disappears. In its turn the former becomes transformed into a Yalmuru, which again splits ; one-half remains, the other perishes, but there is an actual spiritual continuity from generation to generation." [2]

It is now time to give a satisfactory explanation to the idea of a " soul-substance " immanent in every particle of the body. The word is not a real native word, but one coined by Dutch ethnologists to explain the sympathetic magic of Indonesia and New Guinea. Yet, as we have seen, it is coined on the basis of solid ethnological facts, for the natives really believe the soul to be contained in the hair or saliva while they work their spells on these objects. Now if we follow

---

[1] Cf. the idea held by some people that women have no souls. Stones of a phallic shape are found in the Kilimanjaro district. One of these is called the " soul " of the Mbokom, and in war the enemy would try to uproot it. Ch. Dundas, *Kilimanjaro and its People*, 1924, p. 41.

[2] B. Spencer, *Native Tribes of the Northern Territory*, 1914, pp. 270–4.

Ferenczi in his speculations on the autonomous sexual gratifications active in each particle of the body and their migration downward towards and final outlet by means of the genital organ,[1] we may imagine some actual basis for this idea of a soul-substance in the libido quantities contained in each cell and perhaps brought to something like an infinitely reduced copy of the act of coition (ejaculation) in the libidinal connection of the cells with each other.[2]

If, moreover, we stress the latter part of Ferenczi's theory, the gradual migration downward of erotisms from the erotogenous zones to the genital organ, thus constituting the transition from the auto-erotic phase to that of genital primacy, we must regard it as a proof of the relatively undiminished auto-erotism of savages as compared to non-neurotic civilized folk that they experience the castration phobia not only in connection with the expenditure of semen in the genital act, but also in relation to every severed part of their body. Thus my present interpretation of sympathetic magic as a great universal castration phobia and the one given in a previous paper on the same subject [3] (as a proof of the auto-erotism of the savage) can be brought into harmony. Moreover, as symptoms and rites are usually determined by more than one dynamic agency, we can also interpret the same peculiarity of savage life as an indication of an over-powerful castration phobia which radiates from the genital organ to the whole body.

Being familiar with the superposition of eroticisms on each other or the " carrying over " of the peculiarities of an erotic zone into the next, we shall, of course, not be surprised to find oral (food, saliva), anal (excrements, dirt), and urethral (urine) factors playing a part in this castration magic. And the final and most important conclusion of these first two chapters seems to be that the most universal form of magic dreaded by primitive man from the cradle to the grave corresponds exactly to his equally universal animistic belief in what takes place at death. In one case a part of the body is severed, in the other a " something " leaves the body for good. Just as coitus is, in a certain sense, a castration, death appears as the final coitus or final castration of life.

[1] S. Ferenczi, *Genitaltheorie*, p. 22.
[2] Cf. S. Freud, " Jenseits des Lustprinzips," *Gesammelte Schriften*, v.
[3] Róheim, " Das Selbst," *Imago*, vii.

3 Osiris and Other Mortals

Osiris, the son of the Sky Goddess Nut, and the Earth God Sebk, had intercourse with his sister Isis in his mother's womb. He was the inventor of agriculture and the first ruler of Egypt. His brother Set brought a chest into the banqueting room and promised to give it to anyone whose body upon trial it might fit. Last of all, Osiris laid himself down in it. Immediately Set and the other conspirators clapped the cover upon it and carried it to the riverside. As to Isis, as soon as the report reached her, she immediately cut off one of the locks of her hair and put on mourning apparel. Osiris had previously had intercourse with Nephtys, the sister of Isis whom he took to be his wife. Her sister, dreading the anger of her husband Set, had exposed their child as soon as it was born and now Isis made it her business to find this child ; and when by the aid of some dogs (hence the dog is called Anubis) she managed to do so, she bred the child up. At last she found the chest, opened it, and caressed her husband's corpse. But suddenly she remembered her son, or rather her sister's son, Horus, in the swamps at Buto and left chest and corpse to see her son. Set, who was hunting a wild boar by the light of the moon, accidentally found the chest with the corpse of Osiris. He rent it into fourteen pieces. All these were afterwards found by Isis excepting the phallus, which, having been thrown into the Nile immediately upon its separation from the rest of the body, had been devoured by the Lepidotus, the Phagrus, and the Oxyrhynchus, fish which of all others for this reason the Egyptians have in special avoidance. In order, however, to make some amends for the loss, Isis consecrated the phallus made in imitation of it and instituted a festival in its memory. According to native Egyptian sources, Isis conceived Horus from the corpse of Osiris, while Plutarch, whom we followed above, regards Horus as the son of Osiris and Nephtys. Horus, aided by the ghost of his father Osiris, appears on the scene as Avenger. In the battle that followed, Set seems to have assumed the shape of a black swine and in this guise to have blinded Horus by throwing excrement into his eye. The eye was healed by Thoth, and Horus, who had castrated and vanquished Set, gave his father Osiris his own eye. By eating it Osiris gained fresh life and power.[1]

The technique of decomposition is, as I have pointed out before,

---

[1] Plutarch, *Peri Isidos kai Osiridos*, Cap. 12–20. G. Roeder, *Urkunden zur Religion des alten Ägypten*, 1915, pp. 196, 242–71. *Idem*, " Seth " in *Roschers Lexikon*, 63. Lieferung, 1910, pp. 758–79. J. G. Frazer, *Adonis, Attis, Osiris*, 1905, pp. 269–76.

the key that unlocks the secrets of this myth.[1]   Texts are extant that
represent Horus and Set as twins or one and the same person.[2]   If,
moreover, we consider that Set was after a wild boar when he came
upon the corpse of Osiris we have some basis for identifying the boar
Osiris with the swine Set as adversaries of Horus.   Have we not
clearly demonstrated the identity of the Avenger (Horus) and the
Murderer (Set) in the Drama of the Primeval Horde ?[3]   Therefore
if Horus the Avenger is but a mask for Horus the Murderer, must
his adversary not be Osiris-Set ?   And finally it is Set who wounds
the eye of Horus and Osiris who finally devours it.   If then we
consider the drama without paying heed to the names of the actors,
the plot reads as follows :—

A son (who may be Horus or Set), aided by his allies and his mother
Isis,[4] killed, castrated, and devoured his father the wild boar (who
may be either Osiris or Set) but suffered a wound on his eye as the
talion punishment for his temerity.   In the background we have
the love-intrigue of Osiris with Nephtys, who is the wife of Set.
In other words, by a reversal of his own wishes, the son accuses the
father of committing adultery with the mother whom he regards
as his rightful wife, and for this reason kills and castrates him.

We have used this myth as a paradigm for showing the course
of events in the Primal Horde and for proving that as each Egyptian
dead was regarded as another Osiris the cult of the dead in general
was modelled on the traces left by the tragic events of the Primal
Horde.   Now we shall proceed to another aspect of the question
and see what is meant by the death of Osiris.   For we see that this
is represented under at least two, and perhaps under three, aspects.
The first is the whole body in its unimpaired state floating on the
water ; the second is the dismembered or cut-up body ; and the third
is a special case of such a dismemberment—namely the
lack of the phallus, the castrated body.   There can be no
doubt of the fact that this third feature is the real core of the myth

[1] G. Róheim, " Nach dem Tode des Urvaters," *Imago*, ix, p. 84.

[2] Wallis Budge, *The Gods of the Egyptians*, 1904, i, p. 194 ; ii, pp. 241, 242.

[3] Cf. the paper quoted above.

[4] In the manifest myth-text Isis is, of course, the faithful spouse of her
lord Osiris.   But compare the episode in which she leaves the corpse of
Osiris, which thus, for the second time, becomes the prey of Set's malice.
Moreover, she is insulted by her son Horus for her partiality in releasing the
bonds of the captive Set.   And finally the Queen Thueris who, in Plutarch's
version, abets the revolt of Set, is evidently a double of Isis.   In extenuation
of her character we must say that Nephtys is also a double of Isis, and thus
Set (husband of Nephtys) appears to be her rightful lord.

of Osiris, who is the first of mortals, for it is repeated three times in three successive generations. The first hero of the gory scene is Osiris himself who castrated his father Sebk,[1] the second is Set, who castrates Osiris, and the third is Horus who does the same to Set.

This myth of the great gods reappears in a well-known folklore version. It will be instructive to compare these two variants.

Anoupu (that is, Anubis) was the name of the elder brother and Bitiou was the younger. The elder brother had a wife and a farm, the younger had none and worked for his elder brother. There was not such another labourer in the whole world, " and the germ of all the gods was within him." He fetches some grain for sowing and his brother's wife is so well pleased with the strength he shows in doing this, that she tempts him to have intercourse with her. But he rejects her, saying that she is like a mother to him and his elder brother like a father. Now she disfigures herself in a fashion to indicate an attempt at violence committed on her, and tells her husband the whole story but in an inverted manner. It was, according to her, the younger brother who wished to have intercourse with her and she who spoke about her being like a mother to him. The elder brother hides behind the door with a knife intending to kill the seducer, who, warned of the danger by his cows, runs away. Pursued by the elder, he tells him what has happened and takes his oath by the Sun-God that his version is the true one. To attest his innocence he takes a bill-hook for cutting reeds, he severs his virile member, he casts it into the water, where the electric catfish devour it, he sinks down, he faints. The elder brother weeps over him and wants to come to him, but he cannot on account of the lake full of crocodiles between them. His younger brother calls to him, saying : " Thus whilst thou didst imagine an evil action thou didst not recall one of the good actions or even one of the things that I did for thee. Ah ! go to thy house and do thou thyself care for thy cattle, for I shall not live longer in the place where thou art. I go to the Vale of Acacia. Yet here is what thou shalt do for me, when thou art returned to thy business, for know thou the things that will happen to me. I shall take out my heart by magic to place it on the top flower of the Acacia, and when the Acacia is cut down and my heart falls to the ground thou shalt come to seek for it." [2]

[1] H. Brugsch, *Religion und Mythologie der alten Ägypter*, 1891, p. 581. W. Budge, loc. cit., ii, p. 99.
[2] G. Maspero, *Les Contes Populaires de L'Egypte Ancienne*, iii ed., pp. 1–9.

Whereas in the myth Osiris actually commits adultery with his brother's wife Nephtys, in this version moral repression has progressed so far that the motive merely appears as a false charge levelled against an innocent youth.   And while in the primitive heroic fashion, which is far less removed from the grim realities of the Primal Horde, war is fought between the adversaries, here we find merely an oath,[1] a moral indignation on the part of the accused party which, however, is but feebly supported by his deeds.   In castrating himself he appears to avow the very crime he denies, since self-castration is evidently the talion punishment for incest.   Moreover, in the comparison "like a mother, like a father " we see that the brother conflict and sister-in-law incest are merely substitutes for the original Œdipus situation. The departure from this world and the descent to the Valley of Acacia, are here clearly identical with the act of castration.   Just as Osiris-Bitiou after being castrated is still called a Bull, the symbol of fecundity, the mythical Osiris, though a castrated corpse, can still procreate with Isis the Avenger Horus.   The explanation of this contradiction lies in a shifting of meaning between the corpse and the soul.   The corpse of Osiris in whom the germ of all the gods is contained is himself the penis, and in his passage to the other world must again endure the agony of a dreaded castration.

The religion of ancient Egypt is dominated by one idea—the awful anxiety of the dangers that threaten the corpse on its passage to the other world and the efforts made to overcome these dangers, to resist annihilation, and to transform the corpse, the weakest of the weak, into the strongest of the strong.   The deceased hoped to transform each limb into a god and when this was effected to become Ra the Sun himself.   In chapter xlii of the Book of the Dead the deceased says :—

> " My hair is the hair of Nut
> My face is the face of the Disk
> My eyes are the eyes of Hathor
> My ears are the ears of Ap-nuat
>   etc., etc.
> My backbone is the backbone of Suti
> My phallus is the phallus of Osiris, etc.[2]

The corruption of the body seems to have been the supreme calamity dreaded by the Egyptians.   But the words of Thoth and the prayers of the priests caused the body to become changed into a *sahu*, or incorruptible spiritual body, which passed straightway out of the tomb

---

[1] Cf. Reik, *Probleme der Religionspsychologie*, 1919. " Kolnidre."
[2] Budge, *Egyptian Ideas of the Future Life*, p. 197.

and made its way into heaven, where it dwelt with the gods. When, in the Book of the Dead, the deceased says : " I exist, I exist, I live, I live, I germinate, I germinate," or " I germinate like the plants ", the idea conveyed is that a new body which has neither defect nor, like Ra, shall suffer diminution, is ever coming into being, and it is in this new incorruptible body that the soul continues to exist.[1] The whole style of these texts that are regarded as spoken by the deceased is of a peculiarly megalomaniac type.

" Set hath seized Horus who looked with the two eyes but I have released Horus and taken him from Set and Set hath opened the path of the two eyes in heaven. . . Behold me now for I make this mighty boat to travel over the Lake of Hetep and I brought it away with might from the palace of Shu ; the domain of his stars groweth young and reneweth the strength which it had of old." [2]

If we ask for the origin of this peculiar attitude, for the reason why the Egyptians represented annihilation as new life, corruption as the germination of plants, we shall find an answer to our question in the castration complex. For, according to Professor Wiedemann, the oxyrhynchus, the fish that devoured the phallus of Osiris, was the very one which carried the souls of the dead to the other world— undoubtedly after having eaten them. Set, the god who castrated Osiris, appears as the demon who steals the souls, swallows the body, and lives on corpses.[3] There is a town called Oxyrhynchus, the centre of the oxyrhynchus totem, and it is in this town that Set appears as patron deity. Roeder also calls attention to the circumstance that the peculiar snout of the fish is similar to that of the presumably mythical Set animal.[4] In the Pyramid texts, especially in those of the later period, Set appears as the chief of the demons who feed on the corpse.[5] The beast that devours the dead is a fabulous animal with a body combined of that of a crocodile, a lion, and a hippopotamus.[6] Osiris appears as the judge of the dead and he is accompanied by an animal that eats corpses. A specially horrible being called Babai, who is either follower of Set or Set himself, tears the corpse to pieces.[7] On their voyage in the ship of the Sun-God Ra, the dead have to pass a desert full of serpents and especially the dragon Apophis.[8]

In the myth dealing with the fate of Osiris we are told that he

---

[1] Budge, loc. cit., p. 170.   [2] Budge, loc. cit., p. 189.
[3] Cf. article on Set in *Roschers Lexikon*, p. 767.
[4] Roeder, in *Roscher*, loc. cit., p. 781.   [5] Roeder, ibid., p. 767.
[6] Erman, *Die ägyptische Religion*, 1913, p. 117.
[7] Erman, loc. cit., p. 121.   [8] Erman, loc. cit., p. 125.

was cut into fourteen pieces by his adversary. That he was castrated is not expressly stated (except in the tale of Bitiou), but it seems to be implied when we learn that all the other parts of his body were found except his phallus. The question arises, why is this point slurred and the being cut into pieces substituted? In discussing this question with me Dr Ferenczi observed that the motif of being cut into pieces might be used as a substitute for castration because the danger was in a certain sense reduced by being extended to the whole body. Everything is cut up rather than the one member lost, for that loss would be really unbearable. It seems that this view can be applied very well to the myth of Osiris as prototype of the dead. For in a period that preceded the age of mummification, the corpse was cut into pieces like the mythical corpse of Osiris. The decapitation was regarded as especially important, and probably, as in the case of the head-hunters, we must regard it as castration displaced upwards. The severed parts of the body were buried in cultivated land, probably near to the dead man's earthly residence, and perhaps with the idea that they would fecundate the soul. After a time, when the flesh had disappeared from the bones, the latter would be disinterred and finally buried on the edge of the cultivated soil in the sand of the desert. Gradually this peculiar proceeding seems to have given way to its exact opposite, that of mummification. Thousands of years after, when mummification was the general practice, the formulæ still tell us how the dead will get their severed head back in the other world. Corpses have been found that were first decapitated and then, as if people had changed their minds, the corpse was mummified and the head fixed back on it again. There was also a method that looks like a compromise between the two extremes. They let the flesh rot off the bones, which were then reunited and bound together to form a mummy-shaped bundle.[1] Now there is a prototype for this second version also—in the myth of Osiris shut up in a chest, floating down the Nile towards the sea.[2] But here there is a peculiar confession in the tradition as recorded by Plutarch. Isis is looking for the chest containing her dead husband, and finds another swimming chest with her husband's lately born child in it, who had been exposed by the mother.[3] Either there must have been a prodigious number of chests floating about on the Nile at that time or, what seems more probable, the two chests are one and the same. We observe that

---

[1] Wiedemann, *Religion und Mythologie der alten Aegypter*, 1893, pp. 20, 21.

[2] Plutarch, loc. cit., 13.   [3] Plutarch, loc. cit., 14.

a spell originally intended to alleviate the birth-pangs of a woman was also used as a means of procuring easy access for the dead to the other world.[1] An important inscription found on the roof of Hathor's temple at Tentyra shows the connection between these ideas that seem so widely different to the consciousness of modern man. Here we find the description of the ceremonies held in memory of the death of Osiris. For seven days he remained in his shroud as a mummy, from the 24th of Choiak to the last day of that month. Then the god was believed to rest on the leaves of the sycamore trees in the temple of the heavenly Busiris. As for these seven days, they are those that he spent in the body of his mother Nut when she was pregnant with him.[2]

On the 16th of Choiak, at the third hour of the day, the holy female hippopotamus of Nut, who is the mother of the gods, is brought forth and a priest who represents the infant Horus " at his arrival " sits before her.[3] The goddess Nut was also identified with the coffin, and the dead, by being put into the coffin were, in reality, put into the body of the goddess. The following inscription has been found on the lid of the coffin of Teti : " Nut, the shining one, the great one, sayeth, ' This is my son N.N. to whom I have given birth.' Nut, the great vulture, declares ' This is my beloved N.N. my son. I have given him the two horizons that he may grow powerful in them like Harachte ' " (the infant Horus).[4] It is a peculiar feature of Egyptian ceremonialism that this great mystery of the death and rebirth of Osiris was represented in the daily mysteries. At the beginning of every hour his death was represented, towards the middle his resurrection, and the end of the hour saw him again on his deathbed.[5] At six in the evening they brought a vase with fresh water from the Nile. The water of the Nile was regarded as the counterpart of the primeval ocean and the following spell was recited : " Here is your essences, Gods, the Name which gives life to you in its name of Living. This water gives birth to you, as it does to Ra, every day it will make you become like Chepra." By the power of this libation Osiris, or the dead, is reborn of the waters, like the Sun. Now we have the same motif with a varying

[1] Erman, loc. cit., p. 116.
[2] H. Brugsch, " Das Osiris Mysterium von Tentyra," *Zeitschrift für ägyptische Sprache and Altertumskunde*, xix, 1881, p. 96.
[3] Ibid., p. 98.
[4] A. Rusch, " Die Entwicklung der Himmelsgöttin Nut zu einer Totengottheit," *M.V.A.G.*, 1922, xxvii, p. 13. Cf. ibid., pp. 19, 28.
[5] H. Junker, " Die Stundenwachen in den Osiris mysterien," *Ak. d. Wiss. in Wien*, liv, 1910.

symbolism, for there can be no doubt about it that the re-constitution of the corpse, its re-animation and finally its rebirth in plant life and animal life, are all repetitions of one central complex.[1]   It is this latter we intend to discuss, but as the jackal god Anubis plays the central part in this ceremony we shall first try to get some information about him and his African colleagues.

Nephtys gave birth to a son called Anpu (Anubis) whose father was either Osiris or Set.   The animal which was at once the type and symbol of the god was the jackal, and this fact seems to prove that in primitive times Anubis was merely the jackal god and that he was associated with the dead because the jackal was generally seen prowling about their tombs.   It was his duty to guide the dead to Osiris.[2]   In her search for the corpse of her husband, Isis is guided by the dog Anubis who, however, leads the way not to a corpse, but to a new-born child.[3]   However, we have seen that these two ideas are not far removed from each other in Egypt, for the corpse was regarded as an embryo in its mother's womb.   To regard the dead as reborn was but a denial of that annihilation which embalming tried to resist by physical means.   In the Theban recension of the Book of the Dead, Anubis plays a very important part, being connected with the judgment and embalming of the deceased.   Tradition declared that Anubis embalmed the body of Osiris and that he swathed it in the linen swathings which were woven by Isis and Nephtys for their brother ; and it was believed that his work was so thoroughly well performed under the direction of Horus and Isis and Nephtys, that it resisted the influences of time and decay.[4]

If, as seems only just, we inquire into the part played by jackals, hyenas, and similar carrion-eaters in modern Africa, the impression we get will be different.   According to the Yao, one of the chief arts of a wizard is to turn himself into a hyena, leopard, or other animal and dig up graves to eat the flesh of corpses.   Indeed, witchcraft and cannibalism or corpse-eating are regarded as synonymous. The Makanga credit the were-hyena with a human wife who lives in a village and performs the ordinary work of a native woman by day, but by night opens the door of the goat-kraal to admit her husband and then goes with him into the bush to join in the feast.[5] In Nigeria all the inhabitants of a certain city are believed to become

---

[1] Cf. A. Moret, *Mystères Egyptiennes*, 1913, pp. 29–31.

[2] W. Budge, *The Gods of the Egyptians*, ii, p. 261.

[3] Plutarch, loc. cit., p. 14.

[4] Budge, loc. cit., ii, p. 262.

[5] A. Werner, *The Natives of British Central Africa*, 1906, pp. 84, 85.

hyenas at pleasure.[1] The bodies of common people are usually carried away by hyenas, that is, by people who have transformed themselves into these animals.[2] If it is believed that a hyena by treading upon a man's shadow renders him incapable of movement or sound ; it is easy to see that this shadow is merely the substitute for a corpse.[3] The Budas in Abyssinia are believed to be endowed with this uncanny power of self-transformation. The illness of a servant woman was set down to one of these blacksmith-hyenas, who wanted to get her out into the forest and devour her.[4]

After this short survey of facts we shall return to Egypt with the expectation of finding the solution of the riddle. How can the jackal or hyena, the carrion-eater, be transmuted into a god of embalming ?

At the fourth hour of the day the rebirth of Osiris in the other world was announced and victims were sacrificed. They symbolized Set and his allies, and their skin served as a swathing for Osiris. This was the cradle of the god whence he was reborn as a child or an animal. " Be welcome, Isis. Here is thy *meshent*, the house where the divine *ka* renews life." *Meshent* is the skin mentioned above and also a goddess of childbirth. The hide was very often the hide of a cow and is thus assimilated to Nut, the cow of heaven and mother of Osiris.

The presiding genius of these rites was Anubis and his symbol was the hide of a beast attached to a pole. He arranged the sacrifice of the victims by whose hide the rebirth of Osiris was effected. According to the Book of the Dead, Anubis himself passed through the hide and lay in it in the position of an infant in the womb. According to another version this was done by Horus for his father, which amounts to the same thing, as Anubis is also a son of Osiris.[5] Every human being was an Osiris, the son of the Earth God Geb and the Sky Goddess Nut, murdered by Set, thrown into the river, fished out again, cut into pieces, and found a second time. The widow played the part of Isis in the funeral ceremonies, the sons officiated as Horus, and the friends as Anubis and Thoth.[6]

Theoretically the deceased himself was supposed to pass through the hide of the victim, but usually it was done by somebody else for him. Originally human beings who represented Set seem to have

[1] Tremearne, *The Ban of the Bori*, 1914, p. 124.
[2] Tremearne, loc. cit., p. 129.   [3] Tremearne, loc. cit., p. 407.
[4] Parkyns, *Life in Abyssinia*, 1853, ii, p. 46. *Trans. Ethn. Soc.* Waitz, *Anthropologie der Naturvölker*, ii, p. 504 ; vi, p. 288.
[5] Moret, loc. cit., pp. 31–3.   [6] Moret, loc. cit., p. 37.

been sacrificed.   The first substitution was when instead of Egyptians the rite was performed with prisoners of war, usually Nubians. Afterwards the animals of Set were used but they still played the part of human victims.   At the tomb of Montu nerjhepshef, a human personage called the *Tikenou* appears on a sledge with the beast's hide called *mest* or *meshent*.   These words are derived from the radical *mes* = to be born.   The *mest*, the heart of the sacrificed animal, and the hair of the human Tikenou were burnt and supposed to ascend with the defunct from the flames into the sky.   The inventor of this magical proceeding was Anubis who appeared with the hide called *out* which was used for the same purpose as the one mentioned above.   The word *out* can also mean the uterus, and the human figure put into the hide assumes exactly the same position as the victims of animal sacrifice or the embryo in the womb.   In the course of time linen was substituted for the animal hide but still it was spotted to indicate its origin and finally only the ritual of magical rebirth remained for what was originally a human sacrifice.[1]

We have dwelt upon these details at some length as they show how a historical knowledge of ethnology, of the sequence of anthropological facts, may be of some use to the psycho-analyst.   For here we have rites with their unconscious meanings shown with all the distinctness that could be desired, and their mutual relation is the same as that which has been found in individual analysis.   In the beginning, the dead were cut into pieces like Osiris whose dismemberment means castration.   Afterwards, however, the point was just to keep the body intact by embalming to make it possible for the whole corpse to re-enter the maternal womb.   In the beginning, the murder unconsciously committed on the dead, or rather the murder once consciously committed on the Jealous Sire,[2] was repeated on a human victim.   But murder was followed by a compensatory simulated birth till by a series of mitigations the rite came to be nothing but a rebirth ceremony.

Now, according to the latest views of Ferenczi,[3] which I have found reason to accept, the real function of the uterine regression and birth phantasies regression in analysis is quite different from what Rank supposes.   It seems that uterine regression is not a thing to be dreaded on account of the birth-shock.   What is really dreaded is castration—the separation of a part of the body from the whole. The experience of pre-natal life when existence in the desired womb

[1] Moret, loc. cit., pp. 38–50, 86.
[2] Cf. Róheim, " Nach dem Tode des Urvaters," *Imago*, ix.
[3] Cf. Ferenczi, " Gulliver Phantasien," *Zeitschrift für Psa*, xiii.

was possible for the whole body instead of for a part only crops up as a consolation.   It is drawn into the focus of attention by the pleasure principle.   No doubt the birth-shock was a shock but a lesser one than the castration which accompanies every coitus, and at any rate it is a thing of the past, a shock through which we have lived.   Hence its real function in dreams, for instance, is that of consolation, implying that we shall manage to overcome the actual danger just as we succeeded in being born.   In Egypt we observe what was originally the idea and ritual practice of death as castration transformed by the pleasure principle into the idea of death as a new birth.   The idea of Set closely connected as it was with the murder and castration of Osiris gradually became so abhorrent to the consciousness of the Egyptian that it became eradicated from the monuments or supplanted by the name of some other god.[1]   Here most undoubtedly there is proof in history for the work of repression, and it is no wonder that the repression should be directed against a being who stands for parricide and castration.

The orthodox Egyptian attitude towards the problem of death is like that of the Central Australian towards the problem of birth, i.e. to deny what is plain and obvious.   The dead are the " living ones ".   His Majesty Ptolemy the Second is said to have rejoiced in his heart on account of what he had done for his fathers, the very great living (i.e. dead) rams at Mendes.[2]   But for all that there seemed to have been a slight doubt somewhere on the subject, else there would be no explanation for all the efforts made to vivify the corpse.

The starting-point of all these efforts seems to have been the unconscious idea that the corpse is a penis in the state of castration, or at least of loss of the seminal fluid ; so that everything ought to be done to bring it back into a state of erection.   According to an interesting paper by Aylward M. Blackman,[3] the original meaning of libations in Egypt was as follows : " The corpse of the deceased is dry and shrivelled.   To revivify it the vital fluids that have exuded from it in the process of mummification must be restored for not till then will life return and the heart beat again." [4]   The libations are said to be the actual fluids that have issued from the corpse.   According to another version, however, it is not the deceased's own

---

[1] Roeder, article on Set in *Roschers Lexikon*, pp. 766.

[2] Erman, loc. cit., p. 228.

[3] " The Significance of Incense and Libations in Funerary and Temple Ritual," *Zt. f. Äg. Spr. u.A.L.*, 1912, p. 69.

[4] Op. cit., p. 70.

exudations that are to animate the shrunken frame but those of a divine body, the god's fluid that came from Osiris himself.   The king gained his *sa*, which appears to have been a supernatural fluid, from the gods themselves, and it is said that in the veins of the Pharaoh, Son of Ra, the fluid of Ra flows.   The fluid of Ra, that is, the rays of the Sun, were regarded as the source of life and all things. The process by which this fluid was transmitted is called *sotpou*, a word meaning the outpour of water, of flames, the flight of an arrow, and also ejaculation of the semen.   It is used of a father in the act of procreation,[1] so that we are quite justified in regarding the liquid of the gods used in reanimating the corpse as a supernatural seminal fluid.   According to Egyptian views, the statue becomes a " living image " when the eye is introduced, and hence the eyes painted in or other objects (cowry shells, etc.) substituted for them in the empty sockets were really thought to endow the corpse with life.[2]   Having quoted the myth of Horus above we remember that while Set was wounded on his genitalia, Horus suffered the same thing in a displacement upwards to the eye.   If we regard the eye as a substitute for the testicles it becomes clear why Osiris, the dead phallus, the phallus after the expenditure of the life fluid, should be reanimated by eating them.   The works of Elliot Smith and Perry are very well known so that we can do without extensive quotations.   All I wish to say here is that they are quite right in regarding blood in the cult of the dead as a substance containing life ; but that it should be so is because it is a substitute for the seminal fluid and the choice of this substitute indicates a strong castration complex.   Moreover, the other objects used as " givers of life " such as cowry shells and pearls are undoubtedly vaginal symbols, but also, especially the latter, symbols of the penis (testicles) of the child in the womb.   An interesting case to the point has lately been published by Douglas Bryan.   A patient of his called the vulva a pearl and explained this by saying : " The pearl is the result of a wound in an oyster."   Then she said that her vulva was a wound since her father had died and taken away his penis.   That is, the penis is the object that stops the vulva being a wound by filling up the cavity, and death is the castration of the father, the withdrawal of his penis.[3]

---

[1] " Du Caractère Religieux de la Royauté Pharaonique," *Annales du Musée Guimet Bibliothèque d'Etudes*, xv, pp. 47, 48.

[2] Elliot Smith, *The Evolution of the Dragon*, 1919, p. 145.

[3] Douglas Bryan, " The Pearl and Castration Symbolism," *Journal of Psycho-analysis*, vi, 52.

Before taking farewell of Egypt we shall see how they founded their belief in resurrection on their idea of the corpse as a penis in its normal non-erected state.　On the walls of the temple of Dendera we find an interesting group of scenes connected with the story of the death and resurrection of Osiris.　The twentieth scene represents Osiris as a mummy, ithyphallic and bearded, lying upon his bier. Over his head and his body hover two hawks.　At the head kneels Hathor, mistress of the nether world, who weeps for her brother, at the foot is the frog goddess Heget.　The frog symbolizes resurrection.　The twenty-first scene is very much the same. In the twenty-second we find that Osiris has begun to rise, and in the last he is definitely rising out of his basket, while behind him stand Isis with her wings stretched out and before him a bearded god giving him life.[1]　It is easy to recognize this resurrection as the erection of the phallus and the festival of the erection of the dead-pillar can hardly have been anything else.

Thus we have found that the ideas on the basis of savage belief pointed out above are traceable with a peculiar distinctness in Egypt. We see how the ego-ideal is formed by identification with the phallic father-god Osiris ; how death is equivalent to the loss of virile power ; and resurrection means its restoration.　We have been also able, casually, to gain some insight into the relation of the idea of uterine regression to that of castration or coitus, for the former appeared as a substitute evolved on the basis of the dread of castration.

4　The Passage of the Dead

A bridge called Es-Sirat, finer than a hair and sharper than the edge of a sword or a razor, stretches over the Hell of the Moslem. All the souls of the dead must pass across it, but while the good reach the other side in safety, the wicked fall off into the abyss.[2]

The Mohammedan belief is probably the source of similar traditions in Europe,[3] and is on its part derived from Zoroastrian sources. On the fourth day after death the good are separated from the wicked. The bridge Cinvat leads to the Mountain of Judgment in the middle of the world ; it is guarded by two dogs and has the breadth of nine spears.　For the pious it appears to have the breadth of a parasang but to the wicked it appears to be as narrow as the edge of a razor.

[1] Budge, loc. cit., ii, pp. 137, 138.
[2] Cf. Wolff, *Mohammedanische Eschatologie*, 1872, ch. 35, 49.　Sprenger, *Leben und Lehre*, ii, p. 62. Eisenmenger, *Entdecktes Judentum*, ii, p. 258.
[3] Cf. St Patrick's Purgatory.

The good are led by the angel Serosch into paradise, the wicked fall off or they are dragged away into Hell by a devil called " The Dragger ".[1]

In Hinduism we find the dead ferried over the river Vaitarani while holding on to a cow's tail. The river of death is localized at Orissa and pours streams of ordure and blood on the confines of the realm of Yama. The soul is scorched by the heat, attacked by beasts of prey, till at last it reaches the bridge.[2]

Here again there are traces of the idea that the dead pass over the gulf between this world and the next by means of a bridge as sharp as a razor,[3] and we also find the two dogs of Yama. The double rôle attributed to them is undoubtedly somewhat confusing for they both guard the gates of the netherworld and fetch the souls of the living.

At any rate, it seems that the two dogs, the bridge and the water, all belong to the original scenery, the date of which cannot be more recent than the Indo-Iranian period. The river itself is frequently described as a river of fire and for those who are diligent in sacrificing it is promised that the fire, the funeral-pyre, will not burn their genital organ. They shall have plenty of women in the other world, and the god Yama will not rob them of their semen.[4] Passing on eastwards from India we find that these views have found their way to the East Indies, Indonesia, and China. The Karens of Burma tie strings across the rivers for the ghosts of their dead to pass over to their graves. They imagine the Heaven-bridge as a sword and believe that those who cross it become men, while those who dare not become women.[5]

The same general attitude, though without mention being made of the bridge, seems to have fashioned the ideas of the Lushei.

" The first man is said to have been Pupawla, who died before all those born after him. Then Pupawla, this man who died first,

---

[1] F. Wolff, *Avesta*, 1910. *Yashna*, xix, 6. *Jasht*, xxiv, 557. Landau, *Hölle und Fegfeuer in Volksglaube, Dichtung und Kirchenlehre*, 1909, p. 56.

[2] W. Crooke, *The Popular Religion and Folk-Lore of Northern India*, 1896, i, p. 40; ii, p. 55. Weber, *Indische Studien*, i, 1850, p. 398. *Zeitschrift für vergl. Sprachwissenschaft*, ii, p. 315.

[3] L. Scherman, *Materialien zur Geschichte der indischen Visionsliteratur*, 1892, p. 117.

[4] H. Oldenberg, *Die Religion des Veda*, 1894, p. 536, On Yama as carrion-eater cf. E. Arbmann, " Tod und Unsterblichkeit im vedischen Glauben," *A.R.W.*, xxv, 380.

[5] E. B. Tylor, *Researches into the Early History of Mankind*, 1870, p. 359. *Journ. As. Soc. Beng.*, 1865, ii, p. 197.

shoots at those who have died after him with a very big pellet bow.
But there are some he cannot shoot at, for instance, those who have
killed men and sacrificed certain wild animals or those who have
enjoyed three virgins or seven different women who were not virgins ;
but women whoever they may be he always shoots at.   They say
that there is a road between the Mi-thi-kua and the Rihlake.   To
go there, there are seven roads, but Pupawla has built his house
where the seven roads meet.   Then after Pupawla has shot them,
there is a hill called Hringlang hill, and then there is the Lunglo
river (heartless, feelingless, which removes feelings), the water of
which is clear and transparent and the *hawilopar* (look back no more)
flourish there.   The dead pluck these flowers and place them behind
their eyes and drink of the water and have no more desire for the
land of living.   Those whom Pupawla hits with his pellet cannot
cross the river." [1]

The Sea Dyaks of Borneo believe in seven lives or existences.
In the one that follows upon our present life thieves are punished
by an immense sort of pig dragon.   From this state of punishment
a transition takes place to another world, where everything is beautiful
and perfect, peaceful and happy.   It is surrounded by a thick wall.
Here there are lakes and rivers with boats on them.   In the wall
there is a great gate which, divided in two, continually opens and
shuts, the two halves running back in opposite directions and then
closing again.   As the gates open people are perpetually being
admitted.   According to the Idaan, paradise is on the top of Kina
Balu and it is guarded by a fiery dog who is a formidable opponent
to the female sex, for whenever virgins come he seizes them as his
legal prizes, but women who have cohabited he regards as unworthy
of his embrace. [2]   The Muruts believe that the soul of the dead first
paddles across a river, then climbs a hill, and this is repeated several
times.   He comes to a river called the Valley of Tears and when
he leaves this, to a great caterpillar to which he must give some
kladi (a certain plant).   The next thing is a mountain with a lot
of flies and a great bear who is presented with a pig and lets him pass.
Going further he meets a man who holds an iron weir ; he offers him
pisangs and sugar cane and passes unmolested.   Next he comes to
a river which is watched by a man named Tamai Patakloeng to
whom he must give the barbules which grow round the mouth of
a certain species of fish (Silurus).   After this he meets a woman

[1] J. Shakespeare, *The Lushei Kuki Clans*, 1912, p. 63.
[2] Ling Roth, *The Natives of Sarawak and British North Borneo*, 1896,
i, pp. 218, 220.

stamping rice ; she is anxious to persuade him to help her, but he must avoid her ànd pursue his journey.   The next obstacle is a fire in the middle of the road and after that a woman with ears big enough for him to take shelter under from the rain.   He must now jump over the stem of a tree and cut another stem in two.   More mountains and rivers follow till at last he is refreshed by some fruit and safely landed.[1]

This account is too complicated to be very much to the point. We see a series-formation developing from the same motif, but the details probably need a more intimate knowledge of Murut mythology than we can boast of for their explanation.   But one thing seems certain, that these Indonesian accounts have not been developed without historical contact with the Indo-Iranian picture of the bridge and its guardians the two gods, or the two-headed dog.   This is clearly shown by the accounts of the soul's journey we get from the Kayans, Punans, and Malanaus.

According to the Kayans, the ghosts must cross a river by means of a bridge consisting of a single large log suspended from bank to bank.   This log is constantly agitated by a guardian called Maligang. If the ghost during his earthly life has taken a head he crosses the bridge without difficulty, but if not he falls below and is consumed by maggots, or, according to another version, by a large fish called Patan, and so is destroyed.[2]   This Maligang is evidently the Maiwiang of the Malanaus.   Here the soul has to cross a river on a single log the passage of which is disputed by a malign being who tries to frighten the soul by throwing ashes at it while it passes the bridge.   Some Malanaus describe this opposing power as a two-headed dog called Maiwiang whom it is necessary to propitiate with the gift of a valuable bead.   For this reason a bead of some value is fastened to the right arm of the corpse before the coffin is closed.[3] The Punans add some incidents that seem to be of aboriginal growth, that is, to belong to the common stock of Oceanian mythology. According to their version a huge helmeted hornbill sits by the far end of the bridge across the river of death and tries to terrify the ghost with its screams so that it shall fall from the bridge into the jaws of a great fish which is in league with the bird.   On the other side of the river is Ungap, a woman with a cauldron and a spear.   If appeased with a gift she aids the ghost to escape from the monstrous

---

[1] Ling Roth, loc. cit., i, pp. 220, 221.
[2] Ch. Hose and W. McDougall, *The Pagan Tribes of Borneo*, 1912, ii, p. 41.
[3] Hose and McDougall, loc. cit., ii, p. 45.

bird and fish.   Pebbles or beads are put in the nostrils of the Punan corpse in order that they may be presented to Ungap.[1]

Before we pass on to another group of other-world myths in which birds seem to play a conspicuous part we must pause to consider the situation.   The two dogs of Yama appear also as a dog with two heads.   Löschke [2] has interpreted the representation of a naked boy holding two cocks in his hands and attacked by two bitches as representing two female Kerberoi and at any rate the traditional plurality of heads may be the exaggeration of the original two heads. Cerberus is usually represented as a composite beast, between a dog and a serpent,—a sort of dog-dragon.   Pausanias contains a remark of Hekataios about a " serpent that was called the dog of Hades ".[3] We do not believe with Immisch that the idea of a dog of the infernal regions arose from a misunderstanding of this expression, which originally meant merely a servant of Hades.   We are rather inclined to drop natural history altogether and say that the dog was also a serpent or that both symbols represent the same unconscious content. In fact, he was also a frog, for the scholium to Nik. Alexiph., 578, mentions a " dumb " (i.e. chthonic) frog called Kerberos.[4]

A frog is not far removed from a fish, but we have to go as far as Borneo to find a series formed of fish, dog, and woman as the obstacles on the path to the other world.   Serpents are the typical foes of the dead, both in Egypt and Greece, but on the other hand, we find the serpent bridge leading to the other world (cf. below) and the dead themselves reappearing in the shape of serpents.   Again, the dangerous dog of the Indo-Aryan beliefs seems to be connected with the Egyptian Anubis, for the corpse or soul devoured by the ravenous tooth of the beast becomes the dead reborn by the agency of the god. There seems to be some ground for the conjecture that the two dogs were originally the theriomorphic symbols of a female being.   The beads are either for a female being or for a dog.   In Vedic tradition the dogs are sometimes called the dogs of Sarama.   At burial the dead person is told to escape from the two dogs of Sarama, those with the four eyes—the spotted ones—and to approach by the happy path the ancestors feasting with Yama.[5]   We know but little of Sarama, but at any rate she appears to be the mother of the two dogs and herself a bitch.[6]

What can the bridge mean that, fraught with such evident signs

---

[1] Hose and McDougall, loc. cit., ii, p. 44.
[2] *Aus der Unterwelt*, Dorp. Progr., 1888.   [3] Pausanias, iii, 24, 5.
[4] *Roschers Lexikon*, ii, p. 1129.   [5] Landau, loc. cit., p. 66.
[6] Hildebrandt, *Vedische Mythologie*, 1899, ii, pp. 48–50.

of danger, leads into the jaws of a bitch ? It is broad or narrow according to the conscience of him who tries to reach the other shore. It is agitated by the animal, and the bitch of Indian tradition both fetches the soul for the journey and tries to obstruct its path.

Now what takes the soul into another world ? The Batak tell us that the soul of a man in his prime is fetched by a female ghost desirous of a husband ; that of a woman by a male ghost.[1] In a Mabuiag myth the hero has a penis of enormous length that he keeps coiled up by his side. When he hears a woman asking for his assistance to cross the water he takes his penis into his hand and throws it across the channel. Having made herself " fast " the woman is hauled across the channel.[2] Now it can hardly be a coincidence that the word used here, " fast," is the Torres Strait pidgin English expression for coitus. The bridge is the penis ; it leads from earth to heaven and is agitated by a bitch (note the vulgar expression), that is, by the personification of the vagina. Ferenczi has published some cases which showed that this was the meaning of bridge symbolism.[3]

If the bridge is the penis we shall understand the soul passing by means of this bridge to the world beyond the grave as the seminal fluid passing by means of the male member into the womb, and it is anxiety, closely connected as it is with a feeling of guilt, that does not let the souls of the sinners attain the bliss that awaits them beyond the open gate, beyond the gap, beyond the waters. The fate of the sinner is a sort of posthumous *ejaculatio præcox*, and it is fear that transforms the vagina into a ravenous animal that does not let the soul reach its goal. He who does not give his " bead " to the protecting woman naturally falls into the jaws of the devouring fish. Now we can understand why the Karens say that those who pass the sword-bridge are men, whereas those who cannot achieve this feat become women. They are castrated and castration, that is, the dread of something being cut off the body, is symbolized by the same symbol which means the penis, for the bridge is a sword, a razor. The proper sacrifice for the dogs of Yama are the kidneys of the animal killed at the grave,[4] but the kidneys as we shall see in the chapter on magic owe their significance as soul-receptacles to their connection with the genital apparatus. We may well regard

[1] Warneck, *Die Religion der Batak*, 1909, p. 67.
[2] *Cambridge Expedition to Torres Straits*, v, p. 59.
[3] Ferenczi, " Die Symbolik der Brücke," *Zeitschrift*, vii. *Idem*, " Die Brücken-Symbolik und die Don Juan-Legende," *Zeitschrift*, viii, p. 7.
[4] *Roschers Lexikon*, ii, p. 1129.

Thus a Sia Indian goes to his mother in the lower world.[1] " It is the aim of the Sia first to reach the intermediate state at the time their body ceases to develop and then return gradually back to the first condition of infancy. At such a period one does not die, but sleeps, to awake in the spirit world as a little child." [2] Thus it is quite evident that the return to the totem is the return to the mother, to the womb, and that therefore, as we have previously pointed out, the totem must be regarded as a condensation of the father and mother-imago.[3] According to two of the Omaha buffalo gentes, the souls of the dead members return to the buffalo.[4] A dead member of the Wezinshte gens to whom the elk had been taboo all his life receives moccasins made of elk-skin.[5]

But the point we wish to stress is that the idea of return to the totem as mother, or, stating the same thing in more general terms, the idea of another world, is not a primary one in the strictest sense of the word. It is a consolation and the vagina is not an object of dread but the best possible place for the semen. Stating the same thing in reference to the cell, we have first fission and then a living environment regained in conjugation. Perhaps we may therefore say that the dread of castration or autotomy does not originally refer to the vagina at all, that its deepest root is to be sought for in the conflicting forces that work for fission and against it in the overgrown cell. But the attempt to grapple with fear in coitus by the aid of the vagina is only partly successful, for there is a narcissistically resented element of mutual eating up involved in the act of conjugation.[6] The result is that the dread of castration is displaced to the vagina and we see the latter as an organ with oral qualities,[7] as the devouring beast that stops the soul on its dangerous journey to the land of the Hereafter. But this division of the female partner in coitus into the land of bliss as a consolation for the expenditure of the semen and into the devouring beast is not the only complication we have to reckon with. Above we have quoted an account from Borneo according to which the dog cohabits with the souls of women who come his way. While this clearly confirms our interpretation of the soul's passage as coition, it seems that there is

[1] M. C. Stevenson, " The Sia," 11th Report, p. 145.

[2] Stevenson, loc. cit., pp. 144, 145.

[3] Róheim, " Nach dem Tode des Urvaters," Imago, ix.

[4] J. O. Dorsey, " A Study of Siouan Cults," 11th Report, p. 542.

[5] A. C. Fletcher and F. la Flesche, " The Omaha Tribe," 27th Re[...]
p. 589.

[6] Ferenczi, Genitaltheorie, p. 1924.

[7] H. Deutsch, Psychoanalyse der weiblichen Sexualfunctionen, 1[...]

them, therefore, as a substitute for the testicles, the latter reappearing under various guises as beads, honey-cakes, cowries, money, etc., the various objects to be offered to the watch-dog, the ghostly ferry-man, or the women of Hades. Our folklore data show that the principal thing in putting money, etc., on the eyelids or in the mouth of the corpse seems to be that nothing should be open, for an opening of any sort means a second death.[1] The gap is stopped by inserting the penis and anxiety is overcome. This is why nobody can possibly stop a ghost who has enjoyed a certain number of women from getting into a heaven, for the two, coition and the journey to the other world, both mean the same thing.

The dog or other obstructors of the passage are certainly personified representatives of castration anxiety. Thus we are told that the Toradja ghost requires much skill to pass a pig which may bite it, a nut being put into the hand of a child corpse to throw at him. There is also an examining guardian Langkoda, who lames those who are not married or have not killed an enemy. The way to pass him is to recount one's heroic deeds and love adventures so cleverly that he laughs and his great upper lip goes up to his eyes, at this moment the soul can slip by unobserved.[2] Lameness is one of the most frequent symbols of castration, and those who have not achieved the repetition of their infantile Œdipus wishes in marriage and in killing an enemy owe their failure to their " lameness " (castration anxiety) represented, however, by the myth as the consequence and not as the cause of this failure. Victory is achieved by blinding the examining monster (another equivalent of castration), for he who has killed many men and had intercourse with many women is also capable of castrating the monstrous representative of the father imago.

Here, however, we shall pause to consider another question. What man really dreads—this will hardly be questioned—is not the other world but death. The other world is a consolation, an attempt to make death easy, to make it possible for the soul to leave the body by promising another and better place for it to live in. I think this is exactly the point of view taken by Ferenczi in his latest researches on this question. He tells us that the dread of the vagina is not really the dread of the vagina at all. What is really dreaded in the

[1] Róheim, Magyar Néphit és Népszokások, 1928, p. 179. Idem, Spiegelzauber, 1919, p. 213. Elliot Smith, The Evolution of the Dragon 1919, p. 150.

[2] Kruijt, Het Animisme, p. 350. R. Moss, The Life after Death in Oceania and the Malay Archipelago, 1925, p. 279.

act of cohabitation is autotomy, fission, the expenditure of the semen, and the possibility of placing the semen into another favourable environment, in the womb, facilitates its discharge. If we regard mankind's ideas on death as modelled on what is certainly the deepest experience in life, on coitus, we find that this view perfectly covers the facts. In Egypt the dead are protected by a mother goddess : the seminal fluid in the ovum. In chapter cli of the Book of the Dead, Isis kneels at the bier of the deceased and says to him : " I have come to protect thee with the north wind which cometh forth from Tem ; I have strengthened for thee thy throat, I have caused thee to be with the god and I have placed all thine enemies under thy feet."[1] We have seen above how Isis protects the body of the dead but yet phallic Osiris, how—and this amounts to the same thing— she conceives by him. Why are women prominent in the mourning for the phallic sun gods Tammuz, Adonis, Attis, Dionysus, and the maimed (castrated) Grail King ? Why are women the principal mourners in savage mourning rites ; why do they receive the liquid of putrefaction on their bodies ? Because the corpse is a penis ; its rigidity is erection ; the passage of the soul to the other world the ejaculation of semen. Thus we find the dead protected against every danger by the great sky-goddess Nut and at the same time having intercourse with her.[2] If we follow this trend of argument we can understand why among the Baganda the nail-parings are concealed in the garden of a female relative and refuse is eaten by the totem fish among the Kpelle. If they must be lost it is better to have them there than unprotected. If the soul must leave the body another womb must be invented for it. As for placing the severed part of the body in the totem animal, there is no lack in animistic parallels. Thus we saw above how the phallus of Osiris was eaten and how the souls were ferried over to the other world by the totem-fish of Oxyrhynchus. In a myth told by the Iabim one of the ghosts smashes the ghostly ferry-boat and the Charon of the boat in his rage tells them that he will not take them across the water—let them be changed into kangaroos.[3] According to another account, the spirits of the dead are either changed into their respective totem animals or they go to the island other world,[4] which I take to mean that the two are exactly the same thing. The point is that in the Bougainville Straits the corpse is devoured by the totem fish

[1] Budge, *Gods of the Egyptians*, ii, p. 205.
[2] Rusch, " Die Himmelsgöttin Nuth," *M.V.A.G.*, xxvii, pp. 38, 59.
[3] Neuhauss, *Deutsch Neu Guinea*, iii, p. 291.
[4] H. Vetter, *Komm herüber und hilf uns*, iii, p. 21.

and that these totem fish are called grandmothers,[1] man gets back into the inside of his ancestress.[2]

According to a Zuni myth, this is the way death world. The ancestors were trying to cross a river strange anxiety when crossing the water, an anxiety st who do the same. But the women who followed th children on their backs became crazed with these drea of the waters. Wherefore, the little ones to whom the more closely, being yet unripe, were instantly char They turned cold, then colder, they grew scaly, full sharp clawed of hands and feet, longer of tail too, as if and guidance in unquiet waters. Lo ! they felt of a mothers that bore them like dead things, and, wriggli their bare shoulders until, shrieking wildly, these moth hold of them and were even fain to shake them off, fleei in terror. Thus multitudes of them fell into the wailing shrilly and plaintively. For no sooner did the the surges than they floated and swam away, changed even in bodily form ; for according to their several became like to the lizard, chameleon and newt, others l toad and turtle. But their " in-beings " (souls), bec sense of falling, still falling, sank down through the wate itself being started sinks down through the sands in the de There, under the lagoon of the hollow mountain they undying ancients. These little ones paved the way of dy path of the dead, for whither they led in olden times others to seek them followed. But the mothers did not know children had gone to the world whence they themselves and whither constrained by the yearnings of their heart must follow.[3] The place whence, according to their myths, the Zuni came is described by them in so many w openly as the Place of Gestation, the Vaginal Womb, the Parturition.[4] The soul goes to the lake in the depths of K lawa, descends the mystic ladder to meet the council of thence passes on to the undermost world, the place of Zuni

[1] G. C. Wheeler, " Sketch of the Totemism and Religion of of the Islands in Bougainville Straits," *A.R.W.*, xv, p. 26.
[2] Róheim, *Australian Totemism*, p. 208.
[3] Cushing, " Zuni Creation Myths," *Bureau of Am. Ethn.* 13 p. 404–5.
[4] Cushing, loc. cit., pp. 382, 383.
[5] M. C. Stevenson, " The Zuni Indians," 23rd *Report*, p. 308.

here a reversal in the rôle of male and female. The duplication of the symbolism is rather remarkable : for instance, we have the serpent as bridge and the serpent as the demon opposing the passage, the dog as fetcher of souls and as guardian of the gate. Now both serpent and dog are frequent penis symbols, and it seems that the castration here dreaded by the soul would be the one that threatens the penis of the child by another penis, by the man who is in possession of the stronghold, by the father. We must not forget that the myth of Osiris-Set is the narrative of the Primal Horde, of the war waged between the father and the brothers for the women of the horde. Osiris castrated his father and was in his turn castrated by a younger brother. But yet in comparison with a mortal even the evil god Set must appear as a representative of the father and the dreaded passage of the soul to the other world is therefore the dread of the child-adult who is inhibited in his incestuous desires by the idea of the father. And how does a man succeed in overcoming this dread ? By identification with the father. In the language of Egyptian religion, the corpse conquers Set by becoming the god-king of old, Osiris. This explains why the head-hunter has the keys of paradise in his hands ; he will do the same on the passage as he did when a mortal man. Who his opponent is, is made quite evident by the Lushei; it is Pupawla, the father, the first man who died.

In a series of myths from Borneo to Australia we find the passage of the soul to the other world obstructed by a bird. In Borneo it was the hornbill.[1] At Bogota the ghosts of the dead go to an island. In the island of the dead there is a pool of water and thither the ghosts repair to present themselves to the spirit, who is the lord of the dead. Across the pool there is a narrow tree-trunk lying on which they advance, and the ruler of the other-world examines their hands to see if they have the mark of the frigate-bird cut upon them, for this alone admits them to the other world. At Wango, in San Cristoval, the soul on leaving the body makes its way to three small islands near Ulawa. On his first arrival the ghost still feels himself a man and does not realize his real condition,[2] but after some days a kingfisher picks the head of the lately separated soul and it sinks into a ghost. The attitude of the natives towards the kingfisher is the peculiar ambivalent combination of aggressiveness and respect which psycho-analysis so frequently finds in connection with the father imago. They kill the kingfisher because it kills the soul, but young

[1] Cf. the Punan myth quoted above.
[2] Codrington, loc. cit., p. 257.

E

ones spring up from the blood of every one they kill. In the Banks Islands every kingfisher is sacred *rongo*, a spirit is connected with it, and not a single one is ever killed or eaten. The name of the king-fisher is a charm for sunshine, yet the cry is an evil omen for a man who starts on a journey.[1] It is a parrakeet that warns the Fijian killer of souls to lie in wait for the unfortunate traveller[2]; the soul of an Arunta is frightened back by the Recurvirostra,[3] and in Victoria we have an elaborate myth—the crow as principal antagonist of the soul on its journey—the crow being the eponymous animal of one of the two original totem moieties.[4]

Again there is some additional evidence in Melanesia and Australia to demonstrate the main idea of our argument, that the passage of the soul is coition. In a myth of the Solomon Islands, as in the narrative of the Bible, it is the first coitus carried out in the vagina that " brought death into the world and all our woe ".[5] Before that people knew only of intercourse in the armpit. We suspect that by this original intercourse the myth means to indicate an imperfect infantile form of the act, perhaps without ejaculating the semen. However that may be, it is clear enough that the passage of the soul is a posthumous cohabitation. In Fiji every ghost must throw a whale's tooth at a pandanus-tree ; if he hits it it is well, for this shows that people are strangling his wives and they will follow him into the other world. If not, he cannot go on, evidently because without a wife he has no chance of getting admitted. One of the terrors of the path is called the Great Woman, and a bachelor ghost has no chance whatever of getting into paradise.[6] Among the Wathi-Wathi and kindred tribes in Australia, when the soul leaves the body it reaches a pathway divided into two roads. One of these roads is open, the other obstructed by brambles; or one clean and the other dirty. The first road leads to a young and fine woman, the second, the one full of difficulties, to an old one. It is to the latter, the representative of the mother-imago, that the soul must go. Next he jumps across a flaming chasm and over a rope held by two women to trip him. He meets a woman who tries to seduce him and a blind one who tries to trip him. Finally he comes to the All-Father Tha-Thapulli, who gives him a spear to show his skill

[1] Codrington, *The Melanesians*, p. 190.
[2] Williams, *Fiji and the Fijans*, 1856, i, p. 245.
[3] Róheim, *Australian Totemism*, p. 199.
[4] Róheim, loc. cit., p. 206.
[5] Thurnwald, *Forschungen*, i, p. 322.
[6] Williams, loc. cit., i, pp. 243, 244. Thomson, loc. cit., pp. 120, 121.

and strength in spearing emus.[1] In discussing the problems of Australian totemism I have shown both that the emu is the regular mother-symbol of these tribes and that spearing means cohabitation.[2] It is needless to stress the repetition of symbols : it is plain enough what the whole journey means and that it is a passage of the soul into woman, the seducer. But as woman is castrated by coitus, she appears in the shape of a blind woman, and as the woman in question is the emu mother, the soul must get a " spear " from the All-Father before he can remain in the other world that represents her womb.

The Ba Ila tell us that man dies at the very hour which is the hour of his birth.[3] Egypt is familiar with the idea that death is really birth, and the scarab, the symbol of immortality, is the child-god Chep-Ra.[4]

Undoubtedly the beliefs clustering round death could also be described as if they referred to birth. We might remind the reader that the soul was represented as a little child,[5] and that if the other life was a repetition of this one the moment of death must be regarded as the moment of birth. The soul is severed from the body just as the child is separated from its mother. Now we must observe that such a theory would not miss the mark altogether, but only lay the stress on the wrong place. Since the expenditure of the semen in the male is, in the unconscious, equivalent to the act of giving birth in the female, it would be merely a female version of the same solution. But there is something else to be considered. It is not the soul that is anxious, not the part cut off from the whole, but the reverse. It is the loss of a part, of the nail-parings or of the soul, that seems to be unbearable, so that this version would not mean that death is a repetition of the shock suffered in being born, but of that suffered in giving birth to the child, which is the female analogy for the male point of view that death means castration or expenditure of semen in coitus. We have not commented on the gates of the other world. Their peculiar feature is that like the Symplegades of Greek myth, they are continually opening and shutting. The Karens see two massive strata of rocks that are always opening and shutting. Through

---

[1] A. L. P. Cameron, " Notes on some Tribes of N.S.W.," *Journ. Anthr. Inst.*, 1884, p. 364. Id., " Traditions and Folklore of the Aborigines of N.S.W.," *Science of Man*, 1903, p. 46.

[2] Róheim, loc. cit., p. 205.

[3] Smith and Dale, *The Ba-Ila*, ii, p. 103.

[4] Hopfner, " Tierkult der alten Aegypter," *Denkschriften*, Wien, 57 Bd., Abh., 1914, p. 159. Cf. above.

[5] Róheim, " Das Selbst," *Imago*, vii.

them the sun descends at sunset and the soul travels to the abode of the Judge of the Dead.[1]

In the funeral ritual of the Aztecs the soul is said to pass between the two mountains that smite against each other.[2]

The hero of the folk-tale has also frequently to pass through these crushing rocks or smiting door and usually he does not come quite unscathed from the ordeal. The doves fly through the Symplegades to bring Zeus ambrosia, but the last is always crushed by the relentless rocks.[3] Maui, with the pigeon called the Fearless, descends to the nether world where his mother had gone before him. Upon pronouncing the magic word the rock opened and Maui entered. According to one version he entered as a dragon fly perched upon the pigeon, while in another variant Maui is inside the animal. The two fierce guardian demons of the chasm, finding themselves imposed upon by a stranger, made a grab at the pigeon, intending to devour it. But they only succeeded in getting possession of its tail, whilst the pigeon pursued its flight to the shades.[4] In a folk-tale of the Tarantschi, a Tartar tribe in Central Asia, we find the hero passing through the moving rocks on his way to his sister-wife. The tail of his camel is cut off.[5]

If we know what the moving door means we shall understand the missing tail. The motif is very frequent in the mythology of North-West America and its unconscious meaning can be studied there with advantage. The Chilcotin and Shuswap tradition of Little Dog contains a series of episodes which, like the scenes of many dreams, evidently all have the same meaning. Little Dog, warned by his wife not to go in a certain direction, disobeys her and is swallowed by a moose that stands in the middle of the water. Little Dog makes a fire in the inside, cuts the animal's heart and eats it, and thus kills the moose. He comes out alive and well. Soon Little Dog and his children come to a house with a great stone door. Inside the house sits a woman who is weaving a basket. Suddenly, while they are talking to her they notice the stone door beginning to shut and Little Dog quickly places his magic staff so that it holds the door open. The boys slip through, and Little Dog after them, but when he

---

[1] Mason, " Karens," *Journ. As. Soc. Beng.*, 1865, ii, pp. 233, 234. Tylor, loc. cit., p. 348.

[2] Tylor, loc. cit., ii, p. 349.

[3] Frobenius, *Das Zeitalter des Sonnengottes*, 1904, p. 405.

[4] Gill, *Myths and Songs*, pp. 52, 53.

[5] W. Radloff, *Proben der Volkslitteratur der nördlichen Türkstämme*, 1886, vi, p. 243.

pulls the magic staff out behind him his little finger is caught by the door and the end cut off. Now they come to a woman whose vagina is full of teeth. She wants our hero to have intercourse with her, but he first inserts his magic staff into the vagina and breaks her teeth. Then he and all his boys cohabit with her.[1] I think nobody will doubt that the vagina with teeth and the snapping door both made innocuous by a magic staff, through both of which our hero passes followed by his children, mean one and the same thing. If there should still be any doubt our meaning is made perfectly clear by the myth of Maui, crushed between the opening and closing legs, in the vagina of his ancestress Great Mother Night.[2]

If the door is the vagina, the pigeon's tail or the little finger snapped off by it can only mean the penis. The peculiar conclusion arrived at would then be : the other world is the maternal womb, but castration the price to be paid by those who would be admitted. We have called this conclusion peculiar because of the seeming contradiction involved. The passage of the soul is coitus, the soul itself the semen, yet at the gate of the other world we find castration. But then again we have shown that primitive views on death are modelled on the castration anxiety and therefore if by castration we mean death it is natural enough that this should be the preliminary to the entry into heaven. For the soul leaving the body, the chopped off end of the pigeon's tail, and the little finger made shorter all mean the same thing.

In ascending the scale of civilization from the lowest depths of savagery we shall find that up to a certain point the pictures in which the world beyond the grave is represented continually gain in colour. First at the level of the Dyak or the Fijians, the sombre aspects, the difficulties of access, are evolved while at a somewhat higher level all is bliss and happiness.

Celtic heroes have a pleasant way of their own in going to the other world. This is the tale of Bran, son of Febal :—

" One day, in the neighbourhood of his stronghold Bran went about all alone, when he heard music behind him. At last he fell asleep at the music, such was its sweetness. When he awoke from his sleep he saw close by him a branch of silver with white blossoms." Afterwards a woman in strange raiment appears and says :—

[1] L. Farrand, *Traditions of the Chilcotin Indians*, Jesup, North Pacific, ii, p. 7. Cf. Robert H. Lowie, " The Test Theme in North American Mythology," *Journ. Am. F.L.*, 1908, p. 106.

[2] Tylor, *Primitive Culture*, i, p. 344.

A branch of the apple-tree from Emain
I bring like those one knows;
Twigs of white silver are on it,
Crystal brows with blossoms.
There is a distant isle along
Which sea-horses glisten

.   .   .   .   .   .

A delight to the eyes, a glorious range
Is the plain on which the hosts hold games.
Coracle contends against chariot
In southern Mag Findargat [1] (White Silver Plain).

She ends her long description of this land of beauty by inviting him to come to the land of women.[2] He sets out on the journey and reaches the Land of Women. Drawn to the shore by a thread held by one of the women, they go into a large house where there is a bed for every couple.[3] Summarizing the salient features of similar myths, A. B. Cook establishes three principal features :—

1 The Elysian palace has growing beside it a silver apple-tree, or a silver tree glittering in the sunlight like gold and surrounded by trees that drop " rindless food ".

2 A silver branch from the Elysian tree is brought to a king's son, or at least, an apple from the same tree is given to him.

3 The hero mates with the Queen of Elysium and so becomes its king.[4]

Without going into the details of Celtic mythology, we merely wish to lay stress on the importance of the silver branch. It has been pointed out that in this Silver Bough of Irish legend we have the closest parallel to the Golden Bough at Nemi. Both open the way to the other world and in both cases breaking the Bough means the death of a king.[5]

Now we shall attempt to show later on the identity of the king's life-tree with the maypole and the Eiresione and the phallic significance of all these symbols. If we provisionally take this for granted here and make use of our knowledge of dream symbolism, the breaking of a bough from the life-tree would appear to be castration. Nor can the everlasting happy mating of mortal man with the goddess of the other world deceive us—it is evidently a compensation for what cannot be compensated, a beautiful picture

---

[1] Nutt-Meyer, *The Voyage of Bran*, 1897, i, p. 3, 4.
[2] Ibid., i, p. 14.   [3] Nutt-Meyer, loc. cit., i, p. 30.
[4] A. B. Cook, " The European Sky God," *Folk-Lore*, xvii, 1906, p. 151.
[5] A. B. Cook, loc. cit., p. 169. E. Hull, " The Silver Bough in Irish Legend," *Folk-Lore*, xii, pp. 431–45.

conjured up by the unconscious to veil what no man can look upon without terror.

We have hitherto found reason to assume that the one great terror in the life of primitive mankind is the same that plays such a fundamental part in individual neurosis : the dread of castration. This complex rooted in the resistance offered by the narcissistic libido of the cell to fission as the fundamental feature of archaic life is never absent in coitus where there is always a reluctance of the male towards the expenditure of semen. The ideas of primitive man on death are modelled by the pleasure principle, being based on the unconscious view of coitus. The soul separated from the body is either the seminal fluid ejaculated in the act, or what amounts to the same thing, the phallus cut off. This interpretation of the soul is fully borne out by experience derived from the study of psychotic and neurotic patients. Dr Almásy tells me of a case of shell-shock treated by him in a lunatic asylum. The soldier was a Hungarian lad from Transylvania. He declared in the asylum that the shell in question had robbed him of his " double ", and added that the " double " was the Székely,[1] word for the penis.   A patient of mine (character analysis, *ejaculatio præcox* in a moderate degree) has the phantasy that the analyst's easy chairs are transformed at night-fall into stallions and on these stallions the analysts fly through the air and appear as nightmares in their patients' dreams. The couch on which he lies is not a stallion but a hippopotamus (called water-horse in Hungarian), and it goes and wallows in the mud at night. What a fine thing it would be to have a penis as big as a hippopotamus ; he could go and knock the policeman down with such a club. At night his penis would leave his body, assume the shape of a hippopotamus and roam about.   It is hardly necessary to tell the anthropologist that we here have the explanation of the savage dream-soul leaving the body at night and roaming in search of desirable things. " King Gunthram lay in the wood asleep with his head in his faithful henchman's lap ; the servant saw as it were a snake issue from his lord's mouth and run to the brook, but it could not pass, so the servant laid his sword across the water and the creature ran along it and up into a mountain, after a while came back and returned into the mouth of the sleeping king, who waking told him how he went over an iron bridge into a mountain full of gold." [2]   King Gunthram's serpent and the penis-hippopotamus of my patient mean one and the same thing.

---

[1] Hungarian dialect in Transylvania.
[2] E. B. Tylor, *Primitive Culture*, i, p. 442, quoting Grimm, *D.M.* 1036.

From this starting-point the work of repression sets in. The first consolation offered to mortal man is the same as the temptation of coitus ; the valuable part of his personality is not lost but given into the custody of a being with whom he has successfully identified himself in the sexual act. There is another world for the soul after this one and this other world is simply a posthumous projection of the womb. The passage itself is the passage of the penis or the sperm into the vagina. While at a lower level the castration aspect of this passage is emphasized, the grim features of this last journey gradually become obscured by the brilliant vision of everlasting love-life. But just as we know full well that the gods, the " Living Ones " of Irish and other mythologies, are really the dead, we can have no doubt of the nature of the wound that lies behind the phantasy of an Isle of Women.

As, moreover, the sexual act is the portal of life, and as the act of giving birth is the female equivalent of the fission that takes place in the male in the act of coitus, death becomes obscured under the guise of birth and appears as the first step into a new life. In this concept, which it is so easy to find in the phantasies and dreams of individual neurotics, the secondary elaboration due to the tendency to obscure the impending danger probably reached its highest pitch. If we return for a moment to the story of Little Dog our attention is attracted by the series formed of three episodes ; first Little Dog's whole body in the giant moose and his exit from that animal, then his being in a house inhabited by a woman (magic staff holds the door ajar—finger chopped off) and at last his overcoming the danger of castration by the magic staff in actual coitus. The series represents a gradual retransformation of the myth towards the true situation. In the first episode the danger of fission (castration) is completely overlaid by the aid of another phantasy, this time formed on the basis of the pre-natal situation and of birth itself, by means of the idea of evading coitus by returning not with a part but with the whole body into the maternal womb. Therefore, if the recent experiences of Dr Ferenczi and other analysts show that the ideas of birth and uterine regression appear in analysis as a consolation to overlay the dread of castration, we can say that in the history of mankind the function of animism offers.a distinct parallel to these tendencies. The solace found by the pious in the visions of a happy heaven is of the same type as that sought by the neurotic in the various symptoms that correspond to uterine regression.

King Arthur feels his end drawing near. He first commands his sword Excalibur to be cast back into the lake whence it came. We believe that this sword is fundamentally identical with the sword of the Grail romances, the meaning of which has been described in the language of " Life-Symbolism " by Miss Jessie Weston.[1]

Like the supernatural branch, the silver bough, it belongs to the king as long as he lives and returns to its origin at his death.[2] First this phallic symbol disappears into the lake, then Queen Morgan le Fay appears on the scene with her fairies in a barge to take her beloved hero and brother to her realm. And thus spake Sir Arthur :—

> " I am going a long way . . . .
>
> . . . .
> To the island-valley of Avilion
> Where falls not hail, or rain, or any snow,
> Nor ever wind blows loudly ; but it lies
> Deep-meadowed, happy, fair with orchard lawns
> And bowery hollows crown'd with summer sea,
> Where I will heal me of my grievous wound." [3]

However fair the fairy queen may be, mortal man can scarce forget the wound.

[1] J. L. Weston, *The Quest of the Holy Grail*, 1913. Id., *From Ritual to Romance*, 1920.
[2] A. B. Cook, loc. cit., p. 152.
[3] Tennyson, *Morte d'Arthur*. Malory, *Le Morte d'Arthur*, Bk. xxi, chap. v.

II THE PSYCHOLOGY OF MAGIC

1 THE BLACK ART

SO far we have put forward the theory that the ideas of primitive mankind on the subject of death are veiled repetitions of the dread they experience at the expenditure of the seminal fluid. Most primitive tribes live in a perpetual anxiety about what happens to the severed parts of their body, and as this anxiety is a castration-phobia the active part taken by the sorcerer in this connection must be a *displaced repetition of castration*.

Our next aim will therefore be to see whether this view is applicable to black magic or sorcery in general and then to other branches of the magic art, and in a subsequent chapter to draw certain conclusions from the nature of magic to the psychology of the magician.

(*a*) *Opening a Man.*—The first of these practices is chiefly characteristic of South-East Australia with certain affinities in New Guinea and Melanesia that are probably to be regarded as traces of a former ethnological contact between the continent and these islands. The Wiimbaio, for instance, believe that the medicine-men of hostile tribes sneak into the camp at night and with a net of a peculiar construction garrotte one of the tribe, drag him a hundred yards or so from the camp, make an oblique cut in his abdomen, take out the kidney and caul fat, and then stuff a handful of grass and sand into the wound. The strangling net is then undone, and if the victim is not quite dead he generally dies within three days. Club and net are the weapons of these sorcerers. For we also hear that the sorcerer knocks a man down in the night with an " ear-having club ", that is, a club having two corners, i.e. ears. The man being thus knocked down, the sorcerer would remove the fat without leaving any sign of the operation. They believed that the men of other tribes prowled about in the night, like hungry beasts in search of prey, and they called these demons of the dark

" one who spreads a net for the feet " and " one who seizes by the throat ". This seems to develop into a regular group-phobia, as we hear of a case when they asked the protection of a white man against their southern enemies the Wotjobaluk who might come at night, put cords on their throats and, having thus choked them, would carry them off and take their fat.[1] The report of Jamieson from the River Murray Mildure Station probably refers to the same tribe. Death is always attributed to human agency. When anybody dies an enemy is supposed during the night to have made an incision in his side and removed his kidney fat.[2]

In the attempt to trace the geographical distribution of this custom or belief we follow the course of the Murray and from the Wiimbaio we come to the Narrinyeri.

Wyungarre pulls himself up into heaven by means of a line attached to his spear. He still sits up there and fishes for men with a fishing spear, and when people start up in their sleep it is because he touches them with the point of his weapon.[3] If we put the dispersed pieces of evidence together, this dream-experience seems to be of an ominous nature. For it is by the aid of a spear line that Wyungarre himself reaches his father Nurundere in the realm of the dead, and then again it is Wyungarre who throws the line to the dead man and conducts him to the other world.[4]

We shall follow Taplin in his description of *millin*, a species of sorcery which seems to be usually connected with the idea of blood-revenge. " When they see their victim alone, they steal noiselessly upon him, and rushing at him suddenly strike him a heavy blow with the plongge [5] for the purpose of stunning him. Then, as he lies there insensible, they strike him moderately hard with the plongge on the joints of the legs and arms, on the nape of the neck and on the naked chest, the blows not being severe enough to break the bones as a touch of the instrument is considered sufficient. In

[1] Howitt, *Native Tribes of South-East Australia*, 1904, pp. 367, 368.

[2] Th. F. Bride, *Letters from Victorian Pioneers*, 1898, p. 271.

[3] G. Taplin, *The Narrinyeri, an Account of the Tribes of South Australian Aborigines*, 1878, pp. 56-8.

[4] H. E. A. Meyer, " Manners and Customs of the Aborigines of the Encounter Bay Tribes," in J. D. Woods, *Native Tribes of South Australia*, 1879, pp. 205, 206. For a discussion of these myths see Róheim, *Australian Totemism*, 1925, pp. 45-7.

[5] " The plongge is a stick about 2 feet long with a large knob at the end." E. H. Meyer, " Manners and Customs of the Aborigines of the Encounter Bay Tribe," in H. D. Woods, *The Native Tribes of South Australia*, 1879, p. 196.

conclusion they pull the victim's ears until they crack, then leaving him to recover as best he can.   This last operation is for the purpose of rendering the person incapable of telling who attacked him." [1]

The essential features of this description seem to be, that death is preceded by a magical attack, in which the mere touch of a weapon (cf. the touch of the fishing-line above) plays an important part, and that this rather complicated attack is forgotten by the victim; or, at least, he cannot identify the evil-doer.

" By the operation he is delivered over to the power of a certain demon called Nalkara.   The demon will divert his attention from the spear which deals the mortal wound in battle, from the snake along his path, or it will produce disease.   It seems that death from the plongge is specially associated with pains in the chest and that the magical deed is usually perpetrated on a sleeping victim." [2]

" The charming is generally performed upon a person asleep, therefore, when several tribes are encamped near each other, there is always one keeping watch that they may not be charmed by any of the other tribe.   Should a man have an enemy whom he wishes to enchant, and he can steal upon him while sleeping without being discovered, he thinks to throw him into a sounder sleep by striking the air before his face as though in the act of sprinkling it with a tuft of emu feathers which have been previously moistened in the liquor from a putrid corpse." [3]

In general, we can say that over a large area in Australia we find the belief that death is to be attributed to something that happened to the sleeper.   Either his kidney fat is taken out, or he suffers from the effects of strangulation in a dream, or some other peculiar attack is perpetrated upon him at night, which, however, always ends with the infliction of an invisible wound. [4]

Hence their very general dread of going out at night.   Night and anxiety are closely connected in their life.   " They are in perpetual fear of malignant spirits or bad men who go abroad at night, and they seldom venture from the encampment after dusk even to fetch water, without a fire-stick in their hands." [5]   In some of these accounts, for instance, in the beliefs of the Parnkalla and Nauo tribes, the similarity to the *nightmare* of European folklore is very great.

[1] G. Taplin, *The Narrinyery*, 1878, p. 27.

[2] Taplin, loc. cit., p. 27.   [3] H. E. Meyer, loc. cit., p. 195.

[4] Cf. for evil demons of the night, G. L. Stokes, *Discoveries in Australia*, 1846, p. 61. G. Grey, *Journals of two Expeditions*, 1841, ii, p. 340.

[5] G. F. Angas, *Savage Life and Scenes in Australia and New Zealand*, 1847, i, p. 88. Cf. ibid., p. 96.   A. C. Bicknell, *Travel and Adventure in Northern Queensland*, 1895, p. 96.

" Should an individual happen to die without any apparent cause, they imagine that a great bird (*marralya*) which is in fact a man of a hostile tribe, who assumes that shape, pounces upon the sick person, squeezes together his ribs and causes him gradually to expire." [1] They regard the *marralye* as a man of the Kukata tribe who assumes the shape of a bird in order to fly through the air.

It attacks its victims while asleep and somehow inflicts a mortal but invisible wound on them.[2]   All these practices, however they may vary as to the mode of procedure, show two fundamental features ; they are carried out at night and there is no visible wound, or perhaps it would be simpler to say, there is no wound at all.

The Wotjobaluk *bangal* sneaks into the camp at night and darts an invisible bone into the sleeping victim. This compels him to come out of the camp to the medicine man. The latter knocks him insensible with a club or nooses him, and after having thus rendered him helpless the medicine man sits astride on his chest, cuts him open on the right side below the ribs and abstracts the fat. Then bringing the edges together, he sings a spell and bites them together so that they join without a visible scar. The medicine-man then sings a song which makes his victim awake very gradually. He rises, staggers about, and wonders how he came to be sleeping there. The Jajaurung and Mukjarawaint have the same belief. Howitt records the account given by a Jupagalk boy according to which the fat was really taken out, smoked, and carried about to bring luck in hunting. In this case the medicine man killed the victim, but of course he could not make the wound heal again, and therefore I believe that when the rite is actually carried out it is something like the attempt to convert a dream experience into reality. " The effect of dreams in which the sleeper believed that he had fallen into the hands of such a medicine-man may be seen from a remark made by my Wurunjerri informant. ' Sometimes men only know about having their fat taken by remembering something of it as in a dream.' " [3]

In describing the beliefs of the Hunter River natives, Horatio Hale, the learned philologist of the U.S.A. expedition, has found the correct explanation of these beliefs.

" By the tribe of the Hunter River this demon is called Koin or Koen. Sometimes when the blacks are asleep he makes his

[1] Angas, loc. cit., i, p. 110.
[2] Ch. Wilhelmi, *Manners and Customs of the Australian Natives*, 1862, p. 30.
[3] Howitt, *Native Tribes*, pp. 367–73.

appearance, seizes upon one of them and carries him off. The person seized endeavours in vain to cry out, being almost strangled ; at daylight, however, Koin disappears and the man finds himself conveyed safely to his own fireside. The demon is here a sort of personification of the nightmare—a visitation to which natives, from their habit of gorging themselves to the utmost when they obtain a supply of food, must be very subject." [1]

The Bugin of the Wiradjuri, who secures his sleeping victim by the loop-end of a cord of sinew, can change into a stump or other inanimate object just like the nightmare-beings of European folk-lore. [2] The Wurunyerri have an instrument made of sinews of the kangaroo's tail with a loop worked at one end and a pointed bone attached to the other. The most favourable time for the attack was when the sleeper snored. The cord was passed lightly round the sleeper's neck, the bone threaded through the loop, and then pulled tight. By the aid of a second cord he was carried off into the bush, where he was cut open and the fat extracted. " The opening was magically closed up and the victim left to come to himself with the belief that he had had a bad dream." [3]

Kurnai wizards would make the victim of their magic spells rise from his camp and walk to them " like in sleep ". After having thrown pieces of the He-oak at him, his tongue was cut out and he was sent home to die. [4] From the Kurnai we pass on to the Yuin who believed that their medicine-men could make a man go to sleep and then take his fat. [5]

Another peculiar feature of these beliefs is that a person is not supposed to die when he really dies, but to have died previously.

Thus we are told that the Brisbane tribes do not believe they ever die a natural death. Death is always caused through a *turrwan* of another tribe. When a man dies, he has been killed before at some time without it being known to him or anyone. They think that he was killed with the *kundri* (quartz-crystal), cut into pieces, and put together again, afterwards dying by catching a cold or being killed in a fight. In fact, if he is killed they do not blame the real murderer. " He had to die you see," they say, and set out in search of a fictitious person, naturally a member of a foreign tribe, whom they regard as the real cause of death. [6] This is the " dooming "

[1] H. Hale, *United States Exploring Expedition*, 1846, p. 111.

[2] Howitt, loc. cit., p. 374. Cf. L. Laistner, *Das Rätsel der Sphinx*, 1889, i, p. 62.

[3] Howitt, loc. cit., p. 375.   [4] Howitt, loc. cit., p. 377.

[5] Howitt, loc. cit., p. 376.

[6] T. Petrie, *Reminiscences of Early Queensland*, 1904, p. 30.

theory of the Kokoyimidir and kindred tribes. At the Boulia they say he is deprived of his blood which is replaced by a bone or pebble, on the Pennefather River his blood is made bad, on the Upper Georgina River his belly is ripped open or his throat cut, on the Tully River a rope is inserted just below the Adam's apple somewhere into his chest, at Cape Grafton he is choked when asleep, tongue and blood removed and a bone splinter pierced above each nostril into his head, at Cape Bedford he is hit with a stick, his head cut off and put on again, his neck twisted or his ham-strings cut. It may be a quartz-crystal or other object inserted through an invisible wound.[1]

Here we have to do with customs that represent modifications of the South-East Australian idea of abstracting the kidney fat. The existence of the latter in Queensland is proved by what the German missionary Schneider tells us. They have the custom of cutting their enemy's kidney fat out, and therefore when they go on a revenge expedition they say that they are " bringing back the fat of the dead man ".[2] Another link towards the South-East is afforded by the name of the nightmare demon Koin. The Awabakal believe in a being who is sometimes called Ko-in, sometimes Tip-pakal, and sometimes Pórrang. Generally they think he precedes the coming of natives from distant parts, when they assemble to celebrate puberty-ceremonies or dances. When they are asleep he comes and takes them up as an eagle would take its prey. The shout of the other natives who are terrified by the sight makes him drop his prey. In other cases he conveys them to his fire-place in the bush where he deposits his load close by the fire. The person carried off tries to cry out but he cannot, feeling himself almost choked ; at daylight Koin disappears and his human victim finds himself conveyed safely back to his own fireside.[3] Now, on the Tully River any long wasting disease, e.g. malaria, or consumption, is due to Koi (here the spirit of a deceased male) having put a rope into the sick person at night. This rope or twine is inserted through the front of the neck, just below the Adam's apple, somewhere into the chest. On the Proserpine River this magic rope is similar to the implements of black magic used by Wurunjerri, etc. sorcerers. At one end of

[1] Roth, " Superstition, Magic, and Medicine," *Bull. S.*, 1903, p. 28.
[2] H. G. Schneider, *Missionsarbeit der Brüdergemeinde in Australien*, 1882, p. 39.
[3] L. E. Threlkeld, *An Australian Language as spoken by the Awabakal*, 1892, p. 47. Th. H. Braim, *History of New South Wales*, 1846, p. 248. Howitt, loc. cit., p. 496.

the loop there is a pointed stick used for prodding the victim's body to see that he is actually asleep : at the other is a loop which is thrown round the neck and tightened. The alleged strangulation leaves no visible mark next morning.[1]

If we consider the distribution of this custom in Australia we notice that it is an element of " Dual " culture, just as the other form of magic that characterizes Australia, the pointing bone, belongs properly to the Central tribes.[2] In the ethnographical provinces most likely to yield parallels to Australian customs, we find some isolated survivals of a practice that must be attributed to an early stratum of Oceanic culture.

Between Australia and New Guinea we find the Torres Strait Islanders with their practice of *Maid*. If a Murray Islander had some reason to take revenge on another or in case of adultery he would have recourse to the following practice. Having found his adversary in the bush, he would either hurl a stone or a spear resembling the dugong harpoon at him and utter some spells in a half-whisper that his victim might not hear him. The stone would hit the back of his enemy, who thereupon fell down senseless, breathing heavily. The assailant and his helpmates quickly approached the prostrate person and belaboured him with their clubs until he was half dead. Then they rubbed the man with a mixture of herbs and coconut-oil to remove the marks from his body. They placed his bushknife beside him and left bananas and coconuts for him to eat. Finally, while he was still unconscious, they told him that he was to go up a coconut-tree and fall down from it, or to be bitten by a centipede or suffer death in some way. And thus it would happen.[3] The stone is used by day and the spear at night. At Savo and Florida there also seems to be some difference between a night and a day attack. The procedure is called *vele*, a word meaning to pinch. The man who has the secret takes in a bag upon his back the leaves and other things in which the mana for this purpose resides. When he finds his victim alone, he seizes him, bites his neck, stuffs the magic leaves down his throat, and knocks him on the head with an axe but not so as to kill him. He then leaves the man who goes home, relates what has happened, and dies after two days. If the attack is made by night the man cannot tell who his assailant was, but the thing is done also in broad daylight and the assailant does not conceal himself but tells his name and bids his victim make it known.

[1] Roth, op. cit., p. 33.
[2] Róheim, " The Pointing Bone," *Journal of the Royal Anthr. Inst.*, 1926.
[3] Haddon, *Cambridge Expedition to Torres Straits*, vi, p. 223.

But as he goes home the charm makes him forget. At Lepers' Island it is done with a little bow and arrow. He remembers nothing but goes home, falls ill, and dies.[1] The Sulka—a people with the dual organization, but speaking an isolated " Papuan " language [2]—kill a lonely wanderer by what is called *pur-mea*. The sorcerer may knock his victim on the head, choke him, bite through his throat, exercise a pressure on various parts of the body, or drive a magic spear into his anus. Previously, however, he has caught his victim in a string or by throwing stones at him. When rendered helpless they kill the man and then throw some earth on him to make him revive. The man goes home, and unless he makes a clean breast of it and tells his people what has happened to him, he will die shortly. This confession, however, is usually withheld because the man is angry with his relations for letting him go out alone and prefers to get them into trouble by his death.[3] In the Dorch district it is the *Manoin* whose flute allures the luckless wanderer to his doom. He must follow the sound. The spirit cuts his head off and puts some magic stones between the head and the body so that they stick together. Now the poor fellow must dance by command of the spirit ; he goes home perfectly exhausted, and in a few days he is dead.[4]

The next instance comes from the Marind-anim, a people in Dutch New Guinea (near Merauke) with quite evident affinities with Australian culture. According to one of their myths, the Kambara-anim (death magicians) do something to their victim which makes him faint. Then they cut the body from the inside, under the skin, without leaving a visible wound. When the man awakes from his swoon he does not know what has happened and goes quietly home. But in a few hours he feels pains and shortly afterwards he is dead.[5]

Although these cases agree with our Australian data in the sequence death, revival (fictitious), and then death, an important difference still remains : the absence of any reference to the cutting out of the kidney fat. This feature is only found in Australia ; moreover, it is sporadic in Queensland, its real home being the south-east.

Here we have to do with a real custom which may nevertheless

[1] R. H. Codrington, *Melanesians*, pp. 206, 207.
[2] W. H. R. Rivers, *History of Melanesian Society*, 1914, ii, p. 537.
[3] R. Parkinson, *Dreissig Jahre in der Südsee*, 1907, p. 200.
[4] A. Bastian, *Der Papua*, 1885, pp. 25, 26 (Hasselt).
[5] P. Wirz, *Die Marind-anim von Holländisch-Süd-Neu-Guinea*, 1922, i, p. 69.

be reproduced in dream-life. We have the testimony of Curr, who tells us how the kidney fat was abstracted through an incision in the side.[1]

The Bangerang devoured a morsel of the fat of the slaughtered foe as an act of triumph. A piece of kidney fat taken from the slain was wrapped up in opossum skin and preserved for months by the victor.[2]

We are also told by an eyewitness that they cut their enemy's kidney fat out and swallow it raw, with their victim dying before their eyes.[3] In North Queensland various parts of the human body are eaten so as to acquire the forces connected with them ; on the Shoal Haven River a man who killed a convict cut out his tongue on the supposition that as he had eaten the tongue of a white man he would be enabled to speak English.[4] If, therefore, we hear that they indulged in the kidney fat or rather in the kidney itself in preference to any other part of the body and that they regarded the kidney as the centre of life, it will not be difficult to guess the nature of the forces they were after when devouring their enemy's kidney or kidney fat. Wundt reminds us of the close connection between the kidney and the sexual organs, that must have been especially evident for the savage anatomist in the case of the male,[5] and in a Kakadu tradition a new " Numereji " is acquired by cutting out and burning a child's kidney fat.[6] Quite apart from the tradition as an isolated North-Australian case of our rite, it is interesting to notice that the kidney is brought into connection with the patron snake of the medicine-man.

A similar serpent-spirit lives in the body of the Warramunga medicine-man. These practitioners are themselves called Urkutu, i.e. snakes, and as snakes they are allowed special privileges with the women.[7]

It is probably due to this phallic or " life-giving " quality of the kidneys that in mummification the heart and kidneys are left *in situ*

---

[1] E. M. Curr, *Recollections of Squatting in Victoria*, 1883, p. 304.

[2] Curr, loc. cit., p. 264.

[3] W. Howitt, *Abenteuer in den Wildnissen von Australien*, 1856, p. 288. C. Lumholtz, *Au pays des cannibales*, 1890, pp. 351, 352.

[4] Breton, *Excursions in New South Wales, Western Australia, and Van Diemens Land*, 1833, p. 191.

[5] Wundt, " Völkerspsychologie," *Religion und Mythus*, ii, 1906, p. 11.

[6] B. Spencer, *Northern Territory*, 1914, p. 294.

[7] Spencer and Gillen, *The Northern Tribes of Central Australia*, 1904, p. 286.

while the intestines are removed.[1]   In India, the kidneys were placed in the hands of the deceased, and the following verse was recited:—

Escape the two dogs, the sons of Sarama.

Kidneys were used to ward off the second death, the death of the soul, which was regarded as the most terrible of disasters.[2]   The *kelayoth*, or kidneys, are regarded in Hebrew as the seat of lust, but the word *kālāh* means also " to come to an end ".   Some Syriac translations render the word " loins " in such expressions as " Thou gavest to woman thy loins " by " kidneys ".   In the Targum, the word for kidneys is used for testicles.[3]

If we accept this explanation we shall regard the custom of cutting out the kidney fat of the slain enemy as a slight modification of castration.   The substitution of the kidney for the penis might be due to repression ; all the more so as we actually find this custom of castrating the enemy in a cultural area that frequently shows the unrepressed variants of Australian customs.   We are told that the Marind-anim cut off the penis of the dead foe and wear it as a trophy.[4]

This interpretation of what happens here is strikingly confirmed by the only isolated case of this custom or phobia known to me beyond the Australian and Melanesian culture area.   In the Thonga language one of the worst practices of the wizard is called *mpfulo* = the opening.   This designates a mysterious power of the *baloyi* to " open " any kind of thing.   One of them, for instance, has charms to open the kraals of oxen during the night.   He would come into the village, holding the tail of a hyena daubed with medicines, and he would throw on all the inhabitants a deep sleep.   Then, waving the tail, he would open the kraal and let the cattle out.   Another kind of opening is the power to open a hut.   This consists of putting the husband to sleep while the wizard commits adultery with his wife.   The great opening, however, consists in opening a man.   What this consists in we are not told.   But evidently it must be a form of witchcraft in which the victim is opened just as they do it in Australia.[5]

This seems to show that we have here a juxtaposition of two related ideas, the one being that of castration pure and simple with the kidney as a substitute for the penis, and the other the castration or defloration suffered by the woman in the act of cohabitation.

[1] G. Elliot Smith, " Heart and Reins in Mummification," *Journal of the Manchester Oriental Society*, 1911, pp. 72, 79.

[2] T. W. Rhys Davids, " Heart and Reins in India," ibid., pp. 105, 106.

[3] H. W. Hogg, " Heart and Reins," ibid., p. 51.

[4] W. N. Beaver, *Unexplored New Guinea*, 1920, p. 128.

[5] Junod, *The Life of a South African Tribe*, 1913, ii, pp. 469, 470.

The Sumerian expresses the idea of copulation by a verb which means " to open ".[1]   The Thonga case clearly states that the latent content of the " opening " is the penis opening its way into the vagina. The man who, after this attack, is no more than a wandering corpse, has been castrated, that is, transformed into a woman.   This explanation of the phobia becomes particularly obvious, if we remind the reader of the Australian evidence ;   the whole thing happens in dream-life ;   in fact, it is the equivalent of our nightmare.   Now the explanation given by Dr Jones of the nightmare is that it represents the repressed masochistic, female, component in the sexual life of the male.   The inverted situation, the pressure on the chest, the complete helplessness, reflect the situation of the female partner in coitus, and the anxiety is partly due to the repressed character of this wish,[2] partly to its close connection with the castration complex.   It is well known that the nightmare has intercourse with the sleeper and the result of this intercourse (carried to an excess) is usually a lingering illness followed by death.   In Slavic myths we find the demon deeply inserting his tongue into the victim's mouth, and in the light of Dr Flügel's illuminating paper on the phallic significance of the tongue this would mean the demon's penis penetrating into the sleeper's vagina.[3]   In Australia we find an eagle-demon playing this part of castrator, and in my book on Australian Totemism I believe I have shown the close connection of the eagle-hawk with the tragic events of the Primal Horde and the castration complex.   In New Guinea, the women of the Bánara are impregnated by the flute demons, and among the Monumbo the flute is introduced into the vagina.[4]   Shall we not be justified then in regarding the Manoin with the flute as a phallic demon ? Provisionally, therefore, our first investigation into the latent contents of the magic art leads to the following conclusions :—

1 That death is not attributed to an accident or disease, but to a castration previously endured.

2 That there is an element of passive female gratification in this castration.

[1] I. T. Sun, " Symbolism in the Sumerian Written Language," *The Psychoanalytic Review*, 1914, p. 273.

[2] Jones, *Der Alptraum*, 1912, p. 15.

[3] J. C. Flügel, " A Note on the Phallic Significance of the Tongue and of Speech," *Journal of Psycho-analysis*, vi, pp. 209–15.   Laistner, *Das Rätsel der Sphinx*, I, 1889, i, pp. 41, 42.

[4] R. Thurnwald, *Die Gemeinde Der Banaro*, 1921, pp. 21, 22.   F. Vormann, " Tänze und Tanzfestlichkeiten der Monumbo-Papua," *Anthropos*, vi, p. 427.

3 That the magician acts as a point of fixation for these unconscious attitudes. He is the man who undertakes to play the part of castrator. As such he is a *revenant* of that monster eagle, the All-Father, and a representative of the flute, of the weapon that penetrates into another human being, of the phallus.

(b) *The Foot and Footprints.*—It is true that the general law of magic—that anything done to a part equally affects the whole—covers the cases we are about to consider.[1] Nevertheless, there seems to be somewhat more than a normal amount of anxiety connected with the foot and footprints. In some districts of New South Wales, if a man comes across the tracks of a kangaroo he follows them along and talks to the footprints all the time for the purpose of injecting magic into the animal which made them. He mentions in succession all the parts of the foot and then names the different parts of the leg right up to the animal's back. As soon as he reaches the backbone the creature becomes stupid and as an easy prey is overtaken by the hunter.[2] The Kamilaroi on the Gwydir River call a certain form of magic *Dinna-kurra*, e.g. " foot to catch ", evidently because the intention is that the victim should tread into the mixture consisting of the dung of a native cat and a white mossy powder.[3] The Wyingurri, a scarcely known tribe on the border line between Central and Western Australia, use a round magical object called *Tchintu*, the Sun, and supposed to contain the heat of the Sun. By placing it on anybody's tracks the victim will be seized with violent fever and will burn up rapidly.[4] A certain form of evil magic among the Kakadu is associated with the mud that attaches itself to the foot of a native walking through a swamp. If somebody gets hold of this mud he wraps it in paper bark and ties a string round it. In his camp, he pounds it up when it is quite dry till he can roll it into a ball and then he places it in a hole that he makes in the base of an ant hill. By and by the victim's foot breaks into sores which gradually spread all over it. The toes drop off and the hands and feet decay.[5] The Kurnai were very much afraid of " bottle " getting into their feet. The wizard would place sharp fragments of quartz, glass, bone, or charcoal in a person's footprints

---

[1] This axiom of primitive mentality seems also to be based on the castration complex of primitive man. Cf. Herrmann, *Psychoanalyse und Logik*, 1925.

[2] R. H. Mathews, *Ethn. Stud.*, p. 53.

[3] Howitt, loc. cit., p. 362.

[4] Spencer and Gillen, *Native Tribes*, p. 541.

[5] Spencer, *Northern Territory*, iii, p. 261.

or in the impression of his body where he had laid down. A man who was very lame, said : " Some fellow put bottle into my foot." He had an acute rheumatism and believed that somebody had found his footprint and buried the fragment of a broken bottle in it, the magic of which had entered into his foot.[1]

Among the Unmatjera a boy who has been circumcised must hide in the bush and if by any chance he should see a bubra's track he must be very careful to jump over it. If his foot should touch it then the spirit of the louse which is in the woman's hair would go on him and his head will be full of lice. Not only this, but if he were to touch the track he would be sure sooner or later to follow up the bubra, who would ask him : " Why do you come and try to catch me," and then she would go back to the camp and tell her brother who would come and kill him.[2]   According to the natives of the northern D'Entrecasteaux Islands, the effect of a certain sorcery called *ibudoba* is that sores break out on a man's legs. This is caused by any enemy who sings over a piece of wood and lays it in the track. The victim, as he walks along, kicks it by accident with his foot and a sore that grows rapidly worse until he dies is the consequence of it.[3]   At Kiriwina (Trobriand group) the one great dread that darkens the life of every native is the fear of the sorcerer. In the darkness of night he will steal to the house of his unsuspecting victim and place a few leaves of a certain tree, containing his evil magic, near his victim's doorstep. The doomed man on going out of his house next morning unwittingly steps over the fatal leaves and is at once stricken by a mortal sickness. Internal disease of every kind is set down to this agency.[4]

In Fiji a certain leaf mixed with remains from a man's food, clothing, or tobacco is buried near his house or garden.[5]   On Buin and Bougainville they practice magic with footprints and also bury the remains of food and tread on it with their feet.[6]

These practices are well known in European folklore. Either something is done to the footprint that will affect the man, or objects charged with evil magic are brought into immediate contact with the foot. In Mecklenburg the earth from the footprint is tied up in a cloth and hung in the chimney to smoke ; as it dries up, the man

---

[1] Howitt, loc. cit., p. 366.
[2] Spencer and Gillen, *Northern Tribes*, pp. 540, 541.
[3] Jenness and Ballantyne, *The Northern D'Entrecasteaux*, 1920, p. 143.
[4] Brown, *Melanesians and Polynesians*, 1910, p. 234.
[5] Deane, *Fijian Society*, 1920, p. 162.
[6] Thurnwald, loc. cit., i, p. 443.

withers away or his foot shrivels up.[1]   Various methods are familiar
to Hungarian witches.   A girl " lifts " the earth from the footprint
and puts it down again with the toes pointing in the opposite direction
to win a lover back who had gone to another village.[2]   A witch
treads into the footprints of a pregnant woman so that she should
die in giving birth to her child,[3] or witches throw footprints into
a well and thus compel their victim to jump into the well after the
footprints and get drowned.[4]

Another way of inflicting injury on a man is to bring something
into immediate contact with his foot.   In Hungarian folklore this
form of magic is very well known and usually called a " spilling "
(öntés) or " spoiling " (rontás), the latter being also the general name
applied to all form of evil magic.   Witches spill certain objects,
especially the food that is left or beans, on crossways or thresholds,
and anybody who treads upon these objects falls ill.[5]

Another name for " spoiling " is " pouring " (öntés).   If anybody has boils or ulcers he or she will take a bath and have nine sorts
of vegetables boiled in the water.   All the water is poured out on
Friday at midnight at the crossroads, and anybody who treads in
it acquires the disease, to the relief of its original owner.[6]

Now the same method used for " spoiling " a man, the " spilling ",
is also used by a Slovak maid for getting a husband.   She cuts chips
from three times three gates (three churches, three inns, three salt
stores), boils them in water, goes to the road and washes in this water.
Then she spills it and any lad who treads into it must fall in love
with her.[7]

The Huzuls have a similar procedure which they call " strewing
beneath " or " throwing beneath ".   In the former case they will
strew ashes, thistles, mortar, coal, etc., where a person is likely to
walk, somewhere near the door or threshold.   Man or beast who
passes over it will fall ill or suffer some misfortune.   " Laying under "
is the same thing or very like it ;   a part of some unclean animal,
for instance a bat, is covered with a rag and buried under the threshold.[8]
In Silesia they say that a witch who has been making an excursion

---

[1] K. Bartsch, *Sagen, Märchen und Gebräuche aus Mecklenburg*, 1880,
ii, p. 329.

[2] Komáromy, *Magyarországi Boszorkányperek Oklevéltára*, 1910, p. 81.

[3] Komáromy, loc. cit., p. 154.   [4] Komáromy, loc. cit., p. 502.

[5] Varga János, *A babonák könyve*, 1877, p. 44.

[6] Somogyi, " Aradmegye magyar népe," *Aradvármegye Monográphiája*,
1912, ii, p. 341.

[7] Sztancsek, " Privigye vidékén gyüjtött babonák," *Ethn.*, 1908, p. 104.

[8] R. Fr. Kaindl, *Die Huzulen*, 1897, p. 90.

in a whirlwind leaves a bad footprint and anybody who treads on it will get ill.[1]   In Eastern Friesland the same belief is attached to the footprints of anybody who has committed adultery.[2]

Now the remarkable thing about these beliefs is, at least in Hungary, that there is much more of them than one might suspect from a perusal of printed sources. I have heard the *rontás* mentioned very often and when I looked through our collections of folklore I was surprised to find little of it. Another peculiar circumstance in connection with this idea is that it is a perfect focus of euphemisms. In one of the witches' trials at Szeged the witness said : " She said I had trodden into the dish of the Beautiful Women," and when I asked her what that was she replied : " We call it the dish of the Beautiful Women ; we dare not say a spoiling." [3]   In Algyö an old woman spoke about " the spoiling " and " the dish of the Beautiful Women " as the same thing. The Beautiful Woman goes about at noon and midnight and strews the " spoilings " to spoil people. Therefore nobody ought to walk in the middle of the road, that is where the Beautiful Woman has got her dish, and anybody who treads into it catches an incurable disease.   " Spoilings " or " Beautiful Women's Dishes " are dangerous and particularly so at crossroads, yet there is no danger for old people, they can walk where they like.[4]   At Whitsuntide, or rather the night before, the witches dance in a circle and anybody who treads into this circle gets an incurable illness. People should not pour things on the threshold in the evening because anybody who treads into them treads into a " spoiling " or into the " Beautiful Women's dish." [5] The Serbian neighbours of the Magyars say that a person has trodden in the dish of the white fairy.[6]   People who tread where the fairies dance or *kolo* (Serbian national dance), will be paralysed in hand or foot.[7]   At Vinica, people who chance to be present at the rendezvous of witches ought to step three times forward and once backwards to avoid treading into the witches' dish.[8]   Witches are equally susceptible about their " dish " and their footprints,

[1] Kühnau, *Schlesische Sagen*, 1913, iii, p. 23.   Drechsler, *Schlesien*, ii, p. 249.
[2] Wuttke, *Der deutsche Volksaberglaube*, 1901, p. 628.
[3] Kovács János, " A kuruzslás eszközei a szegedi boszorkányperekben," *Ethn.*, x, p. 43. Ipolyi, *Magyar Mythologia*, p. 445.
[4] Kálmány Lajos, *Gyermekijesztök és rablók nyelvhagyományainkban*, 1893, pp. 14, 15.
[5] Kálmány, loc. cit., pp. 13, 14.   [6] *Idem*, loc. cit., p. 15.
[7] Juga, *A magyar szent korona országaiban élö szerbek*, 1913, p. 137.
[8] F. S. Krauss, *Slavische Volkforschungen*, 1908, p. 45.

and indeed the two seem to mean the same thing. In Suffolk you may stick a knife into a witch's footprint and she cannot stir a step till it is withdrawn.[1] In the German Palatinate it is easy enough to tell who is a witch ; step on her footprints, she thinks it is her foot and by doing so betrays her vocation.[2] In a book published in 1920 on Hungarian Folk Lore I tried to show that " recognizing a witch ", " knowing her ", was merely a reduced substitute for having intercourse with her as a representative of the mother-imago.[3] Feet, shoes, footprints, are frequently used in love-magic. A gipsy girl in Yugoslavia cuts her left foot and lets the blood drip on a lad's footprints ; he will always pursue her.[4] In Transylvania a Hungarian girl will take the young man's footprints and bury them under her threshold and the result is that he marries her [5] ; in Szatmár nine footprints are hung up in the chimney.[6]

It seems, therefore, that the foot in these magical practices is the symbol of the penis, so that a man treading into what a witch or a " beautiful woman " has poured out, into her footprints, is really having intercourse with her. The Votiaks tell us that the witch cannot harm a man who has cohabited with her,[7] and among the Slovaks a witch, if she is to work her spells on a man, must be a woman.[8] In Hungarian witch trials " prostitute " and " witch " are perfectly synonymous expressions,[9] and according to a belief of the Yugoslavs, a man gets jaundice if he treads in the footprints of, or has intercourse with, a prostitute.[10] The question is finally settled by one detail that I reserved for the end of my argument ; it is the diseases of a sexual nature, diseases of which people are ashamed, that are acquired by stepping into a " spoiling " or " the dish of the Beautiful Women ".[11] It is hardly necessary to substitute the real words for " dish " for " stepping " and " foot " in this connection ; nobody will deny that we have proof positive both for

[1] Gurdon, County Folk Lore, Suffolk, p. 201.

[2] Schönwerth, Aus der Oberpfalz, 1859, iii, p. 174.

[3] Róheim, Adalékok a magyar néphithez, 1920.

[4] H. von Wlislocki, " Menschenblut im Volksglauben der Zigeuner," Urquell, iii, 1892, p. 12.

[5] Benkö, " Háromszéki babonák," Ethn., 1891, p. 359.

[6] Jakab József, " Szatmármegyei babonák," Ethn., 1895, p. 414.

[7] B. Munkácsi, " Volksglauben der Wotjaken," Urquell, iv, p. 193.

[8] K. Chotek, Narodopisni Vestnik Ceskoslovansky, 1906, p. 230.

[9] Komáromy, loc. cit.

[10] Wlislocki, " A sokacz néphit köréböl," Ethn., 1896, p. 291.

[11] Varga, loc. cit., p. 44.

the symbolic meaning of the foot and for the repression directed against this meaning.

The threshold and the cross-road are favourite places for these " spoilings " or " beautiful women's dishes ". I may refer to a former paper of mine about the threshold and to Abraham with regard to the crossroad.[1] If the crossroad, as shown by Abraham, is the vagina, we can understand why in Herefordshire the coffin should be set down at every crossroad,[2] why a crossroad disperses evil influences in Ireland,[3] and why twins are buried at crossroads on the Lower Congo.[4] In Northern India disease is transferred by being buried under a little pile of earth at a crossroad,[5] and in Ireland a charm or curse is left on a gate or stile and the first person who passes through will have the disease transferred to him.[6] The bat buried under the threshold among the Huzuls is a repetition of the symbolic meaning ; a man who treads on it is treading on a vagina with a penis in it.

We therefore believe that the part played by the foot in savage magic is due to its significance as a penis symbol. Primitive man, with his anxiety about treading on magical objects or footprints, is actuated by the same motive that makes him take care about his nail-parings or hair, viz. by his all-powerful castration complex. Among the Unmatjera, it is specially a circumcised lad who must avoid treading on a woman's track, for doing so would mean that he desires her, and the result of this love affair would be that her brother would kill him. This clearly shows the real meaning of practices connected with the foot and footprints. Just as in the case of the belief in somebody opening people and cutting their kidney fat out, magical phobias and magical practices centre round the castration complex.[7]

(c) *Shooting*.—Another thing a medicine-man or wizard will very frequently do is to shoot some substance into a person's body to make him sick. Loritja wizards cut some hair off their beard,

---

[1] Róheim, " The Significance of Stepping Over," *Journal of Psycho-analysis*, iii. Abraham, " Zwei Beiträge zur Symbolforschung," *Int. Z. für Psa.*, ix, p. 122.

[2] Leather, loc. cit., p. 123.

[3] W. Crooke, " King Midas and his Ass's Ear," *Folk-Lore*, 1911, p. 185.

[4] Weeks, " Customs of the Lower Congo, "*Folk-Lore*, xix, p. 423.

[5] Crooke, loc. cit., p. 164.

[6] Gregor, *Folk-Lore of North-East Scotland*, pp. 46, 157.

[7] For the penis-vagina symbolism of foot and shoe, see both Sartori, " Der Schuh im Volksglauben," *Z.d.V.f.Vk.*, iv, and Aigremont, *Fuss- und Schuh-Symbolik und Erotik*, 1909.

twist it into a rope, and then smear some blood from their subincised penis on this rope. In three days the rope is transformed into a serpent. Then they take some stones from their body and throw them at the serpent. The serpents rise into the air with the stones in their body. There are two serpents; one of them forces its way into the hip, the other into the back part of the victim's head. The two serpents destroy everything they find and death is the speedy result of their work. Women do much the same thing only they take the blood from their vagina.[1] Now there can hardly be a doubt about the matter; we know that the male form of this magic is the original one and the female a copy. The ropes of hair and the serpent are here clearly shown to be projections, really elongated forms, of the penis, and what they do to the victim is a sadistic coitus.

There are reasons to assume that the penis, in its sadistic aspect, is the physical prototype of the magician's weapon. The Dieri variant of the Australian practice called " a pointing bone " is the Mukuelli *dukana*, meaning a " bone to strike ". Two persons join for this ceremony. One of them points with the bone and ties the end of the hair cord which is fastened to it tightly round his upper arm in order that the blood may be driven through it into the bone. The second person holds the end of another cord that is fastened to the bone and goes through the same movements as the one who is holding it. The bone is a human leg-bone and when they intend to kill some influential man of another tribe at a distance they order several of the old men to despoil the dead. Then they take some of these bones, wrap them in fat and emu feathers and point toward the place where their intended victim is supposed to dwell. The blood of the subincised penis is made to drip on to the bone because if it remained dry it could not absorb the blood of the man who is about to be doomed. A string of human hair is attached to one end of the bone with pitch, and the wizard winds the string very tightly round his own arm to transfuse his own blood into the bone. He holds the bone firmly between the middle and index fingers, and another string of hair is wound round these two fingers and the bone; this string connects him with his helpmate. The second man pulls at the string, moving the point up and down. Suddenly he attaches a lump of pitch or clay to the point of the bone. He has now caught the soul of the victim which has been drawn into the bone through the blood (soul) of the magician. The lump of pitch or clay is very necessary as the soul might try to escape at the point. After this

[1] Strehlow, *Die Aranda und Loritja Stämme*, iv, pp. 35, 37.

they bury the bone, wrapping it in emu feathers and in the kuya-mara plant, and leave it in the earth for many months. Then they disinter it and burn it completely. When the bone is quite burnt the man they are killing is dead. The only way to save him is to take the bone out of the flames and put it into water.[1]

If we interpret the blood or soul as being a substitute for the seminal fluid, many details of the ceremony appear in a new light. The point moving up and down would be the action of the penis in coitus. Not only the victim's, but also the magician's, blood rushes into the bone ; it is a coitus between two males who identify themselves by means of the bone as their common penis. *Kuya-mara* means new fish ; it is the plant used in funeral ceremonies.[2] The bone has been transformed into the victim's corpse by imbibing his life blood ; but then the corpse in the grave is the penis in the vagina.[3] The position taken by the Wonkonguru sorcerer, who projects the bone from his hip by means of a string and if he wants his enemy to suffer from venereal disease sings the snake song, is highly suggestive in this connection.[4] Among the Arunta the two men, if they wish to punish a man who has stolen a woman, point the bone in the following manner. One of them kneels down, huddling himself together with his forehead touching the ground in front of his knees, while the other man takes up the magic implement and standing between the knees of the first man throws the thing with all his force in the direction in which his enemy lives. When he has done this he kneels huddled up in the same position as the other man with his head between the latter's feet.[5] The man standing between the other man's legs is playing the part of a penis ; and the dread of castration partly repressed by the sadistic turn given to coitus makes it necessary to have two or more men for the ceremony.[6]

The assistance of other medicine-men is called in if there is some doubt about the matter,[7] and the origin of this doubt or anxiety probably lies in the circumstance that it is not only the victim's blood but also the blood (semen) of the medicine-man that rushes into the pointing instrument. As W. E. Roth tells us, it is most

[1] Howitt, loc. cit., p. 359. S. Gason, "The Dieyerie Tribe," in E. M. Curr, *The Australian Race*, 1886, ii, p. 65. Siebert, "Sagen und Sitten der Dieri," *Globus*, 1910, pp. 97, 55.

[2] Howitt, loc. cit., p. 448.

[3] Cf. Róheim, *Australian Totemism*, p. 370.

[4] Horne and Aiston, *Savage Life in Central Australia*, 1924, p. 150.

[5] Spencer and Gillen, *Native Tribes*, pp. 548, 549.

[6] Spencer and Gillen, *Northern Tribes*, p. 456.

[7] W. E. Roth, *Superstition, Magic and Medicine*, p. 34.

important to bear in mind that when the apparatus is thus pointed—

(a) one of the doctors' gew-gaws, a quartz-crystal, bone, or pebble, passes from the pointer through space into the victim ; while at the same time—

(b) the blood of the victim passes across space into the pointer and so along the connecting string into the receptacle.

It is owing to the insertion of the crystal that the victim contracts his illness ; but it is owing to the removal of the life blood into the possession of the enemy that the latter has absolute control over the victim's person.[1] In this mutual exchange of "life-giving substances" (crystal, blood) the victim's seminal fluid passes into a receptacle. The receptacle, the grave, water, and fire applied to the bone are very suggestive of vaginal symbolism. But the quartz-crystal projected by the medicine-man has another meaning.

In the Awabakal language *Murramai* is the name of a round ball about the size of a cricket ball which the aborigines carry in a small net suspended from a girdle of opossum yarn. The women are not allowed to see the internal part of the ball. It is used as a talisman against sickness and sent from tribe to tribe for hundreds of miles on the sea coast and in the interior. The second "great mystery" of the tribe is the bone called *mur-ro-kun*. Three of the *karakals* (medicine-men) sleep on the grave of a recently interred corpse and during their sleep in the night the dead person inserts a mysterious bone into each, who feel the puncture not more severely than the sting of an ant. These bones remain in the flesh of the doctors without any inconvenience to them until they wish to kill any person, when by magical power they destroy him, causing the mysterious bone to enter his body and so occasion death.[2]

The other substance which enters people and causes illness is the quartz-crystal. The Wurunjerri believed firmly that the *Wirrarap* (medicine-men) could kill anybody far or near by *Mung* or evil magic. The principal substance through which this evil magic acts is the *Thundal* or quartz-crystal, which could be projected into a man either invisibly or else as a small whirlwind. The effect on a man caught in such a way was that he felt a chill, then pains and a shortness of breath. The medicine-man would know that *Mung* had been put into him and he would begin to watch the man, either alone or with another medicine-man, until one of them saw the magical substance about to escape like a little dust whirlwind. He

[1] W. E. Roth, loc. cit., p. 34.
[2] L. E. Threlkeld, *An Australian Language as spoken by the Awabakal*, 1892, p. 48.

would run after it, catch it, and breaking a piece off it, put it in his magic bag for further use. Any article that belonged to the victim would serve to work the evil spell ; it might be a piece of his hair, some of his fæces, a bone picked up by him and dropped, and if, among the Wotjobaluk, he were seen to spit his spittle would carefully be picked up with a piece of wood and used for his destruction.[1] The *bulk* of the Kurnai is a rounded black pebble. If it is buried together with the excreta of any person, that person receives the magic *bulk* in his intestines and dies.[2] There seems to be a close connection between the quartz-crystal and the intestines ; one of the impressive feats of a Yuin magician is that he can bring up Joias from his inside.[3] The Euahlayi magician who could produce the most magical stones would be regarded as the most powerful. The strength of the stones in them, whether swallowed or rubbed in through their heads, adds its strength to theirs, for these stones are living spirits breathing and growing in their fleshly cases, the owner having the power to produce them at any time.[4] It is also worth our attention to note that the medicine-man is the only Australian native who has the inclination to form collections and that the quartz-crystal is prominent among the collected objects. " A wiree-nuns boondoorr, or dillee bag, holds a queer collection : several sizes of gooweras of both bone or wood, poison stones, bones, gubberahs, etc." [5] In the sorcerer's dilley bag we find locks of hair rolled up in thin slips of bark probably belonging to a deceased friend, a piece or two of crystal for magical purposes, two or three bones, and some human fat.[6] Now we have considered two similar cases ; the heads collected by the head-hunting tribes as well as the shell money of Melanesia are both symbols of the fæces.[7] This would explain various details. The black *bulk* put into the victim's excreta, the projection of the substance into the intestines, the whirlwind in which the *Mung* departs (flatus) and the juggling tricks of the

---

[1] A. W. Howitt, " On Australian Medicine-Men," *Journ. Anthr. Inst.*, 1896, xvi, p. 90.

[2] Fison and Howitt, *Kamilaroi and Kurnai*, 1880, p. 251. The *bulk* has the power of motion and appears in the form of a bright spark of fire. Other charms (pointing bone or stick) are also placed where the victim has been defecating or micturating, or again they may be used to touch his food or the " lower posterior portion " of his body. W. E. Roth, *Superstition, Magic and Medicine*, 1903, p. 32.

[3] Howitt, loc. cit., p. 533.

[4] K. L. Parker, *The Euahlayi Tribe*, 1905, p. 35.

[5] Parker, *Euahlayi*, pp. 35, 36.

[6] A. C. Grant, *Bush Life in Queensland*, 1881, ii, p. 192.

[7] See note 1, p. 79.

medicine-men who bring up objects from their inside form a parallel to the hysterical libidinization of the alimentary tract.

A Euahlayi medicine-man acquires his magical crystal at the burial ground [1] and the Awabakal wizard has a bone thrust into him. Would it not be natural to suppose that the quartz-crystal is a symbol for the excrement into which the human flesh has been transformed ? For if the corpse can be shown to be the real source of magical power it could only give a part of itself ; in one case a bone, in the other flesh, but the latter comes transformed into excrement symbolized by the quartz-crystal. A Wiimbaio medicine-man digs up a human body, pounds and chews the bones. He is plastered with human excrement and carries the humerus of a disinterred corpse about with him at which he constantly gnaws.[2] In describing the Kebbarah ceremonies of the Macquarie natives, Angas tells us : " The Mundie is a crystal believed by them to be an excrement issued from the Deity and held sacred." [3] The same ceremony is described by R. H. Mathews as follows : " The novices are taken to goonambang (excrement place). Some old men perform feats of jugglery and exhibit white stones (quartz-crystals) to the novices. These stones are raked out of the heap of earth and ashes in the middle of the ring and are warm owing to the fire which is burning on the top of the heap. These quartz crystals are believed to be the excrement of Goign." [4] This is exactly what we believe ; the crystal is the flesh of the devoured Father-God transformed into excrement or symbolically into a quartz-crystal in the intestines of the youths. The putrefying corpse of the murdered Sire is identified with excrement ; hence the parallel rites of eating a corpse or eating excrement at an initiation ceremony. At the Burbung of the Wiradthuri tribes the old men gave each novice some human excrement which he was compelled to eat.[5] The same is reported of the Kamilaroi.[6]

At the Kombinegherry ceremony the boys swallow small quartz-crystals. " The large rock crystal is venerated by most blacks and is regarded with superstitious secrecy ; it is the symbol of their

[1] Parker, *Euahlayi*, p. 25. Cf. Róheim, " Nach dem Tode des Urvaters," *Imago*, ix. " Heiliges Geld in Melanesian," *Zeitschrift*, ix.

[2] Howitt, loc. cit., p. 404.

[3] Angas, loc. cit., ii, p. 224.

[4] R. H. Mathews, " The Keeparra Ceremony of Initiation," *Journ. Anthr. Inst.*, vol. xxvi, pp. 272–85.

[5] Mathews, " The Burbung of the Wiradthuri," ibid., p. 278.

[6] W. Ridley, " Report on Australian Languages and Traditions," *Journ. Anthr. Inst.*, 1872, ii, p. 270.

Great Spirit." [1]   But even when, as in this case, the excremental symbolism of the crystal has become repressed, it is constantly alluded to as coming from the inside of a human or supernatural being. Thus we are told that Targan, a rainbow and water-being of whom we shall hear more below, vomited them out of his belly. [2]   When the Wiradjuri medicine-man sounds the bull-roarer he is believed to have imparted great power to it by the magical quartz-crystals brought up from his inside. [3]

The Kebbarah ceremony is also performed by the Chepara tribe. At one part of the ceremony the magician holds up a large quartz-crystal and makes it flash in the sunlight.   The boys are told that it came from Maamba and that those who swallow a piece of it will be able to fly a long way out of sight, that is, to become medicine-men and go up into the sky. [4]   But we know that in this same ritual the crystal "comes from" the Supreme Being as his excrement, hence we may say that swallowing fragments of quartz is a sub-limated form of coprophagy.

"The medicine-man then hops backwards and forwards with a staring expression of face, his head vibrates from side to side, and he suddenly shows, sometimes after apparently internal struggles, one of his Joias between his teeth. This is supposed to have been brought from within himself." [5]   In the case of the Gurana or "grave" ceremony the Joia is a quartz-crystal which is considered to be one of the most deadly of magical substances which the medicine-men receive from Daramulun. [6]   Instead of the sacred wand Dhurumbulun, the "stone with a great light" was exhibited to the young men who also used it to exorcise evil spirits. [7]   The Kombine-gherry call it *koree*—it is obtained from the inside of a man when sucked out by the doctor.   Some go in quest of them into the mountains and stay for months fasting and undergoing various privations in consequence of which large stones came up to them at night while asleep. [8]   We have already shown that the origin of the medicine-man's additional power lies in the anthropophagic com-munion ritual ; when he tells us that he has been cut up by the ghost this is a reversal of the rite in which he cut up and ate a man whose

[1] The excrement of the Great Spirit, according to the two former reports. E. Palmer, in *Journ. Anthr. Inst.*, xiii, p. 296.

[2] Howitt, loc. cit., p. 585.   [3] Roth, loc. cit., p. 30.
[4] Howitt, loc. cit., p. 582.   [5] Howitt, loc. cit., p. 535.
[6] Howitt, loc. cit., p. 523.   [7] *Journ. Anthr.*, ii, p. 281.
[8] E. Palmer, "Notes on some Australian Tribes," *Journ. Anthr. Inst.*, xiii, p. 296.

power was thus superadded to his own.[1] The magical substance enters as food and emerges—as what ? As a quartz-crystal, but we know very well that this answer is only symbolical for excrement. This process of transmutation (food, excrements) is the organic prototype of exchange, trade, and barter. There is a brisk barter of intestines going on in Australia to this day between mortals and supernaturals and if proof is needed that trade is only a superorganic sequel of an organic process it is enough to point to the curious idea of an exchange of intestines (and these only) with a supernatural being. The Jonjari and Jonjaringan of the Kabi and Wakka were supernatural beings who haunted mineral springs. The healthful influences of the springs were ascribed to them. After initiation the young man became *jonjariman*, that is, endowed with the favour of the Jonjari. These spirits bestowed the magic stones (quartz-crystals) known as *kundir* in Kabi, *nurum* in the Wakka language, and also the cord or rope called *bukkur*, both of which objects had the power of conferring extraordinary vitality. If a man was *kundirbonggan*, " many crystalled," i.e. he had many crystals in his body, he would lie down to sleep on the margin of Dhakkan's watery abode. Dhakkan was a spirit in the form of a fish or snake who was identified with the rainbow. He lived in the deepest water holes and sometimes slaughtered human beings. What happened to the man endowed with crystals who deliberately sought communion with this dangerous being was this. He would become dimly conscious of a prickly sensation in his limbs ; Dhakkan had now taken him down into his damp dwelling and effected a grand exchange. The black-fellow imparts *kundir* (crystals) to Dhakkan and the latter confers *bukkur* (rope) in return. He was now a magician of higher degree ; he had been party to a barter with Dhakkan ; the latter had given him so much rope for a number of pebbles which he had taken from the man in exchange. He is laid to rest upon the edge of the waterhole and when he awakes he is *maungurngur*, i.e. full of life.[2]

The anal-erotic meaning of the quartz-crystal is quite evident and indeed has already been demonstrated in another paper.[3] But we must not forget that the substance is projected into the body of another living being, a feature that can have no other bodily prototype than cohabitation. We should thus say that shooting the crystal

---

[1] Cf. Róheim, " Nach dem Tode des Urvaters," *Imago*, ix.

[2] J. Mathew, *Eaglehawk and Crow*, 1899, p. 143. *Idem, Two Representative Tribes of Queensland*, 1910, p. 172.

[3] " Nach dem Tode des Urvaters," *Imago*, ix, p. 11 1.

into the patient or victim is an anal version of coitus, that the person who performs or is supposed to perform the ceremony is on the border-line between the anal-sadistic and the genital phase of organization. Possibly the various degrees in the magical profession correspond to so many phases of sex organization, and in this case the medicine-man with his crystals would represent the anal, the one with the rope (penis-symbol) the genital phase. Such a transition might well be effected through descent into a water-hole, and a man full of ropes, i.e. phalli, might well be described as " full of life ".

Recent researches have shown [1] that the act of giving birth is, for the female, the fission that corresponds to the ejaculation of the seminal fluid in the male. At Bartle Bay (New Guinea), disease and death are brought about by a " sending " projected out of the body of the sorcerer or witch. This " sending " is even credited with leading a separate life after the death of the individual to whom it belongs. The " sending " is usually projected from the body of a woman and after her death it may either enter the other world with her spirit or pass on to her daughter. At Gelaria the " sending " was called *labuni*. *Labuni* exist within women and can be commanded by any woman who has had children. By certain processes the *labuni*, which resembles a shadow, emerges from the woman who appears to be sleeping. The *labuni* existed or was derived from an organ called *ipona* situated in the flank and literally meaning " egg " or " eggs ". The *labuni* was said actually to leave the body and afterwards to re-enter it *per rectum*. *Labuni* are shadows with short petticoats. They produce diseases by means of a sliver of human bone or fragment of stone or coral, called a *gidana*, which they insert into their victim's body. The *labuni* throws the *gidana* at the individual to be injured at a distance of about 60 yards and although it was stated that only the spiritual part of the weapon entered the victim's body, it was also said that if the illness was cured the *gidana* would be removed by the medicine-man in its material form.[2]

Why can only a woman who has had a child project a *labuni* ? Because the *labuni* comes from the egg, and the ovum as a diminutive form of the woman herself lives on after her death. That is, the *labuni* is her child, and the act of projecting it is the act of giving birth, although again the fact that it emerges *per rectum* shows that it is the anal-sadistic version of the life-giving act. What follows

---

[1] H. Deutsch, *Psychologie der weiblichen Sexualfunktionen*, 1925.
[2] O. G. Seligman, *The Melanesians of British New Guinea*, 1910, pp. 640–2.

is fission repeated, and the fact that the most potent weapon thrown by the *labuni* is a man's tooth looks as if this second fission was modelled on the part played by the male in coitus.

We have now come to the end of our inquiry into the secrets of black magic. In all three cases investigated by us the action of killing a person by magic was modelled on the unconscious idea of forced coitus carried out as the castration of the victim. The first case is typical of both aspects ; the magician opens a man's body, penetrates into it with his weapon and cuts his kidney fat out. The attack on the foot stresses the castration side of the complex, while the substance projected into the body evidently symbolizes disease as the consequence of a repressed homosexual desire. There is a trace of castration in the life blood or seminal fluid drawn out of the victim.

On the side of the magician, sadism plays an important part in these proceedings. We cannot exactly tell its source and origin, but at any rate we see it at work in transforming the life-giving into a death-giving act. Its association with the anal strivings is quite evident but we suspect that more can be said on the matter.

2   THE RAIN-MAKER

Most ethnologists are inclined to take some simple and straight-forward view of magic, regarding it either as the practice connected with the belief in certain immutable laws that govern nature or as an outpouring of will-power unchecked by the Reality Principle. It is due to these statements that there is a psychoanalytic tendency to regard magic simply as a wish-fulfilment, as a repetition of the intra-uterine phase of existence, without paying any heed to the conditions which govern this manifestation.[1]

At the root of the rain-maker's behaviour we find the tendency to imitate a supernatural being with whom he identifies himself.

For instance, a Shuswap shaman whose guardian spirit was the rain could procure rain by painting his face with red stripes or dots or with both and having done this he went out of the house and walked round in a circle with the sun, singing his rain song and saying : " My guardian spirit will go round the world until he meets rain and brings it here." [2]   From the ethnologist's point of view of course it might be said that the rain spirit is walking round the world because

[1] Cf. Frazer, Marett, and Ferenczi, " Entwicklungsstufen des Wirklichkeitssinnes," *Int. Zeitschrift für Psa*, i, pp. 124–38.
[2] Teit, *The Shuswap* (Jesup North Pacific Expedition), 1909, p. 602.

the shaman is doing the same, that his circuit is merely the mythical reflection of the ritual. But this is not the shaman's view of what takes place. He distinctly believes that in making rain he is imitating what somebody else is doing. We shall see whether, after all, it is not the shaman who knows what he is up to.

Among the Ba-Ila in case of a drought the aid of the sky-god Leza is much sought and recourse is had to a diviner or rain-maker. Taking a pot he puts some tree roots and some water into it. Then he holds a small forked stick in it between the palms of his hands and turns it round, producing froth. Some of this froth he throws in all directions, the idea being that it will collect the clouds. Then another kind of medicine is burnt and throws up a dense smoke which is supposed to have some connection with the clouds. The ashes are put into a pot of water so that the water becomes very black —another reference to the black clouds. Then again he twirls his stick in this mixture—together with the clouds. As the wind brings up clouds, so will the movements of his twirling stick. In the meantime the people are singing and invoking the praise-names of Leza. One refrain is :—

" Come to us with a continued rain, O Leza fall! "

When at last it rains nobody is allowed to hoe for two or three days. This is an act of reverence toward Leza. They say : " Do not wound him with a hoe, do not wound his water, his urine." [1]

If it is Leza who falls down in the rain, may not the proceeding of the magician with a pot of water be an imitation of what Leza is supposed to do in the sky with the clouds ? Thus, for instance, the Suk have a god called Ilat, the Rain. It is his duty to carry water and when he spills it, it rains. [2] According to the Ho, rain is contained in the sky in an immense pot which is filled by the Sons of God. When God tells them to pour it through a filter it rains. Others say that it rains when the pot is overfilled, or that the rain is the tears or the perspiration of God dropping to the earth from the sky which is his body. [3] Indeed, the usual idea of an African is to regard rain as the manifestation of the supreme deity. On hearing thunder at the beginning of the rainy season, a Yao woman would say : " Mulungu is speaking." [4] Evidently, therefore, it is Leza who stirs the rain pot in heaven and the magician who does the same

[1] E. W. Smith and A. M. Dale, *The Ila Speaking Peoples of Northern Rhodesia*, 1920, ii, p. 208.

[2] Beech, *The Suk*, 1911, p. 19.

[3] R. Spieth, *Die Ewe Stämme*, 1906, p. 553.

[4] Werner, *Natives of British Central Africa*, 1906, p. 56.

on earth.   According to Smith and Murray, Leza begins by being
simply Thunder, then he comes to control the clouds to feed his
people, and at last he becomes the Father of Men.[1]   Perhaps,
however, the course of events was the reverse.   At least there seems
to be the trace of an older belief in a Father Sky and Mother Earth,
when we are told that the union of Leza the Sky and Bulongo the
Earth produces grain and all other things.[2]   We think at any rate
that there is no mistaking two outstanding facts : (*a*) that the Rain
God is always the All-Father ; (*b*) that rain is mostly made by
imitating what takes place in the sky.   The Swazies seek to make
rain by throwing water high up into the air, and expect that as the
water falls in drops it will stimulate the clouds which will fall in
rain in sympathy with the artificial shower.   The Pondos kill
certain birds with bright red feathers on their breasts which they
hunt in times of drought.   When they are caught and killed, they
throw the dead birds into the water.[3]

In the Basuto mountains the natives offer beer to the spirits by
pouring it into the earth at the edge of the mealie field.[4]   Turning
now to Australia, we find both a very general belief in the All-
Father as the cause of Rain and Thunder and efforts made by the
magician to imitate him in this field of activity.

Atnatu, the Sky-god of the Kaitish, was the first person to make
a bull-roarer.   He swung it up in the sky when he initiated his
offspring and now he is glad when he hears the natives on earth
making the bull-roarer sound when they initiate boys.   He has a
large number of spears and if he does not hear the men sounding
the bull-roarer when they perform the initiation ceremony he gathers
the spears together and rattles them, and if they still do not sound it
he hurls the spears down and drags the men and boys up into the
sky.[5]   It seems that the spear he hurls down is the lightning and
the sound of the bull-roarer the thunder.   The Yuin regarded the
roaring of the bull-roarer as representing the muttering of thunder
and thunder as the voice of Daramulun, calling on the rain to fall
and make everything grow up new.[6]   The Tully River natives
believe that rain is a person and that certain people who are named
after him can make him come, by hanging a bull-roarer in the water

[1] Smith and Murray, loc. cit., ii, p. 206.
[2] Smith and Murray, loc. cit., ii, p. 196. To-day the earth is male.
[3] Kidd, *The Essential Kafir*, p. 114.
[4] Kidd, loc. cit., p. 115.
[5] Spencer and Gillen, *Northern Tribes*, p. 499.
[6] Howitt, *Native Tribes*, p. 538.

of certain pools.[1]   Again, the Dieri account makes it quite clear that the rain-making on earth is believed to be merely a repetition of what takes place in heaven.   The whole tribe joins under the direction of the medicine-man in making rain.   The sky is supposed to be a vast country inhabited by their ancestors, some of them in hideous forms such as serpents with feet.   The clouds are supposed to be bodies in which rain is made by these rain-making Mura-Muras influenced by the ceremonies of the Dieri.   When the tribe is gathered together they dig a hole about two feet deep and over this they build a hut of logs in a conical form and covered with boughs. The wizards who are supposed to have received inspiration from the rain-making Mura-Muras are selected to have their arms lanced. These are tightly bound near the shoulders to prevent a too profuse effusion of blood.   This being done all the old men huddle together in the hut and the principal medicine-man bleeds each of the men with a sharp piece of flint.   The blood is made to flow on the men sitting round and the two medicine-men throw handfuls of down into the air, some of which becomes attached to the blood of the men, while some continues to float about.   The blood is to symbolize the rain and the down the clouds.   Two large stones in the centre of the hut represent gathering clouds.   After this the men who were bled carry the two stones away and place them as high as possible in the branches of the largest tree near.   In the meantime the other men gather gypsum, pound it fine, and throw it into a waterhole. The Mura-Mura sees this, and thereupon causes clouds to appear in the sky.   Finally the hut is thrown down by the men, old and young, butting at it with their heads ; this symbolizes the piercing of the clouds and the fall of the hut represents the rainfall.[2]   The Karamundi open a vein in the arm of one of their men and let the blood drop into a piece of hollow bark until there is a little pool. Into this they put a quantity of gypsum ground fine which they stir until it has the consistency of a thick paste.   A number of hairs are pulled out of a man's beard and mixed up with this paste which is then placed between two pieces of bark and put under the surface of the water in some river or lagoon and kept there by means of stakes driven into the ground.   When the mixture is dissolved, a great cloud bringing rain will come.[3]   Among the Kurnai it was the Burjil-willung or rain man who squirted water and sang the rain song.   Among the Wotjobaluk a bunch of the medicine-man's hair was soaked in water and then squirted westward.[4]

[1] Roth, *Superstition, Magic and Medicine*, 1903, p. 9.
[2] Howitt, loc. cit., pp. 394–6.   [3] Howitt, loc. cit., p. 397.
[4] Howitt, loc. cit., pp. 397, 398.

So far it seems fairly evident that in producing rain the medicine-man is identifying himself with the Father, for until we can prove it we take it for granted that the All-Father represents the All-Father of the Primal Horde. The question, however, has still to be asked, what is the All-Father really doing and what is the medicine-man trying to imitate ?

Pausanias tells us that at Thebes on the Acropolis they showed the bridal chambers of Harmonia and Semele. The place was taboo. These tabooed places were not only called *abaton* but also ενηλύσια : "places of coming." (Pollux Etymologicum Magnum.) This is the name of a place where a bolt fell from heaven, dedicated to Zeus the Descender. Along with the thunder-bolt that was hurled into the bridal chamber of Semele they showed a log that fell from heaven and it is said that Polydoros adorned this log with bronze and called it " Dionysus Cadmus ".[1] It is evident that the two events represented as separate episodes in the myth, the love of Zeus and Semele and his descent to her in his real shape of Thunder and Lightning, mean one and the same thing.[2] The place where Father Zeus the Thunder " descends " on mortal woman is taboo. The thunderstorm is the bridal of the Earth represented by Gaea or Semele and the Sky represented by Uranus, Zeus, or Keraunos, and their child was Bromius the Thunder.[3] This is symbolized by the thunder axe hafted into an obelisk. Semele is the bride of the bladed thunder.[4] Alcmene is the wife of Amphi-tryon, the double-borer, the thunder-weapon, and Dido is wedded to Æneas in a thunderstorm.[5] The thunder-weapon is the phallic weapon ; in certain Tibetan incantations the priest makes use of the thunderbolt and at the time of the act coitus is performed.[6] It is with this " weapon " that Heaven pierces the Earth when in the *Danaides* of Æschylos [7] Aphrodite says :—

> " Lo, there is hunger in the holy Sky
> To pierce the body of Earth and in Earth too
> Hunger to meet his arms. So falls the Rain
> From Heaven that is her Lover making moist
> The bosom of Earth ; and she brings forth to man
> The flocks he feeds, the corn that is his life."

[1] J. E. Harrison, *Themis*, 1912, p. 91. *Pausanias*, ix, 12, 3.
[2] Jessen, article on Semele in *Roschers Lexikon*.
[3] Harrison, loc. cit., p. 91.
[4] Euripides, *Hipp.*, 555. *Bacch.*, 3.   [5] Harrison, loc. cit., p. 168.
[6] Chr. Blinkenberg, *The Thunder-weapon in Religion and Folklore*, 1911, p. 45. Rockhill, *Ethnology of Tibet*, p. 740.
[7] Nauck frg. 44 ap. Athen. xii, 600.

Everyone in the theatre—Jane Harrison tells us—would remember the final ceremony of the Eleusinian mysteries, how, looking up to heaven, they cried aloud $v\breve{\epsilon}$ " rain ", and, looking down to earth, $\kappa\acute{\epsilon}$, " be fruitful." [1]

Urine being one of the most frequent infantile substitutes for the seminal fluid, we can now understand that the real nature of the Ba-Ila taboo against hoeing was to prevent injuring the urine of Leza, that is, his seminal fluid, his penis.   In the Upper Palatinate, they say if it rains heavily that there is an inn in the sky where people have been drinking more than is good for them and now they are urinating.[2]   Strepsiades, who, in Aristophanes, tells us that Zeus is urinating through a sieve, was repeating a joke of cultured Athens which nevertheless undoubtedly represented the beliefs of his ancestors.[3] But this urine is only a substitute for the real thing.   Thus, the Australians of the Pennefather River believe that Thunder can make lightning men and women, and at Cape Bedford thunder produces lightning by the rapid exposure of his generative organ.   The expression for lightning is " Thunder his penis ejects ".[4]   The Masai tell the old story of how the sky married the earth.   Like the man above his wife, sky lies above earth, and when the earth is fecundated by sunshine and rain this is the same thing as when the woman is fecundated by the seminal fluid.[5]   According to the Koryak, rain is made in the following manner : Universe attaches his wife's vulva to a drum which he beats with his penis, and the liquid that is squirted from the vulva falls on earth as rain.   In order to put an end to the incessant rain, Big Raven and his son turn into ravens and fly up into heaven.   They cause the deity and his wife to fall asleep and then they dry their privates by the fire.   On awakening Universe is no longer able to produce rain by beating the drum and thus it clears up.[6]

We thus come to the conclusion that the rain-maker is the man who has identified himself with the God-Father on basis of the penis as Ego-Ideal, or in other words the child who imitates Father-Sky in having intercourse with Mother Earth.   Among the Dieri the foreskin that has been carefully kept since the ceremony of initiation is believed to have great power in producing rain.   The great council has always several of them for use when required.

---

[1] J. E. Harrison, loc. cit., p. 175.
[2] Schönwerth, loc. cit., ii, p. 128.
[3] Schwartz, *Poetische Naturanschauungen*, 1879, ii, p. 198.
[4] Roth, *S.M.M.*, p. 8.   [5] Hollis, *Masai*, p. 279.
[6] Jochelson, *The Koryak*. Jesup, *N.P.E.*, vi, pp. 26, 27.

They are kept carefully concealed, wrapped up in feathers with the fat of the wild-dog and carpet snake.   After the ceremonial opening of the parcel and the exhibition of the prepuce it is buried again, its virtue being exhausted.[1]   Among the Toradja of Celebes incest committed by animals is regarded as a rain charm.   If it were committed by human beings the actors in this religious drama would have to be put to death, and besides there would be such a tempest that it would do more harm than good.   It is significant, moreover, that even the incest of animals is only indicated.   They carry a cock and a sow to the river, kill the animals and lay them side by side in intimate embrace.[2]   Probably the cock and sow represent the male and the female genital organs—incest desired by man projected into the animal world.   Another method of making rain consists in ploughing.   The plough is the phallus [3] and the Earth-Mother with whom incest is committed appears in the guise of a naked woman.   In Bengal three women of a husbandman's family strip themselves naked ; two of them are yoked like oxen to a plough, while the third holds the handle.   They pray to Mother Earth for rain.[4]   In Southern Hungary a woman draws a plough into the water in case of a drought.[5]   Kapu women in Southern India worship Jokumara.   A small figure of a naked human being is made and they carry it from door to door in an open palanquin singing indecent songs and collecting alms.   Another method they have is to catch hold of a frog and tie it to a new winnowing fan. Then they go singing from door to door : " Lady Frog must have her bath ! "   The woman of the house brings out a little water in a vessel, pours it on the frog, and believes that rain will come down in torrents.[6]   The interesting feature in this ceremony is that it throws some light on the meaning of employing certain animals in rain magic.   The association of frog and rain seems to be world-wide.[7]   In some parts of South-Eastern Australia, when the rainfall is likely to be excessive the natives feared to injure Tidelek, the frog, or Bluk, the bullfrog, because they were said to be full of

---

[1] Howitt, loc. cit., p. 396.
[2] Kruijt, " Regen loken en regen verdrijven," *Tijdschrift vor indische Taal, Land en Volkenkunde*, xliv, 1910, p. 4. Frazer, *Magic Art*, ii, p. 113.
[3] Dietrich, *Mutter Erde*, p. 107.
[4] *North Indian Notes and Queries*, i, pp. 210 and 61. Frazer, *Magic Art*, i, p. 263.
[5] Somogyi, *Arad Vármegye Monographiája*, 1912, iii, p. 241.
[6] E. Thurston, *Castes and Tribes of Southern India*, 1909, iii, pp. 244, 245.
[7] Frazer, *Magic Art*, i, pp. 292, 295.

water instead of intestines and great rains would follow if one of them were killed. Once upon a time a frog drank up all the waters, and the animals were gasping for a drop of moisture. It was evident that they must all die if they could not contrive to make the frog laugh. At last the conger-eel and his relations hung with lake grass and sea-weed reared themselves on their tails and pranced round the fire. The frog laughed and the water running out of his mouth filled the lakes and streams once more.[1]

I have quoted some other versions of this myth in my book on Australian totemism, and made it plain enough that " laughter " means coitus and the contortions of the eel are the movements of the male member in cohabitation.[2]

This agrees well with the world-wide symbolism of the frog ; it means the mother, the vagina, the womb. As a votive offering it symbolizes the uterus.[3]   In Southern Hungary, according to popular belief, if you kill a frog your mother will die,[4] while the Huzuls dread the same calamity for both the father and the mother.[5]   In Udvarhely the mother appears in fetters in a dream to anybody who has killed a frog.[6]   In a saga with variants in every European country the frog-woman asks for a human woman to come and help her in giving birth to her child.[7]   The Suk will not kill lizards or frogs because anybody who kills one of these animals will become poor and his wife will die in childbirth.[8]   The other characteristic animal of rain-making ceremonies is the serpent.   The part it plays in connection with the flute priests and as an embodiment of ancestral spirits in Hopi and Zuni rain-making ceremonies evidently points to a phallic meaning,[9] so that the frog and the serpent would mean the female and male organs of generations in rain-making.   As for the former, we must not forget to stress the fact that the Kapu call it " Lady Frog " and that the part it plays in the ceremony is exactly similar to that played by naked or leaf-clad girls in Southern

---

[1] Howitt in the *Journal Roy. Anthr. Inst.*, 1889, xviii, p. 54.   Frazer, ibid., i, pp. 292, 293.

[2] Róheim, loc. cit., pp. 452, 453.

[3] R. Andree, *Votive und Weihegaben*, 1904, 129.

[4] J. Nagy, " Bácsmegyei babonák," *Ethn.*, 1896, 96.

[5] R. F. Kaindl, " Zauberglaube bei den Huzulen," *Globus*, lxxvi, p. 232.

[6] Balásy, " Udvarhelyvármegyei babonák," *Ethn.*, 1905, p. 41.

[7] E. S. Hartland, *The Science of Fairy Tales*, 1891, p. 37.

[8] Beech, loc. cit., p. 26.

[9] Cf. W. Fewkes, " Tusayan Flute and Snake Ceremonies," xix, *Report Bureau Am. Ethn. Idem*, " The Alosaka Cult of the Hopi Indians," *Am. Anthr.*, i, p. 522.

Europe and elsewhere. In time of drought the Servians strip a
girl to her skin and clothe her from head to foot in grass, herbs,
and flowers. Thus disguised she is called the Dodola and goes
through the village with a troop of girls. They stop before every
house, the Dodola keeps turning round, and the housewife pours
a pail of water over her. One of the songs she sings runs as follows :

> We go through the village.
> The clouds go in the sky.
> We go faster.
> Faster go the clouds.
> They have overtaken us
> And wetted the corn and the vine.[1]

At Egin in Armenia this figure is called " the drenched Mother " ;
at Ourfa she is the " shovel-bride ", and they throw this rain bride
into the water. The Arabs of Moab call her the " Mother of the
Rain " and the Greek Christians of Palestine dress a winnowing
fork in woman's attire and call it " the bride of God ".[2] When the
people near Delagoa Bay want rain the women dress in petticoats of
leaves and put on a head-dress of grass. Then they dance and go
to the water-holes to clean them. The next station is the hut of a
woman who has recently had twins ; she must be drenched with
water.[3] In Zihlahla all the women assemble and start in all
directions to draw water in old calabashes from the lakes and wells
of the neighbourhood. They go skipping along and sing, " Mbelele,
Mbelele, let the rain fall." The mother is seated with the twins
in her arms and they pour the water over her.[4]

Having thus reviewed both the male and the female protagonists
of the drama, we see that the methods used by mortals to procure
rain correspond closely to their beliefs with regard to the celestials.
Just as rain is regarded as the nuptials of Father Sky with Mother
Earth, it can be brought about by incest committed on earth. Corresponding to the phallic weapon of the thundergod, we have on earth
the magician's wand, the stick twirled in a pot by the Ba-Ila, the idea
of producing rain by means of a butter-churn in South Africa,[5]
the plough, the serpent, the foreskin, and the effusion of blood as
effusion of the semen. On the female side we have the naked girl
and the frog, while the part of the male is here represented by the
action of the rain itself. Thus we are told that Hottentot girls run
about naked in the first thunderstorm after their festival of initiation

---

[1] Frazer, *Magic Art*, i, p. 273.   [2] Frazer, ibid., p. 276.
[3] D. Kidd, *The Essential Kafir*, 1904, pp. 114, 115.
[4] Junod, loc. cit., ii, p. 395.   [5] Kidd, loc. cit., p. 118.

so that the rain which pours down washes the whole body. The belief is that they will become fruitful and have many offspring.[1]

If we attempt to determine the degree of libidinal development of these rites we shall probably classify them as phallic, as a playful imitation of what a child conceives to be the coitus of the parents. Each sex has its own little game, the male with a partner who exists only in his unconscious phantasies, the female by opening her bosom to Father Jove himself. There are clear signs to indicate that repression is at work. Among the Nandi a rain-maker who is procuring rain may not have intercourse with his wife, nor may he sleep on the hide of an ox which has recently been slaughtered.[2] When the Karamundi have started their rain-making ceremony their wives are taboo to the men or the charm would be spoiled. The old men said that if this prohibition were properly respected rain would come every time that the ceremony is performed.[3] Here we find the males making rain without the women while at Delagoa Bay the female rain-making is taboo for the men.[4]

It is just possible to indicate the source of this taboo in the Œdipus complex. To begin with, the fact that the bull-roarer (a world-wide symbol of initiation ceremonies) is frequently used in rain magic seems to show that the basic complex of the former is also at the root of the latter. Then we have the positive belief in the connection between incest and rain and the fact that the rain-maker is trying to do the same as Father Sky does with the mother. Perhaps, therefore, it is the sanguinary contests of the Primal Horde that are repeated by the people of Egghiou, a district in Abyssinia, every year in January with the intention of procuring rain.[5] The same past with a different secondary elaboration might be attributed to the ceremonial slaughtering of animals for the purpose of procuring rain. The fact that these animals are usually black, therefore of the same colour as the clouds themselves, seems to show that they are merely older theriomorphic forms of the rain-making celestials. Umbandine, an old king of the Swazies, was famous as a rain-maker on account of his herds of cattle of a peculiar colour. When the ox is killed the blood is caught in calabashes, on no account must it be allowed to fall to the ground. The dish of blood is then placed in a hut together with the meat of the dead ox, on the morrow the meat is eaten, on the third day the bones are burnt. And then— the detail is significant—the priest confesses over the beast the sins

[1] Th. Hahn, *Tsuni Goam*, 1881, p. 87.
[2] Hollis, *Nandi*, p. 52.   [3] Howitt, loc. cit., p. 397.
[4] Kidd, loc. cit., p. 115.   [5] Frazer, *Magic Art*, i, p. 158.

of the people. Dudley Kidd supposes that this confession consists of little else than of the admission that they have not honoured the ancestral spirits sufficiently.[1] That is just the very thing they might confess after having eaten the king's ox !

We shall now proceed to discuss two other methods of magic connected with natural phenomena that may throw some light on the psychology of magic in general. In Hungary it is the custom to hurl an axe, a scythe, or any other sharp tool into the storm to make it stop. Additional conditions are that there should be two weapons deposited crosswise in the court or that the axe should be driven into the threshold. The general belief is that the weapon will wound the witch who is riding in the whirlwind or hail-cloud. But why throw the axe into the threshold ? Now the Roumanians, who have the same belief and practice, do something else besides this. The women undress or throw their skirts over their heads and stark naked they call the prophet Elijah, who is supposed to hurl the thunder-bolts from heaven, to their assistance.[2] According to the Hungarians in Göcsej this is just what a woman ought not to do in a thunderstorm. The reason is that the prophet Elijah is hurling his fiery bolt after the devils. Now the devils are very clever, they do all they can to escape. They crawl into any little hole or crevice, and if a woman were to throw her skirts up she would leave her vagina unprotected and the thunderbolt would follow the devil.[3] Therefore it is easy to see what the Roumanian and Ruthenian women are doing, when they drive a storm away by undressing. They are offering their vagina to the being who hurls the thunder-axe. But the celestial being, be he the Prophet of the Bible or the Thunder God Thor with his hammer Mjölnir, hurls the axe with a double aim. It is both an aggressive movement of the Ego and a coition on the part of the libido. For Elijah aims at his enemies the devils and may perhaps run into the vagina. Thor is after the giants whose wives and daughters he sometimes mates with, but the Mjölnir is laid in the bride's lap at her marriage ceremony. As the celestials, so the mortals ; as the fathers so the children. The Hungarian, German, or Ruthenian peasant hurls his little axe into the storm to stop it ; and with what result ? A witch frequently bleeding and naked falls from the clouds. So he too has his naked woman with the wound, the vagina. There can be no doubt about

[1] Kidd, loc. cit., p. 116.
[2] Cf. A. Herrmann, " Idövarázslás " (Weather Magic), *Ethnographia*, vi, p. 201. R. Fr. Kaindl, *Die Huzulen*, 1894, p. 9.
[3] Gönczi, *Göcsej*, 1914, p. 194.

the matter, for in popular spells at Christmas the penis is compared to an axe. Probably there is another meaning hidden below what looks like coitus pure and simple. We remember the fear of the Ba-Ila lest the hoe should cut the urine of God-Father and probably here too the axe is unconsciously meant to wound the Father first, and then to cleave the threshold, the vagina of the house.

The change that has taken place in the general attitude of mankind from savage life to the Middle Ages is well brought out by the fact that to the savage the magician, a representative of the Father Image, is the embodiment of his castration dread, while in medieval Europe we have the witch as castrator. It is the fluid of Heaven she is after and with this precious substance life and luck disappear. At Cracow witches and shepherds steal the dew from the fields on a Thursday after new moon by means of a rag. They wring moisture from the rag on a kid saying : " I take the fertility (or profit) but not the whole." [1] Naked Palöcz women gather dew on the eve of St George's Day by pulling their blanket through three fields and saying : " I take a part and I leave a part." [2] At Kecskemét the shepherds are the dew gatherers. Their saying is : " I take, I take half of everything." When their blanket is soaking wet they wring the dew into the milking pail that the cows should have plenty of milk.[3] Posen witches collect the dew in sieves at the time of the new moon on the fields and they must be naked to do so.[4] In the Upper Palatinate the same thing is done on St John's Eve. The witch must be naked ; she gathers all the dew of the fields and with the dew she gets all the milk of the cows that have been grazing on those fields.[5] At Puisaye women who desire to get milk in abundance from their cows steal water from their neighbour's well on the first of May.[6] In the Charente anybody who on the first of May steals the dew of his neighbour's field in a blanket will have a double quantity of hay, leaving nothing for his neighbour. On the Côtes du Nord women steal the milk by gathering the dew and they must be naked to do so.[7] Bulgarian women drink milk on the fields on the first of May and at the same time they bathe

[1] Karlovicz, *Czary i Czarownicze w Polsce*, Visla, 1887, i, pp. 15, 16.

[2] Istvánffy, " A borsódmegyei palóczok," *Ethn.*, 1911, p. 295.

[3] Ipolyi, *Magyar Mythologia*, 1854, pp. 56, 123.

[4] Knoop, " Der Tau im Glauben und in der Sage der Provinz Posen," *Z.d.V.f.Vk.*, 1912, p. 95.

[5] Fr. Schönwerth, *Aus der Oberpfalz*, 1859, iii, p. 172.

[6] P. Sebillot, *Le Folk-Lore de France*, 1905, ii, p. 439.

[7] *Idem*, ibid., i, p. 95.

in the dew as this brings luck for the whole year.[1] According to the Southern Slavs a witch who is stealing the cow's milk can be frustrated in her malice by washing the cow in dew acquired by the methods we have been describing.[2] Dew and rain are closely connected ideas. In Little Russia the witches steal from the sky its rain and dew which they carry off in pitchers and bags and hide in their cottages. Once a witch who had stolen all the rain in this manner had to go out one day and she gave strict orders to the girl who was left in charge not to meddle with the pitcher that was left in the corner. But no sooner had she disappeared than the girl opened the pitcher and peeped in. Nothing was to be seen inside, only a voice was heard to say : " Now there will be rain." The frightened girl ran to the door, and, sure enough, the rain was coming down " just as if it were rushing out of a tub ". The witch came running home and closed the pitcher. In a moment the rain stopped and the witch said : " If the pitcher had stood open a little longer the whole village would have been drowned." In other variants of this tale the tubs containing the rain are full of frogs, toads, water-snakes, and other reptiles which set up a strange croaking and crawl away in different directions. Immediately the blue sky turns black and a terrible storm arises only to be quelled by the return of the witch and the restoration of the toads and other reptiles to their prison-tubs.[3]

The dew or rain collected in a tub or rag contains the fertility of the fields and of the cows that graze on them. Whilst the medicine-man or shaman of a primitive tribe is chiefly engaged in procuring rain, a witch is always stealing the moisture by supernatural means. The meaning of this difference becomes evident at once if we know that dew was regarded as the seminal fluid of Zeus.[4] If dew is the seminal fluid we can understand why according to Lushei beliefs the spirits become reincarnated in the form of dew and if this falls on a person the spirit is reborn in his or her child.[5]

Before passing on to the next chapter we shall do well to summarize the results of our inquiries. We have found reason to assume that the dread felt by primitive man of his sorcerers and wizards is derived from the castration complex and more especially from the repressed

---

[1] A Strausz, *Bolgár Néphit*, 1897, p. 307.
[2] Fr. Krauss, *Volksglaube und religiöser Brauch der Südslavien*, 1890, p. 128.
[3] Ralston, loc. cit., p. 382.
[4] Nonnus, *Dionysiaka*, vii, p. 144.
[5] Shakespeare, *The Lushei Kuki Clans*, 1912, pp. 64, 65.

desire of assuming the position of the woman in cohabitation, of suffering castration by the penis of the father. This homosexual component is manifest in the phantasy of having been " opened " or " shot " or of having had the kidney fat cut out by means of super-natural weapons. If we remember the part played by homo-sexuality in the persecutory delusions of the paranoiac we may well compare the general attitude of primitive man to his sorcerers to that of the paranoiac with regard to his assumed enemies. As for the magician himself, he seems to be a person who acts as the scapegoat for the general castration phobia. He accepts the part attributed to him and lives up to his character as far as possible. But he is only playing a part, he is imitating the Father of the Primal Horde. This partial identification is managed by him because he has reached the phallic phase of organization and developed a Super-Ego on the basis of the penis. By means of the Ego-Ideal he identifies himself with the Father both in the act of coitus (weather magic) and in his function as castrator (black magic, axe into thunder cloud). His wonder-working instrument is the penis and the miracle achieved by him is erection. The other side of the castration complex, in which castration is simply fission or the loss of the seminal fluid, is represented by the activity of the witch. But the remarkable feature is that in stealing rain or dew she is in point of fact stealing the milk from the cow's udder. This points to a very primitive phase of organization in the development of the child when before the first teeth appeared he imbibed his mother's milk in an essentially passive attitude. In this phase of development the oral erotic function of the mouth may be compared to the part played by the vagina in coition, while the flow of milk corresponds to the seminal fluid. In the next chapter we propose to consider love magic. Here of course there can be no doubt about the aim of the action, but we believe that in demonstrating the part played by pre-genital phases of organization in these rites some light will be thrown on the parallelism between the non-attainment of erotic reality in the pre-genital organizations and the lack of objective reality that is such an essential feature of magic.

3   LOVE MAGIC

For anybody who is unacquainted with the results and methods of psychoanalysis there can be no more convincing proof of the existence of the eroto-genetic zones and the pre-genital phases of organization than the practices of primitive people in their love magic.

The connection of the olfactory sense with the genital organs is too well known for further comment. It has been explained by Ferenczi and others with reference to the impressions received by the child in its passage through the vagina and thus ontogenetically it would appear to be the most primitive of sex stimuli. At any rate we find more of this type of love magic among savages, while those connected with the oral, anal, and urethral functions are conspicuous in European folklore.

On the Tully River, if a woman has had connection with a boy the perspiration from under the armpits of the latter can be smelt on her and for such an alleged *faux pas* she has often to pay the penalty. On the Pennefather River when a man wishes to inflame a woman's passions he puts a stripe of red clay all the way down his flanks and along the outer sides of his lower limbs while at the same time he smears over the front of his body a preparation made from the inner bark of a certain tree, mixed with charcoal which gives him a peculiar scent. He then passes close to her. She both sees and smells him and has her passions excited. Similarly when a younger brother goes to claim his elder brother's widows he rubs the root and the bark of a certain tree on his face, body, hands, and spear, and she is attracted by the smell.[1] The Yabim make use of various cigarettes for this purpose. Women put the tassels of their skirt in the cigarette ; men have a certain powder that induces strong perspiration in the woman and excites her sexual desires.[2] The smell of perspiration, especially from under the armpits, is much used in European love magic. In Brunswick a boy will secretly give the girl a piece of bread to eat that has been soaked in his axillary perspiration.[3] In Göcsej they proceed as follows ; wine is poured on the axillary hair and given to the girl to drink.[4] In Brandenburg the girl puts some sugar under her armpit and then into the coffee of her beloved.[5] In Oldenburg a piece of bread is soaked in the perspiration [6] ; in Scandinavia three drops of perspiration in an apple are used for the

[1] Roth, *Sup. Mag. Med.*, pp. 22, 23.
[2] Neuhauss, loc. cit., iii, pp. 325, 326.
[3] R. Andree, *Braunschweiger Volkskunde*, 1901, p. 297.
[4] Gönczi, " Szerelmiteemények," *Ethn.*, 1907, p. 35.
[5] H. Prahn, " Glaube und Brauch in der Mark Brandenburg," *Z.d.V.f.Vk.*, 1891, p. 182.
[6] Strackerjan, *Aberglaube und Sage aus dem Herzogtum Oldenburg*, 1909, i, p. 114.

same purpose.[1]   A Gipsy girl will take a part of her clothing that is thoroughly imbued with perspiration, add some hair, burn it to ashes, and put the mixture into the food or beverage of the man she loves.[2] In Esthonia a girl uses a rag to wipe herself in the sweat-bath and then wrings the perspiration into anything her swain will drink.[3] In Bohemia at a dance the lad will wipe his left armpit with a kerchief and apply the same kerchief to the girl's forehead.[4]

The part played by the left armpit is not explained in a totally satisfactory manner by the fact that this part of the body perspires profusely.   Possibly the armpit might be a substitute for the vagina, at any rate it is there that Wend girls put the roll or apple that gets soaked in perspiration and is eaten by the lad.[5]   The fact that it is used by men just as much as by girls might be explained by the suggestion that the vagina symbolized by the armpit was the one through which every individual passes at birth.

However, I will not stress this suggestion, and acknowledge that it is quite hypothetical.   But no such caution is needed in calling attention to the fact that the first phase of libidinal development that is well known to us, the oral organization of the libido, plays a conspicuous part in these forms of magic.   Perspiration is mostly mixed into a food or beverage.   Indeed it seems that the oral introjection of any part of the body seems to be the decisive feature.

According to the Gipsies, the essential thing in gaining the love of man or maid is to mix some part of the body, be it perspiration, blood, or hair, into the food or drink of the person in question.[6] In Silesia they mix some part of the body into a person's food or beverage.   It may be the nail-parings or hair or blood ; the chief thing is that it should be eaten.[7]   At Amboina lovers drink each other's blood.[8]   A Gipsy in Transylvania accused his mother-in-law of having won his love by means of blood mixed into his food.[9]   Still

---

[1] H. F. Feilburg, "Totenfetische im Glauben nordgermanischer Völker," *Urquell*, iii, 1892, p. 59.

[2] Wlislocki, "Szerelmi jóslás és szerelmi varázslás az erdélyi sátoros cigányoknál," *Ethn.*, 1890, p. 276.

[3] Wiedemann, *Aus dem inneren und äusseren Leben der Esthen*, 1876, pp. 391, 392.

[4] Wuttke, *Der deutsche Volksaberglaube*, p. 365.

[5] Schulenburg, *Wendisches Volksthum*, 1882, p. 117.

[6] Wlislocki, *Volksglaube und religiöser Brauch der Zigeuner*, 1891, p. 134.

[7] Drechsler, loc. cit., i, p. 231.

[8] Riedel, *De Sluik en Kroeshaarige Rassen tusschen Selebes en Papua*, 1886, pp. 41, 42.

[9] Wlislocki, *Aus dem inneren Leben der Zigeuner*, 1892, p. 85.

more important from our point of view is the part played by *the mother's milk* in these practices.   In Mecklenburg, if a couple has no children, the man is advised to drink a brandy-glass full of a woman's milk who has just given birth to her first child, then pull a pole out of the earth, urinate into the hole, and put the pole back again upside down.[1]   This is simply a play-imitation of the development of the libido, using the first phase and the phase before the genital one to describe or induce the whole process.   It begins with the mother's milk, and ends in the symbolism of the pole, urinating, and the hole.   The last step, from urinating to the ejaculation of the semen, ought to be achieved in actual life.   In the Hungarian county of Szatmár girls filter milk through the bottom of their chemises and then make cakes with it for the boys to eat.[2]   A mother's milk and a daughter's milk with a piece of menstruous cloth as a potion serve as a love-charm on the Ægean Islands.[3]   In Northern Dalmatia they use the milk of three women who are nursing their children at the same time to bake a loaf.   The lad makes a hole in the loaf, looks through it at the woman, and says : " I look at you through the milk of three women ; may you look at me through three hearts." [4]   At Pórszombat, if there is no love between a married couple and if the woman's mother is nursing a child at the same time as she they bake a cake with the milk of both women.   To repeat the same symbolism ; the cake is baked in an oven with an opening opposite to that of another oven, meaning of course the vagina of mother and daughter.[5]   All object-love is but the repetition of the feelings of the infant towards the nursing mother and the magical act aims at the revival of this ancient object relation through the complete fusion of the mother-imago (represented by the mother-in-law) and the wife.

If, as we suppose, every genital act is a short cut, a reduced repetition of ontogenesis, it is natural that magic should aim at starting the whole process of evolution by beginning at the beginning.   The great stress laid on the oral assimilation of the miracle-working materials shows that the oral phase is represented in all these cases, though of course latter phases of libido development are also conspicuous in these rites.   Thus Burchard von Worms mentions the

---

[1] Bartsch, *Sagen Märchen und Gebräuche aus Meklenburg*, 1880, ii, p. 354.
[2] I. Jakab, " Szatmármegyei babonák," *Ethn.*, 1895, p. 414.
[3] W. R. Paton, " Folk Medicine, Nursery Lore, etc., from the Ægean Islands," *Folk-Lore*, xviii, p. 330.
[4] *Anthropophyteia*, vii, 226.
[5] Gönczi, " Szerelmi teemények," *Ethn.*, 1907, pp. 34, 38.

sinful practices of women who give their husbands pastry that has been kneaded on their anus.[1] In Mecklenburg the way to win love is to swallow a nutmeg, find it in one's own excrement, and then give it to the other person to eat.[2] The same philtre is used in Southern Germany.[3] At Sárhida excrement mixed with an egg is used for this purpose.[4] The Apache substitute animal for human excrement.[5]

As Ferenczi regards coitus as an amphimictic process with anal and urethral tendencies as its chief components we shall not be surprised to find urinating as part and parcel of love magic. At Tutu they spear the ground where the woman has micturated and call her name.[6] The Kai splash her with urine mixed with the juice of a plant.[7]

In Switzerland the girl secretly urinates into the man's wine,[8] and the wise woman in the Middle Ages was inclined to give similar advice.[9] Among the Saxons in Transylvania women dig their own menstrual fluid and the hairs of a corpse into the ground somewhere where a man is likely to urinate.[10] Another very prominent feature is the use of blood in love magic. A girl in Kalotaszeg will prick the little finger of her left hand and smear the blood on the lad's hair ; after which he will not be able to think of anybody else.[11] At Nagylengyel a man will drop a few drops of blood from his finger into a glass of wine the girl is about to drink.[12] A Gipsy woman in Southern Hungary or Roumania will make an incision between her husband's index finger and his thumb on the left hand (this is called " the devil's saddle ") and let the blood flow into a pot. She buries the pot under a tree and after nine days takes it out and pours ass's milk into it. Before going to sleep she drinks the contents and

---

[1] Wuttke, loc. cit., p. 366. Bourke Krauss, " Der Unrat in den Sitten der Völker," *Anthropophyteia*, 1913, p. 193.

[2] Bartsch, loc. cit., ii, p. 353.

[3] Wuttke, loc. cit., p. 366.

[4] Gönczi, " Szerelmi teemények," *Ethn.*, 1907, p. 35.

[5] Bourke Krauss, loc. cit., p. 189. Cf. Krauss, " Liebeszauber der Völker," *Anthropophyteia*, iii, p. 167.

[6] Haddon, loc. cit., v, p. 211.

[7] Neuhauss, loc. cit., iii, p. 120.

[8] W. Manz, " Volksbrauch und Volksglaube des Sarganserlandes," *Schriften d. Schw. Ges. f. Vk.*, 1916, xii, p. 143.

[9] Zachariae, *Z.d.V.f.Vk.*, 1912, xxii, p. 125.

[10] Wlislocki, *Volksglaube und Volksbrauch der siebenbürger Sachsen*, 1893, p. 203.

[11] A. F. Dörfler, " Das Blut im magyarischen Volksglauben," *Urquell*, iii, p. 269.

[12] Gönczi, " Szerelmi teemények," *Ethn.*, 1907, p. 35.

says a spell about the three fairies. The first of them looks for the
blood, the second finds it, and the third fashions it into a child.[1] The
whole action is simply a rehearsal of the pregnancy that is aimed at.
The left hand represents the penis, the blood is the ejaculation of
the seminal fluid, the pot the womb, the tree the mother and the
nine days the nine months of pregnancy.   Gipsy women in Transylvania suck the blood from the little finger of children who die
unbaptized ; this facilitates conception.   In Hesse, Bohemia,
and Oldenburg, blood dripping from the finger in the last hour of
the year is used for a love potion.[2]   A Wend girl cuts her finger
and lets the blood ooze into an apple.[3]   A Gipsy girl will cut her
little finger on the left hand, let three drops of blood fall on a crossroad on St George's Eve and then say : " I offer my blood to my
beloved and whom I see, his will I be."   She sees the phantom
picture of her future husband arising from the blood.[4]   The blood
derived from the finger in the male has a parallel in the use of menstrual
discharge.   A woman is sure of the affection of her husband in
India if she smears her forehead with her own menstrual blood.[5]
Burchard von Worms says : " Have you done what some women
used to do ?   They take their menstrual blood, mix it into some food
or drink, and give it to their husbands to eat and drink so that they
should love them the better." [6]   Serbian women mix their menstrual
blood into the coffee or wine.[7]

According to a general Hungarian belief, there is something
exaggerated in the love of a man for a girl after he has drunk her
menstrual blood ; it is a " mad " love.[8]

Now the essential feature of all these magical ceremonies and
indeed of magic in general is the non-attainment of the post-ambivalent
phase represented by complete genital primacy.

The rites are oral, or anal-sadistic, or phallic, but not genital with
a complete love for the object.   The compulsive feature is akin to
the sadistic strivings of the pre-genital phase ; the magician compels ;

[1] H. v. Wlislocki, " Menschenblut im Glauben der Zigeuner," *Urquell*,
iii, pp. 7, 8.

[2] Wuttke, loc. cit., p. 366.

[3] Schulenburg, *Wendisches Volkthum*, 1882, pp. 117, 118.

[4] Wlislocki, *Volksglaube und religiöser Brauch der Zigeuner*, 1891,
pp. 131, 134.

[5] R. Schmidt, *Liebe und Ehe in Indien*, 1904, pp. 168, 169.

[6] E. Friedberg, *Aus deutschen Bussbüchern*, 1868, p. 98.

[7] F. S. Krauss, " Liebeszauber der Völker," *Anthropophyteia*, iii, pp. 165,
166 ; v, p. 202. *Slavische Volksforschungen*, 1908, p. 169.

[8] Wlislocki, *Aus dem Volksleben der Magyaren*, 1893, pp. 70, 71.

the doomed victim gives up resistance, is masochistically subjected to the object of love. In Wales a love drink consisted chiefly of mead, rhubarb, cowslip, primrose, or elderberry wine. There was something else in it besides which they would not name, although they knew what it was perfectly well. The drink was very pleasant and people said that the person who drank it would forget father, mother, heaven, earth, sun, and moon. A rich man in Glamorgan discovered the secret and used it to obtain the love of a beautiful village maiden, who ever after followed him everywhere. " It was pitiful to see her following him. She would run through pools, over hedges, up hill and down dale only to catch sight of him. At last he got tired of her and wished to undo the spell but he could not. The girl died, worn out with mental anguish." [1]

In Shropshire, to fetch a lover from a distance you must get a pennyworth of " dragon's blood " from the chemist. Then you cut a piece of red flannel into the shape of a heart and stick three pins in it for Cupid's darts. Then you sprinkle the dragon's blood on the flannel and burn the whole thing on a fire of hot embers. A girl who tried this fetched her husband by train from a distance. They had just had a quarrel. " Why, whatever has brought you," she asked when he arrived. " I couldn't rest," he said. " I felt as if I must come." [2] If made conscious, compulsive love easily turns into hatred. In Mecklenburg the way for a girl to get a husband is to begin to wash at midnight on New Year's Eve, and her future husband appears and brings her a piece of soap. But it is a dangerous affair as a word on her part might be her death. Once a lad who appeared under the constraint of the spell left his pen-knife with the girl. She locked it in her drawer. Years after this they were husband and wife. She opened the drawer and he caught sight of his knife. " So you are the one who made me suffer such awful torture," he said, and stabbed her to death with the knife.[3] The ambivalency in love magic is well brought out by the fact that all the devices used to procure love may equally be employed to make love cease. Thus if we were not told we should not know that a Wend lad, in urinating into his boot and giving this to a girl to drink, is not trying to get her love but to get rid of her.[4] His own urine mixed with his wife's blood is a philtre to make a Gipsy husband

[1] Trevelyan, *Folk Lore and Folk Stories of Wales*, 1909, p. 238.
[2] Ch. S. Burne, " Scraps of English Folk-Lore," *Folk-Lore*, xx, p. 223.
[3] Bartsch, loc. cit., ii, pp. 239, 240.
[4] Schulenburg, *Wendisches Volkstum*, 1882, p. 118.

hate his wife.[1]   In Silesia you get rid of your love for a woman by drinking wine out of a shoe that is soaked in perspiration or by smelling excrement.[2]   A Slovak lad who has been jilted will mix some excrement with a piece of his former love's bridal garland and her husband will hate her.[3]   In Macedonia, fumigating a man's clothes with excrement will make him conceive an aversion for the woman.[4]   In Southern Ireland, if a little boy draws blood from a girl when they are playing the nurse will say, " Now you must marry her," [5] while among the Wends it is a reason for not marrying her.[6]   Mother's milk, used in some Hungarian villages as a love charm, is exactly the reverse in others.[7]   In Oldenburg there is a certain form of love magic connected with a frog's bones and they say the chances are that it will *either provoke love or hatred.*   A love philtre of the kind described above is a sure method for making a woman (or man) love you, but marriages concluded on the basis of a love charm are usually unfortunate.   For this love is not love of the normal type ; it is love that is very apt to turn to hatred.[8]

Perhaps the analysis of this compulsion will make it possible for us to understand what love magic really is.   In the Mecklenburg case quoted above we saw that the lad left his knife in the girl's drawer and it was the sight of this knife that roused his sudden wrath. We may therefore infer that he resents the loss of the knife, does not want it to be in the drawer.   What does the knife mean ?   In Macedonia the following measures are taken for loosening a man who is bound, e.g. incapable of intercourse.   When the person who is bound goes to bed he must place a knife with which murder has been committed between his legs and go to sleep, and when he awakes he must utter these words :   " As this knife has proved capable of committing murder, that is to say of killing a man, even so may my own body prove capable of lying with my wife." [9]   The knife between a man's legs is his penis and the constraint he feels under the spell is the tension that is preparatory to ejaculation or the conflict

---

[1] Wlislocki, *Aus dem inneren Leben der Zigeuner,* 1892, p. 85. Cf. on the use of urine for this purpose, Bourke Krauss, *Unrat.,* p. 445.

[2] Drechsler, loc. cit., i, p. 233.

[3] Sztancsek, " Privigye vidékén gyüjtött babonák," *Ethn.,* 1908, p. 104.

[4] Abbot, *Macedonian Folklore,* 1903, p. 232.

[5] W. Crooke, in *Folk-Lore,* xvii, p. 114.

[6] Schulenburg, *Wendisches Volksthum,* 1882, pp. 118, 119.

[7] Gönczi, " Szerelmi teemények," *Ethn.,* 1907, p. 37.

[8] Strackerjan, *Aberglaube und Brauch im Herzogtum Oldenburg,* 1909, i, p. 113.

[9] Abbott, *Macedonian Folklore,* 1903, p. 232.

between the anal tendency of retention and the urethral trend of expenditure. He does not wish to lose the penis or even the seminal fluid.

By retaining the seminal fluid a Yogi conquers death and, we may add, the magician acquires his power. In a Pawnee tale Coming Sun looses his magical power as soon as a woman enters his tipi.[1]

In a Wichita myth Little Man enjoins the Coyote not to marry lest by marrying he should lose his powers.[2] An Arunta medicine-man must keep a fire burning between himself and his wife when he is being initiated, for his magic power might leave him if he were to have intercourse with her.[3] Intercourse ends the tension and it is this tension projected into the world at large that is the source of the magician's power. If, however, the magician's power is derived from tension maintained at a high pitch, from the cathexis that precedes ejaculation, we must ask what induces him to keep this tension up and "prefer power to woman", tension to release? The answer we have given above is "the fear of losing his knife", i.e. his castration complex. It is because he does not wish to lose any part of his body that he is continually operating on the severed parts of other people's bodies, because he is afraid of being castrated that he castrates others. Indeed this is not a very surprising result for our investigations, for having once explained the magical phobia of the savage as the castration complex it is evident that the men who make magic their profession must be individuals in whom this complex is particularly strong. Thus we see that the anxiety connected with coitus is turned into sadistic aggression in the black art with the penis as a magic weapon. The penis as the nucleus of the Super-Ego or Pleasure-Ego [4] makes it possible for the magician to identify himself with the Father in his activity of coition. It is the ejaculation that he shirks, the full genital primacy he cannot attain, because his magic is really the permanent reign of the pleasure principle—an endless erection without ejaculation.

[1] G. A. Dorsey, *The Pawnee*, i, 1906, p. 104.
[2] G. A. Dorsey, *The Mythology of the Wichita*, 1904, p. 254.
[3] Spencer and Gillen, *Native Tribes*, i, pp. 529, 530.
[4] Cf. Ferenczi, *Further Contributions to the Theory and Technique of Psycho-Analysis*, (Int. Psa. Library, xi), p. 85.

III THE MEDICINE MAN AND THE ART OF HEALING

1 THE SUCKING CURE

IN our last chapter we have pointed out that the libidinal process in love magic is a repetition of the phylo—and ontogenetic development of the libido. We shall now consider this process in the case of the medicine-man, partly repeating some ideas put forward in a former paper, partly attempting also to supplement former theories. In the paper to which I refer I stressed the oral and anal fixations in the development of the medicine-man.[1] Our last chapter rather tended to consider magic as based on the genital act, the magician himself as a personification of the penis. We shall now attempt to weld these ideas into a harmonious whole, and trace the carrying over of certain features in the mental make-up of a primitive medicine-man from the oral to the phallic phase and also to consider his functions and personality from the standpoint of the patient and society in general.

As for the oral phase, there are three chief symptoms to be considered. The medicine-man is a being who is born with teeth, he is a confirmed cannibal, and he cures his patients by sucking.

A Hungarian wizard or medicine-man is a person who is born with teeth. He has a similar *táltos* horse also born with teeth for his special use. Every seventh year he must go and fight the wizards of another country for the fertility of the land. The fields will be fertile in the country of the victorious shaman.[2] According to the North Hungarian (palóc) version of this belief, the *táltos* is born with three teeth in the upper jaw. When he is seven years old he disappears because he has to fight the other *táltos* people in the shape of black bulls. This is called his trial and if he can manage to

---

[1] Róheim, " Nach dem Tode des Urvaters," *Imago*, ix.
[2] Karcsay, *Uj Magyar Muzeum*, ii, p. 500.

keep his teeth he will become a *táltos* of a higher degree, for the black bulls try to pull his teeth out all the time. An essential feature of the *táltos* is his supernatural strength manifested in wrestling.[1] At Nagyszalonta he is born with two or more teeth or even with a complete set of teeth. If the midwife notices the teeth and extracts them his supernatural power is done for. When he is seven years old the other *táltos* people run away with him and initiate him into the mysteries of their art. If it is a male *táltos* the initiation must be performed by females and if it is a female by males. They are terribly strong although they feed chiefly on milk. They are always asking for it ; they want milk cream, curds, whey, cheese, and eggs. But they only drink milk if the cream has not been taken off it. If there is milk in a covered pot they can tell which cow it is from. They suck the milk from the cow's udder. They are terribly strong and might bring a second flood that would destroy the whole earth if they were not eternally at war with each other. For every *táltos* hates his colleagues and when they fight there is an awful storm.[2] There are also female wizards and they fight with their male colleagues just like the others. Nor is a female *táltos* transformed into a cow ; just like the males she appears in the guise of a bull. They undress stark naked before they fight and then, at least in the case described by an eye-witness at a witch's trial, the female " bull " is wounded on the left nipple.[3] Then again we are told that in Göcsej these wizards born with teeth suck their mother for seven years. They are terribly strong[4] ; a wizard has the strength of nine other men.[5]

Since Abraham has drawn a distinction between a pre-ambivalent and an ambivalent phase of oral-eroticism and established the fact that the border line between is marked by the appearance of teeth, we fully understand the importance of these data. A man who has had no pre-ambivalent phase in his evolution is probably one who is never destined to attain the post-ambivalent phase of complete genital-primacy. He is from the beginning a sadist, an infant who tries to bore himself into his mother, to destroy the mother by means of his teeth. His addiction to milk, the fact that he sucks the cow and is nursed by his mother for seven years, are symptoms

---

[1] Istvánffy, " A borsódi matyó nép élete," *Ethn.*, vii, p. 364.
[2] Szendrey, " Ember és természetfeletti lények a szalontai néphitben," *Ethn.*, xxv, pp. 315–17.
[3] Lehoczky, *Beregvármegye monographiája*, 1881, ii, p. 250.
[4] Gönczi, loc. cit., pp. 174, 175.
[5] Jankó, *Aranyosszék, Toroczko magyar népe*, 1893, p. 249.

of a strong and sadistic oral mother-fixation that cannot be mis-understood.

A characteristic feature of the oral character as described by Abraham is envy. A wizard wants milk and like an infant he will brook no denial. If this slight gift is refused he mounts his horse, transforms that innocent animal into a terrific dragon, and up he goes into the clouds. An awful storm is the result, crops are spoilt, and there will be nothing to eat for those who have refused him his due of milk.[1] It is no use denying that they have it ; he has a piercing eye for milk and sees it wherever it may be.[2] A farmer who refuses the milk is likely to pine and die with all his family.[3] Wine may be a substitute for milk. In a story I heard in a vine-yard at the Balaton this was the explanation of the bad luck they had had for many years. A wizard asked for a little wine and they said they had none. " Well, if you have none you shan't have any for seven years," he replied, and in fact for three years hail had ruined the vintage.

The Hungarian medicine-man with his teeth and propensity for milk is supplemented by the cannibalistic tendencies of his savage colleagues. An Australian sorcerer must undergo certain rites before he becomes qualified for his profession. Around Adelaide they have at one period to eat the flesh of young children, at another that of an old man.[4]

A person who has eaten human flesh seems to be considered as a minor sort of medicine-man by the Euahlayi, for they say that their shadows must not fall on anyone who has participated in this rite, and it is usually their medicine-men that are after people's shadows.[5] A Ta-tathi medicine-man was carried away to the sky by the ghost of a woman whose powers he invoked by chewing a piece of skin which he had cut from her stomach after death.[6] Among the Wiimbaio, one man, being a *Mekigar*, could initiate another and make him a *Mekigar* in the following manner. They procured a corpse, pounded up the bones, and chewed them. Then the candidate was plastered with human excrement and carried about with him the humerus of a disinterred body which he continually gnawed.

[1] Tóth István, " Kiskunfélegyháza vidéki néphiedelmek," *Ethn.*, 1906, p. 230.

[2] Gönczi, loc. cit., p. 194.

[3] Jankó, *A Balaton néprajza*, 1902, p. 408. On the *táltos*, see also Róheim, *Magyar Néphit és Népszokások*, 1928.

[4] E. I. Eyre, *Journal of Expeditions into Central Australia*, 1845, ii, p. 359.

[5] Parker, loc. cit., p. 38.

[6] Howitt, loc. cit., p. 389.

They were brought to a state of frenzy ; their eyes were bloodshot and they behaved like maniacs.[1] Possibly the fact that a Mungaberra medicine-man can assume the form of an eagle-hawk [2] is connected with the eagle-hawk as the carrion-eater *par excellence* in Central Australia.[3] At Mabuiag a magician will compare himself and his pupil to a fish eagle and its egg and say that the pupil was still in the egg-stage but would some day become as fierce an eagle as himself.[4] A lad who chose this profession was instructed by a *maidelaig* who took only one aspirant at a time. He was taken into the bush by the instructor and the first operation consisted in the old man defecating into a shell filled with water ; when the mixture was well stirred the novice had to drink it all up and in order that he might have the full benefit of it he was enjoined to keep his eyes open whilst drinking. He had to eat the unripe fruit of the kara-tree, which made his eyes red and " inside bad ", and also to chew a plant that made the skin itch. He had to eat other plants and the flesh of a shark or of a fish that bites like a shark. Lastly, he had to eat the decomposing flesh of a dead man which was full of maggots and the effect of this was to make his throat bad. Altogether he was in a very uncomfortable condition, with bloodshot eyes, a sensation of feeling wretchedly ill all over and in a semi-frantic state. A *maidelaig* made a practice of eating anything that was disgusting and revolting in character or poisonous or medicinal in nature, not only during the course of instruction but subsequently whenever he was about to perform a special act of sorcery. For instance, they were said frequently to eat the flesh of corpses or to mix the juices of corpses with their food. One effect of this diet was to make them wild so that they did not care for anyone and all affection temporarily ceased for relatives, wife and children, and on being angered by anyone they would not hesitate to commit murder.[5] Among the Roro-speaking tribes in British New Guinea there is a general belief that sorcerers endeavour to obtain access to freshly dead human bodies.[6] According to the Marind-anim a man called Ugu (the word means skin, hide) was the first sorcerer. People acquired the power of sorcery from Ugu by eating him. Thereby their body became permeated by the substance of magic and anybody who wishes to acquire the power of magic in the future must absorb

[1] Howitt, loc. cit., p. 404.
[2] Spencer and Gillen, *Native Tribes*, p. 533.
[3] See Róheim, *Australian Totemism*, 1925.
[4] A. C. Haddon, *Cambridge Expedition to Torres Straits*, v, p. 322.
[5] Haddon, loc. cit., v, pp. 321, 322.   [6] Seligman, loc. cit., p. 289.

this quality into his own body.   A candidate who wished to become
a *Mesaů* must therefore eat the corpse and drink the exudations of
a dead *Mesaů*.   The exudations of a corpse are a supernatural
substance full of faculties like those attributed to ghosts (*Hais*),
that is, they contain something evanescent, uncertain, and extraordinary.   A person wanting to become a *Mesaů* must have
swallowed extraordinary quantities of this stuff and others into the
bargain.   By eating the fat of birds, he acquires their speed and ease,
by the fat of serpents their qualities and so on.[1]   In Western New
Guinea the Kasoeri dip a piece of sago or taro into a corpse and
swallow it.   This gives them the supernatural power needed for
the vocation of a medicine-man.[2]   The *Talamaur* of the Banks
Islands was also a sort of sorcerer.   A man or woman would obtain
this power out of a morbid desire for communion with some ghost
and to gain it would steal and eat a morsel of a corpse.   The ghost of
the dead man would then join in close friendship with the person
who had eaten his flesh and would gratify him by afflicting anyone
against whom his ghostly power might be directed.   The soul of
such a *Talamaur* was supposed to go out and eat the soul or lingering
life of a freshly dead corpse.[3]   Among the natives of Lake Nyasa
people with a taste for cannibalism are regarded as sorcerers of high
quality.   Although theoretically cannibals when caught should
be burnt alive they are hardly ever denounced, even on the clearest
evidence, for fear of their occult power.[4]   In British Central Africa
the *Mfiti* or wizard frequently turns himself into a hyena or leopard
and digs up graves to eat the flesh of corpses.   The wizard is believed
to kill a person and then when his relations have buried him to send
out messengers to find where the grave is.   When they come back
they tell their master that they have seen the " meat " (i.e. the
corpse).   Then an owl summons all the witches to the feast.   The
animals lead the way to the grave and the chief asks who it was that
killed the person they are about to eat.   Then the wizard who has
done the deed kills his victim over again.   They take the meat
and divide it and eat it in the village.   Witchcraft and cannibalism
are synonymous.   " Why did So-and-So have to drink *mwavi* ? "
" Because he was an eater of men."   This does not mean that he
actually has eaten anyone, only that he has caused someone's death
with the intention of eating the corpse.[5]

[1] Wirz, loc. cit., ii, pp. 63, 64.
[2] *Militair Exploratie van Nederl. Nieuw Guinea*, 1907–1915, p. 260.
[3] Codrington, loc. cit., pp. 221, 222.
[4] L. Decle, *Three Years in Savage Africa*, 1900, p. 513.
[5] Werner, loc. cit., pp. 84, 169.

Among the Ewe, an *Adze* is a spirit dwelling in a sorcerer. This *Adze* sucks blood, drinks coconut water and palm oil. The *Adze* flies about and looks something like a fire-fly and if anybody dares to catch hold of it while in this shape it changes into a human being immediately. For secrecy it offers quantities of shell money. If an *Adze* sees a good-looking little child it may suck its blood until it dies.[1] However, there is a second species of *Adze*. Whilst the first sucks blood and gives (under compulsion) money in return, the second is after the money and makes it gradually disappear.[2] If somebody has no property, these *Adze* will eat his intestines till he dies. They are always after blood, which is their food, and they like to fly to the dust heap.[3] The Thonga word *baloyi* comes from the verb *kuloya, lowa*, to bewitch. The word belongs to the ancient stock of Bantu roots and in Thonga its usual meaning is to bewitch. But the word is also applied to the act of a man who marries his cousin, that is, to incest. However, the technical meaning is to injure or kill by enchantment. The power is hereditary and transmitted through the mother, indeed it is simply sucked from the mother's breast by the infant. In later life it must be strengthened by special drugs to be truly efficient. The *Baloyi* form a kind of secret society in the tribe and they assemble with their spiritual bodies during the night to eat human flesh in the desert. They discuss things sometimes and if one of them is defeated in the discussion (his ideas for evil-doing are rejected) he has to pay a fine. The fine is always a human body, and may be his own child.[4] The *Subachs* of the Western Sudan are a similar category of beings. While among the *Noyi* there is the possibility that only one of them may practise sorcery on his own child and eat him, this is the regular thing in Western Sudan. A man who has no relations, wife, or children, can never be a *Subach* because it is only their lives that are in his power. A *Subach* can attack a stranger only if he has received the power to do so from another *Subach* who is a relative of the victim. If he tried to devour an utter stranger it would mean instant death to him. One day one of them will tell the other : " Take my son " (or brother, or daughter, whoever it may be). Then they begin operations by drumming on a drum that is made of a human skull. Then the *Subachs* congregate and attack the victim. First they change the life-principle of their victim into an ox. If the ox, when questioned by them as to the cause of his death, answers that

---

[1] Spieth, loc. cit., p. 682.   [2] Spieth, loc. cit., p. 724.
[3] Spieth, loc. cit., pp. 832, 850, 906.
[4] H. A. Junod, *The Life of a South African Tribe*, 1913, ii, pp. 461, 462.

it is the *Subachs* who are killing him, they have no power to do so. But they repeat the question day by day until he lays the blame on the innocent ghosts. Now he is in their power. One of them cuts the ox's throat and the others skin it and cut it into pieces. When this has happened to the life-ox the human being begins to feel weak. " His envelope gets weak, he is like the sheath of a dagger when the blade has been pulled out." After a year they burn the head of the ox and then the man dies.[1] These are the sorcerers of the Mande and allied tribes, whereas the Bosso have blood-suckers instead of cannibals. The blood-sucker begins work by undressing and when completely naked it gets out of its own skin. What remains is a mass of red flesh. It sits on the mouth of those whose life-blood it intends to suck. Such a peculiar being has one member more than ordinary humanity. This is a sucking apparatus protruding from the anus like the trunk of an elephant. This member it ejects from its body and inserts into its victim's mouth and nostrils to suck all his blood out. Such a *Subach* appears to his victim in a dream and the first thing he sees is the sucking tusk. Then the *Subach* sits on his lips and he cannot open them, he lies in mortal anxiety like a child without being able to move. Another sort of *Subach* uses a cupping apparatus shaped like a funnel to extract the blood. The *Subachs* of the Tombo are more like usual sorcerers and medicine-men ; they steal shadows. The Mossi see their cannibal sorcerers as fire-flies or toads. Among the *Tamberma*, the *Subachs* eat the bowels, liver, and heart of a sleeping man. The *Subachs* of the Losso are hyenas, but there is also a flying species. The latter have lighted torches protruding from their armpits and anus.[2]

Before we continue our investigation by comparing the curative practices of medicine-men to these uncanny proceedings, we must answer the objections that might be made by the reader. This refers to the black art, the sorcerer, but has nothing to do with the medicine-man, the doctor. Now it is evident to every anthropologist that among primitive people the boundaries between these two types of quasi-supernatural mankind are very uncertain. Usually there is only one kind to be found whose principal work is to make people ill, and in some cases he will also revoke the spell he has cast or counteract the evil designs of one of his colleagues. There may be a differentiation, but the traces of a former identity remain. For instance, a Kobeua medicine-man may receive any objects by way

---

[1] L. Frobenius, *Kulturtypen aus dem Westsudan*, 1910, pp. 76–8.
[2] Frobenius, loc. cit., pp. 78–86.

of salary for his work except arrows.[1]   Why not arrows ?   Because
the arrow is the sorcerer's weapon [2] and well might he think that
it was an allusion to his dark origin.   The Bakairi calls the wizard
an *ome zóto* = a poison possessor.   The medicine-man is a *piaje*,
but they sometimes use these expressions indiscriminately.[3]   In
West Australia the *boylya-gadak* is a medicine-man and yet it is also
the *boylya-gadak* who " eats up " the body of sick people.[4]

In addition to the magician born with teeth and addicted to milk,
to the black wizard as a blood-sucker and cannibal, we have the
medicine-man who cures his patients by sucking.   In North-West
Australia the doctors cure illnesses by expelling the spirits sent by
other tribes.   The doctor stands over the patients and groans aloud,
and then makes a noise resembling the hushing of a child to sleep.
Next he stands with one foot upon the affected part, and then briskly
rubs and squeezes it with his hands.   When he considers this massage
sufficient he puts his mouth to the affected part and proceeds to draw
out the evil spirit.   After all the evil spirits have been drawn out
he runs some little distance with them in his hands and carefully
buries them.   Then he returns, puts his hand to his side, draws out
a good spirit and inserts it into the patient.   He makes a clicking
noise—probably with his finger-nails—which they believe is the
spirit being drawn out.[5]   Howitt says : " Their method of procedure
is that common in savage tribes and which has been so often described
that it may be dismissed in a few words, being, in perhaps the majority
of cases, a cure effected by rubbing, pressing, or sucking the affected
part, possibly accompanied by an incantation or song, and the
exhibition of some foreign body extracted therefrom, as the cause of
evil.   Or the evil magic may be sucked out as a mouthful of wind and
blown away, or got rid of by pinching and squeezing to allay the pain.
As an instance of the methods used by the Kurnai I give the practice
of Tankli the son of Bunjil-bataluk.   His method of cure was to
stroke the affected part with his hand, till, as he said, he could ' feel
the thing under the skin '.   Then covering the place with a piece
of some fabric, he drew it together with one hand, and unfolding it
he exhibited a piece of quartz, bone, bark, or charcoal, even on one

[1] Koch-Grünberg, *Zwei Jahre unter den Indianern*, 1909, ii, p. 157.
[2] Krause, *In den Wildnissen Brasiliens*, 1911, p. 334.
[3] K. v. d. Steinen, loc. cit., p. 299.
[4] G. Grey, *Journals of Two Expeditions to North-West and Western
Australia*, 1841, ii, pp. 321–5, pp. 337–9.
[5] I. W. Withnell, *The Customs and Traditions of the Aboriginal Natives
of North-Western Australia*, 1901, p. 32.

occasion a glass marble, as the cause of disease." [1] Among the
Yayaurung the medicine-man occasionally administers a decoction
of the fleshy-rooted geranium, the only root used as a medicine,
and he sometimes bleeds the arm with a sharp flint, but incantation
is the sovereign cure as well as the cause of all diseases. The doctor
utters a monotonous chant, makes passes by drawing his hands
downward over the affected part and at intervals by rubbing and
blowing upon it. At the conclusion, supposing the disorder to be
rheumatism, hot ashes are applied. [2] The Narrinyeri doctors treat
disease by incantations, mutterings, tappings, and blowings, and partly
by vigorous squeezing and kneading of the affected part. The
doctor will kneel upon his patient and squeeze him until he groans
with the infliction. This is supposed to press out the *wiwirri* or
disease. In cases of rheumatism they employ a sort of vapour bath
which is prepared as follows. They make a fire, and heat stones,
as if for cooking, then they make a sort of stage of sticks and the
patient is put on it. Under the stage they put some of the hot
stones, and having first covered up all but the head of the sick person
with rugs and closed in the place where the hot stones are in the same
way, they put water-weed on the stone and the steam ascends under
the rugs and envelops the body of the patient. [3] A Bangerang
doctor will suck the skin of the sick person over the liver, heart,
or other part affected and, as he declares, draw into his mouth through
the unbroken skin and from the suffering organ bits of wood two
inches long and as thick as slate pencils. [4] The Euahlayi medicine-
man cures a burn by sucking lumps of charcoal from it. If somebody
has pains in the chest he sucks at the affected spot and soon produces
from his mouth a hair, bones, or something similar. [5] The Ngarigo
called the medicine-man *Murri-malundra* or *Budjun-belan* but the
former was the specialist for extracting evil substances which had
been inserted by another *Murri-malundra*. These were in particular
white stones, *thaga-kurha*, and black stones, *thaga-kuribong*. [6]
Besides the more general *Gommeras*, the Yuin also have specialists
of their own for extracting evil substances. These are called
Nungamunga, i.e. " doctor he is ". One of them sucked the place
on a man where there was a pain and spat out a mouthful of blood,

---

[1] Howitt, loc. cit., p. 379.
[2] Standbridge, " Aborigines of Victoria," *Transactions of the Ethnological
Society*, i, p. 300.
[3] Taplin, loc. cit., p. 45.
[4] E. M. Curr, *The Australian Race*, 1886, i, p. 48.
[5] Parker, loc. cit., p. 27.   [6] Howitt, loc. cit., p. 382.

by which the patient felt very much relieved. He would also warm his hands at the fire and place them on the affected part or try to dissipate the evil influence by blowing on the place with short puffs.[1]

The Port Stephens tribes believed that their *Koradjis* could suck out the substances projected into them by the medicine-men belonging to other tribes in the form of pieces of stone or charcoal. One man believed that a ghost had thrown a pebble into him and the *Koradji*, after sucking the place, really produced a pebble as the cause of the mischief.[2] A Chepara medicine-man turns the patient about, presses his body all over, pinches him, and anoints his body with saliva, all the time muttering incantations and finally producing some object, usually a piece of stone.[3] The *Mintapas* remove disease by sucking sickness out of the body. They put their lips to the pit of the stomach and to the suffering part when confined to any fixed spot, and after having sucked for some time, they pull out of their mouths a small piece of wood or bone, declaring that this is the body of the disease which had been thrust in by some evilly-disposed person and sucked out by them.[4] The *Mulgarradock* remove disease by friction with warmed green twigs, puffing as if to blow the pain away. The hand of the *Mulgarradock* is also supposed to confer strength or dexterity ; he will draw his hand repeatedly with a firm pressure from the shoulder downwards to the fingers which he extends till the joints crack.[5] In the North-West the medicine-man swings the bull-roarer and walks round and round the patient. Then he suddenly pounces upon him, rubbing the affected part with his hand or a cowry shell. Then he applies his mouth to the seat of pain and produces a round stone, which he declares he has sucked out of his patient.[6] Among the Larrekiya, Pongo-Pongo, and kindred tribes, it is considered dangerous for a man to receive any food from a woman during her menses or for her to receive any food from him. If this takes place

[1] Howitt, loc. cit., p. 382.   [2] Howitt, loc. cit., p. 384.
[3] Howitt, loc. cit., p. 385.
[4] Ch. Wilhelmi, "Manners and Customs of the Australian Natives," 1862, *Trans. R.S.*, xxi. Cf. C. F. Angas, *Savage Life and Scenes in Australia and New Zealand*, 1847, i, p. 110. C. G. Teichelmann and C. W. Schürmann, *Outlines of a Grammar Vocabulary and Phraseology of the Aboriginal Languages of South Australia*, 1840, p. 23. B. H. Schneider, *Missionsarbeit der Brüdergemeinde in Australien*, 1882, p. 39.
[5] R. Brown, "Description of the Natives of King George's Sound," *Journ. Roy. Geogr. Soc.*, 1831, i, p. 41.
[6] E. Clement, "Ethnographical Notes on the Western Australian Aborigines," *Int. Arch. f. Ethn.*, xvi, 1904, p. 8.

the medicine-man may be summoned, who removes the pain by gestures, pretending to remove an offending body by sucking. Eventually he shows a piece of meat covered with blood to the sufferer. If a medicine-man has a bad case of sickness to deal with he pulls out a few hairs from his armpit, burns them, and places the ashes in the nostrils of the patient, over which he holds his hands in shape of a funnel and blows thereon.[1] In the Yas, Tumut, and Murrumbudgee districts, the magical crystal is called merrudagalle. They say they make it but how they produce it is a secret. The women are never permitted to look upon it ; the crystals are valued according to their size and it is not easy to procure a large one from them. The crystals are used in two ways, either as a curative charm, or to cause a person's death by being thrown at him. A native in the Tumat country was suffering from a spear wound and in his case the crystal was employed in the following manner. The physician sucked the wound and then, without spitting, retired to a distance of 10–15 yards from the invalid ; he muttered for a minute and then placed the crystal in his mouth, sucked it and then removing the stone spat upon the ground. He trampled upon the discharged saliva, pressing it with his feet firmly into the ground. This was repeated several times and the effect attributed to the magical properties of the crystal.[2] Their method of dealing with pustules appeals more to the medical science of Europe and indeed it seems to contain a hint regarding the origin of the sucking cure, at least so far as the reality principle is concerned. They prick the pustules with a sharp pointed fish-bone, squeezing out the fluid contained in them with the flat part of the instrument. The operation must have suggested itself to the *Koradjis* from the observation that the pustules burst spontaneously and discharged whitish matter in the first case of recovery.[3] The *Koradjis* perform their incantations over the sick, waving boughs dipped in water, and throw themselves into various distorted postures, applying the mouth to the affected parts and pretending to suck out or extract the disease. At length after much appearance of labour and pain they will spit out a piece of bone which they represent as the cause of the disorder. Another method is practised by the women only. The patient being seated on the ground has a line passed round the head and the

---

[1] H. Basedow, " Anthropological Notes on the Western Coastal Tribes of the Northern Territory of South Australia," *Trans. Roy. Soc. S.A.*, xxxi, 1907, p. 5.

[2] G. Bennett, *Wanderings in New South Wales*, 1834, i, pp. 190, 193.

[3] C. Bennett, loc. cit., p. 154.

knot is fixed in the centre of the forehead. The end of the line is then taken by the operator who frets her own lips with it until they bleed freely, the patient being led to suppose that the blood proceeds from his head and carrying the disease along with it upon a line passes into a woman's mouth.[1] In some of the Burdekin River tribes of Queensland, the doctors manufacture special articles of wood, somewhat like fish-hooks, which they pretend to extract from the patient.[2] In Queensland, if somebody falls ill he is taken to the *Turrwan*, who pretends to suck a stone out of the affected part.[3]

There is less variety in primitive medical art than one would be inclined to suppose, as rubbing, massage, real and fictitious removal of foreign substances by means of cupping and sucking seem to exhaust the shaman's range of action. On the Western Islands of Torres Straits there was a special group of physicians called *Kekuruk le*. The *Kekuruk le* began his performance by chewing various leaves, spitting the juice into his hands and rubbing it all over his own body. Then he made movements and passes as if he were anointing the sick person and passing some influence from his own body to the patient. He squirted the water and juice of the chewed plants from his mouth towards the patient in little puffs of spray, but he was careful not to let the patient hear anything, indeed he made no noise whatever during the whole performance and the patient was not allowed to open his eyes all the time. The *Kekuruk le* would work himself up into a frenzy passing his hands down his arms or legs as if he were trying to pull something off which was resistant but which finally glided off the finger tips and was wafted towards the sick person. Haddon calls this the nearest approach to hypnotism that was found in the Torres Straits.[4] In the Northern D'Entrecasteaux every sickness for which no immediate cause is evident is attributed to sorcery. The medicine-man would take his seat beside the patient and massage the afflicted part, chanting a magical song. Suddenly with a sharp hiss he would produce a piece of bone, a stone or some other object that was extracted from the patient's body. For afflictions in the lungs, shoulder, sides, or back he would take a leaf of a plant called *ibwadaka* and stroke the arm of the patient upwards from the hand to near the elbow and then downwards from the shoulder to the spot where he had ceased.

[1] G. F. Angas, *Savage Life and Scenes in Australia and New Zealand*, 1847, ii, p. 227.
[2] Curr, loc. cit., p. 48.
[3] T. Petrie, *Reminiscences of Early Queensland*, 1904, pp. 31, 32.
[4] *Cambridge Expedition*, vi, pp. 238–40.

To this point the medicine-man applied his lips and sucked the sick-ness out, producing a stone or similar object from his mouth.[1] The Mafulu believe certain diseases to be caused by the presence of a snake in the stomach which has to be got out. The operator, who is always a woman, takes a piece of bark cloth with which she rubs the front of the patient's body and makes a movement as if she was wrapping the mysterious snake in the bark cloth.[2] In Pentecost, women use leaves as poultices and when they take them off profess to take away with them the cause of pain—a snake, lizard or something similar.[3] The *Gismana* of the Banks Islands worked the cause of pain or disease downwards and extracted it ; he sucked out or bit out from the seat of pain a fragment of wood, bone or leaf ; for swellings he chewed certain herbs and leaves and blew on the place ; he used fomentations and poultices of mallow leaves with some knowledge of the healing and soothing properties in them.[4] In Fiji, disease-causing spirits are expelled by the following procedures. The medicine-man passes his hands over the patient's body till he detects the spirit by a peculiar fluttering sensation in his finger ends. He then endeavours to bring it down to one of the extremities, a foot or hand. Much patience and care are required because these spirits are cunning—they will double back and hide in the trunk of the body if you give them a chance. The demon may lodge in a joint and then it is hard indeed to get him out ! The medicine-man will draw him down to a finger or toe and pull him out with a sudden jerk, throwing him far away and blowing after him lest he should return.[5] In New Britain the magician will suck a worm from the patient's navel,[6] pebbles or bits of wood among the Baining.[7] The Dyak *Manang* pretends to draw bits of wood and needles out of the patient's stomach. To see a party of these doctors feigning to draw by hand an evil spirit or a malady from a person's body is very amusing. At times one can find a circle of them, dancing round and round and feigning to catch evil spirits.[8] Rubbing and massage are resorted to against the cholera.[9] They will also spit saliva mixed with red sirih on the patient's body. " Some Sakarang

---

[1] Jenness, loc. cit., pp. 139, 140.
[2] R. W. Williamson, *The Mafulu*, 1912, p. 241.
[3] Codrington, loc. cit., p. 199.   [4] Codrington, loc. cit., p. 198.
[5] Codrington, loc. cit., p. 198 (Fison).
[6] W. Powell, *Unter den Kannibalen von Neu-Britannien*, 1884, p. 147.
[7] Burger, *Die Küstenbewohner der Gazellehalbinsel*, 1913, p. 66.
[8] Ling Roth, *The Natives of Sarawak and British North Borneo*, 1896, i, p. 263.
[9] Ling Roth, loc. cit., i, p. 290.

wounded were once brought to Sir Chas. Brooke to be spat upon. He declined, so his people gave them a volley of saliva over their wounds in his stead and promised them a speedy recovery."[1] The *Maibas* of the Tangkhuls make use of massage and produce a small stone, picked out of the patients' side, as the cause of the disease.[2] The magicians of the Moi in Annam produce small pebbles, grains of rice, and similar objects, blow upon the affected part and thus heal the patient.[3] The Mohave shaman will blow or spit upon his patients and stroke or rub their bodies to drive the disease out.[4] The shamans of the Mohave Apache are acquainted with the sucking cure but they principally practise cupping on the forehead by cutting and sucking the affected part in case of headache.[5] A Huichol shaman goes through the following procedure to cure his patient : (1) He wrings his hands several times as if washing them, then quickly stretches his fingers one after the other so that the joints crack. This he does in imitation of the crackling of fire, the greatest of all shamans, in order that his fingers may remain well and strong. (2) He breathes into his hands. (3) He holds his hands together, spits into them and holds them out toward the south, north, west, and east and also towards the ground. (4) He places his mouth on the part of the patient's body which is in pain, makes a kind of gurgling noise, and then sucks out the disease in the shape of a grain of corn, a small stone, etc., coughing as he does so. The object produced represents the illness, and is either burned or thrown on the ground that the whirlwind may carry it off. (5) He breathes on the affected part, making passes with his hands as if to waft the illness away.[6] These Huichol medicine-men have their prototypes in the " withdrawers " (*tetlacuicuiliqui*) and " suckers " (*techichena*) of ancient Mexico. These began by rubbing a mixture of aromatic herbs, which had been masticated by the shaman, into the patient and feeling for the seat of pain. When they had located the pain they would " withdraw " an obsidian knife, a pebble, or something of the sort from the affected part. If a child had some ailment in his chest the medicine-man would suck it till blood and matter

---

[1] Ling Roth, loc. cit., i, p. 298.

[2] T. C. Hodson, *The Naga Tribes of Manipur*, 1911, pp. 135, 136.

[3] I. Canivey, " Notice sur les Moeurs et Contumes des Moi," *Revue d'Ethnographie et de Sociologie*, 1913, p. 10.

[4] A. L. Krober, *The Religion of the Indians of California*, University of Cal. Publ. Am. Arch. Ethn., iv, No. 6, p. 334.

[5] B. Freire-Marecco, " The ' Dreamers ' of the Mohave-Apache Tribe," *Folk-Lore*, 1912, p. 173.

[6] C. Lumholtz, *Unknown Mexico*, 1903, ii, p. 239.

came out. " Some get better, some not," as our source wisely
remarks.[1] Among the Indians of the Issá-Japura district there is
a universal belief in the potency of human breath as an evil-expelling
agency. The medicine-man's ceremonial consists in the usual
blowing and breathing over the patient as well as the usual sucking
out of the poison or evil spirit that lurks in the flesh of the sufferer
in the guise of a stick or stone and causes the sickness. Others
besides medicine-men can remove evil by the breathing or sucking
process. They suck each other's shoulders as a cure for rheumatism
and old women breathe on forbidden food to remove the " poison "
in the same way that the medicine-man breathes on the seat of pain
and withdraws the disease. They will also breathe over a delicate
child in the same way to restore its health.[2] For certain cases of
sickness sucking is the recognized cure of the Lengua Indians.
By long practice they develop a power of suction which is quite
surprising—in fact, it amounts to much the same as cupping. If
an Indian spits blood owing to overstraining himself or through some
internal injury he is always in fear of death. Out of this the wizard
makes capital and threatens the people that he will cause them
to die from internal bleeding. To prove his power he shows that
he can produce this bleeding in himself without any harmful effect,
and pictures the terrible consequences that will ensue if he produces
it in them. The medicine-man strikes his head and breast several
times and, looking diabolically fierce, he apparently throws up a
mouthful of blood, which he catches in his hands and rubs upon his
naked chest. The native is terrified for he cannot see through
this simple trick. Certain forest seeds have been secreted in his
mouth by the witch doctor, and after having delivered his oration
he asks for a drink of water, taking care to retain a fair quantity in
his mouth. This water is coloured by the seeds and the contents when
spat out very closely resemble frothy blood. Pustules are opened by
them with a sharp pointed instrument which after use is wiped on
their bare arms and used for cutting their food without any scruples.
They spit upon the wound and suck it to produce the fish-bones
or other objects that have been sent into the patients by wizards of
other tribes.[3]

[1] Ed. Seler, " Zauberei im alten Mexico," *Globus*, p. 78. *Gesammelte
Abhandlungen*, 1904, ii, p. 81. Translation from the Mexican MS. used by
Sahagun. Cf. Starr, *Notes upon the Ethnography of Southern Mexico*, 1900,
p. 59.
[2] T. W. Whiffen, " The Indians of the Issá-Japura District," *Folk-Lore*,
1913, pp. 59, 60.
[3] W. B. Grubb, *An Unknown People in an Unknown Land*, 1911,
pp. 150–4.

The following episode related by Barbrooke Grubb speaks for itself. " We had remarked for some time that this particular wizard frequently requested us as a personal favour to obtain for him several packets of the smallest needles obtainable. He was an ingenious fellow to have invented this new line of business but our suspicions were aroused. What possible use could an Indian have for very small needles ? These suspicions were strengthened when, shortly afterwards, a new epidemic, as it were, broke out among the people. *Needles* became the fashionable disease. But we determined to stamp it out. The supply of needles was cut off, the malady ceased, and the wizard's lucrative occupation with it.[1]

The *Ipaye* of other Gran Chaco tribes, after smoking and sucking the affected part of the patient with great force, pretends to draw out the evil which ordinarily consists in a little worm or some pebble that he had secreted in his mouth.[2] Concerning the River Pilcomayo we have two descriptions. Nordenskiöld tells us that disease is usually attributed to a man having unwittingly swallowed one of his own hairs or some of his own excrement. The medicine-man strokes and spits all over the patient's body and then he sucks at the seat of the pain with all his might. After this has gone on for some time he would appear as if about to vomit something which they bury in the sand. They expect to get quite a feast and all the time that they are not employed in sucking the patient they gorge themselves.[3] The effect of these cures lies of course in the faith placed in them by the Indians. Herrmann tells us that lanolin or a drop of beef tea and in extreme cases, rhubarb pills, which were the ingredients of his medical practice, worked just as well.[4] The sorcerers of South-Western Amazonia would persuade their patients that a serpent had taken possession of their body and then they would suck the affected part, rub green leaves round it and pretend that they had captured the snake.[5] A Bari magician will begin by groaning, assuming all sorts of postures, and continue by smoking and sucking a bone out of the affected part.[6] The *Jakamouch* of Tierra del Fuego shows the material embodiment of the disease

[1] Grubb, loc. cit., pp. 153–4.

[2] G. E. Church, *Aborigines of South America*, 1912, p. 236.

[3] E. Nordenskiöld, *Indianerleben*, 1912, pp. 103, 104.

[4] Herrmann, *Die ethnographischen Ergebnisse der deutschen Pilcomayo-Expedition*, Z. f. E., 1908, p. 129.

[5] Church, loc. cit., pp. 105, 106.

[6] K. von den Steinen, *Unter den Naturvölkern Zentral-Brasiliens*, 1897, pp. 379, 380.

in a spear point or piece of quartz, which he has extracted from
the patient's body and which he can conceal in his own stomach
at will.[1]

We can conclude our survey of facts with some African cases.
In West Africa, the doctor seems to draw from the patient's side
chicken's claws, feathers, bones, sticks, and pebbles and it is supposed
that some witch has caused these things to grow in the man's body.[2]
For South Africa we quote Kidd : " The diviner went over in
the morning and decided to cup the woman in the side and to put
a large cow-dung poultice on the seat of pain. He said the spirits
had told him during the night that the woman had been bewitched
through a lizard and that he would prove this by extracting it from
her side. The children were sent out to fetch some cow-dung
which was made into a poultice and put to the side of the patient,
after a cupping horn had been applied." [3] In the Moschi district
at the Kilimandjaro the medicine-men make incisions in the patient,
suck at the wounded part, and then produce the *corpus delicti*.[4]

To these three aspects of the magician : (1) Teeth and milk, (2)
cannibalism and bloodthirstiness, (3) sucking cure—a fourth may
be added. The black magician sucks his victim's blood till he dies ;
the medicine-man withdraws a smaller quantity of blood and his
intention is to heal.

We shall next consider the principal methods resorted to by the
primitive medicine-man in healing his patients and find that they
can all be derived from the destructive tendencies checked by a
displacement of libido to the patient.

A peculiar weapon or rather instrument that has often excited
the curiosity of the anthropologist is found in New Guinea. A
small bow is used to shoot a miniature arrow at one of the arteries,
the intention being to make the patient bleed and relieve him of his
sickness.[5] The Indian tribes inhabiting the isthmus in Central
America employ the same method. The operator shoots arrows
at various parts of the patient's body till he chances to strike a blood-
vessel. This shooting is done from a not too great distance, otherwise the arrow might penetrate into the patient's flesh and cause

---

[1] P. Hyades et J. Deniker, *Mission scientifique du Cap Horn*, 1891, vii,
p. 257.
[2] R. H. Nassau, *Fetichism in West Africa*, 1904, p. 271.
[3] D. Kidd, *The Essential Kafir*, 1904, p. 166.
[4] J. Raum, " Die Religion der Landschaft Moschi am Kilimandjaro,"
A.R.W., xiv, p. 203.
[5] G. Buschan, *Illustrierte Völkerkunde*, 1910, p. 192.

a fresh wound instead of effecting a cure.[1]   The use of an arrow to
draw blood is also found among the Masai, only here the "patient"
is a cow instead of a human being and the intention is a manifestly
selfish one on the part of the operator.   The Masai are very fond
of blood.   They tie a leather ligature round the neck of a beast
and pierce a vein with an arrow the shaft of which has been blocked.
When the blood gushes forth, they catch it in gourds.   Some drink
it pure, others mix it with milk.[2]   Among the Nandi the animals
are periodically bled by means of an arrow called *longnet*, which is
shot into one of the superficial veins of the neck.[3]   A Nandi myth
even connects this practice with disease and cure.   Milk was first
obtained from the cow by a man whose child pretended to be ill.
The next time the child again pretended to be ill and he said he wanted
some blood to cure him.   The cow told him to tie a ligature round
her neck and to shoot an arrow into her jugular vein.[4]   But this
is only a sporadic variant of the vein-arrow and there can be no
doubt that its original prototype is the disease-arrow of the wizard
or ghost who shoots his disease-bringing substances into mortal
man.   The very idea of procuring another man's blood, whether by
an arrow or scarification or whatever means, represents an almost
undistorted manifestation of the sadistic impulse.   The Boulia
medicine-man tries to get another man's life-blood into his hand
with an avowedly sinister intention,[5] and the ungentle treatment
we find in blood-letting and scarification as curative practices looks
like an unsublimated offshoot of the original aggressivity.   In the
Kaibara tribe a black with a headache would have a rope or
cord tied tightly round the head and be bled with a shell or flint,
the head being beaten with a small stick to cause the blood to flow
freely.   In the Dalebura tribe it was common to find people with
a circular scar round the leg just below the knee and above the calf,
showing that the person had been bitten on the leg by a venomous
snake.   A cord was tied above the knee and the operator would pick
up a quartz pebble, crack it in two and with the sharp edge cut a
circle right round the leg, severing the skin.   Blood poured out, and
though the woman became drowsy and ill she eventually recovered.[6]
A Bukaua headache is cured by winding a plant round the head to
prevent the circulation of blood in the forehead, and besides this they

[1] M. Bartels, *Die Medizin der Naturvölker*, 1893, p. 268.
[2] Hollis, *The Masai*, 1905, pp. 317, 318.
[3] Hollis, *The Nandi*, 1909, p. 22.   [4] Ibid., p. 119.
[5] W. E. Roth, *Superstition, Magic and Medicine*, 1903, p. 35.
[6] Howitt, loc. cit., pp. 385, 386.

scarify the patient over the eyebrows with bits of glass to let the blood out. This sort of blood-letting is in general use for burning wounds. If a snake or scorpion has stung a man they will scarify the skin all round the wound and if possible press the juice of a plant called *i* into the opening. Large wounds are cleaned with a sharp bamboo or obsidian knife and by blowing the matter out. Glowing pieces of wood are used to stop bleeding, but only after an incantation has been pronounced over the fire.[1] Of the inhabitants of the former German New Guinea district of Bogadjim, Hagen says that they even have a rational idea of surgery and draw blood from boils by opening them. "*Bei Kopfschmerz und allgemeinem Übelfinden macht man diese Einschnitte oft mitten auf die Stirn und zwar kräftig, bis auf den Knochen, so dass oft tiefe, eingezogene Narben entstehen.*"[2] In the case of wounds they hold a piece of burning coal quite close to the wound and this is very painful though medically quite correct.[3] Blood-letting is frequently resorted to on the Gazelle Peninsula and the neighbouring islands as a universal cure against pains of all sorts. Blood-letting proper by opening a vein seems to be unknown, but considerable quantities of blood are let by making innumerable scars on the body. Forehead, back, and breast are covered with the memorials of these operations, which are borne with truly stoical fortitude. Such large quantities of blood are let on such occasions that they form pools on the earth, but nevertheless the native seems ready to undergo this operation as soon as he feels the slightest pain.[4] Trephining, which is practised to a great extent by these natives (see Parkinson, mentioned above), may have developed out of these incisions and blood-letting in cases of headache. At Uea (Loyalty Islands) the cure for headache was to let out the pain at the crown of the head by the following surgical operation : The scalp was slit up and folded over, and the cranial bone scraped with a fine-edged shell till the *dura mater* was reached. A very little blood was allowed to escape. In some cases the scraped aperture was covered over with a thin piece of coconut shell ; in other instances the incised scalp was simply replaced. The " cure " was death to some, but most of the cases recovered. To such an extent was this remedy for headache carried on, that sharp-pointed clubs were specially made for the purpose of striking that weak part on the crown of the

---

[1] Neuhauss, loc. cit., i, p. 469.
[2] B. Hagen, *Unter den Papua in Deutsch Neu Guinea*, 1899, p. 257.
[3] Hagen, loc. cit., p. 258.
[4] R. Parkinson, *Dreissig Jahre in der Südsee*, 1907, pp. 114, 115.

head and causing instant death.[1] Among the Land Dyaks bleeding
is performed very rudely by cutting large gashes in the limb which
pains them.   They are also acquainted with a curious method of
cupping.   The wounds are made with a sharp knife or a piece of
bamboo and a small tube of bamboo is placed over them, with fire
at its upper end, so that, the air of the tube being exhausted by the
action of the fire, the blood flows readily and the operation is successfully carried on.   On the Barum River a man will take a small
knife and make slight incisions in another's leg until the whole limb
is smothered in blood.[2]   Scarification is the most frequent operation
at Nias and they believe that with the blood that flows out the
disease leaves the body.   The above-mentioned method of healing
headache by tying a cord round the head and by letting the blood
out is also in use.   Cupping is done through the horn of a *karbouw*,
the blood or matter being sucked out.   Especially when they believe
the pains to be caused by too much blood do they desire to eliminate
the disease by letting the blood out.   Cauterization is in use to hasten
the ripening of an abscess by applying drops of boiling oil to it.[3]
Cupping with or without medicines is largely practised by the Ba-Ila.
The *musuka* (cupping-horn) is the hollow horn of a small ox or
antelope about five inches long ; at the point a small hole is drilled
and covered up with wax.   When applying it to the painful part, the
hole is uncovered and the operator, after drawing out the air with his
mouth, replaces the wax over the hole with his tongue, thus establishing
a vacuum.   Before applying the horn incisions are made in the
skin of the patient with a razor, for instance in the case of headache,
and the method of tying a string round the head is used.[4]   Among
the Pima rheumatism is fairly common and is treated like many other
pains by scarifying the part affected with bits of broken glass.[5]

According to the ideas of the Mackenzie River Eskimo, diseases are
caused by " bad blood ".   The logical cure for most diseases is,
therefore, bleeding.   The incision is usually, but not always, made
over the seat of pain.   In the first operation they seem satisfied
with drawing a small quantity of blood ; but if a second cutting
becomes necessary or a third one, more is drawn each time.   As
this cure is resorted to for disease of all sorts, a man or woman beyond
middle life is sure to have scars on various parts of the body.   Con-
sumptives are cut both on the breast and the back.   Usually the

---

[1] Turner, *Samoa*, 1884, pp. 339, 340.   [2] Ling Roth, loc. cit., i, p. 297.
[3] Kleiweeg de Zwaan, *Die Heilkunde der Niasser*, 1913, pp. 133–6.
[4] Smith and Murray, *The Ba Ila*, 1920, i, p. 231.
[5] Russel, *The Pima Indians*, Bureau of American Ethnology, xxvi, p. 268.

cuts are horizontal, but some pains are treated with vertical cuts.
Boils are cut horizontally across the middle, the cut going as far to
either side as the margin which surrounds the boil.   Headache is
treated with scalp cuts over the seat of pain.[1]

There can be no doubt about the exact situation of the medicine
man's earlier life, the exact phase of fixation to which regression
is carried.   It is the sadistic attitude of the sucking child, " eating
up " his mother.   In a novel written to illustrate Congo life, Weeks
introduces a scene in which his hero is accused of having " eaten up "
his mother by means of witchcraft.[2]   We must all acknowledge
this accusation as well founded, with the qualification, however,
that we are all guilty of the same crime.   Nevertheless there seems
to be a seemingly slight yet all-important difference in the libido
distribution between the medicine-man and ordinary human beings.
The wizard is born with teeth, with a sadistic-cannibalistic appetite.
This feature is certainly carried over to the next phase of libido
organization, the anal.   For has not the substance sucked out of the
patient by the medicine-man previously been projected into him
by one of his colleagues ?   It is the quartz-crystal, the excrements
of the God-Father, the *boylya* which comes from the anus of the
medicine-man that is being sucked out by another wizard.   And
after this act of coprophagy, what does the medicine-man do ?   He
receives a fee—the first case of payment in the history of mankind—
and collects the quartz-crystals in a bag.   The second species of
Adze in Eweland, who are after money and intestines instead of
blood, clearly indicate the progress made by the sorcerer from the
oral to the anal phase of development, while the fact that a blood-
sucking witch (i.e. the child who sucks milk) gives money, a fæces
symbol, in return shows how the transaction is effected.   In the case
of the tusk protruding from the *Subach's* anus and performing the
function of sucking, we have a condensation of the two fundamental
pre-genital libido organizations.

It seems that besides the interpretation we have hitherto given
to the substance sucked out of the wound with reference to the oral
and anal attitude there is a third meaning that is of some consequence.
We have already commented on the fact that the prototype for the
sucking cure from the standpoint of the reality principle is to be found
in the case of ulcers or boils. · Here we have a great tension, a
swelling surface on the body, and release obtained after some alien

[1] V. Steffansson, " Notes on the Theory and Treatment of Diseases among
the Mackenzie River Eskimo," *Journal of Am. F. L.*, 1908, pp. 43, 44.
[2] John H. Weeks, *Congo Life and Folklore*, 1911, p. 201.

substance or putrid matter has been removed. Now this turgescent part of the body may be regarded from the point of view of the unconscious as an equivalent of the swelling nipples, and the matter sucked out in this case interpreted as milk. But the swelling red object suffused with blood is also the penis and the matter sucked out a symbol of the seminal fluid. There are reasons to assume that this second unconscious meaning is also present during the treatment. For instance, among the inhabitants of Nias, incapacity to urinate is cured by the witch-woman sucking a stone from the patient's penis.[1] In cases where the feminine attitude of sucking the penis is not so evident we still have the serpent as one of the most frequent disease-causing agencies, and the fact that besides the quartz-crystal it is minute or supernatural serpents that are most frequently sucked out of the wound by the medicine-man. It would be tempting here to branch off into an inquiry on the nature of disease from the point of view of the unconscious of the savage, yet we resist the temptation for the present and continue the psychology of the medicine-man.

An Australian medicine-man is visibly characterized by two objects. He has quartz-crystals, kept with other gew-gaws in a sack or pouch, and he has a pointing bone. We have already interpreted the latter as the penis that opens another human body in the moment of coition. Having found, from the third interpretation given to the sucking cure, that not only in his capacity as destroyer but also in his function of healer the medicine-man appears as the castrator, we shall suspect that the interpretation given to the pointing bone will be valid for the doctor's wand and other magical weapons in general.

2   Magic Wand and Medicine Pipe

The magician of the Batak has many devices in fighting ghosts.[2] One of the most important, however, is his magic wand called *tunggal panaluan* = man by whom one is defeated. The wands are made of a sort of wood as hard as steel and completely covered with human and animal figures. At the top of the sceptre there is a man, a mythical being called Siadji donda hatahutan, and below him is his wife Sitapi radja na uasan, followed by various carved figures. A new magic sceptre is always made when a part of the tribe breaks off from the rest and a new tribe is formed. They

---

[1] Kleiweeg de Zwaan, loc. cit., p. 76.
[2] Joh. Warneck, *Die Religion der Batak*, 1909, p. 20.

must have a sceptre of their own and it is made with due sacrifices. The essential thing, however, in such a sceptre, what gives it real strength, is the spirit of a murdered child. The spirit is put into one of the carved openings of the sceptre in the form of an ointment. The wand is used in war and they believe that the spirit of the murdered child in the wand will attack the enemy. Therefore it is used as a war flag. Besides this, it helps the chief to make rain by means of a libation offered to Sitapi radja na uasan. Some ethnologists believe that the whole staff with the intertwined human figures means serpentine lightning—the demon is to attack the enemy like lightning coming down from heaven. Siadji donda hatahutan, the top figure, means " magician who makes fear come down like lightning ", while the second figure is a personification of lightning and rain.[1] After having given a phallic interpretation to the thunderbolt, the same suspicion arises in the case of a wand that seems to be connected with the famous thunder weapon as its prototype in heaven. The connection between the two ideas is evident in the case of Kiwai war medicine. On leaving for war a man is given a medicine by his wife consisting of a piece of ginger which she has kept for some time inside her vulva. In the fight he will chew a little of it, spit the juice on himself, and call out : " My wife, all same lightning straight where vulva I go," that is, he attacks, he goes for the vulva like lightning. Or an old man will chew a little ginger and squirt the juice out in the direction of the enemy, saying : " All same I go for thing belonging wife, all same I go for that fighting place, body belong me all same lightning he go." [2] If the force that sways the staff is akin to lightning, this kinship is probably rooted in the phallic origin of the sky weapon. Things are made quite clear by the myth of its origin. This is the way to make a magic wand. Various figures are carved on a staff about the length of a fathom. First a man, below this a woman, then a chameleon, a serpent, a toad, and a rat. The tail of a horse is used for an ornament. Once upon a time twins were born, a boy and a girl. The boy was called Liadji donda hata hutan (the magician who makes fear come down like lightning) and the girl Siboru tapi na wasan (a personification of rain). Twins are considered unlucky and so they were separated. Both grew up and once when they

---

[1] I. H. Meerwaldt, *De bataksche tooverstaf. Bijdragen tot de Land en Volkenkunde van Ned.-Indie*, vi, 10, 1902, p. 297. Warneck, loc. cit., pp. 132, 133.
[2] G. Landtman, " The Magic of the Kiwai Papuans in Warfare," *Journal of Roy. Anth. Inst.*, xlvi, 1916, p. 325.

chanced to meet in the jungle the boy married his beautiful sister.
It happened that they caught sight of a tree with sweet fruit.   The
man climbed up the tree to get the fruit but he stuck there and
could not come back again.   He shouted for help ; his wife came,
and she too stuck fast to the tree.   Then the chameleon, the serpent,
the toad, and the rat came to see whether they might not be able to
get the fruit, but none of them ever came back again.   This got
spoken about and a lot of people came to see what had happened.
They made images of the tree with all the people hanging on it and
this is the origin of the magic staff.[1]   There is only on . episode in
this myth that needs interpretation.   The tree is evidently the
woman herself and the fruit the identical one that brought " death
into the world and all our woe ".   After incest, related openly but
performed unwittingly, that is, unconsciously, by the hero and heroine,
we have the tale of how the phallus climbed up the mother tree.
But man and woman with the symbolic animals [2] get stuck to the
tree—it is a coitus that never comes to an end.

Here we see that our former guess as to the nature of the compulsion brought to bear on the world in general in the magic art
was quite correct.   We regarded it as derived from the tension of
the penis in erection, and said that woman meant a danger to the
magician because the power he had to retain was the seminal fluid
and what he had to avoid was castration.   Here we find a permanent
sticking together, a penis that is permanently repeating incest as
the prototype of the magician's power.   The dread of castration
that underlies this permanent erection becomes evident when,
according to a parallel myth, the figures on the staff are a group
of people who all committed incest and were bitten to death by a
snake in consequence.

Another essential feature of the staff is that it needs murder to
make it complete.   A child, boy, or girl is dug into a ditch with
only its head above the earth.   They make it promise to do their
bidding after death, to attack the enemy, and then they pour lead
into the victim's open mouth.   The ointment made of the corpse

---

[1] Warneck, loc. cit., p. 97. Pleyte, in *Toung Pao*, 1893, p. 11. F. W. K.
Müller, *Beschreibung einer Battaksammlung*, p. 64.   Brenner, *Besuch bei
den Kannibalen Sumatras*, p. 229.

[2] The chameleon with its change in size and colour refers to the penis
in erection ; the serpent is another penis-symbol, the toad probably represents
the vagina and the rat perhaps the anal complex.   All four animals are more
or less typical representatives of magic.

[3] Schurtz, *Das Augenornament*, 1900, p. 49.

or any special parts of the corpse is used as a medium to convey the horrible power of the ghost.[1] It seems that it is an attempt to project the cruelty manifested in murdering their helpless victim as a weapon against the enemy. The fact that besides the symbol of the erect penis committing incest the power of the *panguluba-lang* is needed to make the staff efficient indicates that the magician's wand is a penis used as a weapon. The object symbol is the penis, but the attitude is sadistic, not genital.

However, some of our readers might say that the interpretation of the magic wand as a penis is merely due to our psycho-analytic dogmas without any support in native tradition. We shall therefore describe the rain magic of the Arunta.

Once upon a time it happened that their ancestors were out hunting. They met a number of strange-looking men who were sitting round a pool of pure water and drinking. One of the strangers disappeared into a cave. When the ancestors penetrated into the cave they found that the man had disappeared, but in his place there was a cylindrical stick in the cave. They took the stick and walked towards the pool which had become petrified. Then they beheld the stranger in the sky, and when he saw the stick in the hands of the hunters he took the form of a cloud and water poured down from his hair. From that day onwards the Nangarri, the medicine-men of the Arunta, have kept the spot sacred and taboo to women and children. The stone which used to be a pool they call *Imbodna* (hailstone). The man who escaped to the sky is Nangali = a cloud. The tribe has never since been without water because Nangali left his magic wand in the hands of their sorcerers, and whenever the country was suffering from drought they could call upon him to appear in the sky and bring down rain.

Nangali is one of the celestial beings called *Stua kivatje*, i.e. water men. The water men are believed to have certain mysterious connections with some of the tribal sorcerers, who are their disciples on earth and attend to the rain-making ceremonies. When their people are in need of water, the rain-makers assemble around the *Imbodna* or hailstone, and one or two of them produce the sacred stick known to the Arunta as *kivatje purra*, literally, "water-penis." For a time the "stick is laid beside the great water stone, and the sorcerers kneel while they chant in a barely audible voice. They rise to their feet and one of them raises the stick to the sky. Then he poises the stick horizontally between his hands and rocks it one

---

[1] Warneck, loc. cit., pp. 64, 65.

K

way, then another."[1] It need hardly be observed that this swaying
of the "water-penis" is a repetition of the motion of the human
penis in coitus.

It is generally known that the American medicine-man is the
inventor of the use of tobacco and that the pipe belongs to his original
stock of paraphernalia. In a Pima myth the culture-hero, Elder
Brother, sings :—

> " I am the magician who with sacred pipe
> Of Ten-unarsat increase my magic power.
> I am the magician of the downy feathers
> With the soothing sacred pipe
> I bring sleep upon my enemy.[2]

Smoking customs and pipes are in close connection with the
practices of the medicine-men. Benzoni of Milan tells us that
in 1541, in La España and other islands, when their doctors wanted
to cure a sick man they went to the place where they were to
administer the smoke and when the patient was throughly intoxicated
by it the cure was mostly effected.[3] Hariot, who accompanied
Raleigh's expedition to Virginia in 1584, says : " There is an herbe
which is sowed apart by itself and is called by the Indians *uppowoc* ;
the Spaniards call it tobacco. The leaves thereof dried and brought
into powder they use to take the fume thereof by sucking it through
pipes made of clay into their stomach and head ; from whence it
purgeth superfluous fleame and other gross humors and openeth
all the passages of the body, by which means the use thereof not only
preserved the body from obstructions but also in short time breaketh
them whereby their bodies are notably preserved in health from
many grievous diseases wherewith we in England are often times
afflicted."[4]

The Blackfoot pipe ceremonial is generally given in fulfilment
of a vow. If a child is sick and the father makes his vow known,
he fulfils it after the child is restored to health by giving a feast with
the ceremonials. Of all the Blackfeet medicines the pipe is believed
to have the greatest power but it also brings the greatest burden.[5]
On account of these burdens recruits are not always willing to join

---

[1] H. Basedow, *The Australian Aboriginal*, 1925, p. 265.

[2] F. Russell, *The Pima Indians*, Report, xxvi, p. 229.

[3] G. Benzoni, *History of the New World*, 1541–56, pp. 80–2, Hakluyt
Soc., i. McGuire, *Pipes and Smoking Customs*, Report of the Natural
History Museum, pp. 97, 368.

[4] Th. Hariot, *Hakluyt's Voyages*, iii, p. 330. Guire, loc. cit., p. 445.

[5] W. McClintock, *The Old North Trail*, 1910, pp. 269, 270.

the society but if they catch a man unawares and offer him a pipe he dare not refuse lest sickness or even death come to him or some member of his family. The Medicine Pipe was given to the Blackfeet long ago when the Thunder struck down a man. While he lay on the ground, the Thunder Chief appeared in a vision showing him a pipe and saying : " I have chosen you that I might give you this pipe. Make another just like it. Gather together also a medicine bundle containing the skins of the many animals and birds which go with it. Whenever any one of your people are sick or dying a vow must be made and a ceremonial given with a feast. The sick will then be restored to health." [1] The same connection between the thunder powers and the pipe is found in the case of the Siouan Heyoka society. If a member walks about with the stem of the pipe pointing upwards towards the sky, thunder is sure to strike him.[2] In the Blackfoot ceremony the pipe is called " Sacred Chief ". Slowly raising the pipe they sing :—

> The Great Mystery beholds our chief arise
> The Chief is sacred.

" He shook the Pipe in imitation of a bear, but was careful not to handle it roughly lest a storm should come.[3] There is a long list of taboos connected with the pipe. We repeat them here, leaving out such as seem to be connected with local details of the ceremonial. The remaining ones are as follows : " You must not smoke a pipe or remove your moccasins before we have given you proper instructions. You and all your family should wear necklaces of small shells because they will bring you long life. No one should be allowed to sleep in your bed. Fire, wood, and burning embers must not be taken away from your lodge because they belong to the Pipe. The firewood must lie in the same direction as the Pipe hangs. Ashes must not be removed until the Pipe is first taken outside the *tipi*. You must not be present while the ashes are being taken out, lest you become blind. Permit no one to curse, or talk loud, or aim a gun inside the *tipi* where the sacred Pipe is kept. Allow no one to strike the *tipi* or throw anything towards the owner. Do not cut a horse's tail. This act once caused a Pipe owner to lose five horses. Dangerous storms would arise if you do not drink properly or if you throw water upon children. Never allow a dog to leap against you, for it will cause your body to ache. Never

---

[1] Clintock, loc. cit., p. 253.
[2] Dorsey, *Siouan Cults*, Bureau of Am. Ethn., xiv, p. 470.
[3] Clintock, loc. cit., p. 264.

touch a dead person. Never point toward anyone with your fingers, always use the thumb. Never move anything burning with a knife, lest it start your teeth to ache." [1] The whole list looks like a series of defence formations against the castration complex. The shells are "life-givers"; of which more anon. Then the fear of somebody sleeping in the bed, the fear of fire, symbolizing the seminal fluid, "the fire of life," being taken out of the lodge, the various rules with regard to firewood and ashes, the taboo against cutting a horse's tail, the fear of the dog, of the corpse, of pointing, the worldwide taboo on meddling with the fire (as above, life, the phallus) with a knife, all are unmistakably symptomatic of the castration complex.—The punishment refers to two very frequent penis symbols, the eye and the tooth. Another similar list of pipe taboos exists among the Siouan tribes. If a woman passes between several Mandan who are smoking together it is a bad omen. Should a woman recline on the ground between men who are smoking, a piece of wood is laid across her to serve as a means of communication between the men. The strongest man of the Mandan who had been victor in several wrestling matches with the white people always took hold of his pipe by the head, for had he touched another part of it the blood would have suddenly rushed from his nostrils. Nobody could touch this man's face without bleeding at nose and mouth. This bleeding looks like an ejaculation displaced to the nose, the nose being one of the most usual equivalents of the penis. That there was some hidden unconscious meaning in accepting a pipe from another man is made perfectly clear by the fact that a certain Mandan whenever another offered him a pipe to smoke felt his mouth becoming full of worms which he threw into the fire by handfuls. We should call such an attitude hysterical, and observe that worms are the very objects "sucked" out of his patient by the medicine-man. The trick is, of course, accomplished by previously secreting them in his mouth. The degree of anxiety connected with the pipe and smoking customs is subject to individual variations. It must have been present in a marked degree in the case of a certain Hidatsa, who did not permit anybody in the lodge to speak or move a single limb, except to grasp the pipe, while he was smoking. No women, children or dogs were allowed to remain in the hut and someone was always placed as a guard at the entrance. When any person had a painful diseased place this same man put his pipe upon it and smoked. On such occasions he did not swallow the smoke as the Indians usually do but he affirmed that he could extract the disease by his smoking and he pretended to seize it in his hand and to throw it into the fire. [2]

[1] Clintock, loc. cit., pp. 267–9.   [2] Dorsey, *Siouan Cults*, ibid., p. 511.

A third similar series is that of the Gros Ventre. At present the Gros Ventre have three pipes. Formerly they had more but some of them were buried with their last owners. A sick man sometimes pledged himself to smoke one of the sacred pipes for his recovery. Then he provided food and distinguished warriors were invited. Each of these had to count four *coups* before the pipe could be lighted. A green cherry branch was greased and put into the fire to light the pipe with. If it burnt well the man would recover ; if it burnt poorly they were afraid that he would not become well again. The flame thus being life itself, well might the smoker be afraid when it was taken out of his *tipi*. The keepers of the sacred pipes observed stringent rules. They could not eat the head or back of any animal, nor any part of the white tailed deer nor any eggs. They were not allowed to bathe nor to take any ashes out of the tent. They did not eat dogs or allow them in the tent, nor did they let dogs touch them or walk over their legs or walk before them while they were smoking. It was taboo for them to have their hair cut. The last keeper became so old that he lost most of his hair and the present owner of the pipe, his great-grandson, tied his own teeth, also fallen out from old age, into the same bundle.[1]

Although we regard certain well-known symptomatic actions as perfectly reliable tests of the psycho-analytic interpretation of a given symbol we are not compelled to rely on these in this case if we wish to understand the real, i.e. the unconscious, meaning of the pipe.

In the origin myth of the Arapaho we are told how, in the beginning, there was nothing but water except the waterfowls, and the Grandfather saw that there was a Father of the Indians floating on the water and on the four sticks. Now the person called Father who was floating on the water was really the Flat Pipe, the chief cult object of the tribe. Another variant tells us how on a stand of four sticks on which was a pipe there sat a person. Beneath him something shining was visible. It was water. The man said : " What shall I do ? Where shall I keep this pipe since the water is everywhere as far as my eye can reach ? I am above the man on the stand, continually sitting in the same position. I am unable to do anything for myself and for the pipe." [2] The Father

[1] A. L. Kroeber, *Ethnology of the Gros Ventre*, Anthr. Papers, Am. Mus. Nat. Hist., i, 1908, pp. 272, 273.

[2] G. A. Dorsey and A. L. Kroeber, *Traditions of the Arapaho*, Field Columbian Museum Anthr. Ser., vol. v, publ. 81, 1903, pp. 1–4.

sitting above the Pipe and regarding the pipe and his ego as two equivalent constituents of his personality, would be comprehensible if we substituted the penis for the pipe. Now this is the actual meaning attributed to this symbol by the Arapaho themselves.

The pipe is closely connected with the paraphernalia of the Sun-Dance and plays a conspicuous part in the ceremonial coitus which is, or at least was, an integral part of that ritual. We are told that in former times, in accordance with the fixed rites of the ceremony, the grandfather of the Lodge-Maker and the Lodge-Maker's wife had intercourse on the night following the erection of the Rabbit *tipi*. The wife of the Lodge-Maker would leave the Rabbit *tipi* with the Grandfather, who carried with him the ceremonial pipe. Both of them with the woman in the lead would proceed to a distance of about 100 yards towards the east, during which both emphasized the fact that what they were about to do was a repetition of what had happened at the origin of the ceremony and was in keeping with the wish of their Father. The woman would lie down on her back naked. Then the Grandfather would pray to Man-Above and the subordinate gods for the Arapaho tribe. He then offered the body to Man-Above, the Grandfather, the Four Old Men and various minor gods. During the act of intercourse he placed in the woman's mouth the root brought from the Rabbit's *tipi*. On their return to the Rabbit *tipi* the woman would lead and as they entered she addressed her husband, saying : " I have returned, having performed the holy act which was commanded," whereupon he together with the other dancers said : " Thanks ! " and they prayed for her success. The Grandfather in accomplishing his duties represents Man-Above, the All-Powerful, and the result of the rite is the birth of the people thereafter. According to some informants, the whole thing is symbolic, nothing being really done to the woman. Only if this inhibition were observed would there be an increase in population, stock, and property, otherwise there would be no benefit to the people and the Grandfather's life would be shortened. When the woman approached to about 100 feet from the lodge, she loudly called out for her husband. He came out, put his hands on her head, and received into his mouth a piece of root from her mouth. He then went to the Grandfather and in the same manner received a piece of root into his mouth. Then the husband took the pipe from the Grandfather, proceeded to the Rabbit *tipi* and said : " I have brought back the pipe," whereupon all said " Thanks ".

The pipe and the root seem to be very important actors in this drama and indeed we are clearly told what their meaning really is : " The root given and received by the husband is the seed of the grandfather. The straight pipe is the penis or root of man and so the intercourse happens between the sun and moon for a blessing upon the tribe."

" The husband gives thanks for the seed and goes on to receive it by kissing her. He chews the root and rubs himself with it. The grandfather, being the sun, makes things grow and the woman, being the moon, gives birth to the things of this world ".[1]

For our immediate purpose the important thing is that the medicine pipe used in disseminating evil influences, in obtaining health, and finally in sucking out the disease, represents the penis. We were therefore perfectly justified in regarding the taboos of the keeper as connected with the castration complex and indeed in the case we have been just describing where incest, cohabitation with the mother of the tribe (she represents the tribal mother during the ceremony), is actually performed there are many signs of the anxiety that accompanies the rite. The man who has intercourse with her begins by referring to the origin of the ceremony as a precedent and to the will of the Father. In fact, he offers the woman to Man-Above and when he accomplishes the ceremony he is not himself at all, he is the Father, Man-Above.

Now we shall understand that the whole complex connected with smoking and pipe customs represents a partly aggressive, partly feminine, homosexual identification with the father on the basis of the penis (the pipe) as ego-ideal, or perhaps we should say in the act of coitus. Whenever the Indians travelled they extended the pipe with the mouth-piece towards the sun and said : " Ho, Mysterious Power, you who are the Sun ! Here is tobacco ! I wish to follow your course. Cause me to meet whatever is good and to give a wide berth to anything that may be to my injury or disadvantage." [2] The aggressive elements are well brought out by the action of the Heyoka pointing towards the sky with the pipe and instantly punished by a flash of lightning, and also by the taboos on shooting, cursing, etc. in the presence of the pipe, thus showing a repressed desire to do so. On the other hand, the attitude of the husband in the Sun-Dance ceremony is extremely infantile and ambisexual. He thanks the " mother " for the food received from her mouth but this food is also the " seed ", the semen of the grandfather, with whom he forthwith repeats the ceremony.

[1] G. A. Dorsey, *The Arapaho Sun Dance*, Anthr. Series, vol. iv, 1903, pp. 172–8.

[2] Dorsey, *Siouan Cults*, pp. 377, 378.

The ceremony seems to illustrate an important source for the development both of a well-known homosexual perversion and of the sucking cure in the identification of the mother's nipple with the father's penis. Yet even in this ceremony the aggressive sadistic element on the part of the husband is not completely absent, as he makes up for having received the " seed " of the grandfather by taking the straight pipe from him, i.e. by castrating him.

The part played by the pipes in the *Wawa*[n] ceremony of the Omaha shows both the importance of the father-son relationship and the libidinal basis on which the alliance between the two parties is concluded. Two parties composed of persons having no blood relationship were the principals in the ceremony. One was associated with the man who presented the pipes and the other with the man who received them. Among the Omaha the first was called *wa'wa*[n] *aka*, " the one who sings," and the second was spoken of as *a'wa*[n]*iaka*, " the one who is sung to." A man of a certain gens would carry pipes to a man of another gens within his tribe or to a man of another tribe. The relationship ceremonially established by taking and receiving the pipes was equivalent to that of father and son and the two parties were spoken of by these terms. The avowed aim of the ceremony consists in bringing about good fellowship between the parties and peace in general for all concerned. The " Son " gave many presents to the " Father " but it was declared that these were insignificant and transitory in nature when compared with the one essential gift, the lasting blessing conferred by the pipe.[1] The climax of the ceremony consisted in an esoteric ritual, probably intended to confer " life " on the Son.

We do not know what actually took place, but for a parallel we have the corresponding esoteric ritual of the Ponca. After the pipes had been folded together and wrapped in the wild-cat skin they were raised high over the head of the child and then brought down slowly so as to touch his forehead. Then the pipes were passed down the front of the body to its feet until the mouthpiece rested on the toes, which it was made to press strongly on the ground. This symbolic action was explained as follows. " Firm shall be your tread upon the earth, no obstacle shall hinder your progress ; long shall be your life and your issue many.[2] If this prayer is to be regarded as containing the explanation of the ritual, we must surmise that the

[1] Fletcher and la Flesche, *The Omaha tribe*, xxviith Report of the Bureau Am. Ethn., 1911, p. 400.
[2] Fletcher, loc. cit., p. 401.

movement executed is connected not only with the path of life, but also with questions of issue and generation.

The two objects used in the ceremony were called pipes and were really pipe-stems without bowls and never used for smoking. One of the pipes ornamented with ten feathers from the tail of a mature golden eagle represented the feminine element. The other stem was painted green and had seven feathers from the tail of a young golden eagle. The lower part of these feathers is white with dark tips and they are worn by men as marks of honour. This pipe symbolizes the masculine forces. " It is to be noted that among the Omaha, as among the Pawnee, the feathers which were used by the warriors were put on the stem painted green to represent the earth, the feminine element, while those which were from the mature eagle, and which stood for the feminine element, were fastened to the stem painted the colour of the sky, which represented the masculine element ; so that on each pipe the masculine and feminine forces were symbolically united." [1]

This fully explains why the result of movements executed with the pipes, the benefit conferred by them, should consist in life and a numerous issue. We see that our former conjecture with regard to the libidinal basis of the final union between father and son is fully confirmed, and even the hypothesis that in the pipe symbol we have a condensation of the penis and the nipple, the masculine and the feminine element, is confirmed by the manifest symbolism of Omaha ritual. The meaning of these ceremonies becomes clearer by comparing them with the parallel rite of the Pawnee, known to us by the name of *Hako*.

Two distinct groups of persons were essential to the performance of this ceremony. One of them was called the Fathers and the other the Children. In the Fathers' party there was a man who was an expert in the details of the ceremony. This was the *Kurahus*. Another important person in this party was the rain priest who had also to furnish the pipe and conduct the ceremony of offering smoke to Tirawa. The party also included two doctors, men who had received a knowledge of healing plants, either through vision or by initiation. Each was required to bring an eagle's wing, one the right and the other the left, for the eagle's wing is the official emblem of a doctor.[2] The objects peculiar to this ceremony were two feathered stems about a metre in length made of ash wood. They were rounded and smoothed and the pith was burned out to make an opening for the breath to pass as through a pipe-stem. One of these was called " breathing mouth of wood with the dark moving feathers " and the other the " breathing

[1] Fletcher, loc. cit., p. 377.   [2] Fletcher, loc. cit., p. 19.

mouth of wood with the white moving feathers ". The stem with the dark feathers was painted blue to symbolize the sky and the other one was painted green to symbolize the earth, so that we have here the same union of the female eagle with the male principle in nature and of the male eagle with the female principle as in the case of the Omaha. But here there is a definite splitting of the two trends into a female and a male pipe, for the first stem represented the mother and the second stood for the male, the father and warrior. An especial sanctity was attached to the pipes, which shows that they represented concepts deeply ingrained in the human soul. Few persons ever spoke of them without a brightening of the eyes. " They make us happy " was a common saying.[1] The ceremony of the *Hako* is a prayer for children in order that the tribe may increase and be strong.[2] All the benefit derived from the ceremony is enjoyed by the man who is made a son and gets the help of the supernatural powers represented by the sacred objects. Between the father and the son and their immediate families a relationship similar to that which exists between kindred is established through this ceremony. As for the benefits and gifts brought to the son, they consist chiefly in many children to make his family strong and the gift of long life.[3] But how is a son made, or for that matter, the son of a son ? There is every reason to believe that the dark allusions to this mystical process are but veiled representations of the natural way to beget offspring. One of the stanzas of the song is explained by the *Kurahus* saying that the " spirits " of the singers converge, unite, with the " spirits " of the corn to find the Son. Now the ear of corn represents Mother Earth, or Mother of all things, Mother bringing forth life. Mother Corn opens the way from the tribe of Fathers to the tribe of Children.[4]

If we are to take this literally it would seem to indicate peace restored in the Primal Horde between the Paternal Tyrant and the group of Brothers by the means of the Mother. Friendship is still concluded among various primitive races by common amorous relations with the same woman, and as in these ceremonies the begetting of the child is due to the supernatural powers, this looks like the Son waiving his claim, giving up his incestuous desire, or at least the *ius primae noctis*, in favour of the Father. " In the symbolizing, within the lodge of the Son, of the gift of birth by the power of the Hako, brought thither by the Father, we get a

[1] A. C. Fletcher, *The Hako*, xxiith Report, pp. 18–21.
[2] A. C. Fletcher, loc. cit., p. 26.
[3] A. C. Fletcher, loc. cit., pp. 49, 50.
[4] A. C. Fletcher, loc. cit., pp. 52–4.

glimpse of the means by which the tie between the two unrelated men, the Father and the Son, was supposed to be formed ; namely the life of the Son was perpetuated through the gift of fruitfulness to his child, supernaturally bestowed by the Hako, consequently the Father who brought the Hako became symbolically the father of the future progeny of the Son." [1] If we ponder over the meaning of this passage the only possible explanation seems to be to suppose a rite like the ceremonial coitus of the Arapaho sun-dance as the origin of the *Hako* and similar rites. There we actually have what is merely indicated here in a highly sublimated form of symbolism. The son's " lodge " would mean his wife and the gift of the feathered stems in the lodge would be the act of coitus. Now this is what actually takes place in the Arapaho ceremony : the Lodge-Maker offers his wife to the Grandfather and gets " life " in return. This secondary and ambisexual compensation is represented by two episodes in the *Hako* ritual. On the one hand he enjoys the protection and love of the eagle, the corn and all the male and female forces represented by the pipe stems,[2] that is, if we disregard the symbolic superstructure, of the father and the mother. And on the other, when the child is placed on the robe he seems to be enjoying the safety of the pre-natal situation. The chief puts his hands under the robe held over the child's legs and drops the oriole's nest within the circle so that the child's feet rest on it. " The child represents the younger generation, the continuation of life, and when it is put in the circle it typifies the bird laying its eggs. The child is covered up, for no one knows when a bird lays its eggs or when a new birth takes place." [3] Notwithstanding, however, the show of unity and friendship so prominent in the ceremony, there still remains an element of repressed conflict, for the feathered stem that represented the male was never allowed to be next to the Children. Its place was always on the outside, there it could do no harm, could rouse no contention, but it would serve to protect and defend.[4]

When the Grandfather in the Arapaho ritual returns after the coitus with the Lodge-Maker's wife, his pipe, that is his penis, is taken from him by the husband. In the *Hako* ceremony the male pipe is about to procure issue for the Son instead of letting him do it, and therefore it is evident that proximity would lead to trouble. The aggressiveness that would arise from sexual jealousy is turned to the outside against the common foe, while the unconscious concept of procreating from the same mother with the same pipe establishes

[1] Fletcher, loc. cit., pp. 349, 350.   [2] Fletcher, loc. cit., pp. 204–8.
[3] Fletcher, loc. cit., pp. 244, 245.   [4] Fletcher, loc. cit., p. 21.

good feeling between the parties.[1] A. C. Fletcher says very much the same thing in slightly different words.

" With the growth of social ideas the thought seems to have arisen that ties might be made between two tribes differing from and even competing with each other through a device which should simulate those influences which had proved so effective within the tribe. The Father, representing one tribe, was the incentive force, he inaugurated the Hako party. The tie was made by a ceremony in which the feminine element represented the dominant factor. Through this mother element life was given and a bond was established between a Father and the Son of another tribe. It is remarkable how close to the model this device of an artificial tie has been made to correspond." [2]

It is a remarkable and significant factor that both in the relation of men (" the Children ") to the supernatural, who in their origin and in the concepts of the Indian certainly represent the Fathers, and in the relation of one human group to the other, in treaties, peace-making, etc., the pipe, i.e. the penis, should have played such a decisive part. Unity in libidinal impulses being attained by means of their concentration in the genital organ, the latter also serves as a basis for the attainment of unity in personality and society. At the same time the ego attains identification with a model found in its environment—with the father whom the child desires to imitate in everything, principally because it desires to imitate him in his relations with the mother.

We have followed the evolution of the medicine-man from the oral through the anal to the genital, or, perhaps we ought rather to say, to the phallic phase of libidinal organization. We have not yet been able to find the connecting link, the special feature, that characterizes him in all three phases of this development. But we have noticed that the identification with the father plays an important part in his character and this induces us to reconsider the question of this development from the point of view of the Primal Horde.

3 MANA

Whatever the power of the magician may be, it seems quite evident that it is derived from beings whom we are accustomed to regard as representatives of the Father.

[1] The ceremony itself is the outcome of anxiety and is made as a result of a vow for the recovery of the sick. It represents a self-punishment : the son suffers for having desired his father's wife, by giving his own wife to him.

[2] Fletcher, loc. cit., p. 282.

In the Solomon Islands the position of chief seems to have depended entirely on the belief in his possession of mana derived from communication with the *tindalo* or ghosts.[1] At Eddystone Island the definition of *mana* given in "Pidjin" to A. M. Hocart and Dr Rivers is "you speak true". But the term applies only to ghosts and spirits (*tamate*) and to old men who possess shrines dedicated to ghosts and spirits. For ordinary men the word is *sosoto* (true, right). Truth means efficacy, a lie means defeat in these languages. Take a concrete case. There was a very old man called Rinambesi who was said to be mana. "Rinambesi," they explained, "is like a ghost"; if he says "Go and you will catch plenty of fish," and the man is successful, Rinambesi is mana.[2] According to another native account, "the origin of the power of chiefs (in Florida) lies entirely in the belief that they have communication with powerful ghosts (*tindalo*) and have that mana whereby they are able to bring the power of the *tindalo* to bear."[3] Again, Rivers tells us that the rites of the Banks Islands frequently do not conform to a definition of magic. "It is clear that some kind of spiritual agency is concerned in these rites. Their efficacy depends on the use of certain stones and objects which are believed to possess power (mana) for some special end, and this mana is definitely associated with the belief in the presence of a vui or spirit."[4] It is a general Melanesian belief that spirits and ghosts have power over the weather; it follows therefore that the men who have familiar intercourse with spirits and ghosts are believed to be able to move them to interfere for wind or calm, sunshine or rain. The spirits and ghosts have also imparted power to forms of words, stones, leaves, and other things which therefore of themselves affect the weather, and there is also a natural congruity between some of these things and the effects they produce. The men, therefore, who have and know these things have mana which they can use to benefit or afflict friends and enemies.[5] "The Melanesian mind is entirely possessed by the belief in a supernatural power or influence called almost universally mana. This is what works to effect everything which is beyond the ordinary power of men, outside the common processes of nature; it is present in the atmosphere of life, attaches itself to persons and to things and is manifested by results "which can only be ascribed to its operation". But this power, though itself impersonal, is always

[1] W. H. R. Rivers, *History of Melanesian Society*, ii, p. 100.
[2] A. M. Hocart, *Man*, 1914, p. 98.
[3] R. H. Codrington, *The Melanesians*, 1891, p. 52.
[4] Rivers, loc. cit., ii, p. 406.
[5] Codrington, loc. cit., p. 200.

connected with some person who directs it. All spirits have it, ghosts generally, some men. If a stone is found to have supernatural power it is because a spirit has associated itself with it ; a dead man's bone has with it mana, because the ghost is with the bone ; a man may have so close a connection with a spirit or ghost that he has mana in himself, also a charm is powerful because the name of a spirit or ghost expressed in the form of words brings into it the power which the spirit or ghost exercises through it.[1] In New Britain certain people, the sorcerers, exercise a pernicious influence over others by means of some special mana or supernatural power belonging to them.[2] Spirits of deceased ancestors who had special powers of sorcery (mana) were regarded as *tebarans* (i.e. " nature spirits ", gods).[3] In Guadalcanar, mana (power) seems to be derived from the *tinda'o*. If a Haumbata man wishes to kill an enemy on land he goes to a special place belonging to the naroha bird and calls on this bird for power (mana) and strength (*susuliha*). He offers food in the form of a pudding as well as fish, pork, and tobacco, and the bird gives him the mana which enables him to kill his enemy. The people of Kindapalei reverence a certain snake living on a rock by a place called Koli. The place is forbidden to all except the people of Kindapalei and the people of that division only go there to " worship " him. They take puddings and other offerings to the snake and obtain mana from it just as the Haumbata get mana from their bird naroha. They also obtain mana from the sun and moon and from the sacred fire called *lake tambu*. This is a fire which springs out of a rock at a certain place and the offerings are burnt in the fire. Tongue and lips of a human sacrifice are burnt in the fire.[4] Thus we must note these local deities (*tinda'o*), ultimately probably of totemic origin,[5] as sources of mana besides the ghost, although in a certain sense they are ghost-incarnations of a specific type.[6]

---

[1] Codrington, loc. cit., pp. 119, 120.

[2] Brown, *Melanesians and Polynesians*, 1910, p. 232.

[3] Brown, loc. cit., p. 196.

[4] Rivers, loc. cit., i, pp. 243, 244.

[5] The shark and the pigeon, both of them *tinda'o*, are regarded as their " first men " (cf. Alcheringa ancestors) and are not eaten. Rivers, loc. cit., i, p. 243.

[6] " The belief in Florida and in the neighbouring parts is fixed that every *tindalo* was once a man ; yet some whose names are known to everyone, Daula and Hauri, associated respectively with the frigate bird and shark, have passed far away from any historical remembrance." Codrington, loc. cit., p. 126. *At any rate, the objects of religious worship are all tindalo ; and every tindalo was once a man. Idem*, loc. cit., p. 127. On the other hand,

"In Fiji the word mana is only applied to ghosts and spirits (*kalou*), to chiefs (who are representatives or incarnations of ghosts), and to medicines. As for the last, some are still made effective through spirits and the rest were probably so originally ; anyhow, the mana is not merely in the leaves but always depends upon personality, the leaves are not mana in the hands of any man." [1]

It is therefore evident that the ghosts of the dead are regarded as the principal sources of mana in Melanesia.[2] Human beings come into contact with the mana-category when the results of their actions appear to lift them above the sphere of normal human power, and in this case it is assumed that a second personality is present which is the source of the *super*-natural power-quantity, i.e. the additional power is ascribed to psychical identification with a dead man, to the presence of an ego-ideal. Leg-bones of men are used to make the Lepers' Island arrow called *liwue*. "Not long ago there was a man in that island who out of affection for his dead brother dug him up and made arrows of his bones. With these he went about, speaking of himself as 'I and my brother' : all were afraid of him for they believed that his dead brother was at hand to help him." It is the bone of the dead man that gives mana to the arrow.[3] This state of ghostly communion or of submersion in the ego-ideal is permanently present in the case of the sorcerer ; his work is based on that element of unreality which is implicitly bound up in all identifications and on a disregard of the reality principle. Then again we have the sacred chief who derives his sanctity from a long line of murdered rulers who are all incarnate in him, through identification with his ancestors.

But we must not forget that, as the question stands at present, we are probably analysing the mana-concept in a culture-area where it is not a child of the soil but a concept transplanted thither by a current of immigration. "There are certain Melanesian words, evidently of immigrant origin, which are widely spread throughout Melanesia and Polynesia in a form in which their unity can be recognized by the veriest tyro in linguistic studies. Examples of such words taken from social or magico-religious categories are mana ; *tapu* or *tambu* ;

with each clan there are associated a number of objects, animals, plants, material objects or human beings, which may be regarded as sacred, the name for these objects being in most of the islands some variant of the word *tindalo*. Rivers, loc. cit., i, p. 241. Cf. Rivers, loc. cit., ii, p. 230.)

[1] Hocart, *Man*, 1914, p. 98.
[2] This conclusion has been pointed out by Hocart in the paper quoted above.
[3] Codrington, loc. cit., p. 309.

tamate, tomate, or *atmat* ; *tagataga* or *itokatoka*." " They vary so little in form or meaning, that it is probable that they are relatively recent and could with much confidence be assigned to the ' kava ' people merely on linguistic grounds even if we had no other evidence leading us to associate them with this people." [1]   But of course we have other reasons which cannot lightly be set aside.   As might be expected, the idea of mana plays a considerable part in the ritual of the secret societies.   In the Sukwe of the Banks Island, every man must have a song of his own.   The song-maker retires to some place by himself and with some rite in which he utters formulæ and uses objects with mana, such as sprigs of trees and sea-water, he composes the song. [2]   In the Aurora Qatu, the initiated will take a bit of the *varu* (hibiscus) bark, catch a fish for it, and burn the bark as he cooks the fish, thinking that he will thereby obtain mana (magical power) for catching that kind of fish. [3]   Moreover, we have in the Ingiet of the Gazelle Peninsula a secret society in which the acquisition of magical power avowedly forms the primary aim of the members, [4] but the belief in mana as a force which explains the efficacy of magical action is absent. [5]   If mana is a force primarily connected with the secret societies we shall say (following the line of Rivers' argument) that this brings it into close contact with the " kava " people whose ancient beliefs are embodied in the ritual of the secret societies.   However, this connection between mana and secret societies is far less evident than the contact between mana and another element of Kava culture, the office of chieftainhood.   " It seems clear that all those who are called chiefs or " great men " are high in the Sukwe, and Dr Codrington was unable to decide whether this position in the Sukwe is the reason why men are regarded as chiefs or whether it is their chieftainship which has made it easy to rise to so high a place in this organization.   In Motlav the chiefs are called *etvusmel* or *tavusmel* ('he who kills for the cycas') and here again the derivation of the word indicates a definite connection with the Sukwe." [6]   Still more evident than the connection between chiefs and societies is that between mana and chiefs, indeed we may say that a chief is a man who has mana, or putting the same thing in

[1] Rivers, loc. cit., ii, p. 485.   [2] Rivers, loc. cit., i, p. 78.
[3] Codrington, loc. cit., p. 90.
[4] R. Parkinson, *Dreissig Jahre in der Südsee*, 1907, p. 599.
[5] Meier, " Die Zauberei bei den Küstenbewohnern der Gazelle Halbinsel," *Anthropos*, 1913, p. 8.
[6] Rivers, loc. cit., ii, p. 100.   On the cycas cf. ibid., pp. 228, 237 ; i, p. 207.

a different manner, that mana is the power which distinguishes a chief from a commoner. " In Pentecost the men who are regarded as chiefs by the Europeans are simply individuals especially reputed for their mana." [1]   The real ground on which the power of a chief rests is that of belief in the mana he possesses with which also the wealth he has inherited and all his success in life are connected.[2] The connection between mana and chiefs in Fiji has already been noticed.[3]   Taken together these facts seem to point to a " kava " origin of the Melanesian mana-concept, indeed this concept seems to have referred specially to the superior influence and power of the immigrant Polynesian chiefs. This agrees perfectly with what we find in Polynesia where the connection between mana and the power exercised by a chief is very prominent.   " The old families of Tonga, Hawaii, New Zealand, Samoa, and other Polynesian groups, had an undoubted right to and an absolute power of disposal over large tracts of land whilst they had also a vaguely defined mana— power, interest, or right over common lands and also in some instances over lands in the possession of other families." [4]   Thus it is related of a traditional chief of Hawaiki, whose father came from Rarotonga, while his mother was a native of Rangiatea, that his mana (authority) extended over all three islands.[5]   The *tangata whenua*, the natives of the central part of Northern New Zealand, derive their mana from an ancient chief called Ruatipua and explain their present lack of courage by an unfavourable admixture of alien blood with the ancient race.[6]   But it seems that the mana of a Maori chief or priest was not a virtue immanent in him ; he had to be obeyed (*whakamana*) because of his connection with the gods, because he appeared as their mouthpiece.[7]   White gives us various translations of the word, and then tells us that in all its aspects mana means that irrational element in man which we should call his personality.[8] The mana of a priest is present in all cases when he can be regarded as a mediator between the gods and human beings.   His food, clothes, house, and all the objects which belong to him are sacred or

---

[1] Rivers, loc. cit., ii, p. 99.

[2] Codrington, loc. cit., pp. 57, 58. Rivers, loc. cit., ii, p. 100.

[3] Cf. above Hocart, *Man*, 1914, p. 98.

[4] Brown, *Melanesians and Polynesians*, p. 430.

[5] R. Lehmann, *Mana, eine begriffsgeschichtliche Untersuchung auf ethnologischer Grundlage*, 1915, p. 32. *Journal of the Polynesian Society*, xxii, p. 120.

[6] *Idem*, loc. cit., p. 50.

[7] J. White, in Bastian, *Die Heilige Sage der Polynesier*, pp. 175–8.

[8] Ibid., p. 197.

taboo because his mana dwells in them, and if a commoner touches these things then this mana or the *influence of the gods* (because this is what mana amounts to) causes the death of that man.[1] For Hawaii the translation given by the dictionary is "mana ; supernatural power such as was supposed to be the attribute of the gods ".[2]

In olden days the god abode with the chief and revealed through him things that would happen. If the *Sau* or High Chief of Futuna was not present at kava, the first cup, which should be his, is poured at the foot of the post for the "god", who is supposed to be in the absent Sau. But *Sau* is the same word as *Hau*, and the latter is an equivalent of mana.[3] A man is said to have mana when he possesses genius, good fortune, and audacity in a marked degree. There were cases in which the mana of a man depended upon the facility with which he could communicate with the spirits of departed ancestors.[4]

If therefore we are told that mana is principally immanent in chiefs and priests, but is derived by them from an identification with gods or, what amounts to the same thing, ancestors, we shall again call attention to the psychic phenomenon of identification as the source of mana. It is evident that belief in the mana of a person demands a certain attitude on the part of the mana-bearer, and we shall now proceed to examine a few cases which show what this attitude is. Gudgeon tells us that the mana of a famous warrior is based on his magnificent audacity, on an attitude of uncompromising aggressiveness well calculated to strike terror into the heart of all men.[5] An instructive case is recorded by Gudgeon. Kapi-horo-maunga possessed together with his office as chief the exclusive right to fish from a certain rock. One morning he noticed that somebody had had the temerity to intrude upon his sacred premises. But when he heard from a man of his retinue that his brother was the intruder he began to hesitate, thinking that his father might have intrigued against him and instigated his brother to rob him of his mana. With this doubt in his heart he went home to

---

[1] White, in Bastian, loc. cit., pp. 199, 200.

[2] Tregear, *Maori-Polynesian Comparative Dictionary*, p. 203.

[3] A. M. Hocart, " Chieftainship and the Sister's Son in the Pacific," *American Anthropologist*, xvii, pp. 635, 636, 637. Röhr, " Hau and Mauri," *Anthropos*, xii, p. xiii. " Hau means fame, the nearest equivalent being mana," S. Percy Smith, " Futuna or Horne Island," *Journal of the Polynesian Society*, i, p. 38.

[4] Gudgeon, " Mana Tangata," *Journal of the P.S.*, xiv, pp. 49, 50.

[5] Lehmann, *Mana*, p. 25. *Journal of the Polynesian Society*, xiv, p. 177.

ask his father. The answer he got from the old man was this : " As you have not killed your brother and not taken revenge on him for his insult, you had best stop at home and cultivate his fields for him." What he ought to have done was to kill his brother at once and raise the question afterwards, but he had wavered and, losing his mana, sunk from the position of chief to that of a menial.[1]

Here we again find occasion to go back to Freud's hypothetical Primal Horde. The Leader must hold his own absolutely if he is to hold it at all and must punish all encroachments with instant death. A moment of indecision may prove fatal to him, as he may be torn to pieces by his rebellious sons. His influence over the others rests on an absolutely narcisstic ego-constitution, on a complete submersion of the ego in the ego-ideal, or in other words on a complete self-reliance. Believing in himself he can make others believe in him and can serve as a much-needed riveting point for common human beings who are suffering under the compulsion of doubt derived from their own ambivalency. The Hero is all Ego-Ideal, he can thus serve as a model for all those in whom the conflict between the various tendencies of the Ego is raging. He gives them what they stand in greatest need of—*self-assurance*. This description applies equally well to the chief of the present day as to his ancestor, the Patriarch of the Primal Horde. It is important to remark what this assurance really is, and how in the course of human evolution man has lost this superbly animal quality. Kapi does not kill his brother because he has doubts as to whom his father sides with, the deed which he hesitates in attempting is really a slightly veiled form of parricide. His lack of courage is derived from an ambivalent attitude towards his own father, an attitude in which the feeling of submission plays a larger part than befits a chief. He is there to rule, not to be ruled. Ambivalency is the attitude of the mass ; the superman who attempts to rule them must be " beyond good and evil ", without the moral feeling of guilt, absolutely narcissistic, without regard for the opinions of others. When the famous chief Tama te kapua of the Arawa tribe died he said to his son : " Be very careful to purify thyself correctly when thou comest to bury me lest my mana should harm thee." [2] But as he committed some mistake in the death-rite, the lustration was not successful, and he was overpowered by his father's mana. The fatal mistake

---

[1] Lehmann, *Mana*, p. 35. *Journal of the Polynesian Society*, xiv, p. 62.
[2] Lehmann, loc. cit., p. 36.

made by Tuhoro, when officiating on Tama te kapua was this. The correct spell or *karakia* would have been :—

> By the Priests
> By Tama-te-kapua
> By me this, by this disciple
> Shall this son emerge
> To the world of being
> To the world of light.[1]

Tuhoro, the son, omitted two lines, viz. the second and the fourth. Now if a patient relates a dream but omits two episodes we always suspect that those two episodes contain the clue to the whole plot. In this case the two lines read thus : " By Tama-te-kapua shall this son emerge," i.e. he is not the begetter of his own son, the son was procreated by his father. We thus find a reversal of the original father-son conflict, the jealousy of the son and the suspicion of love relations between the father and his daughter-in-law.

That the father-son conflict contains the true explanation is made perfectly clear by what follows. Tuhoro knew that he would die, i.e. be overcome by his father's mana, and he said to his two sons : " When you have finished handling me strike a wand on my head, then take it to your uncle, Kahu, so that he may purify you from your tapu ; then will you be delivered correctly." [2] We see how the son becomes identical with the grandfather in the aggressiveness against the father and also how the whole complex is displaced to the uncle. Moreover, the struggle between father and son reappears as a fight between two brothers. When Tuhoro tells his sons to go to their uncle, his brother, for purification, he says : " You will find your joint heirloom hidden beneath the window of his home. It belonged to your own grandfather Tama-te-kapua ; it is an eardrop made of greenstone. During a quarrel between your uncle Kahu and myself I tore it out of his ear. But I was sorry for it and hid it. The torn ear will be the sign by which you may recognize your uncle." [3]

One way in which the mana can be passed on to the son is by biting the father's left toe,[4] a rite that evidently contains a rudimentary oral introjection besides the phallic significance of the toe.

---

[1] Takanui Tarakawa, " The Coming of the Arawa and Tainui Canoes," *Journal of the Polynesian Society*, ii, p. 252.

[2] *Idem*, ibid.

[3] *Idem*, ibid.

[4] Takanui Tarakawa, " Explanations of some matters referred to in the paper ' The Coming of the Arawa and Tainui Canoes,' " ibid., iii, p. 200.

It was fear of their father's mana which made it impossible for them to perform the lustration correctly so that they lost their mana and their position as chiefs.[1] The father's mana proves fatal to the son unless he gets rid of his haunting ghost by the ritual lustration—unless he gets rid of the pangs of conscience he feels for having killed his father. But a mistake in performing the ritual means an unconscious resistance against performing it, a will to retain those pangs of conscience which bind him to the father imago. But the death rite itself is only an effort to get rid of the ghost, to bind his fears by a compulsive action. Having learnt what the word fear meant, he has already lost his mana, doubt in the deed has crept into his bosom. The beginning of morality is the end of mana in the old sense ; the first parricide who felt compunction at his deed was the first hero-magician to lose his mana. The mana of the mana-bearers of to-day is not the old stuff but only a successful imitation. They are actors playing a part, identifying themselves with the Leaders of the Horde who ruled before morals were invented. Therefore we find all primitive people declaring that the mana of present days is merely the shadow of the things that used to be and that the dead or the gods (the representatives of countless murdered fathers) are the real sources of mana, who merely endow human beings with this quality in the phenomenon of possession.

It is not difficult to find a parallel in civilized society to this belief of the ancient Polynesians. " In hypnosis the command must be given with so much assurance and certainty that the hypnotized should regard contradiction as quite impossible." [2] Ferenczi has definitely made it clear that the hypnotizer is somebody who assumes the commanding attitude of the father while the patient regresses into an infantile obedience—an attitude which involves a passively directed libido-transference towards the hypnotizer.[3] As Freud points out, there are certain limits to the obedience of the hypnotized, a phenomenon which is probably connected with the fact that the hypnotic state is incomplete, that there always remains a certain amount of endopsychic knowledge, a consciousness of the fact that this situation is merely the repetition, the play-imitation, of another which was completely different and far more realistic.[4] By explaining

[1] Lehmann, loc. cit., p. 37, *Journal of the Polynesian Society*, iii, pp. 199, 200.

[2] Ferenczi, *Introjection und Übertragung*, 1901, p. 23.

[3] Ferenczi, ibid., p. 24.

[4] Freud, *Massenpsychologie und Ich-Analyse*, 1921, p. 87.

the origin of the masses with reference to the brother-clan, Professor Freud tells us, we shall also comprehend the irrational, mystic, attributes of the crowd which are usually expressed by terms like "Hypnotism" and "Suggestion". We should not forget that there is always something uncanny in hypnosis and that the uncanny always indicates something that was very familiar in the past and is now repressed. The hypnotizer asserts that he possesses a secret power which robs the subject of his own will or, what amounts to the same thing, the subject believes that he has this power. This secret power—still frequently called animal magnetism—must be the same which savages regard as the source of their taboo, which emanates from their kings and chiefs and makes it dangerous to approach them (mana).[1] Cases of hypnotic cures in Medieval Europe are still preserved in which the king as a universal father-substitute plays the part of the "medicine-man". Charles II is said to have touched nearly a hundred thousand people for the scrofula, and the kings of France also claimed to possess the same power of healing by touch.[2] The hypnotizer is an imitation of the absolutely narcissistic Leader of the Horde,[3] and the success of his imitation depends upon the degree of identification in him, i.e. as with other actors (conscious and unconscious) on his qualification for the part he is playing. There is another word of a similar nature to hypnotic influence in civilized languages, that is, "prestige". The idea of prestige has been made the foundation for far-reaching sociological speculations in a book of great interest.[4] If we compare prestige with mana we shall find that the similarity is even greater than between "magnetic influence" and mana. To begin with, both prestige and mana are words of a social order. They mean universally acknowledged influence exercised by those of high social standing, by the leader, priest, chief, or king. But it is the etymology of the word prestige which calls for special comment. It is derived from the Latin *præstigiæ*, a word which means the deceitful art of the magician rather than the sober authority of the conservative powers.[5] The unconscious bridge connecting the two concepts would be the endopsychic recognition of an element of fallacy in the authority assumed by the king or any other prestige-possessor, that he is not really the Ruler of the Horde, but only an imitation. The same derived character of the situation is expressed with even greater plasticity in the Pacific ; the chief's mana is derived from his identity

[1] Freud, loc. cit., pp. 106, 107. *Gesammelte Schriften*, vi, p. 328.
[2] Frazer, *Magic Art*, pp. 369, 370.   [3] Cf. Freud, loc. cit., p. 110.
[4] Leopold, *Prestige*, p. 1905.   [5] Leopold, loc. cit., p. 45.

with dead chiefs, ghosts, or gods, i.e. from his identification with the murdered father. The kinship between the Polynesian and civilized concepts has also been recognized by some authors who try to find an adequate English expression for the Maori mana. Gudgeon renders " mana " by " magnetic influence ", " magnetic power " [1] ; Elsdon Best as " prestige, fame, renown ".[2]

For all that, however, there is one important difference between hypnotic influence and mana. The absolute ascendency of the hypnotizer over his medium is obtained by compelling the latter to sleep, i.e. by making him withdraw his cathexis from the phenomena of the outer world and divide this libido-quantity between himself and the hypnotizer. The hypnotizer has replaced the ego-ideal, but as the hypnotizer has acquired his dominant position by an imitation of the Primal Sire (the first ego-ideal) it is quite natural that the ego regards all phenomena as real, if the hypnotizer merely affirms their reality.[3] With mana the case is different. Here we have to do with a social influence exerted over men who are wide-awake and pursuing their business in everyday life. Here the postulate of complete agreement between reality and the ego-ideal is attained by a different route. In the case of hypnosis, reality is modified till it agrees with the ego-ideal, but in Polynesia, where reality is the immovable element, it is the ego-ideal which is dropped if it proves ineffective, i.e. out of harmony with reality. The Eddystone Island definition of mana is " you speak true ".[4] When Mairuru died, a certain man claimed to succeed to his office and declared that the dead man had appeared to him and given him a stone with mana for multiplying pigs. Everybody believed him, but since the pigs failed to increase he was said to have no mana.[5] If, on the other hand, a man's pigs do multiply and his gardens are productive it is not because he is industrious and looks after his property but because of the stones full of mana for pigs and yams that he possesses.[6] If Rinambesi tells a man that he will catch plenty of fish and this comes true, then " Rinambesi mana " ; if not, " Rinambesi lied " (or " was wrong "). One Fijian informant says : " If it is true (ndina) it is mana, if it is not true it is not mana." " A thing is mana if it operates, it is not mana if it does not." [7]

[1] Gudgeon, " The Toa Taua or Warrior," *Journal of the Polynesian Society*, xiii, p. 238.
[2] Elsdon Best, " Spiritual Concepts of the Maori," *Journal of the Polynesian Society*, ix, p. 189. [3] Freud, loc. cit., pp. 84, 85.
[4] Hocart, *Man*, 1914, p. 97. [5] Codrington, loc. cit., p. 57.
[6] Codrington, loc. cit., p. 120. [7] Hocart, *Man*, 1914, p. 98.

The researches of Freud and Ferenczi into the nature of hypnotic phenomena have revealed the fact that the attitude of the hypnotized person is explained by assuming a regression into the primeval state of intimidation (from the side of the Reality Principle) and passive libido transference (Pleasure Principle) which characterized the relations between the Leader and the Crowd in the Cyclopean family. That such a libidinal tie is lurking behind the relations of those who have mana and those who acknowledge it seems probable for various reasons. Activity on the part of the chief and receptiveness from the commoner's side is what we lay stress on ; and thus we shall comprehend why a chief loses his mana if somebody steps over him,[1] i.e. makes him play the passive part in coition. In Samoa, *mamana* means to do wonders, but also to love, to desire, *mana'o*, to desire, to wish, *manamea*, to love, to desire.[2] In Tonga we have *mana*, a miracle ; *mamana* to love, a lover, to be in love, but also *fakamana*, intimidation, terror, the act of intimidating.[3] In Mangarava we have *manawarata*, an unchaste desire ; in New Zealand, *manawas*, heart, *manako*, to love somebody.[4] In other words we shall say that mana is an equivalent of those inhibited sexual impulses which characterize the relation between parent and child, between the Primal Sire and the Brothers, between a Polynesian chief and his subject or between the hypnotizer and his medium. But our researches have not only made it possible to confirm in a striking way the views held by Ferenczi and Freud on the nature of hypnotic phenomena, they have also made it possible to attempt a new solution of a question which has been much discussed in anthropological literature. The question is : Is mana personal or impersonal, animistic or pre-animistic ?[5] We shall answer this by comparing it with similar " power theories " found in the symptomatology of well-known forms of mental disease.

[1] Lehmann, loc. cit., p. 34. *Journal of the Polynesian Society*, xiv, p. 63.

[2] We find *mana matua*, " the supernatural power of a parent bringing a curse on a disobedient child," as if the lexicographer had been prompted in choosing his example by the unconscious knowledge that the parent-child relation was the source of mana.

[3] Tregear, loc. cit., p. 203.

[4] Lehmann, loc. cit., pp. 14, 15.

[5] The general verdict of ethnologists is in favour of " impersonal force " and pre-animism but Hocart, *Man*, 1914, p. 100 (" technical term belonging to a spiritualistic doctrine "), regards it as personal and animistic. Cf. P. W. Schmidt, " Grundlinien einer Vergleichung der Religionen und Mythologien der austronesischen Völker," *Denkschriften*, liii, 1910, pp. 114, 115. K. Th. Preuss, *Die geistige Kultur der Naturvölker*, 1914, p. 55.

In Dr Schreber's well-known case of paranoia his persecution mania consists chiefly in affirming that God, Dr Flechsig and other representatives of the Father-Imago compel him to perpetual lust (= are trying to murder him) by the medium of " rays ", " divine rays ", " nerve-rays ", etc. He evidently regards this connection between himself and the representatives of the father-imago as akin to hypnotic influence, as he asks Dr Flechsig to confess whether he has not been hypnotizing him at a distance all the time.[1] Freud says : " Schreber's ' Divine rays ', a condensation of solar rays, nerve fibres and sperm, are simply objectivated and projected cathexes of libido, giving his delusion a remarkable similarity to our theory." [2]

A patient with schizophrenia complains of the electric current which goes through her whole body.[3] In another case the patient calls himself " radium " because his libido emanates to the universe in general.[4] " Electricity " is a frequent idea of these patients to explain a psychic influence felt by them ; naturally they fall back on any rationalization offered by civilization for the fact that they feel some effect created on them by an object of the outer world, especially if it is not an influence by direct contact. We know that the persecution mania of the paranoiac is the negative projection of libidinal attraction and that hypnotic influence is explained by a regression into that tension of the inhibited sexual impulses which prevails ontogenetically in the relation between father and child and phylogenetically in the formation of the primary social unity. In both cases we find that expressions like " animal magnetism ", " electricity ", " telepathy ", are mere rationalizations, euphemistic substitutes for the libido. The psychotic patient projects his desire to be " influenced " in a libidinal manner to various representatives of the father-imago. The Melanesian and Polynesian does the same with regard to the chief whom he thus endows with all the mana (the " deflected sexual strivings "), which form the psychological correlate of the cohesion of the whole social group. If we find that in certain cases the mana of the chief is regarded as equivalent with the mana of the tribe, we shall say that this is really the case,

---

[1] P. Schreber, *Denkwürdigkeiten eines Nervenkranken*, 1903, p. xi.

[2] Freud, " Psychoanalytische Bemerkungen über einen autobiographisch beschriebenen Fall von Paranoia," *Jahrbuch*, ii, p. 266.

[3] S. Spielrein, " Über den psychologischen Inhalt eines Falles von Schizophrenie," *Jahrbuch*, iii, p. 385.

[4] W. Itten, " Beiträge zur Psychologie der Dementia praecox," *Jahrbuch*, v, pp. 41, 48.

for whilst the mana embodied in his person is derived from the sum total of the deflected sexual strivings of the whole tribe, the mana of each individual is reinforced by finding a father.

Elsdon Best, certainly one of the leading authorities on New Zealand, tells us that " when some one writes a treatise on the word mana it will be seen that mana and ora are almost synonymous terms ".[1] The natives attribute the *ora* (health, vigour, vitality) of the white man to the fact that the *koutu mimi* is in the room at night. For urine represents the *tawhito* (membrum virile) and will avert witchcraft. We thus find the *ora* localized in the penis and *ora* and mana regarded as synonymous expressions.[2] Another synonymous expression is *hau*, a word we recognize in the name given to the chief in Futura (*Sau*). Now the *hau* of man is the vital essence or life principle, the *hau* of land is its vitality and fertility.[3] But then again the *hau* is localized in the sperm, for it is implanted during coition by the father while the mother is regarded as a mere receptacle.[4] The father as owner of the magic wand, the penis, is the *fons et origo* of mana. Thus in time of war the warriors would pass between a priest's legs in order that the mana emanating from the penis should prevent them from being afflicted by the demons.[5]

In our previous interpretation of the primitive medicine-man and his doings we dwelt principally on the traces of anal fixation. Now we have followed the development of the medical art through the three principal phases of libidinal organization but without recognizing the thread that connects these three phases, the specific feature in the structure of the erotogenetic zones that is carried over from one phase of development to the next. If, however, we come to consider that we are dealing with a man born with a tooth, projecting the fæces as a death-bringing quartz-crystal into his fellow-men, and using the penis as a weapon, it is easy to conclude that the differential feature in his make-up is sadism.

It is not merely a question of the sadistic-anal organization, as I thought before [6] (though I still regard this phase as particularly important), but of the sadistic impulses, carried over from the oral

---

[1] E. Best, " Maori Medical Lore," *Journal of the Polynesian Society*, xiii, p. 222.

[2] *Idem*, ibid., pp. 220, 221.

[3] E. Best, " Spiritual Concepts of the Maori," *Journal of the Polynesian Society*, ix, pp. 189, 193.

[4] *Idem*, ibid., p. 181.

[5] E. Best, " The Lore of Whare Kohanga," *Journal P.S.*, xiv, p. 208.

[6] Cf. Róheim, " Nach dem Tode des Urvaters," *Imago*, ix.

through the anal to the genital stage. Indeed, if we come to consider that a magician is quite adapted to his own social reality, that he is somebody whose mana is manifested by " his words coming true ", it becomes evident that since he is in touch with the reality-principle he must also have attained to a certain degree of erotic reality, which as we know presupposes the genital phase of development and on the side of the ego the identification with the father.

That this identification in the Primal Horde was carried out in an oral and sadistic manner is quite evident, and we are also forced to the conclusion that the part of the body which was chiefly incorporated by our pre-human ancestors was the penis. When the Maori chief fails to inherit the ancestral mana it is because he cannot " bind " his father's ghost, and the way to " bind " it is to bite his big toe. If we consider that the chief qualities that distinguished a *toa*, a warrior, were his courage and genital strength, both being supposed to be inherent in the penis,[1] we shall perhaps be justified in regarding the big toe as a penis symbol and the biting as a survival of eating. The Australians who cut out their enemies' kidney fat and eat it are the nearest to what we suppose to have composed the Primal Horde. If we regard the accounts of the initiation of the medicine-man, where he is cut to pieces, eaten, and put together again by the spirits, as reversals of the original scene in which he cut the Father to pieces and ate him, we can find some trace of this supposed incorporation of the penis in the idea of the snake projected into his body by the spirits which he in his turn projects into the patients.

This incorporation of the penis corresponds both to the function of the oral zone in the case of a sucking child and to that of the female organ in coitus. As I pointed out before, the brother horde identified themselves with the father in eating him but their cannibal meal itself was a repetition of the meals enjoyed by the child sucking the mother's nipple. By identifying themselves with the father they were therefore reviving an infantile and organic mother-identification, while in " eating " the father's penis, they identified themselves with the mother from a libidinal point of view. Thus certain quantities of libido were withdrawn from the mother and projected to the body of the father whom they had devoured but who in his posthumous glorification came to represent not merely his own power but also the love-bond between mother and child.

[1] W. E. Gudgeon, " Phallic Emblem from Atiu Island," *Journal of the Polynesian Society*, xiii, p. 193.

4 THE HOLY GHOST

In the New Testament we have an important account of how Jesus was baptized and of the part played by the Holy Ghost in this act. We summarize the versions given by the various sources with all the details that may be of importance. Jesus was baptized by John according to his desire and when he emerged from the water, heaven was cleft asunder and the Holy Ghost descended upon him in the shape of a dove. At the same time a voice was heard from heaven, saying : " Thou art my beloved Son : in thee I am well pleased." [1]

It has been definitely shown by Gunkel and Gressmann that this scene refers to the supernatural succession to the throne. By the descent of the dove or the Holy Ghost the Saviour is recognized both in his capacity of Messiah, the Anointed King of Israel, and as the future King of Heaven. The majesty of the old Persian monarchs left them, in the shape of the Varaghna bird, to fly to their successors.[2] The scene frequently appears in folk-tales.[3] A tale from Kashmir speaks of a land where, when the king died, his elephant " was driven all over the country and his hawk was made to fly here, there, and everywhere in search of a successor and he to whom the elephant bowed or on whose hand the hawk alighted was supposed to be the divinely chosen one." [4] In a tale of the Taranchi Tartars the hero arrives at the gates of a city and the people cry out, " Cuckoo, cuckoo ! " Their ruler had been dead for three days and it was the custom that whomsoever his magical bird alighted on was made ruler of the city.[5] In other tales of this type the birds announce the son as king to be. But his kingdom is connected with the future humiliation of the father, who therefore vainly strives to obviate the inevitable.[6]

A new king can only ascend the throne at the death of his predecessor. The author of The Golden Bough has shown beyond possibility of doubt that the death of the king was not a natural one. The king, when his strength failed, succumbed to the superior strength of another who might be and originally probably was his

[1] John i, 32 ; Matthew iii, 16 ; Mark i, 10 ; Luke iii, 22.

[2] Sacred Books of the East, xxiii, p. 294.

[3] Bolte und Polivka, Anmerkungen zu den Kinder- und Hausmärchen der Brüder Grimm, 1914, i, p. 325.

[4] I. H. Knowles, Folk Tales of Kashmir, 1888, p. 158.

[5] Radloff, Proben der Volkslitteratur der türkischen Stämme Süd-Siberiens, 1886, vi, p. 157.

[6] Radloff, loc. cit., i, p. 208.

son. Gressmann shows that the dove was sacrificed to Jahve and in ancient Palestine, as in modern folklore, was regarded as the bird that embodied the soul of the dead.[1]

Comparative research has made it quite evident that the episode of the Saviour's baptism and of the descent of the Holy Ghost is borrowed by the authors of the New Testament from older sources. Yet even in its new setting it is not difficult for analysis, after thus establishing its history, to interpret the unconscious meaning of the whole scene. The new King of Heaven, like his colleagues of this world, ascends the throne after having killed his predecessor and thus the Holy Ghost becomes truly a holy ghost, the bird descending with the soul of the murdered father to the son and heir.

But we have already observed that the whole scene is borrowed, and this time it is possible to indicate the source or sources with a greater amount of accuracy than is usual in such cases. The voice from heaven is really a voice from Egypt. Thus Plutarch tells us how at the festival of the Pamylia a certain Pamyles, when fetching water from the Nile, heard a voice proclaiming : " The good and great king Osiris is born " or " the lord of all the earth is born ".[2] The parallel gains in accuracy by observing that drawing water from the Nile is in itself a birth ceremony, for Osiris is the Nile and is in the water drawn from the river, just as baptism is ceremonial re-birth. Moreover, the exact words that proclaim Jesus as King are the official title of the pharaoh, and Osiris, of course, is the first divine ruler of Egypt. The pharaoh is called " The beloved Son of Ra or Ptah, or Amon ", as the case may be. Norden, not satisfied with this proof, shows that the Greek εὐδόκησα of the New Testament usually translated, following Luther, by an expression meaning something like " to delight in " really means " to decide for some-body ", to " choose ", and the King of Egypt is called " the beloved of Rê " or " chosen by Rê ". " Thou king whom Rê hath chosen the son of Rê, Rameses beloved by Amon." [3]

If the myth is derived from Egypt and originally represented the death of the old king and the ascent of the new king to royalty, it is additionally certain that the scene involves the death of the father by the son and the transference of the soul or life-power to the latter. Apart from other features of Egyptian royalty, to be considered in the next chapter, there is abundant proof for this view

[1] Gressmann, " Die Sage von der Taufe Jesu," *A.R.W.*, xx, p. 329.
[2] Plutarch, *De Iside*, xii.
[3] Norden, *Die Geburt des Kindes*, 1924, p. 132.

in the myth of Osiris, who is, as we know, a prototype and condensation of all Egyptian rulers.   Now, as we have shown above, Osiris was originally killed and castrated by his son and successor.   But the feature of the myth that is specially relevant in this connection is that Isis, in the shape of a hawk, descended upon the corpse of the murdered and castrated Osiris and conceived from him her son Horus.   Leaving aside for the present all other considerations it is again important to observe the difference made in the text by the literary criticism of Usener.   By going beyond Luther's translation we could recognize the influence of Egyptian court style, but by going beyond the traditional text itself it is possible to show a more archaic idea.   Comparing the references contained in the early Fathers to this passage, Usener shows that the original text must have been, "Thou art my beloved Son whom to-day I have procreated."   This again appears to be a quotation from Psalms ii, 7. Jahve speaks to the king of Israel : "Thou art my son, I have procreated thee to-day." [1]   There are two aspects of this picture. One is that the descent of the Holy Ghost to the Kings of Israel proves that they too, in the unconscious setting, have acquired royal honours by the murderous act, and the other that the passage of the divine spirit from the body is the act of procreation.   The myth of Osiris is not the only point of contact with Egypt for it seems to have been an article of Egyptian belief that every god was destined to die after he had begotten a son in his own likeness.[2]   When the pharaoh ascends the throne he receives from the god his father a sort of divine fluid.[3]   The pharaoh lives by the fluid of Ra, and the same fluid flows in his veins.   This is a fluid like the rays of the sun, like fire, and the apparition of fire in the water heralds the descent of the dove.   We have mentioned this mystical fluid, the *sa* ; it is the seminal fluid containing the germs of life.[4]

When the burning Easter candles as symbols of the Holy Ghost are dipped into the water of baptism, the latter is compared to the uterus and the light is regarded as fertilizing the water.[5]   There can therefore be no doubt whatever that the modern version of the scene given in the New Testament has a past going back untold ages to

[1] H. Usener, *Religionsgeschichtliche Untersuchungen I. Das Weihnachtsfest*, 1911, p. 40.

[2] Wiedemann, *Herodotos zweites Buch*, p. 204.   Frazer, *The Dying God*, 1911, p. 5.

[3] Norden, loc. cit., p. 119.

[4] A. Moret, "Du Caractère Religieux de la Royauté Pharaonique," *Annales du Musée Guimet*, xv, 1902, p. 47.

[5] Usener. loc. cit., p. 69.

when the Brothers fought for the Death of the Paternal Tyrant.
Since the Holy Ghost represents the phallus, the Successor, the
hero who had the ghost in his body, was the man who had taken
possession of the paternal organ of generation. Naturally, the
phallic concept of the Holy Ghost is fully recognized both by
Dr Jones in his analysis of this idea and by Flügel who regards the
fiery tongues of the Apostles as phallic symbols.[1] Indeed, it can
hardly be misunderstood. We must only consider that the Holy
Ghost appears in three principal scenes in the New Testament.
One of these is a conception, the second is spoken of as a conception,
and the third is the ecstasy of the Apostles. In the Catholic liturgy
of the Mass the *spiritus sanctus* is called *digitus dexteræ patris* and
the act of imposition of the hand either for the purpose of healing
or for that of initiation, prophetic enthronization, etc., is regularly
regarded as a means by which the spirit, the Holy Ghost, passes
from the prophet or priest to the new adept. Now Eisler has
collected very important evidence to show that the hand in this
connection was a phallic symbol. A tribe was called B'ne Jamin—
" the sons of the right hand." Phallic gravestones are called *Jad*
—" the hand." [2] The hand is the ideogram of the god Nebo,[3]
and Nebo is the fire-drill. Jewish authorities protest against lifting
the hand to the sky in praying. They regard it as an exhibition
of the genital organs. Maimuni (*Epist. ad proselyt. relig.*) says :
" Why dost thou lift thine hand in prayer like a horse in rut that
lifts its tail." Eisler compares the uplifted hands of Moses as a war
charm,[4] the blessing gesture of the Kohanim, and lifting the hand
to the sky in rain-making. Many centuries later the belief still
survived in the Kabala, where the gymnastic connected with prayer
was regarded as a sort of cohabitation with the celestial sphere.[5]

The symbol of the hand and the dove or Holy Ghost seem to be
interchangeable, for in the oldest illustrations to the Bible, in the
so-called Octateuch of Syriac origin, the Spirit of God [6] above the
waters is not represented as usual by a dove but as a hand and Ishtar
the dove-goddess herself appears as a hand.[7] In connection with

[1] Jones, " Eine psychoanalytische Studie über den heiligen Geist,"
Imago, ix. I. C. Flügel, " Some Unconscious Factors in the International
Language Movement," *Journal of Psa.*, vi.
[2] R. Eisler, " Kuba Kybele," *Philologus*, lxviii, pp. 182, 184.
[3] F. Hommel, *Grundriss der Geographie und Geschichte des alten Orients*,
1904, 101.
[4] Ex. xviii, 11.   [5] Karppe, *Zohar*, 1901, p. 434. Eisler, loc. cit., p. 180.
[6] Gen. i, 2.   [7] Eisler, loc. cit., p. 180. Hommel, loc. cit., p. 101.

the dove, Horapollo says that the dove represented for the Egyptians an ungrateful person because the male dove kills its father and has intercourse with its mother.[1] The New Testament itself makes it quite evident that the state of prophetic ecstasy is regarded as being a sort of supernatural pregnancy. When Elisabeth meets the Virgin who is also " full of the Holy Ghost ", that is, pregnant, the child in her womb jumps for joy and she becomes " full of the Holy Ghost " and begins to prophesy,[2] that is she became ecstatic. It is when speaking of their enemies or opponents that the Fathers of the Church throw off all restraint without, of course, even suspecting that they are telling their own secrets. A passage of Irenæus about the famous Gnostic prophet Marcus runs as follows : " It is probable that he has a demon who serves him and by whom he seems to prophesy himself and can make all those whom he regards as worthy to receive grace into prophetesses. He has a lot to do with women and especially with the elegant ones, those who are dressed in purple and are very rich. He often tries to seduce them by his flatteries. He tells them : ' I wish thee to participate in my grace because the Father of the World sees thine angel always before my face. But thy greatness lies in me. We must be united. Receive the Grace from me and by me. Prepare thyself like a bride waiting for the Bridegroom, that thou shouldst become what I am and I should become what thou art. Receive in thy bridal chamber the seminal fluid of Light. Take it from thy Spouse, take hold of it and let thyself be held by it. See, Grace hath descended in thee, open thy mouth and thou art a prophetess.' "[3] Here it appears as a charge brought up against an enemy worse than heathen, but we may, with all the probability that can be had in these cases, generalize the statement and say that the " mystic " union with the divinity, the state of possession, derives its " mystic " quality from repression ; that it is, originally, the highest degree of unity that can be attained by one living being with another, namely, coition, and that the seminal fluid, that is light, is identical with the Holy Ghost, with the *sa* descending from the Sun-God of Egypt to the King and with the spirit or soul in general, these beliefs being all moulded on the biological basis of the seminal fluid.

Having thus far shown to our full satisfaction that the dove and

---

[1] Hopfner, " Tierkult der alten Aegypter," *Denkschriften d.K.Ak.d. Wiss.*, 57, 1914, 125.

[2] Luke i, 35.

[3] Irenæus, i, 13 3. H. Leisegang, *Pneuma Hagion* (Veröffentlichungen des Forschungsinstituts für vergl. Religionsgeschichte), Leipzig, p. 33.

the Holy Ghost represent the male member in coitus we shall now
proceed to prove the exact opposite—that they represent the female,
the mother.

The voice from Heaven says : ἐν σοι εὐδόκησα—" I have
chosen thee," but in the older version restored by Usener ἐγω σήμερον
γεγέννηκά σε. We have followed Leisegang is translating γεγέννηκα
as " procreated " and in referring it to the activity of the male in
coitus. But Usener and Gressmann translate it as " I have given birth
to thee to-day ".[1] The festival of Epiphany, the day of the Descent
of the Dove, was originally celebrated as Christ's birthday.[2] Now
this would point to a goddess and, indeed, Gressmann clearly shows that
everywhere in the Semitic world the idea of the dove is associated
with the belief in Ishtar or similar mother-goddesses representing
love both in its tender and in its unbridled, incestuous aspect. Ishtar
is the virgin mother and also the prostitute. The ambivalency of the
original idea could hardly be expressed more forcibly than by the fact
that Langdon uses the word " virgin-harlot " in translating the
original Babylonian adjective of Ishtar.[3] The inhabitants of the
harem, i.e. the virgins consecrated to the Ishtar cult, are referred to
as " birds " (hu), a euphemistic expression for prostitutes, or more
especially as " doves " (tu hu) and their habitations are dovecots.[4]
In an old Syriac version of our text we find the following modification : " Thou art my son and beloved whom I have chosen,"
and Gressmann explains this modification by the Babylonian view
of the King as Son and Spouse of the dove-goddess.[5] Origen,
quoting from the apocryphal Gospel to the Hebrews, has the following
passage : " My mother the Holy Spirit took me a moment ago by
one of my hairs, and carried me away to the great Mount Tabor."
The Ophites represented the Holy Ghost as the " first woman ",
the " mother of all living ", who was beloved by " the first man "
and by " the second man " and who conceived of both (i.e. of father
and son) the light which they call Christ.[6] Consequently we
must suppose two distinct sources for the Christian idea of the Trinity.
One of these sources goes back to Egypt and in it the ghost is the

[1] Usener, loc. cit., p. 40.
[2] K. Holl, " Ursprung des Epiphanienfestes," Sitzungsberichte der
kngl. Preuss. Akad. Wiss., 1917, p. 404.
[3] S. Langdon, Tammuz and Ishtar, 1914, p. 75.
[4] Radau, " Miscellaneous Sumerian Texts from the Temple Library
of Nippur," Assyriologische und Archæologische Studies H. v. Hilprecht
gewidmet, 1909, p. 399.
[5] H. Gressmann, A.R.W., xx, pp. 11, 12.
[6] Frazer, The Dying God, p. 5. H. Usener, loc. cit., p. 116.

procreating soul of the murdered father. This idea, as shown by Dr Jones, was used to repress the all too manifest incestuous connotation of the dove that came from Babylon—the king ascending the throne, becomes the husband of the dove-goddess who is also his mother. But we believe that this general trend is very ancient indeed and that its source lies in the cannibal communion after the death of the Jealous Sire. For there are two ways of becoming united with a god, either by eating him or having sexual intercourse with him. If we wished unduly to simplify matters we could say that from the point of view of the Brothers in the Primal Horde, the being who was eaten represented the father and the one with whom they were united by means of cohabitation stood for the mother. Taking matters from the female point of view and considering the analogy of vaginal and oral functions, we should, however, say that the god who was eaten, incorporated in the act of intercourse, and spoke from the inside of the prophetess was the Father completely introjected by the woman and identified with the child in her womb.

However, as shown in a previous paper of mine, when the Brothers devoured the Paternal Tyrant they repeated a scene of their childhood and regained the forgotten libidinal satisfaction once enjoyed at the mother's breast.[1] By this act libido was displaced from the mother to the father and the Tyrant became a beloved deity, the ghost or the corpse of the father became a Holy Mother. I have also shown that excrement being from an infantile point of view the equivalent of the milk, the father (mother) whom they had eaten became identical with their own excrements and this agrees exactly with the flatus symbolism of the Holy Ghost pointed out by Dr Jones.[2] But now, considering the results obtained in examining the pipe-symbolism of North American Indians, I am inclined to stress another symbolic equation—that of the penis with the nipples. The new formula would be somewhat as follows. The brothers, having eaten the father's penis, repeated their original "eating" of the mother's nipples and were filled with his "ghost"—the seminal fluid—as in their infancy they had been with their mother's milk. The result of this situation would seem to be a peculiar series of ambiguities making for femaleness on the side of the libido and for maleness on that of the ego. For by eating the father's corpse, kidney, or penis they were performing the functions of a woman in coitus, were becoming identical with the mother who had also and frequently "eaten" the living father. This is from the point of view

[1] Róheim, "Nach dem Tode des Urvaters," *Imago*, ix.
[2] Jones, op. cit.

of the libido and object relations, while from the point of view of identification and the ego, it was precisely by eating the father that they had become true fathers, i.e. males. The normal male will repress the female attitude by the aid of identification with the father. But the medicine-man, the seer, and prophet derives his supernormal power from being both father and mother at the same time. The former trend is prevalent, though not exclusively, in his attitude towards humanity at large whom he dupes by his assumed and over-done identification with the Father of the Primal Horde. But in his relation to the Supernatural World he is the Female, the Receiver completely overcome in his ecstatic state by a Will that imposes itself from without and penetrates into his body. The shaman sublimates the female libido dormant in the male and, narcissistically maintaining the libidinal relations between the male and female components of his own Ego, transforms the former into a series of supernatural beings. In his ecstatic fit he re-condensates the two acts of the Primal Tragedy, the struggle with the male and the coitus with the female. Whereas, however, in the original struggle he was the victor, victory became transformed into defeat by posthumous obedience. He is overcome by the father whom he has overcome and takes the part of the mother in the scene that follows. Or rather, he plays both parts but his male attitude is split off to appear as a separate being that enters his body and leaves it after the fit. When the divine spirit departed from Saul, David began to prophesy.[1] The presence of the Spirit of God in the Old Testament is regularly manifested by an ecstatic condition. The prophet is " overcome " by the Spirit and becomes the tool of a will stronger than his own. In the case of Pythia there is sufficient evidence for the belief that her inspiring demon Apollo entered her body through the vagina.[2] Reitzenstein shows how generally accepted in Hellenistic circles the belief in the cohabitation of the divinity with a man or woman was, that the divine spirit was transfused by means of this cohabitation so that the new shaman became " full of god ", that is, fell into an ecstatic state.[3]

Similar phenomena have been described in detail from Siberia to South Africa. In Siberia an essential feature of the phenomena is that inspiration is brought about by beating a drum. We refer to the Koryak idea of Universe making rain by beating a drum and using

[1] Josephus, viii, 2.
[2] Leisegang, *Pneuma*, 32, quoting Suidas. Origen, *c. Cels.*, vii, 3. John Chrysost. *Homil.* xxix. Norden, *Aeneis*, vi, 1903, p. 144.
[3] Reitzenstein, *Poimandres*, 1904, pp. 225–33.

his penis as a drum-stick. Perhaps the lizards and toads used as drum ornaments by the Tunguz and Ostyak have also a sexual significance. The process itself is described as "the heat of the god" coming upon the wizard and the heat is described as a sort of hot wind.[1] The shaman women, when they expect the spirit, uncover their head and loosen their hair, a ceremony that must probably be interpreted as a survival of nakedness. The demon seizes the shaman but he is often reluctant to give answers. They wrestle, the shaman is completely exhausted, tortured, transfixed by spiritual arrows.[2] The following is a description of what takes place among the Yakut. "When the shaman who has been called to a sick person enters the *yurta*, he lies down on a white mare's skin and waits for the night till it is possible for him to shamanize. The host chooses the best latchets and forms them into a loop which is placed round the shaman's shoulders and held by one of those present during the dance in order to prevent one of the spirits from carrying him off. Slowly the shaman begins to get ready. He sometimes has a nervous and artificial hiccough which makes his whole body shake ; his eyes are fixed on the fire. Now the fire is allowed to die out. Dusk descends on the room, voices become hushed, everybody talks in whispers. The shaman slowly takes off his shirt and puts on his wizard's coat or failing that he takes a woman's coat. Then he is given a pipe ; he smokes it for a long while, swallowing the smoke. His hiccough becomes louder, he shivers more violently. When he has finished smoking his face is pale, his head falls on his breast, his eyes are half closed. At this point the white mare's skin is placed in the middle of the room. The shaman asks for cold water and when he has drunk it he takes the drum. He kneels on the mare's skin and sprinkles the water to the four corners of the world. Gradually the soft sounds of the drum are audible. At first the music is soft, delicate, tender, then rough and irrepressible like the roar of an oncoming storm. It grows louder and louder and like peals of thunder wild shouts rend the air, the crow calls, the grebe laughs, the seamews complain, snipes whistle, eagles and hawks scream." All the while the shaman has been possessed by his spirits and these ventriloquistic performances represent the guardian spirits that have taken possession of him. At last the crescendo ceases and the shaman begins to chant some obscure fragment.

---

[1] Cf. the Holy Ghost as flatus.
[2] Munkácsi, loc. cit., pp. 373–400.

" I, Mighty bull of the earth
   . . . . Horse of the steppes
I, the mighty bull . . . bellow
I, the horse of steppes . . . neigh
I, the man set above all other beings
I, the man most gifted of all !
I, the man created by the master all powerful
Horse, of the steppes, appear ! teach me !
Enchanted bull of the earth, appear ! speak to me !
Powerful master command me ! " [1]

A man clad in a woman's cloak, on a white mare's skin, is possessed by bull and horse. It is easy to show the phallic nature of these symbols by comparison with Hungarian beliefs.[2] In the beginning of his ecstatic incantation he seems to be the bull himself, he identifies himself with the father till by gradual transition the bull seems to be a powerful being who has completely subjugated the shaman. Troschanski has put forward several important arguments for the female origin of Yakut shamanism. We repeat them here not in order to follow this line of argument but to demonstrate the ambisexual attitude of the male shaman.

1 The shaman has on his coat two iron circles representing the breasts.

2 He parts his hair in the middle like a woman, and braids it, letting it fall loose during the shamanistic ceremony.

3 In the Kolyma district neither a woman nor a shaman lies on the right side of the horse skin in the *yurta*.

4 A shaman wears his own garments only on very important occasions ; on lesser occasions he wears a girl's jacket made of foal's hide.

5 For three days after the birth of a child no man may enter the room where the woman is lying, only women and shamans.[3]

While among the Neo-Siberian tribes we find merely ritualistic survivals of the shaman's ambisexuality, this feature is in full evidence among the more primitive people called Paleo-Siberians. Thus the homosexual shaman of the Chukchee called " soft man " is supposed to have a special protector among the spirits who usually plays the part of a supernatural husband. This husband is supposed to be the real head of the family and to communicate his orders by means of his transformed wife. On the other hand, normal male shamans

---

[1] Czaplicka, *Aboriginal Siberia*, 1914, pp. 233–6.
[2] Cf. Róheim, *Magyar Néphit és Néposokások*, 1928, chap. i.
[3] Czaplicka, loc. cit., pp. 246, 247.

have supernatural females as wives.[1] The sexual organs play a large part in Chukchee shamanism. A "mischievous shaman" when performing an incantation must strip himself naked and show his private parts to the moon. At some thanksgiving ceremonies they appear naked and perform an incantation addressed to their assistant spirits. The incantation refers to their genital organs.[2] That the shamanistic trance itself, described by the Chukchee as sinking into another world, should be an act of sexual communion with the spirits seems very probable, although not openly stated.[3] At any rate this would explain why this gift of inspiration should be bestowed more frequently on women. *If we regard the spirit that penetrates into the human body as the male member or when already inside as the embryo in the womb we can understand why although women are more likely to be inspired than men, the bearing of children should be regarded as adverse to shamanistic inspiration.* A woman with considerable shamanistic power may lose a great part of it after the birth of her first child. She will recover it only after several years—with the ending of the period of her maternity.[4] Among the Koryak we are also told that *childbirth may result in a complete or temporary destruction of shamanistic power.*[5] *If being possessed by a spirit is equivalent to pregnancy, the exit of the demon would be childbirth.* Naturally women would be more likely to be inspired than men and naturally they would cease to be in a state of supernatural pregnancy and to give birth to supernatural children when they had real ones.

Among the Hausas of North Africa a *bori* frequently chooses a human conjugal partner and the *bori* is also responsible for the phenomenon we call inspiration.[6] Among the Ba-Ila the demoniacs or possessed are spoken of as dancing *busala*. Mr Heath furnishes the description of this state. "I found the wife of Chungwe face down on the ground and covered with dust. The limbs were rigid, the eyelids quivering and only the whites of the eyes visible. The feet moved spasmodically and the head wagged from side to side." Playing drums is the regular cure for these fits. As soon as she hears the drums she will twitch and jump about. Then she grovels on the ground, shakes a rattle violently and seems to be quite unconscious of what she is doing. If the drum is beaten long enough the afflicted woman

---

[1] W. Bogoras, "The Chukchee," *Jesup North Pacific Expedition*, vii, 1907, p. 452.

[2] Bogoras, loc. cit., pp. 448, 449.

[3] Bogoras, loc. cit., p. 441.   [4] Bogoras, loc. cit., p. 414.

[5] Jochelson, "The Koryak," *Jesup N.P.E.*, vi, p. 54.

[6] Tremearne, *The Ban of the Bori*, 1914, pp. 393, 396.

will rise to her feet and utter the name of the spirit troubling her.
By having spoken the name she recovers. But this kind of possession
passes into another not different in nature, but different in degree.
This is called *kushinshima*, " to prophesy," the word being applied
primarily to the low, muttering tone in which such a person speaks.
When the ghost enters the chest of the prophet, he will prophesy.
He may prophesy famine or the death of a man. It is interesting
to observe what the ghost says on entering the chest of a man. Such
a ghost will say " So and so is pregnant, I shall come to be born by
her ".[1] The same transition from a disease to a profession is found
in the case of the Zulus. Their symptoms are usually ascribed to
possession by an ancestral spirit. From some the trouble departs of
its own accord, others have the ghost laid which causes it, while some
let the affection take its course and become professional diviners.
The best description is that of a hysterical visionary " who had the
disease which precedes the power to divine ". He describes the well-
known symptoms of hysteria, the heavy weight creeping up within
him to his shoulders, the sensation of flying in the air, etc.[2] Among
the Baganda a medium had only one duty to perform, that of being
the mouth-piece of the god whom he represented. It was always
the god who chose his representative ; in some cases women might
be chosen as mediums, in others only men. In each case the choice
was indicated in some such manner as the following. The person
was suddenly possessed by the god, and began to utter secrets or to
predict future events which without divine influence it would have
been impossible for him to know. The bystanders thus knew that a god
had selected the man to be his medium and he was at once taken to
the temple. Possession was called " being married to the god " at
the time when a person first became possessed ; whilst subsequent
possessions were called " being seized by the head ". When a medium
wished to become possessed in order to give the oracle he would
smoke a sacred pipe and sometimes drink a cup of beer. He sat in the
temple near the fire and gazed into the fire until the spirit came upon
him. During the time that a medium was under the influence of a god
he was in a frenzied state and his utterances were only intelligible
to the priest. As soon as the god had left the medium he became
prostrated. When a woman was chosen to be the medium she was
separated from men and had to observe laws of chastity for the rest
of her life ; she was looked upon as the wife of the god.[3]

[1] Smith, *Ba-Ila*, ii, pp. 136–41.
[2] C. Callaway, *The Religious System of the Amazulu*, 1884, pp. 183, 259.
[3] Roscoe, *Baganda*, p. 275.

We have traced the steps of the savage wizard or medicine-man from his pre-human beginnings up to antiquity. His professional activity consists of substitute formations or sublimations of the oral, anal, and genital functions. In his relation to the lay world on the one hand and to the supernatural on the other we see him assuming both the part of the threatening father, of the protecting mother, and of the sucking child. The three phases of psychoneuroses that correspond to the three phases of libido-development are easily discernible in his mental make-up. His fits of maniac raving and melancholy depression occurring in conjunction with ceremonial cannibalism are characteristic of the initiation period. In his professional activity, in shooting the anal quartz-crystal into his enemies or in withdrawing it from his patients, he is full of obsessions, taboos, spells ; for as we know very well *obsessional neurosis is the particular form of disease that is connected with the anal organization.* As a shaman possessed by a demon or god, the medicine-man is producing a hysterical fit, and since Freud there can be no doubt about the fact that a hysterical fit *reproduces coitus and that the hysteric plays the part of both the male and the female partner.*[1] For a person who is possessed, as the Baganda tell us, is married to a god.

5 Disease and the Art of Healing

I acknowledge that my explanation of the medicine-man lacks the advantage of simplicity but I shall now proceed to make things clearer or even worse by linking it to a libidinal theory of disease. For, as we shall see, a primitive doctor regularly identifies himself with his patient ; indeed, he would never be what he is without this. It is evident moreover that the views held by primitive man on disease and cure having no other source than his own unconscious cannot fail to reflect the unconscious meaning of these phenomena. If we know what disease means and how it is healed we shall also be on more familiar terms with the healer.

The relation of the medicine-man to his patients is built up on his original sadism, but this sadism is repressed and sublimated by two circumstances. We have already pointed out how the idea of *projecting* substances into the body of another human being must be derived from its only organic prototype, from the act of coitus where the male emits a substance into the body of the female. The Arunta

[1] Freud, " Hysterische Phantasien und ihre Beziehung zur Bisexualität, *Gesammelte Schriften,* v, p. 246.

smear the pointing bone with blood derived from the subincised penis.[1] Loritja medicine-men smear the " ropes " they project into their enemy with blood derived from the same source,[2] while the women make these ropes of the pubic hairs and smear them with blood taken from the vagina. The medicine-man who tries to suck this rope out of the patient's body only succeeds in securing a small part as the rest remains inside and becomes transformed into a serpent which is fatal. That the ropes are again " serpents ", i.e. the missing penis of the woman is shown clearly by the case when the victim of feminine spite is of the stronger sex. They smear the pubic hair ropes with blood taken from their vagina and put it into earth where they have urinated. The two ropes emerge out of the earth, enter the body of the women themselves *per vaginam*, leave it again through the head and bore themselves into the man's heart, who dies in great agony.[3] Another clue comes from the sacred songs of the Omaha medicine society. We have mentioned that arrows, besides shells and crystals, figure among the projective missiles of the medicine-man and it will therefore be no surprise to us to hear that the sacred shell, which was shot like an arrow, should be called " arrow " in the mystic song.[4] Another of these mystic songs says : " Wife, what else are you afraid of ? Are you afraid of my magic medicine (or arrow) ? " The magic power, that which is shot into somebody, is here spoken of as an arrow. " This song is said to have a double meaning and to be phallic in character," [5] i.e. the " arrow " or shell stands for the phallus and the " shooting " is equivalent to coition.[6]

A common feature of all myths on the " false cure " is that it is a human being whose missile penetrates into the body of an ogre, spirit, animal-being, at any rate a " supernatural ". Now there is another group of myths which may be linked to this first one by the presence of the same common feature, only in this case the end is more in accordance with the curative aspects of the medicine-man for he really pulls out the arrow he has shot into the unfortunate ogre. Nevertheless the connection with the former group is quite evident ; in the first instance on account of the identity of actors (human being sends disease into supernaturals ; a reversal of the real situation) and

---

[1] Strehlow, *Aranda und Loritja*, iv, p. 33.
[2] Strehlow, loc. cit., iv, p. 37.   [3] Strehlow, loc. cit., iv, p. 38.
[4] Fletcher, " Omaha Tribe," *Bureau Am. Ethn.*, xxvii, p. 524.
[5] Fletcher, loc. cit., p. 549.
[6] The Hungarian vulgar expression for coitus is to shoot. Since the introduction of fire-arms the Arunta call magic *tarinama*, i.e. shooting. Strehlow, loc. cit., iv, p. 32.

then because the shaman presents himself here in an ambivalent aspect as disease-causer first and healer only as an after-thought. Big-Light, the Koryak equivalent of the North-West American Raven, went seeking adventures with his brother. They arrived at the country of the Kamak (man-eating demons). But there was one human girl living with the ogres and when Big-Light saw her coming out of the lodge he said : " I wish she would only untie the bands of her coat." The girl immediately untied the bands of her coat. Then Big-Light shot an arrow from his bow and it hit the girl's chest. She fell down dead. Her people find the tracks which lead to Big-Light's house and call him to come and revive the girl he has killed. He does so, presumably (although this detail is omitted) by extracting the arrow he shot into her, and marries the girl.[1] Grebe-Man marries the woman whose heart he took out. Here we have first death and then revival.[2] The episode is given in its original unmodified form for the whole context of the tale leaves no doubt about the fact that Big-Light's arrow is what we call Cupid's arrow. He is in love with the girl, he shoots her, coition appears to her as death but as death followed by a revival. The American variants are less direct but not less instructive. Ya'qstatl shoots the *Tsonokoa* (ogress) for stealing his salmon. He goes after her to get his arrow back, meets a girl fetching water who recognizes him as a shaman and asks him to cure her mother. His arrow is invisible to all eyes except his own, he withdraws it and receives the " water of life " (the power to resuscitate the dead) and the girl as his reward.[3] The " shooting " is here told in connection with the mother, the marriage with the daughter. In the Koryak variant it is the daughter who is shot and married ; here the psychic censor is at work in obliterating the sexual meaning of the shot. The means by which this end is accomplished are of some interest ; the doubling of persons (mother and daughter) and the regression of the symbolic action (shooting) towards the first infantile ideal (mother). In a Heiltsuk variant the daughter is a great medicine woman and brings the gift of reviving people with her.[4] The Tlatlasikoala have the same story [5] ; while in a Heiltsuk variant it is the father who is shot and not the daughter.[6] In the Comox [7] and Nootka variant [8] the supernatural people to whom the shaman

[1] Jochelson, *The Koryak*, pp. 238, 239.
[2] Jochelson, loc. cit., p. 240. Cf. ibid., pp. 223, 277.
[3] Boas, *Indianische Sagen von der Nord-Pazifischen Küste Amerikas*, 1898, p. 194.
[4] Boas, loc. cit., p. 255.   [5] Ibid., p. 190.
[6] Ibid., p. 238.   [7] Ibid., p. 94.   [8] Ibid., p. 99.

comes are really sea-animals and he fetches a wife from their submarine abode. Instead of an arrow we have a harpoon thrown at a whale in a fishing expedition and withdrawn. But the sea-lady proves a doubtful benefit to the shaman ; by coition with her he suffers castration as her hard scales rub his penis off.[1] These variants again are closely connected with the myths of the " wife-angler ". A mythological hero can do more than merely " fishing for compliments "—he fishes for a wife.[2] Atmolokot causes the submarine old woman to spit his lost fish-hook out ; instantly she gets better and recognizes the hero as her grandchild. (Instead of giving him her daughter as wife.) In Japan a fish swallows the hero's magic fish-hook but spits it out again. The hero marries the daughter of the sea-king who herself is a sea-animal, whilst on the other hand the fish who swallowed his hook is called " the red woman ". The two are doubles of the same figure and when the sea-princess follows her terrestrial lover to his home and is already in the family way, it is quite in accordance with the latent meaning of the myth to say that this has been caused by her *swallowing his fish-hook*.[3] The identity of fish-hook and disease-making arrow in these myths gives additional importance to certain cases in which *human* materials are used to fashion the fish-hook. Mauis' bait was his own ear,[4] and he fashioned his fish-hook from the jawbone of his children, or from the jawbone of his ancestress Mahuika.[5] The fish-hook or arrow which causes death gives life, and the reason why after a certain time the destructive wizard becomes the father of the healing art is that his destructive actions are connected with a certain amount of libido-transference on his victim ; they must be termed cases of sadistic coition rather than of destruction pure and simple.

The second bond between the medicine-man and his patient is *identification*. When a Kai magician is trying to kill a man whose soul he has " bound " he imitates every movement of his intended victim. He shows how the man feels pains in his side, he groans and cries like a sick man. His assistant offers consolation as friends usually do if somebody is ill. His friends come and see him and they are all very sympathetic about the sad state he is in. At last the moment

---

[1] Ibid., loc. cit., pp. 99, 100.
[2] L. Frobenius, *Zeitalter des Sonnengottes*, 1904, p. 280.
[3] K. Florenz, *Die historischen Quellen der Shinto Religion*, 1919, pp. 76–84.
[4] J. J. Polack, *Manners and Customs of the New Zealanders*, 1840, p. 13. Ibid., p. 13.
[5] Westervelt, *Legend of Mauis*, 1910, p. 82.

of death draws near. The wizard acts the part of an agonizing man, heaves a last sigh and falls prostrate. After some time the dead wizard gets up again ; for that day he has finished his drama.[1] One of the methods used by Dyak medicine-men is called " wrapping with Lantai " or floor laths. One of the Manangs personates a dead man. He is vested with every article of Dyak dress and ornament and lays himself down as dead. Then he is bound up in mats, wrapped up in slender bamboo laths tied together with rattans, taken out of the house and laid on the ground. He is supposed to be dead. After about an hour other Manangs loose him and bring him to life, and as he recovers the sick person is supposed to recover.[2] It is true that the magician cures by becoming possessed, but the disease he cures is frequently ascribed to the same supernatural reason.

Badi is the name given to the evil principle which according to the views of Malay medicine men attends everything that has life. It is described as the enchanting or destroying influence which issues from anything—from a tiger which one sees, from a poison tree which one passes under, or from the saliva of a mad dog. It is the contagious principle of morbid matter. There are a hundred and ninety of these mischiefs and the first originated from Adam's brood, or, according to another version, from the iguana or again from the " Heart of Timber ". The principal feature in the ceremony of " casting out " these mischiefs consists in repeating the appropriate charm, at the the same time taking a brush of leaves and stroking the patient downwards all over, from head to foot.[3] The evil spirit or " mischief " is supposed to leave the body of the patient and to proceed, guided by the many-coloured thread which the latter holds in his hand, to enter into a choice collection of " scapegoats " ready for him on a tray. These are little dough images of various kinds of birds and animals arranged on a tray and finally carried away by a " disease-boat ". It is a peculiar fact that the disease-boat is originally a two-masted vessel with galleries, fore and aft, armed with cannon, in fact the type of boat used by Malay Rajas on the Sumatran Coast. To make it still more acceptable the model was stained with turmeric or saffron, yellow being recognized as the royal colour among the Malays.[4] We can get some notion as to the real meaning of casting out the demon by ceremonies supposed to represent it or by things it is

[1] Ch. Keyser, " Aus dem Leben der Kaileute," *Deutsch Neu Guinea*, ii, p. 137.
[2] L. Roth, loc. cit., i, p. 280.
[3] W. Skeat, *Malay Magic*, 1900, pp. 426–30.
[4] Skeat, *Malay Magic*, p. 433.

compared to. A Negrito woman of Kedah was seized with one of her paroxysms and rushed away in a frantic fit to the jungle. The chief began to exorcise the demon by uprooting trees. When he had succeeded in uprooting the first stump he took some soil from the hole and rubbed it on her back and stomach. The stem of the stump was pinched in ; a sure sign of the presence of the demon. A second root was a creeper whose roots had grown across in the manner of a mandrake. The next thing he did was to eject saliva with chewed betel-leaf on the patient's stomach, and to conclude the ceremony two of the audience picked up a couple of fallen saplings and hurled them forcibly that the evil spirits might go with them.[1] A Dyak doctor will declare that there are *hantu* in the patient's body ; and he proceeds to extract them. Striking two or three times over the part where the pain is, he brings the charm down to the floor with a crack and he produces some fragments of wood or stone as the demon whom he has dislodged. They bring forth inimical demons from a patient's body just as a dentist extracts a tooth in civilized countries.[2] The state of a possessed patient in Bengal is described by Dalton as follows : " The affection comes on like a fit of ague lasting sometimes for a quarter of an hour, the patient or possessed person writhing and trembling with intense violence. He springs from the ground to the air with a succession of leaps all executed as if he were shot by an unseen agency. During this stage of the seizure he is supposed to be quite unconscious and rolls into the fire or under the feet of the dancers without sustaining any injury. He passes into the spasmodic stage, jerking his head with a circular movement." This ecstatic dance or, as we might also call it, hysteric fit reappears in the Vaishnava sect where it is supposed to represent the dance of the Gopis with Krishna, e.g. a love scene. Moreover it is performed at a Brahman marriage by a boy and a girl with the purpose of scaring away the spirits of evil.[3] Again among the Ainu we find the association of snake phobia with a certain kind of hysteria and with the theory of possession. This kind of hysteria, called *imu*, attacks mostly, though not exclusively, the women. Women who were bitten by snakes were always subject to these fits; and men sometimes. Nobody who is subject to these attacks can bear the sight of a snake or viper or even hear these animals mentioned. Once a man went off into this kind of hysteria by killing a large snake and taking a rat out of

---

[1] Skeat and Blagden, *Pagan Races of the Malay Peninsula*, 1906, ii, pp. 229–31.

[2] L. Roth, loc. cit., i, p. 260.

[3] Crooke, *Popular Religion*, i, pp. 154, 155.

its stomach. Women went off into hysterics when the missionary told them of the part played by the serpent in the fall of man. The eyes of the patients open very wide, stare fixedly, and glitter. The whole demeanour of such persons is one of abject fear. But the snake phobia is also acquired by psychic contagion alone, without having been bitten by snakes.[1] The Ainu regard the disease as a case of snake-possession,[2] and what kind of snake is really meant becomes pretty evident by another piece of information. Snake worship is particularly practised when an addition is being made to the family, especially when there is any difficulty in the matter. The image of the snake is placed upon the woman's shoulders and worshipped by her.[3]

The case we quoted from Borneo and others of a similar nature show the close connection between the universal sucking cure and the theory of disease caused by demoniac possession. The serpent or another penis symbol has been projected into the patient by a medicine-man or has taken up its abode definitely in the patient's body ; in either cases the patient appears to be a pregnant woman, and the relief obtained by the removal of the disease substance is delivery. The medicine-men of Hispaniola cured by suction and when they had extracted a stone or other alleged cause of sickness it was preserved as a sacred relic, especially by the women who looked upon it as of great aid in parturition.[4] If a child has a swollen spleen, the Kai invoke a spirit called Aidolo—" Come and help this child ; he is *pregnant with a disease-lump*. Cut it open, press and squash that blood and matter should come out and my child should get healthy." [5] As relieving a swollen part, making blood, matter or small objects (that may be penis, fæces or child symbols) come out of the patient seems to be the regular cure, we might say that the unconscious idea of being transformed into a woman, a pregnant woman, was regularly lurking in the background of disease. Now this is just one of the features of identification between the patient and the medicine-man. A Gipsy witch acquires her supernatural power by having intercourse with the demons who leave a serpent in her body.[6] In describing the stages of transformation from the normal attitude

[1] Batchelor, *The Ainu and their Folk-Lore*, 1901, pp. 299–303.
[2] Batchelor, loc. cit., p. 303.
[3] Batchelor, loc. cit., pp. 366, 368.
[4] I. G. Bourke, *The Medicine-Men of the Apache*, ix, Report 472. Gomara, *Hist. de las Indias*, pp. 172, 173.
[5] Keysser, loc. cit., p. 153.
[6] H. v. Wlislocki, *Volksglaube und religiöser Brauch d. Zigeuner*, 1891, p. 55.

to that of a " transformed ", i.e. homosexual shaman, Bogoras says that in the first stage of transformation the person subjected to it personates the woman only in the manner of braiding and arranging the hair. This usage is widespread among the Chukchee and is adopted not only by shamans at the command of their spirits but also by sick persons at the bidding of the shamans.[1] Indeed it would be no exaggeration to say that the calling of the medicine-man is simply *disease made permanent and sublimated into a vocation.* A Dyak doctor at initiation behaves like a patient and suffers the others to cure him.[2] A Chukchee suffering from syphilis had recourse to spirits to heal himself and after two years he had become completely restored and a shaman.[3] The process of acquiring inspiration appears to be so painful as to be regarded as a peculiar kind of sickness and every preparation for a performance is a sort of repetition of the initial process.[4]

It is a good argument for the validity of a result, though it may be monotonous as a piece of literature, if the same conclusion can be reached from several starting points. We have found the ontogenetic source for the shaman's addiction to sucking out " diseases " in the fixation to the mother's breast, and it would be only natural to suppose that in the happy feeling of satiety at the breast the baby identifies itself with the mother. Trying, however, to ascertain the explanation of this attitude on the patient's side we shall find that he regresses to exactly the same phase of development as the shaman. We must reconsider the evidence for the practices of the *Subachs* in the Western Sudan.

If the *Subach* begins by withdrawing his victim's soul, opening him, cutting him to pieces and letting him die in about a year, we have to do with one of the cases of opening explained in the previous chapter as passive homosexual phantasies. This is pretty evident when we are told that a long snout is projected into the victim's mouth. But then we are told that the victim is paralysed like a fearful child. If so the dream must refer to some episode in infantile life. Now the *Subach* appears to be a huge mass of flesh sitting on the victim's lips and the origin of the *Subach*-power is from women.[5] The *Subach* therefore seems to represent not only the father's penis but also the mother's nipple and behind the homosexual regression to a female attitude we find the regression to the impressions received by the child at the first introduction of the nipple into his mouth.

---

[1] Bogoras, loc. cit., p. 450.
[2] Ling Roth, loc. cit., i, p. 281.
[3] Bogoras, loc. cit., p. 428.
[4] Bogoras, loc. cit., pp. 420, 421.
[5] Frobenius, loc. cit., pp. 81, 82.

However, in Australia this opening is only the introduction to another operation, the removal of the kidney fat. As the treatment of boils, swelling parts of the body, the tension and the relief that follows the evacuation of putrid matter probably contributed to the origin of the sucking cure, we can regard the swollen part as a displaced penis and the relief obtained as derived from a sort of fission or self-castration. Frequently, as we know, the disease-causing agency appears in the guise of a snake, an indication of its phallic origin. The removal of the snake would therefore be castration and the medicine-man, like the black wizard, has inherited the quality of castrator both from the Father and Mother-Imago.

All this is not new in psychoanalysis. Ferenczi [1] has shown that there are libidinal forces set into action in organic disease and has described what he calls a pathoneurosis as a displacement of the genital function, as a genitalization of some other part of the body. We find that anthropological data agree with this view, and add that the treatment offered by the primitive medicine-man is adapted not to the organic but to the libidinal side of the process. This adaptation is produced by a Dialogue of the Unconscious between doctor and patient made possible by the identity of unconscious attitudes. For if we can say that disease from the unconscious point of view is a symbolic castration, we can also show that the medicine-man begins his career by being " opened ", that is castrated. Indeed we are occasionally told that before the *manang bali* in Borneo can assume female costume he is sexually disabled.[2] We decidedly doubt the accuracy of this statement; instead of taking it as a fact it seems rather to be an unconscious and correct interpretation of the initiation ceremony. He acquires his power in an initiation ceremony called *Bekliti*, i.e. " Opening ". The other *Manangs* cut his head open, take out his brains and wash and restore them, to give him a clear mind to penetrate into the mysteries of evil spirits and the intricacies of disease ; they insert gold dust into his eyes to give him keenness and strength of sight powerful enough to see the soul wherever it may have wandered ; they plant barbed hooks on the tips of his fingers to enable him to seize the soul and hold it fast ; and lastly they pierce his heart with an arrow to make him tender-hearted and full of sympathy with the sick and suffering. Of course these actions are not carried out but replaced by symbolic imitations. For instance a coconut shell is laid upon the head itself, etc. After this the man is no longer an *Iban* (Sea Dyak), he is a *Manang*. He is lifted from his earthly surroundings into a different

[1] S. Ferenczi, *Hysterie und Pathoneurosen*, 1919.
[2] Ling Roth, loc. cit., i, p. 270.

sphere of existence, and when engaged in his functions he makes a point of emphasizing this distinction by constant use of the two words in contrast to each other.[1] The next higher degree in the *Manang* hierarchy is acquired in a similar ceremony, the concluding act of which consists in the candidate lying down flat on the floor whilst the *Manangs* walk over him and trample upon him.[2]

Similar methods are frequently found in the initiation ceremonies of Australian medicine-men. In all these cases we find that a man is lifted out of the sphere of mere mortals by being killed (and resuscitated) ; we find that death is the path to this terrestrial Olympus. The shaman is a man who has been killed and thus lifted into the category of spirits. About fourteen miles to the south of Alice Springs there is a cave inhabited by the Iruntarinia or spirit individuals, each one of whom is the double of one of the ancestors of the tribe who lived in the Alcheringa, or in other words of some living member, as each one of these is but the reincarnation of one of the ancestors. When any man feels that he is capable of becoming a magician he lies down to sleep at the mouth of the cave but does not venture to go inside, for in that case he would not become a magician but would be spirited away for good. At break of day one of the Iruntarinia throws an invisible lance at the sleeping man. The lance enters his neck from behind, passes through the tongue, and, making therein a large hole, comes out through the mouth.[3] A second lance thrown by the Iruntarinia pierces the head from ear to ear ; the victim falls dead and is at once carried to the depths of the cave. In this cave the Iruntarinia remove all the internal organs and provide the man with a completely new set of them, after which he comes to life again.[4] The Iruntarinia may be replaced by very old members of the medical guild both in the Arunta and neighbouring tribes. A celebrated medicine-man of the Unmatjera tribe was initiated when a very old doctor came one day and threw some of his atnongara stones at him with a spear-thrower. Some hit him on the chest, others went right through the head from ear to ear, killing him. The old man then cut out all of his intestines, liver, heart, lungs—in fact everything. In the morning the old

[1] Ling Roth, loc. cit., i, pp. 281, 271. E. H. Gomes, *Seventeen Years among the Sea Dyaks of Borneo*, 1911, p. 178.

[2] H. Ling Roth, loc. cit., i, p. 281. Gomes, loc. cit., p. 179. *Manang* is the magician ; *manadak*, to sing incantations. Wilken, *De Verspreide Geschriften*, 1912, iii, p. 353. Cf. ibid., iii, p. 354 (*manang*).

[3] Cf. Strehlow, loc. cit., pp. 38–43.

[4] Spencer and Gillen, *Native Tribes*, pp. 522–4.

man placed some atnongara stones inside his body, in his arms and legs and covered over his face with leaves. He sang over him till his body was swollen and then he provided him with a completely new set of inside parts and patted him on the head, which caused him to jump up alive. When he awoke he could not remember what had happened and said : " I think I am lost." But when he looked round he saw the old medicine-man standing beside him and the old man said : " No, you are not lost ; I killed you a long time ago." [1] In the Warramunga tribe the medicine-men are made by the *Puntidir*, a spirit who lives out in the Mulga scrub and is the equivalent of the Iruntarinia of the Arunta. This is the account of how a Tjupila man of the Varanus lizard totem was made a medicine-man. He had been engaged in a fight near Renners Springs and was out in the scrub alone, spearing euro on the hillsides. He noticed two men walking about but at first did not pay any heed to them. He went down to a rock hole to get a drink and there he saw the two men again. Then he noticed that they were not some of his companions but strangers, so he became afraid of them and went to another water hole. Still more to his astonishment he found them seated down there by the water when he arrived. In his alarm he ran away expecting to be attacked every moment. Next day he spent wandering about but still he saw the two men who appeared to be watching his movements. The day after this he had just stooped down to drink, when he saw the two strangers once more standing close to him. He was very frightened and had just got the spear poised on the thrower when they said : " *Don't kill us, we are your father and brother." He knew then that they were really spirits,* but this evidently rather augmented than diminished his alarm. He wished to return to his *lubra* from these uncanny folk, but go where he would the two men always came up in some inexplicable manner. They told him to come with them and they would show him a big corroboree. But he said, " No, I want to go back to my own country," and so the two strangers whom he now recognized as *puntidirs* or spirit men, walked off. He sat down for some time and then got up and danced. The two *puntidirs* returned after a time looking very angry and bringing with them pointing bones. At night the man made a big fire and lay down to sleep, but while he slept the *puntidirs* came and " boned him " so that he died. While he was lying dead they cut him open, took all his organs out, providing him, in the orthodox manner, with a new set. Finally

---

[1] Spencer and Gillen, *Northern Tribes*, p. 481.

they put a little snake inside his body which endowed him with the powers of a medicine-man.[1]

This little snake is a characteristic animal of the medicine-man's craft.[2] He is also found in the other group of Warramunga doctors. These are initiated by old men of the Worgaia tribe. The candidates are not allowed to have any rest, but are obliged to stand or walk about until they are thoroughly exhausted and scarcely know what is happening to them. Sides are cut open, internal organs removed, and a new set provided as usual. A snake called Irman, the great efficacy of which is derived from the fact that it comes from the Worgaia country, is put into their head. Finally the *kupitja* supposed to have been made by the snakes in the Alcheringa is put through a hole into the nasal septum. Having thus two snakes in their body it is no wonder that this set of medicine-men should be called *Urkutu* (the general term for snakes) themselves. Whilst in certain respects they are very careful of their conduct they are allowed peculiar licence in other directions. On one occasion one of them lost his powers simply because during a fight he had struck a tribal father, who was a doctor much older than himself, with a boomerang. On the other hand they had certain privileges with regard to women and they could not be punished when interfering with other men's *lubras*.[3]

In the Binbinga tribe the doctors are stated to be made by two spirits, Mundadji and Munkaninji, father and son. The father catches the novice and kills him. He cuts him open right down the middle line, takes out all his organs and exchanges them for his own which he inserts in his body. When it is all over the younger spirit Munkaninji comes up and restores him to life, telling him that he is now a medicine-man and showing him how to extract bones and other forms of evil magic out of men. Then the spirit takes him up into the sky and he sees his friends in his own camp mourning for him. But gradually he recovers from his dazed condition and everybody knows that he has been made into a medicine-man. When he takes the bone out of other people the son-spirit is supposed to be near at hand watching him.[4] In the Mara tribe the proceedings are very similar.[5]

In the Boulia district a nature spirit called Malkari will insert a pebble, bone, or quartz-crystal in the inside of the future medicine-man. Or the *Karnmari* (water snake) may point a bone at a man ;

---

[1] Spencer and Gillen, *Northern Tribes*, pp. 481–4.
[2] Cf. the serpent of Aesculapius.
[3] Spencer and Gillen, *Northern Tribes*, pp. 484–7.
[4] Spencer and Gillen, *Northern Tribes*, p. 487.   [5] Ibid., p. 488.

one day he sees the dreaded monster undulating along the surface of the water. He runs home to the camp, recounts what has taken place and is sick for many years afterwards. The years roll on and he will suddenly blossom forth with all the powers peculiar to his profession. Another being who can initiate medicine-men is a ghost who haunts the grave.[1] At the Pennefather River the medicine-men are said to have learnt their profession at the graveside from the spirits of deceased persons.[2] Threlkeld tells us that Murrokun is the name of a mysterious bone obtained by the *karakals* (medicine-men). " Three of these sleep on the grave of a recently interred corpse ; during their sleep in the night the dead person inserts a mysterious bone into each who feel the puncture not more severely than the sting of an ant. These bones remain in the flesh of the doctors without any inconvenience to them until they wish to kill any person, when by magical power they destroy him, causing the mysterious bone to enter his body and so occasion death." [3] When the old wizards of the Euahlayi tribe desire to initiate a boy into their profession they take him to a tribal burial ground at night and tie him down. Various supernatural beings appear ; a big star, his totem animal, a snake, a giant who drives a yam stick through his head and inserts a sacred stone into him, and last of all the spirits of the dead who corroboree round him, instruct him in songs full of sacred lore and tell him how he can call upon their aid.[4] Perhaps the crudest and most savage form of the rite has been noted in the Wiimbaio tribe. Here one *Mekigar* could initiate another in the following manner : They procured the corpse of a man, usually by digging one up. The bones were pounded up and chewed. The candidate was plastered with human excrement and carried about with him the humerus of a disinterred body wrapped round with twigs at which he gnawed. These men are at such times brought to a state of frenzy, their eyes are bloodshot, and they behave like maniacs.[5]

Seeing ghosts was the qualification for becoming a medicine-man in the Mukjarawaint tribe. The Wotjobaluk had the " opening " method of initiation. The medicine-man's power is derived from the quartz-crystal and from that time on he can " pull things out

[1] W. E. Roth, " Superstition, Magic, and Medicine," *North Queensland Ethnography Bulletin*, No. 5, 1903, p. 29.

[2] Roth, loc. cit., p. 30.

[3] L. E. Threlkeld, *An Australian Language as spoken by the Awabakal*, 1892, p. 47.

[4] K. L. Parker, *The Euahlayi Tribe*, 1905, pp. 25, 26.

[5] Howitt, loc. cit., p. 404.

of himself " such as quartz, wood, charcoal and also out of his arms
something like feathers which are considered to have healing
properties.[1] In the Jajaurung tribe we have a trance-visit to the
world of spirits [2] ; in the Kurnai tribe the ancestral ghosts visit the
sleeper.

The Narrangga medicine-man communicated with departed
spirits.[3] According to the Port Jackson tribes (Cammeraygal),
a man becomes a *Car-rah-di* by sleeping at the grave of a deceased
person. " During that awful sleep the spirit of the deceased would
visit him, seize him by the throat, and opening him, take out his
bowels, which he replaced and the wound closed up." [4] In a detailed
account which we have of the making of medicine-men in the
Wiraduri tribe the novice tells us that when he was taken into the
bush he began to see things that his mother could not see. He was
beginning to see the ghosts. At his initiation his old father showed
him a piece of quartz-crystal in his hand and when he looked the old
man went down into the ground and then he saw him come up again,
covered with red dust. That is, the old man dies and is reborn
before the eyes of his son. His father led him to a grave ; he went
inside and saw a dead man who rubbed him all over to make him
clever. When he came out of the grave his father pointed to a tiger
snake and said : " That is your guardian spirit ; it is mine also." [5]

In the case of the Umnatjera medicine-man we find, just as in the
case of a person who has been " opened ", a complete oblivion
of all that took place. When we are told that the Arunta
medicine-man is wounded on his tongue we may assume that
the tongue is a substitute for the penis. The Arunta medicine-
man has a lance thrown into him, the Warramunga has Atnongara stones put in—the same that he, in his turn, projects into
the patient. The arrow in the Dyak medicine-man is to make
him feel sympathy with the sick, i.e. to identify himself with them.
If we regard the arrow as Cupid's dart (cf. the case of the Omaha)
we understand the point ; at the root of the *identification we have
the sublimated homosexual coitus-phantasy of patient and doctor*. It is,
however, among the Warramunga that we find direct authority
for our views ; a snake is injected into the body of a medicine-man

---

[1] Howitt, loc. cit., p. 404.

[2] W. Stanbridge, " On the Aborigines of Victoria," *Transactions of the
Ethnological Society*, i, 1861, p. 300.

[3] Howitt, loc. cit., p. 405.

[4] D. Collins, *An Account of the English Colony in New South Wales*,
1804, p. 383.

[5] Howitt, loc. cit., pp. 406, 407.

by other medicine-men ; this same serpent endowing him with supernatural power, he becomes as a serpent himself and is entitled to do what he likes with the women.

We can distinguish two phases of the initiation ceremony ; one of them, the injection of a new phallus into the medicine-man's body, is a homosexual coitus, the other, the removal of the intestines, is castration—castration of course compensated by the new penis and the new indestructible intestines that replace the old ones. On going into the details of the whole situation we see that this passive function as a form of gratification is not original ; its seems rather to be a punishment re-elaborated into a gratification by the unconscious. If we try to ascertain the phylogenetic past of the initiation scene we are struck by the fact that the initiators are either old men or ghosts, in both cases representatives of the Father Imago. This endopsychic knowledge makes an attempt at breaking through the veil in the vision of our Warramunga medicine-men with the spirits appearing in the guise of his father and brother, and in some cases we have the father himself as the initiator. But why should the father cut the medicine-man to pieces ? It seems that if our neophyte is symbolically eaten by the spirits, this form of initiation represents the reversal of another type in which we find the novice eating a corpse. Probably it represents also the reversal of the primal scene, the sons killing and devouring the father in order to gain access to the women of the horde. In this obedience after death a reversal of the original scene takes place ; it is not they who eat the father, it is the father who eats his children. Moreover they deny their male striving that lies at the root of the whole tragedy ; they have not killed the father and cohabited with the mother, for they are women, symbolized by being possessed by the ancestors, or castrated men (the intestines removed). In the second act of the drama the compensation follows, or as the Binbinga put it, there are two spirits—the father who kills the medicine-man and the son who resuscitates him.

Having put forward the theory that disease for the unconscious of primitive man is a symbolic castration and that the initiation of the medicine-man really represents the play repetition of the same phobia and therefore a reaction to it, we have also found that in the case of the medicine-man this castration appears to be the unconscious punishment for the Great Sin. This interpretation of *disease as a punishment* for a violated taboo or something done against divine will is frequently found.

Madness is regarded by the Ainu as a case of possession by the devil and should be treated accordingly. However, none are supposed to be thus afflicted unless there has been some special sin committed or a direct selling of oneself to the demons.[1] Among the Nandi if a person falls ill it is attributed to one of his or her deceased ancestors or relatives and a brother or other near relation is sent for to propitiate the angry spirit.[2] In Nias, disease is regarded as due to the sins of the ancestral gods and there are special demons of disease whose wrath against immortality brings disease to mortals and who must be propitiated to obtain recovery.[3] In China the family may perhaps attribute disease to some unknown god or goddess who has been offended through some act or word of the person. Sometimes however the disease is due to the spirit of his or her former wife or husband, that is the wife or husband in a previous state of existence. After a long search this spirit has finally succeeded in finding his partner. The sick person sometimes declares this to be the fact, or rather the mouth of the sick is used by the spirit to make this disclosure.[4]

If disease appears both as a punishment and as a renewal of conjugal partnership we have the well-known condensation of libidinal gratification and punishment in the same symptom. The Ainu use of the word *turen* applied both to good and evil seems to convey our meaning. It signifies " to be inspired by the gods " as when a prophet prophesies ; then " to be possessed with a devil " ; then " to be afflicted with disease " as a punishment for evil deeds ; next " to have special blessing from God " ; and lastly " to have God's protection " as when engaged in some great or dangerous under-taking.[5]

On the punishment side, disease appears to be castration, but it is also the fundamental form of libido gratification ; it represents coitus. The affected part is genitalized ; tension followed by relief is what the female experiences in giving birth and the male in the ejaculating of the seminal fluid. Therefore the swollen part may be a symbol of pregnancy, the object withdrawn being the child, but from a male point of view the swollen part is the penis and what is removed is the seminal fluid.

The fact that sub-incision, a typical castration ceremony, occurs in Fiji and Tonga as a therapeutic practice, fully demonstrates our point of view. The urethra is opened and a thread passes in so that

---

[1] Batchelor, loc. cit., p. 312.

[2] Hollis, *Nandi*, p. 69.

[3] J. P. Kleiweeg de Zwaan, *Die Insel Nias bei Sumatra I. Die Heilkunde der Niasser*, 1913, p. 12.

[4] Doolittle, *Social Life of the Chinese*, 1866, i, p. 146.

[5] Batchelor, loc. cit., pp. 584, 584.

one end hangs from the artificial opening and another from the meatus. The thread acts as a seton and is occasionally drawn forwards and backwards so as to produce pain and a discharge of blood. It is employed for tetanus and for various diseases, the idea being to get rid of the blood by way of the urethra.[1]

Now there are two fundamental animistic theories of disease found in mankind : possession, that is, a foreign demon or substance in the body, and ecstasy, the idea that the soul has left the body and must be brought back accordingly. In a book recently published by no less an anthropological authority than Rivers these two theories are ascribed to different cultural areas. Rivers says : " The belief in the production of disease by the abstraction of the soul or one of several souls appears to be limited to Indonesia, Papuo-Melanesia, and America. We do not know of it in Asia ; and though disease may be ascribed to absence of the soul or of the vital principle in West Africa, this belief does not appear to have given rise to the organized system of practices which we find in Indonesia and to a less extent in America.

" India and Africa, on the other hand, are pre-eminently the seat of the belief in the production of disease by possession. These two beliefs . . . are more or less opposed to one another. If the phenomena of disease are much the same all the world over, and if the similarities of belief and action are due to the uniformity of the human mind, how comes it that men should have been led to these very different beliefs and why should these beliefs have different distributions ? "[2]

This long quotation serves to show the attitude of the new migration school in anthropology. Rivers was the head and most cautious representative of this school and of course everybody would expect that the facts taken as a starting point for these views are correctly stated. I am sorry to say they are not. It is always a dangerous thing in anthropology to rely on an *argumentum ex silentio*. Now, according to Rivers, the hunt for the truant soul ought not to occur beyond the area given above.

In the Wimmera district in Australia, when a person is ill the wizard is sent for to throw a good spell on him. He takes something like a rope out of his stomach and climbs up to the sky to have an interview with the shadow. On his return if the man is to recover he says : " Your shadow is come back and you will soon be well,"

---

[1] W. H. R. Rivers, *Medicine, Magic, and Religion*, 1924, pp. 104, 105.
[2] Rivers, loc. cit., pp. 79, 80.

but if he is to die, he says : " I could not get your shadow." [1] Now Australia is not so important for the ethnological question concerned, as it may be regarded as an extension of the Papuo-Melanesian area. But there is plenty of evidence in Asia itself, as I shall show below, and as Rivers himself describes the existence of the practice in all other continents, his whole argument, drawn from an alleged limited distribution of the soul-hunt, falls to the ground.

One of the methods used by Chinese medicine-men is to bring back the departing spirit of the sick man. A bamboo eight or ten feet in length is provided with fresh green leaves and a white cock at the end. One end of a red cord is tied around the centre of a two foot measure and the other end is made fast around the bamboo among the green leaves. A coat belonging to the dead man and very recently worn is suspended on the measure, its end being put into the arm-holes of the garment. A metallic mirror is tied to the measure in such a manner as to be a few inches above the shoulders of the garment in the place where the head of an individual would come if the coat were worn. A member of the family takes this bamboo pole and holds it loosely in his grasp. The priest now begins to call the name of the sick person, to ring his bell, etc., trying to induce the sick man's spirit to enter the coat. The white cock and the mirror are important, they represent the soul. After a while the pole is observed to turn slowly round in the hands of its holder—a sure proof of the presence of the sick man's spirit in the coat. Then they take the coat from the bamboo pole and as soon as possible place it on the body of the sick man.[2] The next Asiatic instance is quoted by Frazer, and as Frazer is the only authority for customs connected with the absence and recall of the soul, it is interesting to observe that Rivers managed to overlook it. The Mongols explain sickness by the absence of the patient's soul. The soul either does not want to go back into the body or he cannot find his way ; therefore one thing is to make the body as attractive as possible for the soul and the other is to show him the way back by means of a coloured cord.[3]

A frequent reason for disease among the Chukchee is that one or all the souls of a certain person are stolen by the demons. The shaman can find and restore the missing soul, usually in the shape of a black beetle. When put on the body of the patient it will crawl all over

[1] H. Livingstone, *Grammar and Vocabulary of the Minyung people*, p. 24. Bound with Threlkeld, *Awabakal*.

[2] Doolittle, loc. cit., i, pp. 150, 151.

[3] Frazer, *Taboo and the Perils of the Soul*, 1911, p. 44. (Another Australian case is quoted by Frazer.)

his head, trying to find a hole to slip in. Then the shaman will open the skull and put the beetle in its proper place. The beetle may enter through the mouth, armpit, fingers, toes, intestines, etc.[1] The capture of the lost soul is effected by dreams or in a shamanistic trance. Then he will begin to blow the soul into the patient's body through the breast, the ear, or the crown of the head. Sometimes the shaman refuses to put the soul back personally and orders that the mother or the sister of the patient, or in their absence his father or brother, sometimes his wife, should go out at dawn next morning and pick up a blade of grass, saying : " Here, here I found the little fellow." The " little fellow " is the soul represented in this ceremony by the grass and it is tied to the collar strings of the patient. Sometimes a shaman of sufficient power who cannot find the lost soul may blow a part of his own soul into the patient's body. The patient is then said to become the son of the shaman.[2] An Altai shaman chases the truant soul of the sacrificed bird.[3] When offering a sacrifice as a substitute for the sick man, a Yakut shaman says that people will feel sympathy for the patient and that the goddesses called " the *Mothers* " will restore his soul.[4] Exactly the same theory and practice is found among the Gypsies in Hungary and Roumania, namely that the demons have stolen the patient's soul but will give it back for a sacrifice.[5]

If we consider that the soul is drawn out of the body by " the Mothers ", that among the Chukchee a mother is said to be the right person to restore it, that when the Chukchee shaman transmits a part of his soul to the patient he by this act becomes the patient's father, we cannot fail to see that the exit of the soul is a supernatural equivalent to the act of procreation. The soul leaving the body is the seminal fluid. The Gypsies say that the chief of a tribe must give his demission after the birth of his third son. For with every son a part of his guardian spirit leaves him and when he has had three the small amount of spiritual power he retains is supposed to be insufficient for keeping the tribe from danger. A person is completely forsaken by his guardian spirit if he (or she) has become a widower or widow four times and remarries once more or if he (or she) has begotten or given birth to nine children.[6] The soul leaving the body is birth from the woman's point of view or ejaculation

---

[1] Bogoras, loc. cit., p. 333.   [2] Bogoras, loc. cit., pp. 463–5.

[3] W. Radloff, *Aus Sibirien*, 1893, ii, p. 23.

[4] F. S. Krauss, " Das Schamanentum der Jakuten nach Priklonskij," *Mitt. d. Anthr. G. in Wien*, xviii, 1888, p. 175.

[5] Wlislocki, loc. cit., pp. 60, 61.   [6] Wlislocki, loc. cit., pp. 45, 46.

of the semen from the point of view of the male. We can therefore explain the two animistic theories of disease as built upon the male and the female function in coitus. The exit of the soul from the body is what the male does in cohabitation, while being possessed by a demon is what happens to the female. Or we might also say that the anxiety in the former case corresponds to reluctance against the expenditure of the semen ; in the latter the anxiety is a displaced erotic tension, and can be relieved by a simulated expenditure of the seminal fluid.

Should we therefore ask what disease means and what the therapy offers to the unconscious of the savage, our answer would run as follows. Disease is a displaced erotic tension, a genitalization of a non-genital part of the body. This process is due to what Ferenczi calls the " genitofugal " current of the libido, to a reflux of libido from the genital member to other portions of the body. The reason for this reflux is evidently a resistance against the final loss of the germ-plasm as the ultimate outcome of genital centralization. This state being in itself due to the castration phobia (dread of fission), it appears also as castration to the unconscious. Disease being in itself both castration and coitus, or rather a non-genital coitus connected with the dread of castration, it can only be relieved by the medicine-man, who, accepting this unconscious attitude, acts an autotomy, a fission, a process that involves the two aspects of castration and coitus. The essence of primitive therapy, therefore, seems to be libidinal gratification. Having maintained the oral, anal, and the displaced genital fixation, the medicine man is in a position to satisfy all the libidinal demands of the patient arising from the same sources. As the medicine-man plays in this drama the rôles of the phallic father, the loving mother, and the sucking child [1] he can do anything the patient really desires. For the helpless patient is really regressing to the state of an infant in arms while the affected part of his body is playing the nipple or the phallus.

By indicating above what disease is and what the cure can be we are also in a position to unify the manifold aspects in the character of the medicine-man. The disease is a reflux of the genital libido ; the medicine-man, the agent that stops this reflux, turns it into the right channel and obtains an outlet for this tension. Now Greek healing gods, Aesculapius among others, are symbolized by the serpent.

[1] The Masai story of the origin of the medicine-men is as follows. The first medicine-man was such a small person that he was first of all believed to be a child. He was taken by the Aiser clan to their kraal where it was discovered that he was a medicine-man. Hollis, *Masai*, p. 326.

Among the Kurnandaburi the seminal fluid is the healing agency.[1] The first medicine-man of the Marind-anim is born from male sperm without female intervention.[2] The Kagaba medicine-man heals by stones that are called "seminal stones" or phalli.[3] We shall therefore say that just as the genital act summarizes or condenses all pre-genital organizations, the medicine-man with his numerous pre-genital fixations is still from the patient's point of view a personification of the penis. It is he who obtains relief from tension, procuring release for the libido that has flowed back from the genital organ to the body. According to the belief of the Kabi and Wakka, a man went to sleep at the margin of a water hole and when the usual exchange of organs had been effected by Dhakkun, the rainbow serpent, he awoke with a rope in his inside as a *manngurnur*, i.e. a man full of life.[4] Following our usual incredulous method, we shall regard this statement with some degree of suspicion ; if he is said to be so very full of life it seems that we are groping in the darkness somewhere near the grim reality of death. All the accounts of the medicine man's initiation begin by the statement that the spirits kill the candidate, that he falls into a death-like sleep, sleeps on a grave, eats a corpse, and is inspired by the ghosts. May we hazard the conjecture that behind the identification with the father this shows a love for the dead, for death in general, that what we see here is the death-impulse at work ? If we believe with Freud that the two main components of a human being are the Impulse of Life and the Impulse of Death, we shall be astonished at noticing that very little reference to the activity of the latter is to be found in psychoanalytic literature. It lies deep and there is a strong resistance against noticing it. Yet we have the clue to its work in Freud's view that sadism is the death-impulse projected out of the individual. We have seen that the sadistic impulse is carried over by our medicine-men from the oral through the anal to the genital phase of development, while on the other hand they commence their career by a simulated death or by closest contact with a corpse. Indeed they preserve as long as they live a morbid attraction for the phase of life that is a transition to death, to disease. It will therefore not be too much to say that the choice of a life-giving vocation is determined by the effort made within them to counterbalance the activity of the death-impulse, that during his whole life the medicine-man is fighting against his own tendency to die when he finds that tendency in others.

---

[1] Howitt, loc. cit., p. 411.   [2] Wirz, loc. cit., i, pp. 91–2.
[3] Preuss, " Forschungsreise," *Anthropos*, xiv–xv, p. 1052.
[4] Mathew, *Two Tribes*, p. 172.

All his " phallic " activity is merely a brilliant mask, a veil used by the life-impulse to cover what no man can see without horror. And the patient ? Is it a commonplace to say that the death-impulse manifests itself in disease ? [1] Commonplace or not, it is evidently true. Life hides death by genitalization, resists the attack by simulating the great life-giving act. Compared to death itself, the idea of death as a coitus, even of castration, is merely a substitute, a consolation offered by the unconscious.

6 ADDENDA

(a) Death and Castration

The view of the relation of the death-impulse and castration anxiety and all that follows from that view as held by the author in 1925, when delivering his course of lectures at the Institute of Psycho-Analysis in London, is not the only possible conclusion that can be arrived at from a psycho-analytical point of view. Indeed the fact that in most cases when we find the notion of death in the open version of the dream, analysis shows that the latent content of the dream is castration is a very strong argument against connecting our conscious concept of death with the metapsychological hypothesis of a death-impulse. It must also be observed that the situation is really strictly analogous in both cases, i.e. in clinical and anthropological psycho-analysis. What we find in our patients is that they dream of death and really mean castration, or, as it has been put by psycho-analysts, there is nothing that corresponds to our notion of death in the unconscious. Primitive races have a universal fear of sorcerers who kill them, but if we analyse the mode of procedure we find that the sorcerer kills by castrating his victim. Again we may reconsider the situation in animism and animistic myths. Death is the conscious side of the picture while the latent content can easily be disclosed as castration. We may go even further and show that even what might be expected to be a reality-fear assumes the form of castration anxiety. " If a man dreams before a fight that he is carrying a baby girl with a large vulva, it portends his death, and the vulva represents the arrow wound he will receive." [2] This dream shows both the connection of the genitofugal or regressive trend with anxiety representing the adult man as a baby girl and the

[1] Cf. since these lectures have been delivered, F. Alexander, *Psychoanalyse der Gesamtpersönlichkeit*, 1927, p. 209.

[2] G. Landtmann, *The Kiwai Papuans of British New Guinea*, 1927, p. 278.

castration-complex underlying the reality-fear of the wound; a man who is wounded is castrated, has a vulva instead of a penis, and is merely a baby girl. Crocodiles are undoubtedly a very realistic cause for anxiety in New Guinea, nevertheless the deaths caused by these saurians are invariably attributed to magic.[1] What this means is easy to see if we know that all magic is directly or indirectly derived from the female sexual organ " just as fingers branch off from the hand ", and therefore the mere idea of nudity in the case of woman evokes the greatest abhorrence.[2] There is therefore much to be said in favour of an interpretation that does not go beyond the idea of castration and regards the concept of death as merely the conscious equivalent of the unconscious dread of castration.

It is evident that there must be some other arguments on the opposite side that induce me not to cancel the daring hypothesis which attempts to correlate a psychic system with the death-impulse. A similar suggestion has been made of late by Dr Hermann, who believes that the conscious part of our psychic apparatus must be built up on energy derived from the death-impulse. The function of establishing relations he regards as somehow belonging to the order of formalistic, lifeless phenomena in contrast to the more vivid affective attitude of the unconscious, and he is therefore inclined to suppose that the conscious system and the super-ego are more closely connected with the death-impulse and the unconscious with the life-impulse. We should therefore have to suppose that a defusion of impulses, a release of the death-impulse, takes place in the conscious.[3] If we accept this position we might also suppose that the typical defence mechanism of this system, repression, being essentially a withdrawal of (preconscious) cathexis, the opposite attitude embodied in the unconscious or rather in the Id is based on an accumulation of cathexis, and that this (libidinal) cathexis was accumulated as a defence mechanism against a psychic system correlated with the death-impulse. In other words we should have an alternation of accumulation and withdrawal of cathexis of life and death as under-lying the strata of our psyche. Death conquered by life (accumulation of cathexis, genitopetal trend) would mean the superposition of a libidinal system (the unconscious) on a system of destructive energies. These two systems [4] might be regarded as connected with the Id

[1] Cf. *Papua, Annual Report*, 1916, p. 85.

[2] Landtmann, loc. cit., p. 238.

[3] Hermann, " Das System Bw," *Imago*, xii, 203.

[4] I.e. the unconscious that corresponds to the death-impulse and the libidinal unconscious.

while in the ego and super-ego we have a defusion, a liberation of the death or destructive impulse that gives rise to our conscious psychical system. Thus the conclusions arrived at by Dr Hermann fall into line with the avowedly tentative suggestion put forward in this book, viz. that taking the destructive trend (death-impulse) and a correlated psychic system as our starting point, the unconscious as we know it might be due to a tendency to accumulate libido as a defence mechanism against the death-impulse (the genitopetal trend of Ferenczi) while the higher psychic systems originate as defence mechanism of the ego against an over-drainage of libido, against the loss of too much seminal fluid, against castration (the genitofugal trend of Ferenczi). There is at least one important fact in favour of this suggestion. Although the usual thing is that death in dream-life means castration or is a substitute for castration, yet there are dreams in which we find the reverse, i.e. that castration appears as a substitute, a milder form of death [1] (*Pars pro toto*). It might therefore be suggested that as the idea of death is latent in these dreams and absent in the unconscious (meaning the psychic system we usually have to deal with), the latent death-concept is here rooted in a still deeper layer, i.e. in the death-impulse itself.

(b) The personification of the penis

In order to avoid misunderstandings that would very probably arise from the use of this expression, I think it is necessary to explain what I mean when I call, not a mythical, but a real human being, the personification of the penis.

[1] Dream of a patient, age 30, journalist.

" I call on the fair woman but am told by her father that I must wait, as she is in the dining room, having her luncheon. I know that this is not true, that she is washing her vagina and not eating. Her father, an ugly dwarfish hunchback, speaks in an improbably deep, exaggeratedly virile voice. He disappears and I find myself talking to my mother in the antechamber of the flat we occupied in my childhood. I try to talk to my mother in the style or voice of the dwarf but I can keep it up only for a few minutes. Taking my watch from my pocket I tell her that I must go home ; it is late. My watch is covered with fluid enamel under the glass, I move it up and down so that a part of the real watch becomes visible under the enamel."

[1] Daly, " Hindu Mythologie und Kastrationskomplex," *Imago*, xiii, p. 198.

The day before he dreamt this dream the patient had really visited the fair lady. He found her with her father, the dwarf, and her mother having their afternoon coffee. The lady shared her coffee with him and he was, of course, obliged to do as if he relished it. But it was disgusting, lukewarm, like urine. At home he wouldn't have thought of drinking it if it had been served in this manner. This reminds him of horses urinating in the street and of their powerful penis. The woman's father is disgusting and uncanny and really has an unnaturally deep voice. The scene of his trying to imitate this voice reminds him how in his childhood he used to imitate the clergyman whom he saw in church at the very same spot in their old lodging where he talks to his mother in the dream. She was amused by this performance. After visiting the fair lady he felt a terrible nausea and he does not know whether the coffee or the father (the dwarf) were the chief objects of his disgust. Finally he remarks that the position of his watch (a present from his mother, which he is very proud of and regarded as indestructible) reminds him of a picture in a book on caricatures. A gentleman hands a bonbon to a lady in a *chambre separée* so that only a small part of the sweet is visible, the rest is wrapped in silver paper. The drawing is evidently an allusion to the penis as it emerges from the foreskin when the erection takes place.

The dream shows the whole structure of his neurosis. He refrains from having intercourse with the lady he loves because of the disgust connected with the coffee. Besides the urinating horses, this calls up a traumatic episode of his infancy : the disgust he felt when some bigger boys smeared his face with human excrement. His failure to imitate the girl's father is evidently the great failure of his infancy in imitating his own father in his relation to his mother. A small part of the watch comes out of the enamel ; an incomplete erection. The disgust felt at the sight of the hunchback dwarf is derived from a repressed homosexual attitude, from the desire to be impregnated by the father's penis. The glans penis coming out of the foreskin reminds him of circumcision (he is not a Jew), and then of how he used to take a bath with his father and see his father's big penis, and how his father told him that if somebody had a small penis the girls would not like him. Thus the uncanny dwarf also represents this anxiety, and in connection with circumcision it must be interpreted as his own penis after castration. From this point of view the appearance of the dwarf is an attempted consolation ; the penis survives as an independent being after castration. Evidently, envy was provoked by the father's remarks in the bath and by the sight of his big penis, and the desire to cut it off would follow as a natural consequence. The dwarf in real life is uncanny because he represents an unexpected realization of this desire, and the reaction of course is complete submission to the father and identification with the mother in the sexual act instead of the desire to possess her. The associations pointing towards urine and excrements are rudiments of infantile sexual theories and remind us of Ferenczi's views of the genital impulse as a condensation of the anal and urethral trends.

2. Second dream of the same patient, several months later.

" I am an apprentice in a big building, a sort of factory, but at the same time I am going to give a lecture in another big public building. I want to leave the factory and the inspector says : ' You are here the first day and go away during work-hours. All right, but we shall not pay you for this half-hour, not even half-pay, the time of communist rule is over ! ' ' More's the pity,' I say, ' a new communism would be highly desirable ! ' The inspector winks as if that was quite his opinion. In the public building I am astonished to see that one entrance is dirty, the other clean and very beautiful. The room where I should give the lecture is in the clean part of the building. Suddenly I remember that I have forgotten to prepare the last and most important part of the lecture. I rush home down a winding staircase, but there is somebody, I think, a woman, who goes before me. I want to outdistance her and manage to do so by relinquishing my hold on the rails of the stairs and simply floating down in the air. On my way home I meet a very disgusting fellow G. L. ; he is dressed in white like an apprentice in a candy shop, and presses a hot-water bottle to his stomach. I tell him I am in a great hurry, and invite him to come to my lecture."

The fact that he is now capable of dreaming a dream that is a sort of compromise between the demands of reality (factory) and his own desires (lecture) he regards as due to the last hour of analysis. Then he begins to talk about G. L., who is a degenerate, disagreeable fellow. Rabbis respect him very much, because they say his family is of old Jewish nobility, indeed of royal descent. He calls this acquaintance of his, ironically, the King of the Jews. There is something clammy about him. Then quite abruptly, " *He is just a penis* " (using the Hungarian colloquial term). I remind him of the fact that he complains of the same soft clammy feeling if he takes hold of a pigeon and we have had abundant proof that this means the same thing. Then it is again something to do with onanism, he thinks. He begins to talk about the house, which reminds him of other houses in previous dreams. When I suggest the womb-interpretation derived from previous dreams he remarks that in that case the dirty entrance would be the anus and the clean exit, where he is to deliver his lecture, the vagina. Finally, he says that he would like to be an analyst himself and he thinks that he is serving his apprenticeship to the craft here, in being analysed. I point out that in that case the factory in the dream is also analysis (a dream factory), that he feels he is making progress, but there is one thing he must run home for before he can give his lecture, and that is his genitality. It seems that the disagreeable clammy King of the Jews whom he meets on the way is not only a penis but also the analyst. " Quite possible," he says, " the King of the Jews is Jesus, quite a good idea to call the penis a little Jesus. Now I think of you," he says, " with a crown on your head."

The dream figure, who is also a real friend of his, is thus a personification of his own penis and represents all the ambivalent feelings linked up with onanism. But he is also the analyst, i.e. the sorcerer, and the part of analysis which must be worked through is just the fact that the analyst appears to him in the light of a penis, i.e. his homosexuality. The chief progress from dream 1 to dream 2 is that instead of the father we now find the analyst in the focus of attention and that instead of being pregnant in his phantasies he has now impregnated the father-analyst (hot-water bottle is what his wife, who is now in her seventh month, uses).

Now we can see what is meant by interpreting the sorcerer as a collective personification of the penis. The tendency to personify the penis is an overcompensation of the castration complex, an attempt to find a substitute for what one might be deprived of. At the same time this penis which appears as an independent human being is the father's penis, the realization of a desire to have a penis as big as the father's member. It is therefore always connected with the negative aspects of the Oedipus complex—with homosexuality. As the sorcerer is one of the central elements, or perhaps the great central element of every primitive social organization, this is also in harmony with the very general interpretation of the social trends which regard these as due to sublimated homosexuality. A theory of Ferenczi which distinguishes between the prohibitive aspects of the super-ego and what he calls the pleasure-ego based on the personification of the penis must also be mentioned in this connection. For the similarity of the magician and his realm of wish-fulfilment and the pleasure-ego is quite evident, so that the merging of the prohibitive (paternal) super-ego with the pleasure-ego as a psychical process might explain the sociological process of how the parts of chief and magician tend to be acted by the same person.

(c) Savage and Medicine-man in modern Europe and the Origin of the Super-Ego

Two years after I had written this book, but before I sent the manuscript to the publisher, I had a case in analysis which gave me such striking proofs for all that has been said in the first three chapters of this book that I decided to publish these data before the analysis was finished. The patient is a young man, the son of a German mother and a Hungarian father. He had spent all his life in Germany and the colonies and yet he came to Budapest for analysis. Besides certain infantile memories the chief reason why he came to Budapest was that his father's surname was Sándor—like Ferenczi's. After having been in analysis (obsessional neurosis with schizophrenic and paranoid tendencies) for about ten days, he related the following dream :—

"I am in a very beautiful boudoir with my mother. She is in bed and I am standing before the bed. She catches hold of me, draws me to the bed and I have intercourse with her. I have the feeling of *ejaculatio præcox.*"

At this juncture he interrupts the story and tells me that he would like to hit me. Then he goes on :—

"I had intercourse with her a second time but this time without ejaculation."

A year before, and even after the death of his father which happened when he was about 17, he frequently dreamt of intercourse with his mother, but usually he was interrupted in the coition by dreaming that his father came into the room. The boudoir in the dream reminds him of the following episode. A boy called Bauer, some years his senior, caught hold of his penis once in the playground. He noticed that the boy's penis was in erection and evidently what the boy wanted was to masturbate him. This was when he was about 9 years old. For a moment he felt quite helpless when he felt his friend's hand on his penis, then he ran away ; but at the same time he asked the boy to hypnotize him. Now this boy told him a story about a brothel (boudoir) as follows :—

Women drew him into the brothel. One of them was lying on the floor naked and they compelled him to have intercourse with her. After that his pubic hairs were shaved off and they used the hair to make a sort of potion or love-philtre.

The patient had a young cousin called N. with whom he tried to reverse the rôles and play the active part. He urinated in the garden and this reminded him of a scene at a German summer resort where he urinated in the street when he was quite a little boy and a madman threatened to castrate him.

Homosexuality and the struggle against it are very marked. He masturbates in the lavatory and imagines that a man is having intercourse with him *per anum*. Then he tells me about another summer resort where he stayed with his father. There were pictures of dragons and devils there and he was awfully afraid. There was also a performance in the hotel by a conjurer who hypnotized people and made a lady disappear. The conjurer reminds him of the devil. He begins a seemingly very learned metaphysical argument in which he attempts to prove that both God and the Devil really exist and that they are in reality one and the same person. Suddenly he interrupts himself and declares : " I am trying to show off how clever I am ! " " You are playing the devil yourself," I say. " Yes," he answers, " When I was a child I used to play that I was the devil or a conjuror." He is always arguing with himself, i.e. with the devil. Before leaving the rooms he says :—

" Now I remember, I dreamt about the devil and the devil looked just like my father."

Some weeks after this he tells me that I look like death. His mother used to tease him and his father by telling them that they looked like death. He had a favourite folk-tale as a child and although it was a gruesome affair yet he kept reading it over and over again. It was the story of Death and his god-child (Grimm No. 44). This is the story :—

A poor man, after having refused God and the Devil as godfather for his child, accepts Death. Death teaches the child to become a great doctor ; if he sees Death standing at the head of the patient the patient can be cured, if at his feet he is lost. Once when the king was ill he came to the conclusion that he could cheat his godfather by changing the position of the patient. The next time, however, it was the beautiful princess whom he is to marry if he saves her. Death was again standing in the wrong place and not withstanding the warning of his godfather he again changed the patient's position. This time Death blows out his candle of life and kills him.

The extraordinary importance of this folk-tale for his infancy is explained by another dream in which he is compelled to marry Death. Now death is the father or the analyst and as he is afraid that the father will kill him if he tries to love the princess (mother), he withdraws his libido from women and tries to love the father, i.e. to marry Death.

After a period of six or seven months in which he did not even attempt to go to a prostitute he had a love affair with a prostitute or third-rate actress.   He let his friend have intercourse with her first and then it was his turn.   His friend was an astrologer whom he often confused with the analyst.   After this adventure his whole attitude changed from melancholy to mania.   He thought that he had something extraordinarily important to tell me.   When he used to masturbate and the seminal fluid was ejaculated he had the phantasy that somebody was castrating him.   Now he thought his friend represented his father.   He let him have intercourse first because this was the way to kill a person.   The seminal fluid leaving his penis meant death.   The trouble was, he said, that his seminal fluid went to the wrong place.   It ought to have gone to the mother but it was directed into the wrong channel by Bauer, his friend, and this was the origin of his perpetual anxiety.   *" Man muss sich im Orgasmus mit dem Sperma identifizieren,"* he said.   *Ruah,* the Hebrew word for the soul, is the spermatozoon and also anxiety. His one wish was to masturbate and then castrate Bauer, whom he identified with the analyst.

Now we can understand his whole life.   He was terribly depressed after the adventure with Bauer.   His father asked him again and again why he was so sad, but he could not tell him.   The reason why he could not tell him was simply this : Bauer was a substitute for his father.   Instead, he told him a story about having seen a girl's vagina just as he began analysis by telling me about incest-phantasies regarding his mother.   After his father's death he was troubled so terribly by these incestuous phantasies and the compulsion to masturbate that he went to a doctor and asked to be castrated. The doctor told him not to talk nonsense ; then he was hypnotized by a friend of his.   But he wants to get rid of this hypnotic influence and goes from one hypnotist to the other, from one analyst to the other, always seeking refuge against the over-powerful father-image in a new father-imago.   At the same time he produces an extraordinary series of castration traumas (people threatening to castrate him) which lasts from his fifth to his twenty-fourth year.   He continually identifies all the various castrators whose prototypes are Bauer and his mother, with all his doctors, hypnotizers, conjurers, and analysts. He cannot keep any post he gets, because the employer is always the father with whom he would like to play the mother's part. Finally he has a real homosexual adventure with mutual immission of the penis into the mouth and soon after this he manages to get a job and to keep it for the first time.   The employer he identifies with the analyst and gives both of them a name that indicates homosexuality (*Bock-schiessen*, in Hungarian *bak-löves* to have coitus with a he-goat, i.e. to make a mistake). On the 17th of August, 1928, he brought the following dream :—

He was walking up a street in Graz where he spent his childhood. It is the street that leads to the house of Uncle H. There is a sort of hypnotizer or conjurer showing the tricks he can do with cats. They are little black cats and they have to be transformed into tigers. The tigers are piled up, one on the top of the other. He is torturing the cats terribly, stabbing knives into them, in fact castrating them. Finally he takes them home and the dreamer plays with one of the cats. They look quite healthy, nobody would believe that they are (or were ?) neurotic. Uncle H. is the father of young N., a boy with whom he performed mutual masturbation. I have forbidden him to masturbate [1] ; this morning he held his penis in his hand ; he wonders whether that is also forbidden ? I have a cat here and the other day when he played with it, I told him not to stroke it. That was because the cat was full of wounds. I told him that workmen had been torturing the poor animal, but he thinks I must have been the culprit. This shows clearly the identity of the conjurer with the analyst. What do the tigers remind him of ? A picture book with tigers, one of which looked just like his father. In the last hour he talked a lot about the Freudian view of the super-ego, so I ventured to suggest that perhaps piling up one tiger on top of the other indicates the super-ego, the male attitude he is to develop through analysis. Clemenceau, he says, was called a tiger and Clemenceau reminds him of the Bordeaux or Borderaux in another dream.[2] My face is like the muzzle of a beast of prey. This morning when he dressed he noticed in the looking-glass that he was trying to imitate me. I have a watch he wants to purchase—a watch (*Uhr*) or rather a prostitute (*Hure*). He ought to have a prostitute as a sort of formality. Why formality ? I ask. Because the coitus he performs is not a real coitus—the vagina always appears as a mouth. Like the mouth of the homosexual or like the analyst's mouth. A street performance reminds him of urinating in the street ; that would be a performance. This is what happened when he was a boy at a German summer resort and he would like to kill the man who threatened to castrate him.

He again takes up the topic of marriage or a prostitute. Well, it might be a real marriage, not a matter of form, but that would be the *ultima ratio*. What does he mean by *ultima ratio* ? I ask. The

---

[1] I only advised him to abstain and tell me the results in analysis.
[2] An equivalent of Bluebeard or the analyst.

ultima ratio is death, but according to the dream he says this would mean to become a tiger, i.e. to be cured. In other words, if there is no hope of carrying through his homosexual desires in analysis he may as a last resort, rather than bear the torture of being analysed, i.e. castrated, any longer, even think of being cured.

This one case contains data that confirm almost all the theories I have put forward on the basis of our anthropological material. To begin with we have the direct identification of the seminal fluid with the soul, of ejaculation with the moment of death. Both these phenomena are, as we should expect if Ferenczi's views hold good, identified with castration and then again castration with coitus. The next striking confirmation is that of the equation-magician (medicine-man) and castrator.

He is continually expecting to suffer castration (or to play the passive part in coition) in analysis and brings dreams in which his father has intercourse with him instead of his mother.

We have seen that the primitive medicine-man is a condensation of the father and the mother imago. But so is the analyst in this case and in all other cases. In one of his dreams I am a witch with a peaked hat (penis) who acts by the orders of his mother. Whenever the witch gives him a peaked hat like her own he turns round and the witch becomes a beautiful girl, but then again it is a muzzle with teeth, a beast of prey, like my face. Then again he has phantasies of sucking my penis, and of my giving him food, and goes on to talk about his mother who used as a joke to offer him her nipples when he was a big boy and made him terribly ashamed of himself.

We can therefore repeat our interpretation that primitive society with the medicine-man as its chief is centred round an uncanny representative of the father and mother and based on a displaced castration anxiety.

The next day the patient brought the following dream :—

1 An electric lamp is burning and a young man is standing beside my bed. I awake with a start ; it is only the moonlight.

2 A locust and a lizard fight with each other. The lizard has taken the locust's head into his mouth or it might be vice versa. The lizard is much stronger but both are long, green, disgusting things.

The lizard and the locust remind him of the tiger. The idea of taking each other's head into their mouths is like the affair with the homosexual (mutual *fellatio* in the episode mentioned above), " I saw a locust on the stairs here and drove it out of the window fearing that it might be crushed. A locust ; perhaps it was a dragon-fly. A dragon-fly is like a girl with a tail (tail = penis in German). The homosexual spoke to me as if I were a girl."

It hardly needs much argument to show that the analyst (father) is represented by the big penis, the lizard and the patient (see his solicitude for the locust) by the smaller animal. Analysis here appears as a homosexual scene between two male genitals ; or in the archaic language of the Id, as the mutual eating up or conjugation, the original form of union. It is significant that this same scene is brought into connection with the tiger, i.e. with the super-ego. The first scene is a more sublimated equivalent of the second. The patient says that the lamp glowing beside the beds is a " lamp of resistance ". That is why the young man disappears from his bedside. He looks like the first " homo-analyst " (instead of homosexual). Of course this lapse of speech convinced him that my interpretation of the dream was correct. The next day the patient came with the following dream.

" I am trying to pray in the Synagogue. An old Jew is reading the Bible and I am repeating what he says. He uses the Ashkenaz pronunciation and I can hardly follow him because I pronounce the words according to the Sephardi way. Suddenly there are no vowels between the consonants, that is, I have the original text. I feel great anxiety. Mrs Krauss comes with her little boy, a cheery, healthy-looking chap. They are accused of having committed incest and there is going to be a public trial in the Synagogue. I am acting for the defence, somehow playing the part of the psycho-analyst. That doesn't matter, I tell them ; why shouldn't he ? It is much better than if he had something to do with a man. Great speeches are delivered from the pulpit for and against the boy, I defending him, but I feel that I have not convinced the public. I go to console the little boy and he cries ' Now I shall never be a boy any more '. I bend over him (this is the super-ego !) and have a sort of homosexual feeling. We both cry and I try to comfort him."

Mrs Krauss is a person who occurs frequently in his infantile memories. Her chief distinctive features are a long knife used by her for some carving purpose in the dining room and that when asked as to what profession she would like her son to choose, she answered : " To cut coupons." Living from the yield of one's fortune is like having intercourse with the mother while work is like intercourse with other women. " To cut coupons " reminds him of something else that is cut in the Synagogue, viz. the foreskin. He relates a story about the doctors in one of the French colonies. People were analysed in public there and the patient had simply to repeat what the doctor said (in German, *nachbeten*). The French call psycho-analysis " Austrian psychology " ; this is the Ashkenaz pronunciation. The Sephardi pronunciation might be the Stekel school, that is, his first analyst. Then the " original text " without commentary would be the real unconscious, and the story of Mrs Krauss, the castrating mother and her son, fully explains what we must regard as the fundamental trend of the unconscious.

The public discussion in the Synagogue represents public opinion as a sublimated representative of the place where the circumcision, i.e. castration, happens. The whole story means : *he fled from the castration threats of the mother to the love of the father, and developed a Super-Ego on the basis of deflected homosexuality.* This would explain a theoretical difficulty regarding the origin of the Super-Ego. In melancholia it is the heterosexual love object that is introjected, but the Super-Ego is derived from the parent of the same sex.[1] If we take the double aspect of the Oedipus attitude as our starting point we might suggest that one of these aspects is likely to develop into a regular object cathexis, while the other would be withdrawn and regress from cathexis to identification. Thus the normal boy gives up loving the father (genitally) and replaces this love by identification while the homosexual would do the same on the mother's side— instead of loving the mother he would raise her to the level of a Super-Ego. If sublimated or deflected homosexuality is the origin of the Super-Ego, we could also understand the Pleasure Ego as a personification of one's own penis and its fusion with the prohibitive aspects of paternity as represented by the father's penis. Again we must distinguish the two components united in what is usually called a Super-Ego. One of these components is derived from paternal sadism as a sort of introjected castrator.

Here is another dream of the same patient to illustrate my meaning.

" I go to Uncle N.'s house and he reproaches me for leading an idle life. I want to tell him that he is no better, when he begins to wrestle with me. We both have a tight grip of each other and each of us is trying to castrate the other."

Uncle N. is a substitute for the analyst and the reproach shows his connection with the Super-Ego. He would like to imitate the father (analyst) as castrator, i.e. to develop a Super-Ego of his own. In the lizard dream this same effort is represented as a mutual immission of the penis, i.e. here we have the libidinal (homosexual) basis in the

[1] Cf. Jones " Der Ursprung und Aufbau des Über Ichs," *Zeitschrift für Psychoanalyse*, xii, 1926.

development of the Super-Ego. If we agree to call the destructive "ethical" phase of our psyche the Super-Ego and the libidinal phase the Ego-Ideal we might say, with reference to a recent paper of Ferenczi's,[1] that analysis is finished when we have the pure Ego-Ideal without any traces of the Super-Ego.

[1] S. Ferenczi, "Die Elastizität der psychoanalytischen Technik," *Zeitschrift für Psychoanalyse,* xiv, 1928, p. 209.

IV THE DIVINE KING

I INTRODUCTION

OUR analysis of the psychology of patient and medicine-man, of the libidinal factors at work in disease and therapy, gains additional importance by the circumstance that the world-wide organization of primitive societies is certainly what we could call a pharmako-cracy, a rule of the wizard or medicine-man.

Among the Wiradjuri, for instance, the headman was always a medicine man and there was one for each local division.[1] Jalina piramurana, who was regarded as superior headman of the Dieri tribe, was also a great medicine-man. He was the head of the *Kunaura murdu*, the Kunaura totem, and boasted of being the " tree of life " for the seed Kunaura forms at times the staple vegetable food of these tribes. He was also spoken of as the *Mamgura murdu*, that is, the plant itself of which the Kungaura is the seed.[2] A Ngarigo or Wolgal headman was also the medicine-man of the tribe.[3]

Summarizing the evidence for Australia, Frazer says :—

" On the whole, then, it is highly significant that in the most primitive society about which we are accurately informed it is especially the magicians or medicine-men who appear to have been in process of developing into chiefs." [4] The power of a Melanesian chief depends entirely on the belief in his mana.[5] In the Marshall Bennet Islands it was the duty of each chief of a clan to charm the gardens so as to make them productive.[6] In New Britain people who possessed extraordinary powers, sorcerers and wizards, were regarded as chiefs.[7] Among the Semang by far the most important

---

[1] Howitt, *Native Tribes*, p. 303.
[2] Ibid., p. 299.   [3] Ibid., p. 302.
[4] J. G. Frazer, *The Magic Art*, 1911, i, pp. 336, 337.
[5] Codrington, op. cit., p. 46.
[6] C. G. Seligman, *Melanesians*, p. 702.
[7] Brown, *Melanesians and Polynesians*, p. 270.

member of the tribe was almost invariably the shaman or medicine-man. Under ordinary circumstances the chiefs of the Semang tribes are always *Blians* of more or less repute.[1] The *Manangs* or medicine-men of the Sea Dyaks rank next in importance to the village chiefs, and it is by no means unusual for the medicine-man himself to be the chief of the village.[2]

Considering the evidence brought together by Frazer for the ascent of the magician, we must say that this seems to be the regular path to monarchic rule. For although cases might certainly be found in which a paramount person in a savage community owed his influence to the strength of his arm, his sagacity, or even his wealth, it is easy to show that the historic kings of ancient civilization really derived their power from men who represented the link between the worlds of mortals and immortals. Everywhere in antiquity the ruler of a community wields supernatural powers and appears to be a representative or incarnation of the deity. In proceeding to investigate the psychic meaning of these kings we are extending the scope of our research from a society consisting of medicine-man and patient to society itself. If we should find that the interpretation given to the medicine-man holds good for his successor, the king, we may infer that society is held together by forces that are analogous to those we have found in action between the doctor and his patient.

2 TAMMUZ AND THE KING

Taking the ancient kingdoms of Sumer and Akkad, afterwards continued as the empire of Babylon and Asshur, as our starting point, we observe that the king is not what he seems to be. He is either an earth-born power projected into heaven or the shadow of heaven upon earth. Sin, the Moon God, is said to be King of Heaven, who "rules with his crown ". The Moon God chooses the king and confers his sceptre on him. In the great hymn of Ur the king is said to shine like the new moon and his head is covered with radiance. Bur-Sin is "the son beloved by Nanna ", Gimil-Sin "the beloved of Nana ", Enneatum "the dear priest of Nanna." Hammurabi calls Sin his creator and himself a scion of royalty created by Sin. He is the one whom Sin has endowed with the regalia, and

---

[1] Skeat and Blagden, *Pagan Races of the Malay Peninsula*, 1906, ii, pp. 225, 226.
[2] Ling Roth, *Natives of Sarawak and British North Borneo*, 1896, i, p. 265.

Agumkakrime's vow is "may Sin eternally renew the seed of Royalty ". Asur-ah-iddin tells us that month by month, Sin and Samas, at their appearance, will " renew the gods, finish the temples, consolidate my Government, the throne and my priesthood ". " Every month, unceasingly at his rise and at his setting, Sin will not leave the king, to prolong his days, consolidate his throne, and to give omnipotence to the king my master." [1]

Some interesting inferences might be drawn from this connection. For just as the king is connected with a specific idea of " life "—to behold his face means to live,[2] it is alleged of the Moon God that he is the " father of the great gods ", that he " procreates gods and men", that to see him is " life", and that he is the " king of living beings ".[3]

But like a savage medicine-man he is the sender of disease and also the healer. "Sin is medicine." [4] At the feast of the new moon, offerings were made to the statues of King Gimil-Sin.[5] Sacrifices were offered to the dead king on the day of the new and full moon in the month of Tammuz, and it seems that all departed kings were connected with the moon and vegetation.[6]

It is, however, the identification of the king with Tammuz that calls for our special notice both on account of its antiquity and because Tammuz seems to have been not a specific case but one of many— the representative of a type of divinity with which Sumerian, Syrian, Phrygian, and Egyptian kings were identified.

At Isin, the capital of one of the Sumerian dynasties, at least five kings are named and they are spoken of as those that sleep.

> " The lord Idin-Dagan sleeps.
> And the gardens of themselves restrain their growth.
> The city weeps for Isme-Dagan who slumbers
> And the gardens of themselves withhold their fruit.
> The city weeps for Bur Sin who sleeps
> The sturdy youth is in the land of weeping." [7]

---

[1] A. Jeremias, *Handbuch der altorientalischen Geisteskultur*, 1913, p. 172. Et. Combe, *Histoire du Culte de Sin*, 1908, pp. 24–30.

[2] Jeremias, op. cit., p. 178.

[3] Combe, loc. cit., p. 25.

[4] Combe, loc. cit., p. 25.

[5] L. W. King, *A History of Sumer and Akkad*, 1910, p. 310.

[6] S. Langdon, "Three New Hymns," *Proceedings of the Society of Biblical Archeology*, 1918, p. 36.

[7] S. Langdon, *Tammuz and Ishtar*, 1914, p. 26. Ishme-Dagan is the " beloved spouse " of the goddess. L. W. King, *A History of Sumer and Akkad*, 1910, p. 310.

The passage, Langdon tells us, evidently refers to kings who in their day played the rôle of Tammuz in the mystery of this cult.[1] If we had no other clue to the nature of ancient kings the cult of Tammuz alone would hardly be sufficient to enlighten us. For all we seem to know of him is that he is the faithful son, the " son and consort ", who dies, is mourned for by his mother and probably also revived by her. Characteristic of this worship is the figure of the desolate mother wandering in the barren fields or desolate sheep-folds, or sitting in the temple wailing for the lost son and lover. The people, too, take part in the mourning.

> For the removed there is wailing.
> Ah me, my child the far removed,
> My consort, the far removed,
> My anointer,[2] the far removed,
> For the sacred cedar where the mother bore him.[3]

But Tammuz is more than a single human being, even if that human being is a divine ruler. He is the " fecundity of the country " the " master of the country's vital power ".[4]

We are therefore told that the wailing is not for him alone, it is for the plants ; " they grow not " ; for the flocks " they produce not ", for the perishing wedded ones, for perishing children it is, the dark-headed people create not. There is no grain, the fish will not spawn, the tamarisk refuses to grow. Life itself has disappeared with the Lord of Life for " life unto distant days is not ". It seems, though this is merely an inference, that a pantomime was performed by weeping men and women. A wooden figure of the dying god was placed in a boat and launched into the waters of the Euphrates or Tigris. When the figure of the god disappeared beneath the waves the god passed into the underworld. Perhaps his death was also represented by throwing grains and plants upon the waves. " He lies in the submerged grain." [5] The liturgies represent Ishtar descending from her chamber in Eanna in search of her son and lover. At last she finds him in the waters, in the nether world. As the virgin mother was identified with the star Sirius and that star was invisible for two months (April and May), about 3000 B.C., this period seems to have been regarded as the descent of the goddess.

---

[1] Langdon, loc. cit., p. 26.

[2] The priest who employs oils in healing disease and casting out devils.

[3] Langdon, loc. cit., p. 10.

[4] Zimmern, " Sumerisch-babylonische Tamuzlieder," *Berichte der philologisch-historischen Klasse der Sächs. Ges. d. Wiss.*, 1909, p. 228. W. W. Baudissin, *Adonis und Esmun*, 1911, p. 100.

[5] Langdon, loc. cit., p. 13.

She is warned away by her imperious rival, the queen of the netherworld, with whom she has a nearly fatal contest for the possession of Tammuz. But it seems that the " child-begetting courtesan " (Ishtar) and the queen of the shades are originally one and the same person, for in the oldest Babylonian prayers there is no rival queen to encounter. " The obstacle in the way of bringing back the lord of fertility was rather the difficulty in arousing him from the deep sleep which fell upon the souls of the dead." [1]

This assumed identity of the mother-wife with the cause of the hero's death gains in probability if we remember that she is said to be not only the restorer of life but also the murderer of her lover. For when Gilgamesh, the King of Uruk, spurns the love offered by the divine harlot, he reminds her of the dangerous nature of her love. " Whom of thy husbands didst thou love for ever ? Tammuz was the love of thy youth and year by year thou makest wailing for him. The shepherd whom thou didst love thou hast changed into a bird with broken wings, the lion whom thou didst love was caught in traps." The horse had to suffer whip and lash, the shepherd was changed into a wolf, the gardener into another animal.[2]

Epic poems are the products of ages of many generations. There is a nucleus like the dream-thought and many layers of secondary elaboration. In this case two things are evident : (a) the text shows that the love of Ishtar meant death ; (b) circumstances indicate that originally Gilgamesh, the King of Uruk, was the rightful consort " the damu " (consort = Tammuz) of the goddess. The kings of the Isin dynasty who were also the rulers of Uruk regarded themselves as the chosen consorts of Innina (Ishtar) the pure one.[3] These kings were, as we have seen above, every one of them a Tammuz, or a Gilgamesh, for both seem to mean the same. We possess a long liturgy which celebrates the marriage of Idin-Dagan, third king of the dynasty of Isin with the mother-goddess Innini.[4] According to Radau this marriage of Tammuz and Ishtar was celebrated on New Year's Day, the 1st of Nisan, and it was the spring festival symbolizing the resurrection of nature. Dumuzi and Ishtar do not signify any particular god or goddess, but every god or goddess who played the rôle of " son " and his " bride ", the " bride " being also the " virgin mother ", " the wife of the father ".[5]

---

[1] Langdon, loc. cit., pp. 15–18.
[2] Ungnad-Gressmann, *Das Gilgamesh-Epos*, 1911, p. 33.
[3] Ungnad-Gressmann, loc. cit., p. 122.
[4] Radau in *Hilprecht Anniversary Volume*, 1909, pp. 391–409.
[5] Radau, loc. cit., p. 404.

Thus far we have shown that the leading feature in the character of the ancient Sumerian kings and their Semitic successors was their marriage with a god who was also their mother. While the king symbolized for the people a super-ego, something desirable and therefore a projection of their heart's desire, this same super-ego for the king was represented by a divinity, the "Consort", the "Master of Life", who was also the son of his beloved spouse. There is also royal pride in the statement of Sargon who reigned in Agade, in 2850 B.C.

"Sargon, the mighty king of Agade am I. My mother was a divine harlot, my father unknown, while his brother lived in the hills. My divine mother conceived me and gave birth to me in secret. She put me into a chest of reed and it swam on the waters. The river carried me down to Ahi, the drawer of water. He drew me out of the water and brought me up as his child. I became the gardener of Ahi and as gardener I became beloved by Ishtar and for many years ruled the dark-headed ones." [1]

The king is the beloved of the goddess and a son of a divine harlot who represents the heavenly Ishtar on earth. The fact that Gilgamesh appears on the scene as a mythical king of Uruk makes it probable that further variations of the Tammuz theme will be found in his epic. If we eliminate episodes with a historic basis (as for instance, the war with Humbaba), the marriage of a king with a goddess, his encounter with a bull of heaven and his subsequent descent to the nether world seem to be the original contents of the epic. This scene is related once as a contest between Gilgamesh and the bull-like being Engidu, once as a fight of the two heroes Gilgamesh and Engidu with the bull of heaven.

In both cases somebody asks the gods to create an opponent to withstand the might of the indomitable Gilgamesh. In the first scene the bull-man Engidu is called the image of Anu and in the second Ishtar asks her father to create a bull of heaven to destroy Gilgamesh. Moreover in the first scene we have the bull-man coming into the town accompanied by a harlot at the very moment when the festival of the *hieros gamos* between king and goddess is about to take place, and presumably the king must conquer his semi-bestial foe before he can consummate the marriage. [2] In the second scene the original and natural attitude is inverted. For if we remember that the King of Erek was regularly regarded as the "damu", the consort, of the goddess, that the right to the throne itself seemed to

---

[1] Jeremias, loc. cit., p. 211. King, *Chronicles concerning early Babylonian Kings*, ii, p. 87.

[2] Ungnad-Gressmann, op. cit., pp. 16, 29–35, 90, 114.

depend on the fact that the king has been " chosen " by a mother-
goddess, we shall picture a scene more in keeping with the natural
and inevitable order of things, the male being the wooer and the
female protected by a mighty bull. But the bull is killed by the
youthful hero and its right thigh is thrown with contempt into Ishtar's
lap. Ishtar assembles her harlots and great is their wailing for the
right thigh of the bull. Nearly all Assyriologists agree in regarding
the right thigh as a euphemism for the phallus.[1] But it seems that
the victory is fatal to the heroes. Engidu dies, Gilgamesh descends
to the nether world in search of his friend. He desires " Life "—
again the same word always connected with kings and gods. This
" life " is inherent in a plant of life or youth. The condition is that
he should not go to sleep. Finally, although it seems that he breaks
this taboo, he gets what he is in search of, but when he thinks that
he has conquered death, the old enemy of mankind, the serpent
steals the plant of life and man is mortal for evermore.[2]

What does this scene represent ? We believe that it is a survival
of barbarous times when the ascent to monarchy and to the couch
of the goddess was not so easy. Like his adversary, Gilgamesh himself
is called " the mighty wild bull "[3] and the bull in general is the
emblem of the king.[4] There must have been a time, though very far
remote, in the prehistoric period of these people when the young bull,
the hero of a bull-clan, had to kill and castrate the bull of heaven,
his predecessor, before he could become the " damu ", the consort,
of the mother. For we know that the marriage of the king
and the mother-goddess was celebrated at the Zagmuk festival of
New Year and this seems also to have been the critical period for the
tenure of kingship. " For every year at the festival of Zagmuk the
king had to renew his power by seizing the hands of the image of
Marduk in his great temple of Esagil at Babylon." " According
to the historian Berossus, the festival of Sacaea was celebrated annually
for five days in the month of Lous. During these five days masters and
servants changed places, the servants giving orders and the masters
obeying them. A prisoner condemned to death was dressed in the
king's robes, seated on the king's throne, allowed to issue whatever
commands he pleased, to eat and drink and enjoy himself and to live

---

[1] H. Schneider, *Zwei Aufsätze zur Religionsgeschichte Vorderasiens*,
1909. *Die Entwicklung des Gilgameschepos*, p. 57. Ungnad-Gressmann,
op. cit., p. 133. O. Weber, *Die Literatur der Babylonier*, p. 78.

[2] The plant is called " the aged become young again ", Gressmann, p. 143.

[3] Ungnad-Gressmann, loc. cit., pp. 7, 12.

[4] Schneider, loc. cit., p. 45.

with the king's concubines. But at the end of the five days he was stripped of his royal robes, scourged, and hanged." [1]

Moreover, the Zagmuk festival was the time when the fates were determined by Marduk and Nebo for the ensuing year. Now the creation myth relates how Marduk wrested these tablets of destiny from Ningu after he had killed the dragon. " We may therefore conjecture "—says Sir James Frazer—" that the dramatic representation of this incident formed part of the annual determination of the fates at the Zagmuk ". [2]

Langdon believes that Tammuz was the name of a prehistoric Sumerian ruler of Erech, who became identified with the Sumerian dying god Abu. The Old Sumerian calendar contained two new-year festivals, one in spring and one in autumn. The new year celebration of Zagmuk was held in honour of Ishtar at Erech. At the same time a carnival was celebrated at Lagash as the wedding festival of Ningirsu [3] and the goddess Bau. One of the important details of the Zagmuk ritual was the temporary abdication of the king of Babylonia. On that day the king went in the early morning to the chapel of Marduk in the great temple of Esagila. The high priest met the king at the door of the chapel but did not permit him to enter. The king's crown and sceptre were taken from him together with all his royal garments. These were taken to the chapel and placed before Bêl. The high priest returned to the king who was kneeling at the door of the chapel. He smote the king's cheek, boxed his ears, and scourged him. If the king wept the reign of the next year would be prosperous. If he would not weep it would end in sudden disaster. The king was temporarily reduced to the rank of a layman and punished by God's vicar upon earth. The high priest then spoke to the royal penitent, promising him God's blessing and the augmentation of imperial power. [4]

It seems highly probable that reducing the king to the rank of layman was an attenuated survival of regicide. At the same time, the ceremonial slaughter of the dragon was enacted. [5] Frazer thinks

[1] J. G. Frazer, *The Dying God*, 1911, pp. 113, 114.

[2] Frazer, *The Dying God*, pp. 110, 111.

[3] Ningirsu is Nin-gish-zida (Jastrow, *Die Religion Babyloniens und Assyriens*, 1912, i, pp. 86, 88, 92), and Nin-gish-zida is Gilgamesh (Schneider, loc. cit., p. 49).

[4] Langdon, " The Babylonian and Persian Sacaea," *Journal of the Royal Asiatic Society*, 1921, pp. 67–70.

[5] For a Hittite parallel cf. A. H. Sayce, " Hittite legend of the War with the Great Serpent," ibid., 1922, p. 177.

that the old king must have played the part and worn the mask of the dragon in the original form of the ceremony.[1]

Our explanation of the Gilgamesh epic offers a parallel to Frazer's conjecture. Bull and serpent are both frequent emblems of royalty. Schneider has given good reasons for the assumption that in certain seals of Sargon representing a naked man or god giving water to a bull, the bull represents the king himself, the water is the water of life and the naked divinity the god Gish.[2]

Now this god Gish is the divine prototype of the hero Gilgamesh. He is sometimes called Gisch-zida or Nin-gisch-zida and in the latter case appears as a human being with dragon's heads protruding from his shoulders.[3]

If the ancient kingdom of Sumer was the due of the serpent or bull hero who defeated the old serpent or bull and had access to the Divine Mother we can understand why her love appears to be a dangerous boon in later ages. For year by year the chosen of Ishtar has to encounter a foe of his own blood and one of the two " bulls " is dispatched to the country without return.

But here there is a difficulty. It is the bull who is killed and castrated, and yet the double of Gilgamesh, and then Gilgamesh himself descends into the other world. He ought to be marrying the goddess ; can the two mean the same thing ? Now Schneider observes that the fact that Gilgamesh, or his prototype the god Gish, is represented as a powerful naked man seems to indicate his phallic nature.[4] So does the name Gish-zida which means " wood-standing-erect ".[5] The historic continuity in these Oriental traditions makes it a pardonable offence in method if we adduce the views of early Christendom that Christ's descent to the lower world was compared to a return into the womb of the Virgin.[6]

Then the marriage of the god would be his descent to the womb and the resurrection of the sleeping " wood-standing-erect " can only be effected by the mother-goddess. The idea that the descent to the other world is really coitus is suggested not only by the regular appearance of a male and a female partner on the scene, but also by the gradual unveiling and final nakedness of Ishtar, who is trying to resuscitate her lover. The trouble is that Gilgamesh,[7] like Tammuz, is " asleep ", i.e. the penis in its non-erected state.

[1] Frazer, *The Dying God*, pp. 110, 111.   [2] Schneider, loc. cit., p. 44.
[3] Schneider, loc. cit., pp. 48, 49.   [4] Schneider, op. cit., pp. 46, 47.
[5] Schneider, op. cit., p. 48.   [6] H. Schmidt, *Jona*, 1907, p. 178, note
[7] Cf. Ed. Stucken, " Beiträge zur orientalischen Mythologie," *Mitteilungen der vorderasiatischen Gesellschaft*, 1902, No. 4. H. H. Figulla " Istars Fahrt ins Toten-Land," *Memnon*, ii, S.A., pp. 55.

It is by the help of the naked goddess that he becomes a " wood-standing-erect ", a " plant of life ".[1] In several inscriptions of Judea we read of the " wedding " of Ningirsu and Bau celebrated on New Year's Day. Bau is the " one who brings forth ", who " quickens the dead " and " restores the green things of the earth to new life ". Later on, the wedding of Ningirsu was transferred to Marduk and his wife. It is the union of Marduk with the earth that makes the earth " give up her dead ", i.e. effect their resurrection.[2]

We have found it necessary to explain the myth and ritual of Babylonian royalty by a double interpretation. In the first instance we stress the fact that the king represents somebody else—a great god who lived in incest and ruled by the grace of his muscles—that is, the Jealous Sire. On the other hand, he was the " father ", the " begetter ". Like the moon god, he gave life, he was like Tammuz pre-eminently a consort, a Master of Life, or like Gilgamesh a " wood-standing-erect ", and the vicissitudes of his career corresponded to the vicissitudes of the phallus. He was the common super-ego of his people, the Great Man of the country, and we know that the penis as representative of a pleasure-ego (Ferenczi) is the organic starting point for the formation of an ego-ideal.

3 Adonis and Other Lords

The city of Byblos was sacred to Adonis,[3] and the river Nalir Ibrahim, which falls into the sea a little south of the city, was called Adonis.[4] Gingras the father of Adonis was king of the city.[5] Now Adonis is the Greek form of the Phœnician and Hebrew " Adon ", a word meaning simply " lord ", and therefore like the title of " damu " (consort) applicable to any deity or king. Hebrew kings were frequently styled *Adoni-hamelech*, " My Lord the King," or *Adoni Messiah*, " My Lord the Anointed," and although the names of the rulers of Byblos only show that they claimed affinity with Baal, there can be no doubt about the essential identity of this Baal, or Master, with Adon, the Lord.

---

[1] The trick of the Raven in North-West America. A girl complains that she is unwell. Raven tells her to sit on a plant that stands erect in the woods. He is hidden under leaves, the plant is his penis. F. Boas, *Indianische Sagen von der Nord-Pazifischen Küste Amerikas*, 1898.

[2] H. Radau, *Bel, the Christ of Ancient Times*, 1908, pp. 42, 45, 49.

[3] Strabo, xvi, 1, 18, p. 755.   [4] Lucian, *De dea Syria*, 8.

[5] J. G. Frazer, *Adonis, Attis, Osiris*, 1907, p. 10.

According to Apollodorus, Smyrna, by the aid of her nurse, prevailed upon her father Theias to have intercourse with her. When he recognized his daughter he pursued her with a drawn sword. She prayed to the gods and they came to her rescue by transforming her into a myrrh tree. In due time the tree was cleft asunder and Adonis was born. Aphrodite, smitten by the child's beauty, hid him in a chest and gave the chest to Persephone. But she too fell in love with the infant and refused to let him return to the world of mortals. The strife of the goddesses was judged by Zeus, and accordingly Adonis spends two-thirds of the year with Persephone and one-third with Aphrodite.[1]

As for the opening of the tree-mother, Servius, who usually seems to furnish us with myths of importance, says that it was either done by the tusk of a boar or by the sword of the father.[2] It is remarkable that the boar should be connected both with the death and the birth of the god. For we are also told that Ares, jealous of the illegal amours of his wedded wife the love-goddess Aphrodite, sent a boar or changed himself into a boar to kill Attis. The beast's tusk wounded the young hunter on his knee, and it is of this wound that he bled to death. Now this shows that there was a definite historic connection between the body of Semitic myth transported into Greece under the name of Adonis and the fate of the young King-God of Babylon. For the month Tammuz is sacred to the god Ninib whose animal is the wild boar and who was called a wild boar himself. The festival of the death of Tammuz was celebrated when the star that represented Ninib became visible and therefore the belief that the boar was the murderer of Tammuz seems very likely.[3] We have noticed that Tammuz, or rather the particular Tammuz who was called Gilgamesh, goes to the shades after fighting and castrating a bull and that a human being, his father and predecessor, is represented by that bull. Just as Anu sends a bull to destroy Gilgamesh, Ares sends a boar to kill Adonis. But the advantage in the case of Adonis seems to be that here we can definitely show the identity of the boar with the human father. For it is the father's penis that opens the mother's body and in our myth this is accomplished by the tusk of a boar. Moreover,

[1] Cf. article on Adonis in *Roschers Lexikon* for the references.

[2] Servius, *Ad Verg. Aen.*, v, p. 72. *Eclog.*, x, p. 18.

[3] Jeremias, Tamuz, in *Roschers Lexikon*, 70. Lief. Sp. 53. Baudissin, *Adonis und Esmun*, 1911, p. 150. Jensen, " Das Wildschwein in den assyrisch babylonischen Inschriften," *Z.A.* i, 1886, p. 309. Zimmern, " Der babylonische Gott Tammuz," *Abh. d. phil.-hist. Kl. d. sächs. G. d. Wiss.*, xxvii, 1909, p. 717.

we have an alternative version ; the tree is cleft either by the boar's "tusk" or by the father's "sword", in both cases by the father's penis. As Adonis is said to be born of incest, it is not astonishing to find him killed by his father the boar, for his love to his mother. Nor can there be a doubt about the meaning of the knee wound. It is generally known that the idea of castration is closely connected with the punishment for incestuous wishes. Why this should be so is not made quite clear by Freud, but he assumes that the attack on the male genitalia was part and parcel of the fights of males in rut.[1] Gilgamesh throwing the bull's phallus at Ishtar, Osiris castrated in the shape of a swine, his son Horus castrating his adversary Seth, and being wounded in the eye by him, and finally Adonis wounded to death by a boar on his knee are all offshoots of the same myth. Born of an incestuous wedding and beloved by his mother, the god who was the prototype of Syrian kings is killed and castrated by the father.

As for the cult of this deity, we again find the close connection of marriage, death, and resurrection. The other outstanding features of the ceremony were that Adonis was dressed like a corpse, that the images of the deity were thrown into the sea, and that women were the principal mourners in these rites.[2] At Alexandria the images of Aphrodite and Adonis were displayed on two couches and beside them were set ripe fruits of all kinds, cakes, plants growing in flower-pots, and green bowers twined with anise. The marriage of the lovers was celebrated one day and on the morrow women attired as mourners with streaming hair and bared breasts bore the image of Adonis to the sea-shore and committed it to the waves. Their songs concluded with the hope that the lost one would come back again.[3] This is the scene implied in the Tammuz and Gish myths ; the wedding of the god is his descent to the nether world, while in the ritual at Alexandria it is followed by that descent. At Byblos the death of the god was followed by his coming to life again and his ascent to heaven. The women shaved their heads as a sign of mourning, or if they were reluctant to do this they had to give themselves to strangers on a certain day of the festival.[4] Now it is hardly probable that coitus should be a substitute for the loss of hair. For once Lucian is mistaken and the shaving rite is a later modification of coitus. If we view the festival in this light, the female worshippers having intercourse and the god descending to the nether world under the surface of the water,

---

[1] Cf. Freud, *Totem and Taboo*, 1919.   [2] Frazer, *Adonis*, p. 183.
[3] Frazer, *Adonis*, p. 183.   [4] Lucian, *De Dea Syria*, 6.

the two actions appear to afford some clue to their mutual interpretation. For I have shown that in the Sedna cult of the Eskimo
(a fertility festival), both the descent of the shaman to the Mother of
Sea Animals and the exchange of wives that was going on in the
meantime meant one and the same thing.[1] And if Adonis like
Tammuz means the phallus it becomes evident why his marriage,
death, and resurrection should be so closely connected with each
other, why his death should be equivalent to castration, and why his
descent below the water should be the same thing as the cohabitation
performed by his worshippers. Indeed we might apply the modern
interpretation of a god as a projection of his *thiasos* to this particular
case and say that the god in Syria and among the Eskimo are both a
part and parcel of their worshippers ; they represent the organ of
life itself.

There is not much difference between our view and that held by
Greek lexicographers ; they regarded Adonis as the father of Priapus,[2]
we believe that he was Priapus himself. The " gardens of Adonis ",
the rapid growth of wheat or barley under artificial circumstances,
were certainly intended to promote fertility in the crops by means of
a magical analogy, but their associations with love-magic in European
folklore clearly indicate that the plants meant something more
important than plants for human hopes and desires. Indeed, Frazer
has recognized this feature of the ritual though he regards it as
an extension of the original idea of vegetation magic.[3] Thus it
was the custom in Italy in the sixteenth century to sow barley and
wheat a few days before the festival of St John and it was believed that
the person for whom they were sown would be fortunate and get
a good husband or wife if the grain sprouted well. In various
parts of Italy it is still customary to put plants in water or in earth on
the Eve of St John, and from their blooming or fading oracles are
drawn with regard to the future of the love of those who plant them.[4]
In Sardinia, about the first of April a young man of the village presents
himself to a girl and asks her to become his *comare*, a word meaning
gossip or sweetheart. The invitation is considered as an honour by
the girl's family and is gladly accepted. At the end of May the girl
fills a pot and sows a handful of wheat and barley in the earth. On
the day of St John they break the pot by throwing it against the church
door. We recognize the sad fate of Adonis, indeed as pointed out by

---

[1] Róheim, " Die Sedna Sage," *Imago*, x.
[2] Quoted by Roscher, vol. i, p. 72.
[3] Frazer, *Adonis*, p. 209.
[4] Ibid., p. 210.

Wünsch there is reason to assume that St John in these festivals has replaced Adonis.[1]

For, at Ozieri, images used to be placed in the gardens of Adonis as in the Adonis festivals of the East. The image was either a doll dressed like a woman or a Priapus-like figure made of paste. The same method of obtaining oracles by making plants, especially branches of the cherry-tree, blossom, is well known in Central Europe in connection with the winter solstice,[2] and although the oracle sometimes refers to the crops its usual meaning is that the girl who broke the branch will get a husband.[3]

The branch is Priapus or Adonis, the chosen spouse of the love-goddess and also of maidens less lofty and divine. No doubt the early Semitic kings played the part of their divine patron and the marriage they consummated with the mother-goddess was the prototype of all human mating and of fertility in general. For were they not the representatives of Baal on earth ? And was not Baal or Adonis, both meaning exactly the same thing, conceived as " the male principle of reproduction, the husband of the land which he fertilized ? "[4]

The rest has already been pointed out by Frazer.[5] For Cinyras, like Adonis, was also noted for his exquisite beauty and like his son was wooed by Aphrodite herself. These stories of the love of Aphrodite for two members of the royal house of Paphos can hardly be dissociated from the corresponding legend told of Pygmalion, the Phœnician king of Cyprus, who is said to have fallen in love with an image of Aphrodite and taken it to his bed. Pygmalion, the father-in-law of Cinyras, Cinyras, the father of Adonis, this gives three successive generations of love-intrigue between Aphrodite and the king so that we can hardly help concluding that the early Phœnician kings of Paphos or their sons regularly claimed to be not merely the priests of the goddess but also her lovers, and that by having intercourse with the sacred harlots who represented her on earth they personated the phallic god Adonis.

---

[1] R. Wünsch, *Das Frühlingsfest der Insel Malta*, 1902.

[2] Cf. about the gardens of Osiris in Abydos H. Brugsch, " Das Osiris mysterium von Tentyra," *Zeitschrift für äg. Sprache und Altertumskunde*, xix, 1881–4. Plutarch mentions Harpokrates lying among the flowers made to blossom prematurely. (Plutarch, *De Iside*, 65*b*.)

[3] Róheim, *Adalékok a magyar néphithez*, 1920, pp. 67–80.

[4] W. Robertson-Smith, *Lectures on the Religion of the Semites*, 1907, p. 108.

[5] Frazer, *Adonis*, pp. 37, 73.

4 ATTIS AND MIDAS

The kings of Phrygia bore the names of Midas and Gordias in alternate generations, but an early king of Lydia was called Attis.[1] According to the version of Herodotus, Attis was the son of the Lydian king Croesus,[2] and Frazer, after showing that the priests of Attis were regularly called Attis and therefore probably played the part of Attis in the ritual, conjectures that these priests were members of the Phrygian royal house who were perhaps castrated and killed instead of the king himself.[3]

However, a peculiar feature in the myths and cult of Attis is that while his name simply means " father " and another name of his was Papas, " the Father," [4] he regularly figures as a son in the myths and cult. The simplest explanation we can suggest for this peculiarity would be that the part of Attis was originally played by the king himself.[5] Subsequently, however, for some reason the rôle was shifted to his son and a parallel transformation took place with regard to the myth and cult.

According to Pausanias (vii, 17) and Arnobius (v, 5), Zeus the Father of mortals and immortals desired the love of the Great Mother who was sleeping on the rock. But his desire was frustrated and his semen fell to the earth. Impregnated by the father, Earth bore a wild androgynous being called Agdistis. He was indomitable and cared neither for law nor order. The gods not being able to overcome him by force managed to do so by stratagem. Bacchus mixed wine into the spring he was accustomed to drink from and when he fell into a heavy sleep, he bound the monster's penis to a tree with a strong rope, so that on awakening he castrated himself. The penis penetrated the earth and became an almond-tree (or a pomegranate, according to Arnobius). Nana, a daughter of the river-god (or king) Sangarios, took one of the almonds and hid it in her lap. The almond disappeared, and Nana was pregnant. Her royal father was none too pleased at the probable increase of the family and Nana was locked up in a tower and left to perish with her child. Rescued, however, by divine intervention, she gave birth to Attis, who on account of his supernatural beauty was beloved by Agdistis. Agdistis accompanied him wherever he went and gave him the spoils of the

---

[1] Herodot., i, 94, *Journal of Hellenic Studies*, ix, p. 379; x, p. 156.
[2] Herodot., i, 34, 35.   [3] Frazer, loc. cit., pp. 239–41.
[4] Frazer, loc. cit., p. 235.
[5] The Attis priests were originally secular rulers. Strabo, xii, 5, 3.

chase. He kept this secret and vaunted his own prowess as a hunter. Once, however, when he was drunk he blurted out the truth and since then wine is tabooed in the cult of Attis. When he was of age, Midas, the king of Pessinus, desired him to become his son-in-law. But Agdistis seems to have objected to this plan. As an unbidden guest he appeared at the wedding and all the guests were seized with the mania of castration. The King instantly castrated himself and cut off his daughter's breast. Attis wrenched the flute of Agdistis from him and rushed away raving and in a trance. Under a pine-tree he killed himself by self-castration.

Agdistis was sorry for what he had done and asked Zeus to revive Attis. Zeus would not grant this boon, but by way of compromise, he decreed that the corpse should not rot, his hair should continue to grow, and his little finger alone should remain alive and in perpetual motion.[1]

This is a long myth and contains some lessons worth learning. The first of these is that the almond-tree is a symbol of the penis. Now the almond and the pine are the two particular species of trees that are prominent in the cult of Attis.

" In the Phrygian cult "—Arnobius tells us—" that was dedicated to the Mother of Gods, year by year a pine-tree was felled and the image of a youth bound to its trunk."

In the cult of Isis they fell a pine-tree, cut out a part of its trunk and fashion the image of Osiris from this wood. The image is buried.[2] Frazer compares the pine-trunk with the image of Attis to the may-pole ; and we may also remind the reader of the Sardinian " gardens of Adonis " with a Priapus-like image among the flowers. In Greece the Bacchic sacrifice seems to have taken place under a pine-tree and at the Thesmophoria pine-cones with pigs and phalli were thrown into the sacred vaults of Demeter to quicken the ground and the wombs of women.[3] It is therefore quite possible that the regular association between royalty and a branch or tree or plant is due to the identity of the king with the " Wood Standing Erect ".

The second point is the peculiar parallelism between the fate of Attis and Agdistis who, although an androgynous being, must in this connection certainly be regarded as the father of Attis.[4] Both are

---

[1] H. Hepding, *Attis, seine Mythen und sein Kult* (*Religionsgeschichtliche Versuche und Vorarbeiten*), 1903, pp. 104–10.

[2] Arnobius, *Adversus Nationes*, xxvii.

[3] Scholiast on Lucian, *Dial. meretr.*, ii, 1, ed. Rabe. Quoted by Frazer, *Adonis*, p. 232.

[4] The almond which makes Nana pregnant is his phallus.

castrated, in both cases castration is connected with a tree (almond, pine), wine proves dangerous to both, and castration is regularly followed by new life. Our suspicion is increased by the circumstance that Attis and Agdistis are said to have been inseparable and that Agdistis did all the work while Attis in his beauty seems to represent pleasure. If we stress the identity of penis, almond, and child the conclusion would be that Attis is the penis of Agdistis. In dream symbolism the penis is frequently represented as the " son ", the " little one ", so that we should not be surprised if father and son meant the Body and the Penis. Then we should say that Zeus has granted the request of Agdistis, for the little finger that keeps moving, the hair that grows, even the indestructible corpse is Attis himself, the penis. This accounts for the parallelism between the two castrations, for in a variant of the myth Attis is the high priest of the Great Mother. But the king of the town loves the youth and Attis, to escape from his advances, flees into the woods. The king finds him but Attis prevents him from obtaining his desire by castrating him. The dying king does the same to Attis and the priests of the Great Mother find the castrated corpse under a pine-tree.[1] If we interpret Attis as the " son " or penis of the king it is easy to understand why they should both be castrated at the same time. Moreover, we know that the narcissistic love of the boy for his own penis, the phallic phase of organization, is the starting point of homosexuality and our myth appears to contain a statement of this fact. If we interpret Attis and Agdistis as one and the same person we shall say that the bi-sexual or narcissistic features in him resist his attempt to marry the king's daughter, or rather it is the appearance of Agdistis (ambisexuality, narcissism) that makes marriage seem castration.

However, Agdistis, the male being who is also a female, is merely another aspect of the Great Mother.[2] In other variants of the Attis myth it is the Great Mother who by her jealousy disturbs the wedding and transforms what ought to have been the beginning of new life into the horrible death suffered by Attis.[3] Nor can there be a doubt about the nature of the relation between Attis and the Great Mother ; the young Phrygian shepherd is both her lover and son.[4] And if we

---

[1] Servius, *Aen.*, ix, 115.
[2] Strabo, x, 3, 12, p. 469; xii, 5, 3, p. 567c. *Philologus*, vii, p. 198. *Journ. Hell. Studies*, iii, p. 56. Hepding, loc. cit., p. 105.
[3] *Fasti*, v, 227. *Metam*, x, 103–105. Hepding, loc. cit., pp. 116, 118, 120.
[4] Clemens, *Protr.*, ii, 15. Arnob., *Adv. nat.*, v, 20. Jerome, *Adv. Jovinianum*, i, 7. Hepding, loc. cit., p. 125. Hepding, loc. cit., p. 135. Frazer, loc. cit., p. 235.

combine this version with the variants that explain the death of Attis like that of Adonis and Tammuz by an accident that befell him on a boar hunt,[1] and with the version we have just referred to representing Attis the son as killing and castrating his father and suffering the same punishment for this outrage, we have all the actors of the Primal Oedipus Drama. In the son who kills and castrates his father, the boar, because he loves his mother and can only procreate children with her after the father's death, and then in the repression that sets in, we have the reversal of the whole bull situation, the castration and death of the son in consequence of his incestuous desires.

Thus far we have tried to explain the myths of Attis and perhaps there is some contradiction between the two interpretations we have given. Is the myth a reflection of what took place in the pre-human epoch of the Primal Horde or does it reflect the process of coitus itself ? Is Attis the Son or the Penis, the castration complex ? Before we attempt even a provisional answer we shall follow Hepding and Frazer in describing the cult of Attis.

On the 22nd March a pine-tree was brought into the sanctuary of the Mother Goddess.[2] It was the duty of the guild of Tree Bearers to swathe it like a corpse and deck the trunk with wreaths of violets, for violets had sprung from the blood of the castrated Attis. The image of the young Attis was tied to the trunk. The second day of the festival seems to have been devoted chiefly to the blowing of trumpets. The third day was called the Day of Blood. This was the day of the burial or descent of the god, and his worshippers seem to have imitated his fate in several ways. The High Priest drew blood from his arms and presented it as an offering and the inferior clergy followed suit, dancing about and gashing their bodies in wild ecstasy. Although it is not expressly stated by the sources, there is sufficient circumstantial evidence brought forward by Frazer for believing that it was on this day that the priests not merely gashed their body but actually cut their penis off and that the male members of the devotees were wrapped up and buried in the subterranean chambers of the Mother Goddess. The laity did not go as far as this although at any rate they abstained from eating flesh and from having sexual intercourse.[3] But when night had fallen, the sorrow of the worshippers was turned to joy. For suddenly a light shone in the darkness ; the tomb was opened, the god had risen from the dead, and

---

[1] Hepding, loc. cit., pp. 100, 101.

[2] Cf. Hepding, loc. cit., pp. 150–6. Frazer, loc. cit., pp. 222–7.

[3] Hepding, loc. cit., p. 155. Hippolyt, *Refut. omn. haeres.*, v, 9, p. 170. Deubner, *De incubatione*, 1900, p. 17.

as the priest touched the lips of the weeping mourners with balm he softly whispered in their ears the glad tidings of salvation. The resurrection of the god was hailed by his disciples as a promise that they too would issue triumphant from the corruption of the grave. The resurrection was a festival of Joy, called Hilaria in Rome, and followed by a sort of Carnival.

What is the function of the god in this festival ? He descends to the other world. And the phalli of the priests ? They are put in a subterranean cave that belongs to the mother-goddess. And the lay brethren ? They abstain from coitus and believe that the fate of Attis their god is their own fate.

These three degrees remind us of Ferenczi's description of coitus.[1] The spermatozöon is really segregated from the body and enters the womb ; this is Attis, the god. Then the penis : it does the same thing but only partially and symbolically ; these are the priests with their male members put into the subterranean cave. Lastly the body : it participates in the adventures of the first two in a hallucinatory fashion. Now why does the laity abstain from intercourse ? Because for the time being they have found a common penis or ego-ideal in Attis, whose resurrection testifies that they, too, will triumph over death.

In trying to explain the beliefs of primitive mankind about death and the other world we saw that the grim horror of death was first glossed over by the allied horror of castration. Now the whole festival from the point of view of the laity is intended to allay the great anxiety of mortals, and it is the priests who castrate themselves for the community.

But here the pleasure-principle cannot stop and the unconscious substitutes coitus for castration. Both are derived from the same pre-genital root, from the time when fission meant death and at the same time new life for organic beings. Therefore in the third stage of displacement the thanato-phobia of the laity and the castration of the priest is reflected in the coitus of Attis. For it is as a coitus that we have interpreted the descent of Tammuz and Adonis, and according to the conjecture of Hepding the bath of the Mother Goddess[2] at this festival is the survival of her marriage feast with her son and lover. Moreover, the vernal feast was evidently meant to be a fertility charm, and fertility charms are always represented by some unconscious equivalent of coitus. But if the descent of the god is coitus what can his reappearance mean ? We shall answer this question after describing the initiation of the novice. The neophyte descended into

[1] Ferenczi, *Versuch einer Genitaltheorie*, 192–4.
[2] Frazer, *Adonis*, 234. Hepding, loc. cit., pp. 215–17.

a pit, the mouth of which was covered by a wooden grating. A bull adorned with garlands of flowers was driven to the grating and stabbed to death with consecrated spears. The blood poured through the grating on the worshipper below till he emerged dripping with blood and scarlet from head to foot to receive the homage of his fellows. For his sins had been washed away in the blood of the bull and he was born again to eternal life, and the fiction of a new birth was kept up by dieting him on milk like a new-born babe.[1]

Now it is a fact that in this cult the testicles of a bull or a ram were sometimes substituted for the testicles of the devotee.[2] Hence we may regard the bull as symbolizing the neophyte himself and the death of the bull atones for his sins. The same feature is also symbolized by his descent into the pit and is made still clearer by the circumstance that the whole ceremony took place at the same time as the descent and reappearance of the god. But the bull is also a symbol of fertility and the blood gushing forth from the wound means the semen. With the expenditure of the semen all anxiety (that is, sin), is washed away and a new being procreated in the mother's womb. He emerges as a new-born babe, and this explains the reappearance of the god. This is the last and final consolation offered by the unconscious and by life itself for death : re-birth in the child. Perhaps we may try and form some hypothesis as to the origin of the unconscious equation penis = embryo. It would be in keeping with our general view on the function of the psyche if we regarded this equation as due to a wish to offer a consolation, a medicine against the dread of castration or reluctance to emit the seminal fluid. The segregated penis lives on in the womb in a new organic environment that consoles it for what it has lost.

We shall therefore conclude that the myth and cult of Attis really represent coitus itself or death regarded by the unconscious as coitus. But on the other hand the bull is the symbol of the father and the death of the bull as an atonement for sins, a repetition of the primal sin. If therefore we find that these myths and cults can equally be explained by reference to the individual act of coitus and to the historic background of our psychic life in the conflicts of our ancestors, we shall both acknowledge that our own individual attitudes are modelled on phylogenetic experience represented by the Primal Horde, and suppose that that phase of man's existence itself was determined by a yet older phylogenetic experience which in the course of ages had become organic. The organism is the product of its environment and reacts on it, fashions it, modifies it according to its own innate

---

[1] Frazer, *Adonis*, p. 229   [2] Hepding, loc. cit., p. 191.

tendencies. Is not super-organic evolution traceable to organic, and the form of society with a single male as procreator a repetition of the evolution that led to the specific function of gametic cells? Returning, however, to the Phrygian kings we are discussing, we must observe that while their identification with Attis is merely conjectural (though of course the parallels are all in favour of that conjecture) there is no doubt about their identity with Midas. The mythical prototype of their dynasty intoxicated Silenus [1] in the same way as Bacchus caught Agdistis, thus forming a link between the myths of Attis and Midas. The latter, as we know, was the gentleman with the ass's ears. The myth connected with these ears travelled a long way, from the Aegean to Ireland and to Central Asia. But as a dream often told becomes more accessible to interpretation, it is from these variants that we can guess the latent contents of the original myth.

The king of Black China, east of India, had never shown himself to his subjects. Every day he sent for a barber, who, when he had finished his office, was executed. At last a barber came who was nibbling a cake made with his mother's milk. The youth discovered that the king had the ears of an ass. But the king tasted the cake, heard the story, spared the boy and swore him to secrecy. The boy fell ill through the secret which dwelt upon his mind and his physician told him that he would never recover till he got rid of it. He whispered it into a tree and a squirrel chattered the secret out. This variant has a happy ending : sometimes, however, the barber's head is cut off as a punishment.[2]

Now to touch the head of a chief or to be the barber of a king is a dangerous matter. " There is such a holiness ascribed to all parts of his (the Mikado's) body, that he dares to cut off neither his hair, nor his beard nor his nails. However, lest he should grow dirty they may clean him in the night when he is asleep . . . without prejudice for his dignity." [3] The wife of a Maori chief is tabooed for seven days after she has shorn his hair and in Fiji the danger of hair-cutting could only be warded off by the chief eating a human victim.[4]

If somebody has to be killed for hair cutting, evidently it ought to be the barber. Perhaps the royal taboo was prominent in the Phrygian dynasty and their hair could only be cut on condition that the barber was instantly put to death afterwards. In this case we

---

[1] Frazer, *Pausanias*, ii, p. 74. W. Crooke, " King Midas and his Ass's Ears," *Folk-Lore*, 1911, p. 183.

[2] Crooke, " King Midas," ibid., p. 192.

[3] Frazer, *Taboo*, p. 3. [4] Ibid., pp. 264, 265.

must ask, why should the king have such a phobia of losing his hair, and by way of an answer refer to the general care shown by savages in disposing of their hair and nail-parings. We saw that this was really a neurotic castration phobia and (if we interpret the king as a sort of embodiment of a phallic demon) it is easy to see why such a phobia should be particularly prominent in his case. But why an ass's ear ? It is very probable that as Crooke suggests the ass was the royal animal of Phrygian kings and that on special occasions they wore the hide of an ass as a mask or costume.

" In the ritual of the sacred marriages of gods, a piece of sympathetic or mimetic magic intended to promote the fertility of men, animals, and crops, the god was represented at his marriage in animal form, Dionysus for instance appearing as a bull.[1] On the other hand, A. B. Cook has proved the existence of an Aegean ass cult in which the ass had certain well-marked phallic qualities.[2]

The simple explanation of our tale seems to be that the shocking sight seen by a common mortal, the king's ass's ears or horns, is simply the father's phallus. The child sees the member in erection, the king celebrating his marriage festival, and the shock is too much for him. Repression is of no avail and the physician, evidently an early forerunner of analysts, tells him he will not get better till he discloses the secret. This is done to the mother or mother substitute, and in many cases brings about an ending happy for all.

The conclusion established by the analysis of the secret about King Midas' ass's ears tends to confirm our views on the phallic nature of the Phrygian king. It is perhaps possible to guess at a repartition of functions between the king and his son : the king as Midas enjoyed the advantages of his ass's ear and the son as Attis had to take the consequence.

5 THE PHARAOH AND OTHER AFRICAN KINGS

Towards the end of an hour of analysis, during which I was particularly successful in unveiling the latent contents of a patient's day-dreams, he suddenly exclaimed : " Well, I suppose I ought to have been king. But no, even that would have been of no use, for even the king can't simply say : " Well, please mother, now I want to have intercourse with you."

[1] Crooke, loc. cit., p. 199.
[2] " Animal Worship in the Mycenæan Age," *Journal of Hellenic Soc.*, xiv, p. 100.

Now this is just what the original rulers were made for, as realizations of and scapegoats for the unconscious desires of their subjects.

Frobenius calls the king in Africa a symbol, a fiction, a phantasy, carried into reality. " In direct contradiction to the customs of his subjects, the King marries his own sister or daughter. The Lumba-Humbe declared that this characteristic was decisive for genuine ancient kings between the Tanganjika and Bihe. The Hausa regarded this as a matter of course, but they were very much shocked by the idea of doing the same thing themselves. And similarly, everywhere where the old customs are still adhered to the other daughters of the king are free to fornicate wherever they may in the country as real priestesses of sexual desire. Besides the king another member of the royal family called the ' King's Mother ' is prominent. She may be either his mother, aunt, or elder sister, but at any rate she is regarded as the ' mother of kings ' and occupies a high position ".[1]

Three features characterize African monarchy : 1 The king is not himself, not what he seems to be, but the representative of an ancestral god, a being who lived in the infancy of humanity. 2 Acting up to this ego-ideal the king lives in an incestuous union with his sister, and is killed by his subjects. 3 He represents fecundity, he is regarded as the great source of life.

Now the Egyptian rulers, who appear in every respect as true representatives of African royalty, represented either the sun-god Ra (in a latter period Amon) or Osiris or his son Horus. As for Osiris and Horus, we have discussed the elements of their myth. It contains incest with the sister, regicide, and castration, and the reappearance of the dead king in his son.

" As a god of vegetation "—Sir James Frazer tells us—" Osiris was naturally conceived as a god of creative energy in general, since men at a certain stage of evolution fail to distinguish between the reproductive powers of animals and of plants. Hence a striking feature in his worship was the coarse but expressive symbolism by which this aspect of his nature was presented to the eye of the multitude. At his festival women used to go about the villages singing songs in his praise and carrying obscene images of him which they set in motion by means of strings." [2]

The phallic nature of this divinity and his identity with the king is made quite clear by some rites connected with the bull Apis,

[1] Frobenius, *Atlas Africanus*, Heft 2, p. 7.

[2] Frazer, *Adonis*, p. 343. Herodotus, ii, 48. Plutarch, *De Iside*, 12, 18, 36, 51. Diodorus Siculus, i, 21, 5 ; 22, 6 ; iv, 6, 3.

who was the image of the soul of Osiris.[1] This Apis carries mummies
on his back to the other world and Osiris is called the " Bull of
Aneenti ".[2] When the Apis died its soul went to Heaven, joined
Osiris there, and continued to exist as the double divinity Asar-
Hapi, Osiris-Apis.[3] According to another version, it is not the
soul of Osiris which passed into the Apis, but the members of Osiris
were thrown by Isis into an ox made of wood and covered with
ox-hides, and hence the name of the city Busiris.[4] We shall see
that this is exactly what happens to African rulers when they die,
and just as the hawk which stands both for Osiris and Horus was
the double of the pharaoh in pre-historic times,[5] the bull Apis may
have been the double of other rulers. Like the rulers of yore the bull
was reverenced as a god as long as he lived and he was drowned in
the holy spring when the term of his rule (25 years) had expired.[6]
After the death of an Apis, mourning lasts till the new Apis is found
and installed. The spirit of Osiris is infused into one bull after the
other as each of them enters on his divine functions.[7] His death
and burial are affairs as secret as those of a murdered king. Bulls
were sacrificed to this divine bull and this sacrifice must have been
regarded as a sinful yet necessary act, for we are told that the sacrificers
declared that any misfortune which might fall on them or Egypt in
general might strike the cut-off head of the sacrificed bull.[8]

It seems that the sexual functions of the bull were regarded as of
primary importance. Once a year a cow was brought to the divine
bull, an honour for which she had to pay with her life.[9] But the
bulls seem to have been compensated for this modest allotment of
cow-wives by human consorts, or rather, we should say, that the
tendency in this isolation was to reserve all the male strength in the
bull for the benefit of humanity. Diodorus Siculus tells us that
before he came to Memphis the bull was brought up in Nilopolis
for forty days where the women showed him their genitalia.[10]

Now Ramses is " king of the throne of Ra " and from the fifth
dynasty every ruler of Egypt was a *sa Ra*, a son of the Sun-God.[11]

---

[1] Plutarch, *De Iside*, 20.   [2] Budge, *Gods of the Egyptians*, ii, p. 350.
[3] Budge, loc. cit., p. 349.   [4] Ibid., p. 348.
[5] V. Loret, *L'Egypte au Temps du Totemisme. Ann. M.G.*, xix, 1906,
p. 203.   [6] Frazer, *Spirits of the Corn*, ii, p. 34.
[7] Budge, loc. cit., ii, p. 348.   [8] Herodotus, loc. cit., ii, 38–41.
[9] A. Erman, *Die ägyptische Religion*, 1909, p. 190, quoting Pliny, *Hist.
nat.*, viii, 185.
[10] Diodorus, i, 85. Plutarch, loc. cit., 160.
[11] A. Moret, *Du Caractère Religieux de la Royauté Pharaonique*, 1902,
p. 10.

The Egyptians called the sun *Kamephis*, "Bull of his Mother," that is the bull who has intercourse with his own mother and procreates himself.[1] In a hymn probably belonging to the XXth or XXIst dynasty Amen-Ra the god is spoken of as the lord of the tchefan food, the bull of offerings, in the name of " Amen, Bull of thy mother ".[2] The connection of Ra with the king is specially emphasized by the fact that every king was regarded as born from the mystic union of the queen with the Sun-God. This union is effected by the rays of the sun, and the rays contained *sa*. The Sun continued to confer *sa* on the Pharaoh and this *sa* appears to have been regarded as a sort of magnetic fluid passing from the god to the king. The technical expression used is *sotpou*, a word that originally means the ejaculation of seminal fluid.[3] It is by this perpetual supply of seminal fluid that the king becomes capable of discharging his holy office, of playing the part of the fecundating principle for the country and his subjects.

The third divinity with whom the king was identified is Amen, frequently appearing as a deity united to the Sun-God as Amen Ra. This Amen, originally a local god of Thebes, is represented with a feathered hat and like Min he is a purely human divinity with no animal incarnation. His head-dress and blue skin, and especially the fact that he is represented as an ithyphallic divinity, remind us of Min so that Erman regards the two as originally identical.[4] Now the great god Min, the local divinity of Koptos, is purely and evidently a personification of the phallus. His head is crowned by two big feathers and his right hand is raised holding a whip. He is the god who performs coitus with his own mother, the god who steals women, the master of maidens. He appears holding his penis in his hand.[5]

If the king is Osiris, the god of phallic festivals, if he is Ra, the " bull of his mother ", the source of seminal fluid, if he is Amon and Amon is Min, the phallus, there can indeed be no more doubt as to the phallic nature of royalty. Still it does no harm to make assurance doubly sure and we shall quote the opinions of Egyptologists on the regalia.

Before giving these opinions in detail it is worth while considering the nature of regalia in general. They refer either to the head-dress or the sceptre. In the case of Midas, the starting point of the myth seems to have been the mask of an ass assumed by the king for special occasions and Crooke's conjecture was that the special occasion in question was the moment when the king representing the god of

[1] Erman, loc. cit., p. 8.   [2] Budge, loc. cit., ii, p. 11.
[3] Moret, loc. cit., p. 47.   [4] Erman, loc. cit., p. 18.   [5] Ibid.

fertility consummated his marriage with the queen-mother. Moreover there are two peculiar facts that have not been duly emphasized till now, firstly that Greek gods frequently assume animal form for the purpose of some love adventure and secondly that the bestial attributes of Egyptian gods are always manifested on their heads. The explanation for this peculiarity lies in the custom of wearing animal masks. Evidently these divinities were connected with the usual form of African secret societies and represented by men who danced about in animal masks. But this is no solution of the question ; we do not know why the peculiar ornaments are connected with the head. In my book on Australian Totemism I have found that the churinga, a source of creative energies and a penis-symbol, is put in the head-dress of the performers at Intichiuma ceremonies. These ceremonies, as I have shown, are survivals of the pre-human rutting season so that the head-dresses of the Australian ceremonies, the masks worn by secret-societies, the bestial appearance of the god's head in Egypt, and last but not least the crown of royalty seem to be super-organic equivalents of the secondary sex characters. It is well known that the males of certain animal species develops antlers, crests, manes, and all sorts of appendanges during the rutting season which they frequently discard when the rutting season comes to an end. These secondary sex characters are regarded as closely connected with the primary ones by zoologists ; they appear to be simply the penis displaced upwards ; and it seems that this displacement upwards, this erection displaced to the head, is a necessary fore-pleasure phase, an introduction to coitus in the case of some animals.[1] If we are right in regarding masks and crowns as derived from the same source, we shall expect to find (a) that the symbolism of the crown should be connected with ideas of fertility, (b) that we should find " kings " and " queens " as leading actors in ceremonial survivals of the pairing season.

All the symbolism of the regalia, Moret says, is connected with the head-dress and the sceptre. The gods have crowns and the king imitates them. During the number of centuries that passed from the beginning to the end of Egyptian royalty and with the many local cults that played a part in the political and religious history of the country, an endless variety of crowns was evolved and it is impossible to ascertain the meaning of each symbol. But it is enough for our purposes that the chief insignia are understood by Egyptologists and the others are probably formed on the same lines.

[1] Róheim, op. cit., p. 243. Cf. M. Bonaparte, " Über die Symbolik der Kopftrophäen," *Imago*, xiv, p. 100.

The typical crown of the pharaoh is the *pshent*—a combination of the white crown of the north and the red crown of the south. The white crown is evidently a peaked hat. De Rochemonteix regards it as something more : the outline or the short-hand equivalent of the divine crown *atef*. The *atef* is a series of lotus plants with a disc above and a disc below, as according to Egyptian myth Horus, who in this case appears to be a sun god, rises in the morning from the lotus and returns into the calyx of the flower at nightfall. Now the king is said to rise in the morning like the sun, and before each divine service he is reborn to divine life. Thus Rochemonteix concludes that the white crown symbolized this idea of perpetual youth or rebirth. His theory of the red crown ($\bigvee$) is no less ingenious. He regards it as a conventionalized sign formed of the hieroglyphics, the stalk of a plant ℮, the earth || and a vase ▽. In other words the king puts a vase on his head and in this vase earth is fecundated by water, thus giving rise to vegetation.

When the king has this crown put upon his head, Horus declares that the union of the two countries, south and north, is achieved. However, according to Moret, the union of the two countries may also be interpreted mythologically as the union of Sky and Earth typifying the union of male and female. According to Soldi, whom Moret seems inclined to follow, the spiral is a projection of the solar disc, a spiral ray "*qui vient féconder l'union des germes solides et liquides*". This spiral reappears in connection with the sun and with the sanctuaries of the phallic god Min. The details may still be open to doubt, Moret says, but at any rate for the period of the full development of Egyptian symbolism these interpretations seem to be correct, so that the whole crown *pshent* certainly conveys the idea " *de la fécondation de l'univers par l'action du soleil perpétuellement renaissant* ".[1] Various other symbols were added to this central idea, for instance the feather of an ostrich as symbol of the god Shu. This divinity sometimes appears as the patron of the pharaoh ; mythologically his function consists in taking his mother Nut, the Sky, from his father Sebk, the Earth, thus separating the father from the mother. Then again we find the horns of a ram representing Khnoumou the potter-god, who fashions human beings ; according to Rochemonteix " *elles rapellent l'énergie fécondatrice* ". But no crown is complete without a hoop formed of the tail (*sed*) of the Uraeus serpent. The Uraeus was a goddess and she received the same adoration in Lower Egypt as the vulture in Upper Egypt. When the king wished to proclaim his sovereignty over all Egypt he gave himself the title

[1] Moret, loc. cit., p. 286.

of " Lord of the shrines of the Vulture and Uraeus ".[1] The city of the vulture-goddess was called " Eileithyiaspolis " by the Greeks, thus indicating her maternal functions.[2] The Uraeus projects flame from its mouth, and this flame may either be lightning descending on the enemies of the king and " eating " the enemies of the gods, or the fiery milk, the food that makes the gods immortal. The deified dead drink the milk of the Uraeus.

But the phenomenon called *over-determination* by analysts is very much at home in the rich growth of Egyptian symbolism. Not only is the hoop a serpent's tail but the two crowns are also identified with the goddesses of the North and the South, the Uraeus and the Vulture. The vulture-goddess protects ; she hides the dead under her wings. The name of the Uraeus goddess means " *raverdir, rajeunir* "— she is the goddess of perpetual youth. Thus, says Moret, two great goddesses are symbolized by the two crowns " *qui s'unissent corporellement au roi* ".[3]

In the petty rulers of Central Africa from the Nile to the Congo we have living representatives of the Egyptian monarchy. Each king of the Bakitara had a new crown made and they were put on his head in quick succession. They were made by experts from palm leaves and the fibre of the bark of a certain tree. There was a woven frame of the crown with beads and a chin strap covered with the long hair of the colobus monkey which looked like a beard and hung to the waist. These skins were obtained from the eastern side of the Nile. Round the edge of the crown of the reigning king were eighteen eyeless needles of iron, brass, and copper called the *Amasoke*. They were all six or seven inches long and two made of iron had twisted ends and were known as " the males ". [4]

If we regard magic head-dresses as the secondary sex characters of the rutting male, all this Egyptian symbolism looks like a return of repressed elements. Everything is as clear as could be desired. The king is a phallic divinity, the crown represents the union of the sexes, of Father and Mother and by way of the solar symbolism it stands for incest.

The ostrich feather and the horns of the man-making god are evidently phallic symbols, while the female symbolism can be explained by the hypothesis that the king's head itself stands for the phallus and the head in the crown is the penis in the vagina.

We shall now follow Moret in his explanation of the sceptre.

---

[1] Budge, loc. cit., p. 24.   [2] Ibid.
[3] Moret, loc. cit., pp. 284–9.
[4] J. Roscoe, *The Bakitara*, 1923, pp. 130, 131.

The objects that appear in the king's hand are a crooked staff, stone-headed club, a sceptre, and a whip. As for the first, it evidently represents the king as the shepherd of his people, just as Tammuz, the dying king of the Sumerians, appears as a shepherd. The stone-headed club is used by the king to kill the victim at the sacrifice or to give the consecrating touch to the sacrificial food that transmutes it into food fit for the gods. The stone-headed club being an ancient throwing weapon, it signifies the idea of projecting something, as the gods created the universe by emitting sound and light. The sceptre represents strength and might, sometimes gods and kings hold the sceptre out to each other with the *ankh*, symbol of life, issuing from its end, thus exchanging their vital fluids. Finally the whip is the attribute of Osiris and the gods connected with him. It means " to project light " ; the phallic god Min projects " life " and " light " by uplifting his whip.[1]

I think there cannot be the slightest doubt about the fact that all these sceptres, whips and clubs with " light ", " voice ", and " life " emanating from them represent the penis and that the often-quoted vital fluid is simply the real vital fluid, the seminal fluid that gives life.

The king is a " good deity ", he who " creates " the sacrifice for the gods. " His palace is the House of Life," the " place where magic fluid is ejected ".[2] The word translated as " ejection " above could also be given as " ejaculation " for it is again the same word *sotpou* which conveys the idea of the life-giving act. The king being the principle of life itself, it is no wonder that a ceremony should be held to renew the life of the king. For this seems to have been the avowed aim of the Sed festival, or Osirification of the rulers of Egypt. The following occurs in a Sed festival for the king. " Thou re-beginnest thy renewal, beginnest to flourish again like the infant god of the Moon, thou art young again year by year, like Nun at the beginning of ages, thou art reborn by renewing thy festival of Sed." [3] The rebirth alluded to here seems to have been really performed, at least at Bubastis, by pulling the king through a hide (the *tikenu* mentioned above),[4] but here if anywhere we can see distinctly that the " birth shock " is only a consolation for something more serious. A whole series of very competent authorities agree in regarding the Sed festival as a symbolic survival of regicide.

At this festival the king's soul is said to be lost and found again.[5]

[1] Moret, loc. cit., pp. 290–3.   [2] Ibid., pp. 296, 297.
[3] Moret, loc. cit., p. 256.   [4] Moret, *Mystères Egyptiens*, 1913, p. 73.
[5] Moret, *Royauté*, p. 249.

Originally, we may conjecture, the soul was lost for good and the ceremony is called the tail, i.e. the end, the end of the king's rule. We quote the summary given by Seligman. "The sed festival of ancient Egypt seems to be a survival of the custom of the ceremonial killing of the king. The essential point of the ceremony was the identification of the king, though still living, with Osiris the god of the underworld with whom every Egyptian was united at his death." The oldest representation of the ceremony which has come down to us, is on the mace head of the god Narmer. This shows the king as Osiris, seated in a shrine at the top of nine steps and holding the flail commonly held by the god. At one side of the space in front of the king are a number of standards, the first of which is the jackal Upwawat, " the opener of the ways," described on the seal of King Zer as " he who opens the way when thou advancest towards the under-world ". This seal shows King Zer as Osiris preceded by Upwawat and the ostrich feather, called the *shed-shed*, which is in front and upon which the deceased is supposed to ascend. " Here then "—says Professor Petrie, " the king identified with Osiris, king of the dead, has before him a jackal god who leads the dead and the ostrich feather which symbolizes his reception into the sky." [1]

It seems that the effigy of the king as Osiris was solemnly buried in a cenotaph.[2] In pictures of the Sed festival we see the king enthroned as the dead Osiris ; he is wrapped in tight bandages like the mummified god.[3] Having thus become identical with Osiris, that is with the dead, there is no need for him to die in good earnest. Thus he has escaped from the hands of his pious and devoted subjects, and this truly meant a new lease of life, a life that seemed eternity.

A representation of the festival discovered at Memphis shows the stuffed or dried arms and chest of a man being carried behind the king. Professor Petrie believes that originally it was the actual dried mummy of the dead king Osiris, whilst in historic ages probably the cartonnage models of a chest and arms were carried to the investiture and laid on the shoulders of the new ruler to confer the virtue of the royal office.[4] We may perhaps regard the ghostly appearance of the corpse originally as a *memento mori*, a reminder of the days when it

---

[1] C. G. Seligman, " Some Aspects of the Hamitic Problem in the Anglo-Egyptian Sudan," *JRAI.*, 1913, p. 665. Flinders Petrie, *Researches in Sinai*, 1906, p. 183.

[2] J. Capart, " Bulletin critique des religions de l'Égypte," *Revue de l'Histoire des Religions*, liii, 1906, pp. 332–4. Frazer, *Adonis*, p. 381.

[3] Frazer, loc. cit., p. 380.

[4] *Palace of Apries*, 1909, p. 10.

was time for the king to become really identical with his ghostly predecessor. However, Osiris, the ruler of the dead, is also the phallus —the source of life. Hence there is the emblem of *ankh*, the life symbol, emanating from this corpse,[1] and the identification of the king with the phallus—the union of earth and sky—means life in a different sense than the one indicated above.

For death is coitus and coitus is death. Miss Murray says that Osiris is the king and the king is Osiris—in other words that the spirit of fertility is incarnate in the king. She distinguishes four chief features in the Sed festival : (1) the king is represented as Osiris, (2) before him is carried the figure of the jackal-god, (3) the royal daughter, seated in a litter, is the most important figure after the king, and (4) in most instances there are one or more running or dancing men.

" This presence of the royal daughter and the running men "— Miss Murray tells us—" is due to the scene being one of marriage. The throne went in the female line so that the queen was queen by right of birth, the king was king by right of marriage. The dancing men were probably the suitors for her hand ; but whether the dance was a contest before marriage or a fertility dance after marriage is uncertain." [2] From the fact that in the representation of the Sed festival of the XIIth dynasty the king dances alone before Min, the god of generation, it would seem to be a fertility dance to promote the increase and welfare of the crops, animals, and people of his kingdom.[2] Miss Murray further points out that Rameses II possibly had six Sed festivals because he had six marriages ; at any rate we know of four marriages of his, first with his sister and then with three of his daughters in succession.[3] In holding a marriage festival at the moment of his death the king only repeats the history of his divine prototype. For it is the dead Osiris who procreates Horus with Isis. Coitus being a partial castration (expenditure of the semen), the member of Osiris is missed by Isis, and if the king dances before the phallic god we shall say that he is acting the penis, *so that his death is truly a sort of self-castration of the social body.*

Before passing on to what may either be the *débris* of Egyptian ideas among other African people or perhaps in some cases the primitive germs of this system, we shall take leave of the pharaoh by considering the Baganda equivalent of the Sed festival.

The ceremony held for prolonging the life of the king of Uganda

[1] M. A. Murray, " Evidence for the Custom of Killing the King in Ancient Egypt," *Man*, 1914, p. 22.
[2] Murray, loc. cit., pp. 20, 21.   [3] Ibid., p. 21.

is connected with the chief of the Lung-Fish clan called Nankere. This Nankere lived in the north of the Busiro district and he was never permitted to see the king except when he performed the ceremony for prolonging his life. When the time came for performing the ceremony, Nankere selected one of his own sons, or, if he had no son, a near relation, who was then fed and clothed and treated in all respects as a prince and was taken to live in a special house near the place where the king had to go to perform the ceremony. After the youth had been guarded and fed for a month and treated in all respects as a prince, the king set out from the capital. At the temple of Mukasa he stopped and changed his clothing, leaving his anklets behind, for he received new ones from Nankere. When the king arrived at his destination, Nankere handed him a gourd of beer and he handed another in exchange. The king's mother was present at the ceremony and she was to see her son for the last time. Nankere turned to the king : " You are now of age, go and live longer than your forefathers." Now Nankere's son was brought in and presented to the king. The king passed him on to his bodyguard who took him outside and killed him by beating him with their closed fists. The muscles from the back of the body of the murdered youth were removed and made into anklets for the king and a piece of skin was cut from the body to make a whip, which was kept in the royal enclosure for special feasts. The body was thrown upon waste land and guarded against wild beasts but not buried. The king then returned and after playing a certain game under a large tree, he was met by a chief of the Mushroom clan who conducted him to his wife Naku. Here the king planted a plantain-tree and cut some grass which he handed to his wife. Then followed his ceremonial meeting with a chief called Walusimbi. The king again played the game with the fruit stones ; under a tree he would call for the fruit stones to play with and whoever ran to bring them would be caught and speared to death on the spot with the object of giving the king long life. Some boys carried cooking pots before him ; his attendants killed as many of them as they could. The king and his train passed on to the Princess Naluwembi, where the king stopped until the anklets made from the muscles of Nankere's murdered son were ready for him to wear. It was the Princess Naluwembi who had to superintend the making of them. When they were finished they were put on the king and the party went on to Kibibi, where he took his stand upon a hillock, saying : " I want a hut built here, go and cut the grass and bring the materials." The man who first arrived with grass was caught and killed and his head placed on top of the hut.

The king entered the hut when it was ready and his wife Naku cooked him a meal there. The hut was called Naku's hut and was kept as a fetish shrine during the king's lifetime. After this he sent a farewell message to his mother whom he was not allowed to meet again.

Just as the Egyptian monarch repeated the ritual of his enthronization, it was customary for the king of Uganda to give a feast to his people from time to time to commemorate his accession. After the Nankere ceremony, a feast on a larger scale was arranged. At this feast a priest called Mutebi went about carrying under his mantle the whip which had been made from the skin of Nankere's murdered son ; any person whom he struck with it had to pay either nine or ninety cowry shells to the goddess Namulondo to prevent sickness and death from falling upon him. When a person who had been struck with the whip went to pay the cowry shells to the priest, the latter struck him on the shoulder with his hand and by this means removed a curse which the whip had laid upon him and which deprived him of his generative powers. At the end of the feast all the drums were removed excepting the drum called Busemba. Someone in the crowd would notice the apparent oversight and bring the drum along ; this person was instantly caught and killed and the bones from his upper arm were made into drum-sticks for that particular drum.[1]

What has this wholesale slaughter of innocent human beings got to do with the prolongation of the king's life ? We are reminded of the fact that the Sed festival involves the right of burying a model instead of the king and that the victims drawn through the *tikenu* were originally killed outright. Perhaps at one phase of its development human victims were killed to " prolong the king's life ", that is, they died as substitutes for His Majesty. The Baganda slaughter many human victims as sacrifices to the dead king [2] and perhaps the same feature of ritual in the ceremony we are concerned with is intended to indicate that the king is dead. Moreover, it seems that the slaughter is an introduction to what looks like a marriage ceremony, especially if the tree planted by the king when conducted to his wife Naku should be interpreted as a Tree of Life. The human sacrifice is repeated later on, and a hut is built by the king for his wife Naku. Now the Sed festival had something to do with the erection of a temple and Naku's hut was kept as a fetish shrine during the king's lifetime. It is the hut of the king's wife. Osorkon's Sed festival at Bubastis is described in the following words, " assumption of the protection of the two lands by the King, the protection of the sacred

[1] J. Roscoe, *The Baganda*, 1911, pp. 209–13.
[2] Roscoe, loc. cit., p. 284.

women of the house of Amon, the protection of all the women of this city." [1]

The first and most important of human victims is Nankere's son. He is treated like a prince before being killed, evidently because he is a substitute for the king. We might describe the ceremony as the ritual murder of a son by his father, and as we shall see that other African princes kill their fathers on their accession to the throne, it would seem that the reversal of the original situation is a natural substitute for the king's death. Looking more closely into the details, however, we find that at this ceremony the king is said to come of age, and like the members of any savage tribe at their initiation, only in a more accentuated manner, he is separated from his mother. Some Egyptologists regarded the Sed festival as the thirtieth anniversary of the king's appointment as crown prince [2] and it would seem therefore that there is some allusion to this phase of his life in the evidence. The initiation ceremony is the period when the youths of a tribe are symbolically " killed " by the ghosts or their fathers and our ritual looks like a condensation of initiation and regicide. Psycho-analysis derives both these ceremonies from the original conflict in the Primal Horde, from the incest desired and fought for both by father and son. This is the myth on the origin of the life-prolongation festival :

Tembo, the grandson of Kimera, had two children, a son and a daughter. The son fell in love with his sister and married her—thus following the example of Osiris and the rulers of Egypt. She gave birth to twins and at the place where she felt the birth-pains a river sprang forth. At the place where she gave birth to the twins two rivers with their twin springs sprang forth. Later on, Tembo became insane and could not be cured until someone suggested taking him to the chief Nankere where he derived benefit from a human sacrifice and from the anklets made out of the sinews of a man of the Lung-fish clan ; and this was the origin of the life-prolongation ceremonies. [3]

But if Tembo's son committed the incest why should Tembo become insane and be cured by a life-prolongation ceremony ? There are sure indications in the myth that the incest is only carried over to the son but originally belonged to the same actor in the drama for whom substitutes were killed in the Nankere ritual. For Tembo is responsible for the other part of what forms a connected whole ; he committed what must be regarded as the equivalent of parricide.

[1] Murray, loc. cit., p. 20.   [2] Murray, loc. cit., p. 20.
[3] Roscoe, *Baganda*, p. 216.

Tembo killed his grandfather when the king was out hunting bush-buck, but the ghost haunted the king and wished to be avenged on him. To appease the ghost Tembo made a drum and directed that the sticks used for beating it should be made from the bones of a human being. When the bones were provided, the ghost of Kimera was quieted. This is the final ceremony in the series of human sacrifices described above. Here it becomes evident that the human sacrifices are the substitutes for the death of a king killed by his grandchild. And the Baganda take good care that the king should not be permitted to forget the deed which gave him power, life, and will give him death. Like the mummy of Osiris appearing as a *memento mori* at the Sed festival to remind the ruler of his impend-ing fate, this human sacrifice and the original parricide it was established to atone for was from time to time brought to the memory of the king. The priest called Mutebi occasionally went into the king's presence dressed in a mantle of cow-hide which covered his body from neck to foot. At such times he concealed under his robe the arm-bones of the man killed for the drum. As he stepped before the king he quickly produced the bones and shook them before him, then he quickly hid them again.[1]

Again, there are reasons for connecting this death of Nankere's son and the other victims with the idea of castration. It is remarkable that all these human beings should be killed when the king is separated from his mother and it looks as if this were more than a mere coincidence. Nankere's son represents the king, Nankere would be the king's father and henceforth the king is tabooed from seeing him just as he may not see his mother. It seems that the death of a son who was treated like a prince had a specific meaning besides the idea of substitution. We remember the account of Berossus of the Sacäa—the man sacrificed instead of the king previously has access to the king's wives. Perhaps this circumstance is of greater importance than we could guess till now ; the sacrifice and the forma-tion of substitutes seems to be specially connected with this side of the king's functions. The whip formed of the skin of Nankere's son deprives people of their generative power [2] and his death separates the king from his mother. We find another similar substitute for the king in the person of the Kauzumu who is the king's half-brother. It is his duty to fulfil certain ceremonies and taboos for him and thus to save him from inconvenience. It was his duty to take for one night to his bed the women who were to become the king's wives. When one of the king's wives went away to mourn the death of a relative

<hr>

[1] Roscoe, loc. cit., pp. 213, 214.　　[2] Roscoe, loc. cit., p. 213.

it was the Kauzumu who on her return brought her back to the king and before presenting her jumped over her ; thus she was restored to His Majesty free from any restrictions.   When one of the king's wives died, the Kauzumu was the chief mourner instead of the king, and when a clan sent a woman to fill the deceased wife's place the Kauzumu jumped over her before he presented her to the king. When presented she took a goat with her ; the king placed his hand upon her head and then upon the goat's head, after which the Kauzumu took the goat, killed it, and gave her the liver to eat.[1]

The distinctive features in this ceremonial complex are :—

1 The Kauzumu acts as a sort of scapegoat for the king.

2 The functions of the scapegoat are closely connected with the sexual sphere.

3 The taboo resting on the new wife is removed by a real scapegoat ceremony.

In Urundi a number of girls follow the funeral of the king to the country of the Wanganje.   Presumably all these girls were once given to the dead king as his wives, that is, sacrificed to his ghost. At present they all return safe and sound excepting one girl. This is the one chosen by the chief of the Wanganje to become his wife and by marrying her he acquires the right to the hereditary royal title of *Mwesi* (Moon).   A second chief of the Wanganje is also called *Mwesi* and this one is the keeper of all the sacred seed stored up during many generations.   This second *Mwesi* is killed when the ruler dies.[2]

One of the two royal substitutes in Urundi marries the king's concubine, the other is the " keeper of the seed ".   We suspect that the seed originally meant human seed and that the process of substitute-formation is analogous to that " genito-petal " migration of the libido which makes the penis a substitute for the whole body.

We shall continue to study the function of these royal substitutes in connection with the ascent of the king to the throne.   The peculiar conclusion we are arriving at is that the ascent to the throne is the death of the king.   Before we finally explain the meaning of this contradiction, we must observe two features of African royalty ; the ambivalency connected with king-killing and the incestuous marriage of the ruler.

If a king of Baganda was killed in a rebellion, the successful prince assumed the throne and went through all the accession ceremonies. He mourned for his fallen brother as though his death was the greatest calamity which the country could have sustained and he pardoned the chiefs and the people who had supported the late king. The

---

[1] Roscoe, loc. cit., pp. 205, 206.   [2] Meyer, *Die Barundi*, p. 186.

person who struck down a king or a rival prince, provided it happened in a civil war, was belauded on all sides as a great hero ; and he was loaded with gifts and honours at the same time. The new king, however, when he was established on the throne would seek out the person and put him to death, as one who had shed royal blood.[1] Behind this ambivalency we find incest. Like many a Pharaoh whom he perhaps imitated in the life-prolongation ceremony, the king of Uganda married his half-sister. It was essential that the princess selected should be a sister of the king, though not by the same mother, and further that her own mother should have no sons.[2] Besides this, the peculiar taboo-relations between the king and his mother look like the repression of a former incestuous marriage. For instance, the queen-mother is treated in much the same fashion as the king's chief wife. When the royal enclosure was ready for the king, he took possession of it with his wives but the queen had her own residence at a distance of about a mile. It was necessary to have a stream of running water dividing her court from the king's because she was also a king with her own independent establishment and two kings could not live on the same hill. The same applied also to the king's mother ; she too was called a king and her residence had to be divided from the king's by a stream of running water.[3] The king's mother owned estates of her own and had her own court. Like the queen, she was carried on men's shoulders when travelling. She was not permitted to marry again, though it was known that she had paramours. We believe that the prohibition of marriage rested on the unconscious ideas of the queen as the wife of her son, while her indulgence in love affairs was a corollary of the symbolic meaning of royalty in general. She had a guardian, a man from her own clan, whom she regarded as her brother. She was forbidden to have children and if the king heard that any man was becoming too familiar with his mother he ordered him to be executed.[4] Similarly among the Wawanga, the king's mother is a most important personage who possesses great influence over the king in domestic and tribal matters. She exacts large contributions in money and in kind from the king and if these contributions are not forthcoming she threatens to make use of the power vested in her by virtue of her custody of the sacred spears ; a threat that rarely fails to have the desired effect.[5] She plays a very important part in the reaping and sowing ceremonies ;

---

[1] Roscoe, loc. cit., pp. 347, 348.   [2] Ibid., p. 191.
[3] Ibid., p. 203.   [4] Roscoe, loc. cit., p. 237.
[5] Kenneth R. Dundas, " The Wawanga and other Tribes of the Elgon District," *JRAI*, 1913, p. 30.

before the people begin to sow a black ram must be strangled before the hut of the king's mother or chief wife. In the family of a chief it is always his mother or chief wife who must commence sowing the wimbe crop.[1] Frobenius tells us that according to the old ritual of the Mossi empire a king or emperor always married one or more of his own daughters. But one daughter, usually the eldest, had to remain a virgin as long as her father was alive.[2] Weeks knew a king of Congo who had one of his own daughters living with him in his enclosure as his wife.[3] Perhaps this was not an individual freak but the survival of a feature closely connected with the ritual of African monarchy. The return from the taboo attitude to an attitude of unbridled wish-fulfilment characterizes the king, but even here we see that the king's other daughters are merely substitutes for his eldest who remains under a taboo. And as for the eldest we may regard her as a substitute for the king's mother who is under a similar taboo in Uganda.

After this digression we return to the problem of substitutes and of scapegoats who die to prolong the king's life when he ascends his ancestral throne.

Among the Banyoro a boy was appointed whose duty it was to drink the surplus of the king's milk. Should the boy fall sick during the term of his office he would be strangled, and should he have sexual relations with a woman he would be put to death. He had to be guarded against scratching his flesh or doing anything that might draw blood. To strike this boy was an offence punishable with death because the boy's life was bound up with that of the king and anything that happened to him was liable to affect the king.[4]

That the life of the king is bound up, in this case not in an adult but in a boy, is a significant feature. The same infantile attitude inherent in royalty is indicated by the first thing the king of Ruanda does after his accession to the throne ; he drinks milk.[5] The origin myth of Banyoro royalty shows the real meaning of this infantile attitude.

The oracle said that if King Bukulu's daughter had a son the king would surely die. So he guarded his daughter in a tower, but nevertheless it happened that a man from the priestly clan called Bucwezi

[1] Ibid., p. 48.
[2] L. Frobenius, *Und Afrika Sprach*, 1913, ii, pp. 176, 372.
[3] John R. Weeks, *Among the Primitive Bakongo*, 1914, p. 38.
[4] J. Roscoe, *The Northern Bantu*, 1915, p. 9.
[5] John Roscoe, *The Bagesu and other tribes of the Uganda Protectorate*, 1924, p. 189.

had intercourse with her and she had a son. The king gave the boy to the guard to be drowned but the child's umbilical cord was tied to its wrist and when the child was cast into the river the string by which the cord was tied to the wrist caught on a branch and saved the child from drowning.[1] This was regarded as an intervention of the gods and the boy grew up as the son of the guardsman who attempted to kill him. Finally, a struggle ensued between the boy and the king's herdsmen in which the king was fatally speared. The regicide became king and disappeared in his old age because it was not customary for kings to die.[2]

The boy kills the king because his pseudo-father attempted to kill him, although in the myth the situation is reversed from the standpoint of retribution anxiety and the attempted murder of the boy is motivated by his future as a king-killer. It is this eternal boy, the representative of unbroken infantile wish-fulfilment, who is embodied in the boy mentioned above. There is something in a king of " His Majesty the Baby ", that is, his life is bound up with the life of a boy. He retains the traces of the Oedipus constellation period before the Oedipus attitude becomes sublimated in a super-ego in consequence of the castration-threat.[3] The king subsisted on milk and beef but chiefly on milk. He drank the milk from a herd of nine cows jealously guarded against a bull,[4] that is, he remains a child who has realized the Oedipus wish, eliminated the father and become sole possessor of a series of mythical mothers.

The king as an infant drinking milk reminds me forcibly of the dream of a patient of mine. First he related a novel of Goethe's about children's fights and struggles and how, in after years, a lad and a lass who were the chief antagonists in these fights meet again and the reviving memory of their infantile pugnacity develops into a deep love. Then he went on to tell me how he saw a " Manna-battle " in a dream. Two groups of children fight each other with snow-balls and with great good humour and pluck. Manna falls from the sky. Suddenly there is an eruption of a volcano (Mount Sinai) and a complete change in the attitude of the children. Their games are broken up by a panic, the ceiling (or sky) opens above his head and he sees a vagina.

---

[1] This episode is a striking confirmation of Rank's interpretation of the exposure as a repetition of the intra-uterine situation. The child who is thrown into the water hangs from his umbilical cord.

[2] J. Roscoe, *The Northern Bantu*, 1915, p. 6.

[3] Cf. S. Freud, " Untergang des Oedipus-komplexes," *Zeitschrift*, 1923.

[4] J. Roscoe, *The Northern Bantu*, 1915, p. 10.

The associations and other dreams show what is meant by the period when manna fell from the sky. It is the time when nourishment could be obtained without any effort. This was the happy age of unbroken wish fulfilment of the infant who was nourished by the nurse's milk. In dim outlines we see an episode of childhood ; at the age of three he caught sight of a servant-girl's vulva who was on a ladder above him masturbated in his excitement and had deep pangs of conscience after it. His whole attitude towards life changed and although everybody noticed it and he would have been greatly relieved by the confession he did not dare to tell his father. It seems probable that there was not only the sight of the female genital and masturbation but also a castration-threat on the part of the maid and that his homosexual tendencies in after life represent a flight from the maid (mother) to the protecting father.

The king as the boy or man who drinks the milk of nine cows certainly represents the pre-castration stage. But on the other hand the decomposition into king and boy, the security sought by hiding the soul or penis in another human being, and the boy as a detachable penis show strong indications of castration anxiety. For what has the boy to be guarded against ? Against a wound and against sexual intercourse. " The Mugabe had to be careful not to hurt himself and not to lose blood." [1] The night when he visited his wives and had intercourse with them was the critical period. It was never known with which wife he was going to sleep lest he might be attacked during the night by anyone who wished to kill him.[2] The king finds but a poor rest at night for he is hurried on from one house to the other, from one wife to another, to escape his would-be murderers.[3] Both in connection with boys as royal doubles and otherwise the castration-complex is perhaps the most prominent feature of royal ritual.

A dairymaid who took care of the king's cows was called " wife of the king " but she was always a virgin and in constant attendance to give him milk.[4] A special herd of not fully developed animals was reserved for the king's use. These animals must not be hurt and they must not mate.[5]

" A boy herald drove the two cows to the place where they were to be milked. While on duty the herald wore the skin of a calf which had been killed at birth. The boy was too young to think of marriage

[1] J. Roscoe, *The Banyankole*, 1923, p. 40.
[2] J. Roscoe, loc. cit., pp. 42, 44.
[3] Roscoe, *The Northern Bantu*, p. 13.
[4] Roscoe, *The Bakitara or Banyoro*, 1923, p. 98.
[5] Roscoe, loc. cit., p. 101.

or to have sexual desires but during his term of office he had to avoid playing with girls or even with other boys lest he should be hurt. He must use no profane language, lose no blood and therefore had to be careful not to walk where thorns might scratch him. His person was sacrosanct and no man might hurt him for anything done to him would affect the king. Should he be seriously ill, he was killed.[1]

The whole complex of royalty shows a peculiar ambiguity with unusual freedom on the one hand[2] and ceremonial routine on the other,[3] an anxious avoidance of sexuality (castration-complex) with a ubiquituous sexual symbolism and a marked tendency to decomposition or formation of substitutes.

Among the Bakitara, a virgin slept at the king's feet so as to cover them. At cockcrow she arose, went to a vessel that was placed in readiness and urinated into it. Then she dipped some bark cloth into the urine and touched first one and then the other of the king's feet with the urine. The ceremony was called *kyonzire* and was regarded as a purificatory rite removing evil from the king in order that he might step forth without fear.[4]

If we connect this with the virgin who was the king's wife[5] and with the symbolic meaning of walking, of the step,[6] it is quite evident that the feet symbolize the penis, and this is why a purificatory ceremony has to be performed before they can be used without fear. This purificatory rite has a double aspect ; the woman covers the feet, i.e. the penis is in the vagina, and then the woman who covers the feet is a virgin, i.e. the penis is not really in the vagina. What we find here as a result of interpretation is in full agreement with the general style of these ceremonies, as for instance when we are told that the washing of the king was performed by mixing hot and cold water. The hot water was called male and the cold female and the washing might not be done outside lest the gods should see him naked.[7]

In order to understand the psychology of the royal ritual it is necessary to explain what is really meant by *kyonzire*. The definition given by Roscoe is " anything offered in sacrifice alive and not for killing ".[8] Therefore in this case the king would be the *kyonzire*,

[1] Roscoe, loc. cit., p. 96.
[2] "A prince might have any girl by simply sending a messenger to fetch her." Roscoe, *The Banyankole*, 1923, p. 58.
[3] The king was completely absorbed in the sacrificial ceremonies by which he brought prosperity to his people. Roscoe, *The Bakitara*, 1923, p. 91.
[4] Roscoe, *The Bakitara or Banyoro*, 1923, p. 91.
[5] Roscoe, ibid., p. 98.
[6] Cf. Róheim, "The Significance of Stepping Over," *Journal*, iii.
[7] Roscoe, *Bakitara*, p. 92.　　　　[8] Ibid.

i.e. touching his feet with the urine (a symbolic castration) would be regarded as a substitute for regicide. On the same principle, when the appearance of the new moon had been proclaimed a man was caught and taken away secretly. His throat was cut and the blood was smeared on the royal fetishes. That this innocent victim is a substitute for the king is proved by another part of the ceremony. When the moon appeared, the principal chief and head of the Sacred Guard went to the king and said : " You have outlived the moon, and our people are a fighting people and rejoice with you." [1] It is evident therefore that at the end of the month the king is in a critical situation and that a substitute is found who is killed in his place. Evidently the *kyonzire* proper, or animals kept in the temples alive instead of killing them, are substitutes for something or somebody and the practice of keeping them in the temples a substitute for killing them. Thus we find the king reappearing under the guise of innumerable substitutes. On entering the bathroom in the morning the king went to the doorway to meet two young bulls. These animals were brought to the bathroom each morning. One of them called Ruhinda was black with a white forehead, the white being intended to drive away evil, and the other, Lutimba, was red and black. The king took the black bull by the horns and laying his head against its forehead said : " Take away from me, O Ruhinda, all evil magic and enemies." Taking the second bull in the same way, he said : " Pour thy blessing upon my country and upon my people." He then released the bulls and went away. If during this ceremony one of the bulls made water a page caught a little in his hand and touched the king's forehead, with it for it brought blessing to him and to the land.

The bulls were called *kyonzire* (living sacrifices) and had to be relieved of this office before they were old enough to serve cows. The old bulls were killed [2] but their mouths were tied up so that they could make no noise which would be beneath their dignity. [3]

The phallic bull is intimately linked up with the king in ritual in modern Africa, in ancient Egypt and Asia Minor. As we have seen above how a man is killed at the new moon instead of the king, we may also mention the case of the Bagesu who kill a bull for the royal drum every month. [4] The process of decomposition sets in when the phallic aspect of royalty is embodied in the bull and proceeds when the bull is replaced by two bulls, i.e. a cathartic phallus to take away evil, and a fertilizing one to confer blessing.

[1] Ibid., p. 107. [2] Roscoe, ibid., p. 92. [3] Roscoe, ibid., p. 115.
[4] Roscoe, *The Bagesu and other tribes of the Uganda Protectorate*, 1924, p. 193.

The regalia are also equivalents or representatives of the king and owe their existence to the process of decomposition. "If the king were quite unable to perform this sacred function he would send the royal spear to represent him." [1] The royal spear must always be held upright, it must never be laid down. [2] The royal spear is evidently the same thing as the rain-spear of the Lango. A new rain-spear is consecrated with the following prayer :

> " May the harvest be a rich one.
> You, spear of the rain,
> Bring good rain and fruitfulness
> That our granaries may be filled,
> That the hearts of our daughters may rejoice
> And that they multiply unto us sons and daughters." [3]

The royal spear has an important function in the annual ceremony for blessing the country. The throats of a white cow, a white fowl, and a white sheep are cut and the blood is caught in a vessel. The king stands at the door holding the spear and looking on in silence. When the meat is cooked some is put on the spear and the king raises the spear up to heaven with the following prayer :

> " God, hear me in heaven,
> The ruler of living and dead.
> Enable me to increase and surpass all.
> To have children and surpass the nations." [4]

A spear that brings fertility is evidently a phallic symbol and therefore an appropriate representative of the king. The throne is another royal double of the same type. It was covered with lion and leopard skins, might never be left alone and two wives of the king slept at night on either side of it. They had to be virgins and when menstruating might not go to the throne. [5]

On the coronation day the king appoints two women from his mother's clan, called " little mothers ", to take charge of the crown. They are also the guardians of the king's nail-parings and hair-clippings and have to cut his hair and nails when necessary. These were kept in a special bag with the umbilical cord and the teeth knocked out at initiation. There must be two mothers because if one of them were menstruating she might not approach. While the inter-relation of the menstruation taboo and the hair and nail-clippings points decisively to the castration-complex and to the crown

---

[1] J. Roscoe, *The Bakitara or Banyoro*, 1923, p. 118.
[2] Roscoe, loc. cit., p. 92.
[3] J. H. Driberg, *The Lango*, 1923, p. 249.
[4] J. Roscoe, *The Bakitara*, 1923, p. 111.
[5] J. Roscoe, *The Bakitara*, 1923, p. 77.

as a royal phallus displaced upwards, the fact that the " mothers " of the crown taken from the clan of the king's mother are nominally the king's wives [1] shows the ultimate identity of wife and mother and the incestuous background of royalty.

It is in connection with the act of regicide and of mortuary ceremonies for the king that the tendency of substitute formations is most prominent. At the anniversary of the burial a poor man was chosen to impersonate the dead king. He lived in royal state in the royal tomb and was called by the name of the monarch he represented, for he was said to be the old king revived. He lived in the tomb, had full use of the king's widows, and the reigning king sent him presents and cattle. For eight days he lived like a king ; when the ninth day came he was taken to the back of the tomb and strangled.[2]

On the evening of the day on which the mourning for the king of Uganda was ended the chief of the Grasshopper clan brought a gazelle for the king to hunt. It was turned out near his enclosure and the king hunted and killed it. Then the king's head was shaved and in the evening the drums were beaten to show that mourning was ended. During the evening a man was brought before the king who speared him slightly, whereupon he was put to death and the body was thrown into the river under the papyrus roots ; he was called " the fowl ". The drums warned the people to cease mourning : no sign of it might be found anywhere under penalty of death. After the king had been crowned, two men were brought to him bound and blindfolded. The king took a bow and arrow and wounded one of the men, but after he had been wounded by the king he was not killed, as we might have expected. He was taken with a cow, a goat, a dog and a fowl and the dust and fire from the king's house to Bunyoro. He was a " scape-goat " (*kyonzira*), designed to do away with all uncleanness which might attach to the king or the queen. One of the leading chiefs conveyed him to the Bunyoro frontier and after maiming the man and the animals he left them alive, looted all he could from the Bunyoro and returned to the king.[3]

It is evident that the man who carries away all uncleanness from the king, who is a substitute for the king, must mean the same thing as the king himself. They carry the remains of the king's fire away beyond the frontier, but this fire seems to be the dead king himself.[4] But it is the destiny of the other man that explains the real meaning of the fire and the lot of his colleague. For he is spared, not even wounded. He is called "*he who escaped*" (Kawonawo) and

[1] Roscoe, loc. cit., p. 131.   [2] Roscoe, ibid., p. 126.
[3] Roscoe, loc. cit., pp. 109, 110.   [4] Cf. Roscoe, loc. cit., p. 103.

henceforth lives in the royal enclosure where he has charge of the king's wives.[1] From the king's presence Kawonawo was conducted together with a number of captives to the sacrificial place Seguku ; there he was blindfolded while seven men were clubbed to death but he was allowed to see the eighth and last man killed. As the men were killed they were ripped open and their bowels taken out and hung round the neck of Kawonawo. These deaths were said to add to the king's vigour and to make Kawonawo strong and faithful.[2]

Evidently there must be a reason why the prisoners should be killed in the presence of " the man who escaped ". Their bowels are hung round his neck to show that their fate might have been his fate. Their death gives him vigour, which he needs since he is to be the guardian of the king's wives. But the sacrifice adds not only to his own health but to the health of the king, showing that like the Kauzumu he is fundamentally identical with the king.

What is the function of the Kauzumu ? He is not only guardian of the king's wives but the scapegoat who cohabits with them instead of the king. Presumably this was the original function of the Kawonawo and thus we find him as identical with the man who is chased and maimed—the bearer of the sacred fire. For there are two aspects of coitus. From the libidinal point of view it is the goal of our strivings but from the point of view of the narcissistic retention in the ego, coitus is death or castration.[3]

If the ascent to the throne really meant coition—and such a hypothesis is fully legitimate in the case of a phallic being—we could understand the whole ceremony as a repeated decomposition of the original concept. The principal thing is done by His Majesty ; he ascends the throne. His action is glossed by " the man who escapes " ; he obtains the king's wives. But as coitus is fission, castration, " the man who escapes " has a colleague and this colleague is a scapegoat, driven out and maimed. Castration is death, therefore another equivalent of this scapegoat is killed and thrown into the water and eight men are killed for the " man who escapes ", i.e. for the king.

When the old king of the Wemba had been safely buried and the millet was ripe a great concourse of Awemba gathered together in the chief village. That same evening the heir entered one of the huts of the inner harem courtyard and with his head wife " slept within the fence ". Before the dawn of the next day it was the special duty of a certain chief to carry the ceremonial bowl used at all the

[1] Idem, loc. cit., p. 109.   [2] Roscoe, loc. cit., p. 200.
[3] Cf. Ferenczi, *Genitaltheorie*, 1924.

consecrations of the Wemba kings into their hut. A fire was lit and the bowl—filled with water, which was, it is said, mingled with herbs of sanctifying potency—was held over it by the chief, who joined hands with the king's wife. When the water boiled the chief spoke the customary sentences, saying that now " the country was hot " as the " fire again flamed in the land " and anointed the limbs of the king and his wife.[1]

If proof was needed, here we have it. The ascent to the throne is coitus and followed by " the country being hot ", " fire again burning in the land." What else could this fire be than the *sa*, the solar fluid of vitality animating the ruler of Egypt, the outflow of which was described with the same word as the ejaculation of the seminal fluid ? When a Shilluk king is elected, various sticks or stones that represent the royal princes are thrown into the fire. If the fire burns with a big flame and blazes up, then the people laugh. " This is the king " they say.[2]

When the king of Uganda died, the people said : " The fire is extinguished,"[3] and a sacred fire with a guardian of its own had to be kept burning during the life of a king.[4]

Besides the fire-symbolism, the life of Baganda royalty was believed to be closely connected with certain trees. We should guess that the symbolic meaning is the same as in the case of the fire, for the castration related in the folk-tale equivalent of Osiris (Bitiou) takes place under a tree, Attis castrated himself under a pine-tree, Osiris himself, the phallic god, is a tree-spirit and early Sumerian rulers the representatives of the " Wood standing erect ". In Uganda the particular species selected was the bark-cloth tree. Bark-cloth trees were planted near the main entrance to the temple by the priests of each principal deity, because it was believed that as they grew and flourished so the king's life and power would be increased.[5] At his " coronation " the king ascended a mound and repeated after the priest : " I am the King of Uganda." Then the priest handed him a stout branch of a bark-cloth tree and this the king planted in a hole near by. Again he ascended the mound and recited the words : " I am the King to live longer than my ancestors, to rule the nations and to put down rebellion." Then the king received the royal

---

[1] Gouldsbury and Sheane, *The Great Plateau of Northern Rhodesia*, 1911, pp. 19, 20.
[2] D. Westermann, *The Shilluk People*, 1912, p. 102.
[3] Roscoe, *Baganda*, p. 103.
[4] Roscoe, loc. cit., p. 202.
[5] Roscoe, loc. cit., p. 202.

spear which was only used on these occasions. Spear and tree seem
to be intimately connected, for after this they went down the hill to
a place where some trees were grown for making spear shafts ; one
of these trees was cut by the priest and handed to the king with the
words : " With this overcome your enemies." [1]

The spear, or its equivalent, the staff, play an important part among
the regalia of monarchs. We have very good reasons to assume that
the king is merely an exalted rain-maker and the rain-maker uses a
staff ; in the case of the Batak the staff was described as belonging,
properly speaking, to their sacred kings. It can hardly be a mere
coincidence if the Batak staff represents incest and castration, and if,
on the other hand, incest and regicide figure so prominently in the
life-history of kings. The sacred spears of Shilluk royalty were kept
in the shrines called the graves of Nyakang. At the rain-making
ceremony, which is held at the beginning of the month *Alabor*, a
bullock is slain with the sacred spear before the door of the shrine while
the king stands by praying in a loud voice to Nyakang to send down the
refreshing showers on the thirsty land. The sacrificial bullock is
speared high up in the flank so that the wound is not immediately
fatal. Then the animal is allowed to walk to and from the river before
it sinks down and dies. As much of the victim's blood as possible is
collected in a gourd and thrown into the river.[2]

We have seen that Moret has noticed the double meaning of the
sceptres, staffs, whips, etc. used by Egyptian rulers. They represent
both life and death, both the phallus and a mortal weapon. The whip
in Baganda means a loss of the generative powers to the man it touches.
At a ceremony performed a year after the election of a Shilluk king
" the people of Nyakang " whip everybody they can catch. In the
meantime the king catches hold of a girl.[3] Now it is the
second meaning of the spear that seems to be prominent in this
Shilluk rain ceremony and in the case of Wawanga royalty. For the
sacred spears of Wawanga royalty are used in connection with the
funeral of the dead king and here, as in the Shilluk rain-making
ceremony, a bull is killed. The king's nominee is given a spear and
entrusted to kill the bull. The son appointed to act as co-chief holds
the bull by a rope at its neck whilst his brother spears it behind the
shoulder before the door of the hut in which the body of the late king
is lying ; the dying animal must then run inside the hut and falling
on the corpse expire on it, otherwise the late king is presumed to have

[1] Roscoe, *Baganda*, pp. 94–6.
[2] Frazer, *The Dying God*, pp. 19, 20.
[3] Westermann, loc. cit., pp. 124, 125.

reconsidered the matter.[1] The spear that killed the father and the life-giving spear have a common source in the biogenetic past, for, as Hesse and Doflein show, the male first developed weapons, protruding parts of his body, to master the resistance of the female.[2]

The Kabyles have a bull-cult and they tell a myth about the bull-calf who desired intercourse with his mother and succeeded in driving off his father.[3] The Hausa attribute a fertilizing virtue to the bull-sacrifice and they regard it as a substitute either for killing the king or for killing the totem animal.[4] A pharaoh as child of the Sun-God is a " bull of his mother " and the Wawanga king becomes king by killing a bull which, in the ritual, is identified with his predecessor.

Till now we have done nothing but *interpret* these rites but we cannot go on doing so without considering the origin of royalty from a historical point of view. All the African monarchies we have come across in this research seem to be connected with Egypt.

The ruler of the Mande sits on a carpet of ram's skins and in Darfur it is only members of the royal family who may eat the flesh of the holy ram,[5] while the pharaoh represents Amon, the ram-god, on earth and has ram's horns as a part of his crown.

The coronation ceremony of the Ewe ruler reminds one forcibly of the ram-headed divinities of Egypt. The crown is here made of a ram's head and ornamented with feathers. The king kneels at the throne and the priest puts a ram on his shoulders. Then they lift the ram from the king's back, swing it up in the air to the gods and cut its head off. A sacrificial meal in which the king himself consumes the principal parts of his divine *alter ego* finishes the ceremony.[6]

As royalty is mostly connected racially with the Hamite invaders, we must regard it as an institution of theirs transmitted from the north to the aboriginals of Africa. But we can go back still further in the history of this institution. It is impossible to separate the pharaoh from the first pharaoh, Osiris. However, Osiris and Isis are Tammuz and Ishtar, for nobody will be bold enough to assert that the myth of the dying god, killed by a boar and revived by his mother, connected with the pine or other trees, with water, with royalty and incest has been invented independently in these two centres of ancient civilization. From Babylon to Uganda we have only one type of royalty.

---

[1] Kenneth R. Dundas, "The Wawanga," *Journal R.A.I.*, 1913, pp. 27–9.

[2] Hesse-Doflein, *Tierbau und Tierleben*, 1914.

[3] L. Frobenius, "Volksmärchen der Kabylen," *Atlantis*, i, 1921, p. 64.

[4] A. J. N. Tremearne, *The Ban of the Bori*, 1914, p. 39.

[5] L. Frobenius, *Und Africa sprach*, 1913, i, p. 249.

[6] J. Spieth, *Die Ewe-Stämme*, 1906, pp. 101, 102.

When Tammuz sleeps his sleep of death the seven demons who are trying to revive him seek him in the sheep-folds :—

> " Tammuz the lord slumbers in woe, they sigh much.
>   The sacred consort of the heavenly queen, the lord, slumbers, in woe they sigh much
>   Because the lord has gone forth. In his sheepfolds there is no creating
>   Because Tammuz has gone forth, in his sheepfolds there is no creating." [1]

But Tammuz is simply the prototype of royalty. At Isin, the capital of one of the Sumerian dynasties, five kings are named as " sleeping ".

> " The lord Idin-dagan sleeps
>   And the gardens of themselves restrain their growth
>   The city weeps for Isme Dagan who slumbers
>   And the gardens of themselves withhold their fruit." [2]

Fertility ceases with the representative of fertility, but we have to go to Africa to see that what the liturgy refers to is not simply a figure of speech and is more even than a psychic attitude ; it is carried out, realized, in the shape of ritual. When the king of Ruanda died the whole tribe shaved their heads and all men kept apart from women during the two months of mourning. Males of cows, goats and sheep were separated from their females.[3] At the death of the Mugabe, the ruler of the pastoral Banyankole, all the fires in the royal kraal were extinguished, all the goats and dogs were killed, as they were supposed to contain the evil death. Every full-grown bull in the royal herds had its scrotum tied, to prevent its mating with the cows. All work ceased in the land and the blades of all weapons had to be wrapped up in grass or fibre.[4] We may compare the appearance of Tammuz as shepherd, the search for the god in the sheepfold, with the king of the Banyoro who has his official bed in the dairy[5] and whose enclosure is said to be very like a cattle kraal [6] ; or the harlot mother-goddess Ishtar, who was nevertheless regarded as a virgin, with the king's mother among the Bakitara, who after the ascent of her son to the throne was supposed to lead a chaste life, and had innumerable lovers.[7] And just as the life of the king is renewed with the moon in ancient Babylon, Assyria and Israel, African kings are congratulated for

---

[1] S. Langdon, *Tammuz and Ishtar*, 1914, p. 20.
[2] Ibid., p. 26.
[3] J. Roscoe, *The Bagesu and other tribes of the Uganda Protectorate*, 1924, p. 187.
[4] J. Roscoe, *The Banyankole*, 1923, p. 51.
[5] J. Roscoe, *The Bakitara or Banyoro*, 1923, p. 91.
[6] J. Roscoe, *The Northern Bantu*, 1915, p. 9.
[7] S. Langdon, *Tammuz and Ishtar*, 1914, p. 42.

having outlived the period of moonless night and renewed their life with the moon.[1]

This must be traced back to a period of evolution in the past of these races when they all formed a cultural unity and were beginning to evolve the germs of the civilization of the ancient East.

Only people acquainted with the elements of agriculture have Divine Kings and there is certainly a close connection between the two institutions. Agriculture means incest with Mother Earth ; among the Ho a good king is a good farmer,[2] and ploughing is the chief ceremonial duty of the Chinese emperor.[3] It is evident that the transition from a phase of existence that has been called that of food-gatherers to an economic basis where man produces the food he consumes (i.e. from the unconscious point of view " cohabits with his own daughters ") can only be accomplished by the aid of the return of repressed elements, a revival of the incestuous attitude.

We have repeatedly pointed out that the king is " living up to a character ", playing a part. He represents a god who lived on earth in the infancy of mankind, a god who lived in incestuous union with his mother, sisters, and daughters and was killed by his rebellious offspring.

This archaic picture survives in a slightly modified form in Africa. At the death of the Bakitara king the princes fight for the throne. Before the fight began the rival princes each sought out his mother from the king's widows and carried her away to a hiding place because the mothers would try to kill each other and the new king would certainly kill the mothers of his former rivals. Fighting princes would endeavour to steal some of their father's young widows for their own use.[4]

The whole life of the king is nothing but the repetition of these primeval tragedies and it is the period of the return of repressed elements represented by royalty that makes it possible for us to gain some insight into the libidinal mechanisms of the Primal Horde. For if the king and his fate represent the phallus, evidently the same must have applied to the Jealous Sire in the Primal Horde. That it

[1] Cf. Ròheim, *Mondmythologie und Mondreligion*, 1927, p. 99.

[2] J. Spieth, *Die Ewe Stämme*, 1906, p. 104.

[3] O. Franke, " Ackerbau und Seidengewinnung in China," *Abh. d. Hamburgischhen Kolonialinstitutes*, xi, 1913, p. 27.

[4] J. Roscoe, *The Bakitara or Banyoro*, 1923, p. 123. It is also most significant that the Mugabe and his sons never meet except at the moment when the Mugabe is about to die. J. Roscoe, *The Bagesu*, 1924, p. 51. Even the " family-romance " myth of foster-parents is realized in this situation. Roscoe, *Bakitara*, p. 123.

applied to him fully we know quite well, for as long as he held sway over the horde procreation was his prerogative. Again, the libidinal processes that made this state of things possible may be interpreted as the repetition of what takes place in the organism when the superfluous amount of libido is drawn out of the cells and the whole surface of the body in order to be concentrated in the penis. At this phase of our development, genital primacy is attained by one individual (the Jealous Sire) and by society as a single unity.

If for a very deep organic layer of the unconscious the fission taking place in the sexual act is the equivalent of death and castration it is no wonder that the first form of society formed by these beings should be a social organization in which death comes before coitus. Before losing their own vital fluid the Brothers killed a being who in their unconscious must have been the phallus of the whole group. The murdered Father was not merely a being existing in actual life ; for the men who obeyed him and were swayed by him he was also a projection of their own penis.

When the pain-producing quality of the sexual matter accumulated in the genital organ became absolutely unbearable the Brother Horde was moved to an action, meaning a partial death for them (the ejaculation of the semen) but death in good earnest for the Being they had made the representative of the male organ. At this juncture the " Osirification " of the king takes place, for the dead king is the penis of the whole society.

Now we remember the significant liturgies at Nippur when Tammuz the King died or, to use a polite phraseology, descended to the nether world.

> The wailing is for the plants ; they grow not.
> The wailing is for the barley ; the ears grow not.
> For habitations and the flocks it is ; they produce not.
> For the perishing wedded ones ; for the perishing children it is ; the
> dark-headed people create not.[1]

The Lord of Life has descended into the other world, his consort and mother the love-goddess after him, libido itself is withdrawn from the social organism with its representative. When a king of Urundi dies there is deep mourning for all men, and for a year no Murundi is permitted to sow or do any other agricultural work. Dancing and all noisy pursuits are interdicted and the head-dress, the pride of every African male, is shaved off. The bull is separated from the cow, the ram from the ewe, the cock from the hen, the husband from his wife, for a child conceived at this period would be a monster with teeth on

---

[1] Langdon, *Tammuz*, p. 11.

his nose and the conception would kill the new king.[1] We conjecture that the liturgies reflect a similar ritual at Erek and wherever the Tammuz kings ruled, the death of the king was a period of general sexual taboo, in him the penis of the whole male population had departed to have intercourse with the Earth Mother.

This is how a priest-king of the Baja lives and dies. In the lodging of each of these kings there is a holy serpent. It is a serpent of a large species ; it lives, sleeps and eats with the chief. Indeed it is his own god as he is the god of his people ; he prays to it for success in war, for a plentiful harvest and for children and he calls the animal *nakom*, that is, grandfather. If the serpent dies the king is immediately killed, whereas if the king dies before the serpent, his son inherits this deity. No Baja king may live for more than 14 years and his son and successor is also his murderer. He manages this by making his father eat of the royal totem animals. Having thus repeated the Original Sin, which gave him the right to the throne, death must follow. A process of mummification takes place as the corpse is shrivelled for nine days. This is the same period as in the festival of Choiak when the dead Osiris is said to be in the womb of his mother Nut.[2] When the corpse is shrivelled to a mummy it is sewn into the skin of five white goats. At the same time a ceremony takes place in the bush where the initiation ceremonies are usually conducted, in fact analogy permits the guess that what takes place is the initiation ceremony itself. The corpse is buried in a grave and covered by a river that has been deflected on purpose from its course to receive the royal corpse.

At the beginning of the next sowing season the king's brother sacrifices eight red cocks to the memory of the deceased. But they have to be held very firmly lest by wriggling or falling to the earth they should foreshadow the death of another important member of the royal house. When he wrings the neck of the first cock, the king's brother says : " If it was I who killed my brother may my neck be wrung as I wring the neck of this cock " and when he kills the second his words are : " If anybody else has killed the king let his neck be wrung as I wring this cock's neck." When the harvest begins to ripen there is a sort of repetition of this ceremony. This time a couple of red goats and a white she-goat are sacrificed at the grave by the king's brother. When the first red goat is killed the royal priest says : " I kill this so that no disease or misfortune should befall anybody in

[1] Meyer, *Barundi*, p. 187.
[2] Hopfner, " Tierkult der alten Aegypter" *Denkschriften d. kais. Ak.*, 57, 1914, p. 109.

the country. Everything evil may stick to the animal." And so it happens that the scapegoat becomes a vehicle of evil. Nobody except the very old people will touch its flesh for to eat it would mean death. As for the old people, it seems that the Baja do not care very much if they die, nor do they themselves care either. Then the other goat and the she-goat are killed with a prayer that there may be a good harvest and that the women of the country may bear children. From this day till the next festival no Baja may cohabit with his wife and the same taboo applies to eating sorghum. At last the new king appoints the time for the last feast. This is a family affair. The head of each household goes to the grave of his grandfather with an offering of beer and says : " You died ? That was your affair. (That is, he pleads not guilty.) But now take care that there shall be plenty of corn on my fields ". [1]

The king's death does not clinch affairs. He must die again as a red cock and presumably a third time as a red goat. For the corpse has been covered with red and the red cock is the symbol of a member of the royal family. We know very well that the royal brother stands in great need of the cock that is to take his guilt away, for the members of the royal family are regularly guilty of regicide. And when the second cock is killed, representing anybody who might have killed the king, this is regicide openly repeated, for the king's brother must know as well as we know that the man who killed the old king was the new king, his own son. But evil is not dispelled yet and the goat is killed as a second scapegoat after the cock. Why it should be these two animals is explained by a myth of the Lakka.

Umadje was bathing in a river. A ram approached and from a long distance he politely saluted Umadje so that the latter had time to cover his nakedness. Next day when he was again bathing a cock and a goat came. They saw him but they did not care, so that he had no time to cover himself. Thus they caught sight of his male member and Umadje in his rage said : " You, ram, shall always wear your tail downwards, but you two, cock and goat, shall wear it upwards so that everybody can see what shameless animals you both are." And therefore it is taboo for Lakka women to eat the flesh of these two animals.[2] The tail standing upwards is the phallus and the " shameless animals ", cock and goat, are taboo to women and used as a substitute for the king as phallic symbols. For again there are two goats. One is killed and becomes a vehicle of death, the other is eaten with a prayer for children.

[1] Frobenius, *Und Afrika Sprach*, 1913, iii, pp. 176–82.
[2] Frobenius, *Und Afrika Sprach*, iii, p. 173.

After the death of red king, red cock and red goat society becomes a body without a penis. Coitus is taboo till in a final ceremony all guilt is disclaimed and the dead grandfather invoked to fertilize the women of the country.

We suspected that the ceremony performed at the circumcision place after the king's death is circumcision itself. This conjecture is confirmed by what happens among other tribes. The Wawanga circumcise the new king three months after his father's death. At the same time his brothers are circumcised together with representatives of various clans practising this rite.[1] So we might say that an initiation ceremony takes place after the king's death.

According to tradition, a king of the Mundangs can only rule for seven years. If one of the kings survives this period it becomes the duty of his maternal uncle to remind him what his people expect him to do. His father's skull, wrapped in a cow-hide, is brought before him as a reminder of how he ascended to the throne and of the fate that is in store for him. When the king is dead it is time for the young men to be circumcised. The ruler of the Dakka always dies at harvest time and before the new king is appointed a circumcision ceremony must be held.[2] There are several connecting links between initiation and regicide. One of these is the leopard. The priest appears at circumcision in the guise of the leopard, the bull-roarers are called leopards, and if among the Durru a boy does not survive the hardships of initiation they say that the leopard has killed him.[3]

The priest who was concerned with the " Osirification " of the king wore a leopard's skin at the Sed festival, and the leopard throughout Africa is the totem animal of royal families.[4] The Baganda ruler kills a leopard when he ascends the throne and the king of the Mundang must die if he sees the foot-prints of a leopard.[5]

There is a strong unconscious bond in these communities that unites king and people in a common fate. The Hausa, or at any rate some Hausa clans, express this by saying that the soul of the totem dwells in the chief and the soul of the whole clan is in his keeping.[6] We know what happens to the novices in the bush ; they are killed symbolically by the leopard, that is, they share the lot of their ruler in a reduced imitative manner. For the king, himself a leopard,

[1] Dundas, loc. cit., *Journ. R.A.J.*, 1913, p. 29.
[2] Frobenius, loc. cit., iii, p. 141.
[3] Frobenius, loc. cit., iii, p. 142.
[4] Moret, *Mysteres*, p. 75. Frobenius, loc. cit.
[5] Frobenius, loc. cit., p. 254.
[6] Tremearne, *The Ban of the Bori*, 1914, p. 43.

dies for having killed a leopard (his father) and is killed by a young leopard (his son). This chain of parricides accompanied by an always well-founded dread of retribution seems to be symbolized by the Hausa customs of king killing.

In the lion, leopard and kindred clans the totem-animal was controlled by the priest-chief, whose official title was the " Lion of the Town ", and four other priests. When the people had seen that the totem was becoming powerless or was allowing some other town to become more prosperous than that actually worshipping the animal, the five priests would burn incense and the totem would appear and lie down on the place appointed. The chief would then lay his complaint and the lion would nod or shake his head according as he admitted or denied the accusation. If the charge could be proved the priestly king would say to the lion :

" We have found you out, you have been a traitor to us and we are going to kill you." The lion would not struggle, for it would know that it was in the wrong, and the chief would catch hold of its mane and pull back its head and one of the four other priests would cut its throat. If, on the other hand, the priestly king had held his position for two years and all was going well with the community, he might be allowed to remain in office for another year, but probably the four priests would declare that his power was waning and a new man was required for the good of the town. The lion would therefore be summoned in the same manner as before and one of the priests would stand forth and accuse the chief. The lion would first deny the charge, for the chief was his brother, but on proof being adduced he would consent to kill him.[1]

The king kills the lion and the lion kills the king ; but when he has killed him he goes on to do the same to the novices. Moreover, it is impossible to have an initiation ceremony during the king's lifetime, for the blood that flows from the circumcision wound would certainly kill the king.[2] The whole situation reminds us of what took place in Phrygia. Attis dies and descends to the nether world, the priests castrate themselves while the laity perhaps gash their arms till they bleed or perhaps only enjoy the benefits of the ceremony. Circumcision is a mitigated form of castration and just as the severed parts of the eunuch priests were hidden in the vaults of the Great Mother, probably as emblems of fertility and instruments of resurrection, the prepuce was put into a ditch as a sacrifice to Mother Earth.[3]

The youths lose a part ; but for the king or Attis the part means

---

[1] Tremearne, loc. cit., pp. 34–8.
[2] Frobenius, loc. cit., p. 255.   [3] Frobenius, loc. cit.

the whole.   Just as the body participates in the " death " of the penis in coitus in its descent to the other world, the king—a symbolic phallus of the community—appears as chief protagonist on the scene and the youths are the chorus who share his fate but share it through identification and in a reduced manner.   For we must not forget that there is truth in what the savages themselves say, that initiation ceremonies are preparatory to coitus ; the fission that will take place when the seminal fluid leaves the body is indicated by cutting a part off the penis.   On the other hand the priest-king of the Hausa is the man with large testicles,[1] the man who is all pleasure-principle, all penis.   The Shilluk believe that the king must not be allowed to become ill or senile lest with his diminishing vigour the cattle should sicken and fail to provide their increase, the crops should rot in the fields, and men stricken with disease should die in ever increasing numbers.   To prevent these calamities it used to be the custom with the Shilluk to put the king to death whenever he showed signs of failing health and strength.   One of the fatal symptoms of decay was taken to be an incapacity to satisfy the sexual passions of his wives.[2]   " Taken along with the other reasons which are alleged for putting the king to death, this one suggests that the fertility of men, of cattle and of the crops is believed to depend sympathetically on the generative power of the king, so that the complete failure of that power in him would involve a corresponding failure in men, animals and plants and would thereby entail at no distant date the entire extinction of all life, whether human, animal or vegetable." [3]

If the king represented the penis of the universe his death is an act of self-castration.   Therefore it is a sort of " mythical " exaggeration of the puberty ceremony.   In the latter, the youths are prepared for the functions connected with puberty by a partial loss of the penis ; here society regains its impaired fertility either by severing its organ of procreation or we might also say by sending it into the womb, into the grave, by transforming the king into an ideal penis, into a penis remaining in the womb.   When the Shilluk king had been duly murdered a hut was built for the occasion, the king was put in it with his head resting on the lap of a nubile virgin and the door of the hut was then walled up.[4]   In Urundi a young woman was " married "

[1] Tremearne, loc. cit., p. 46.
[2] Frazer, *Dying God*, p. 21.   C. G. Seligman, *The Cult of Nyakang and the Divine Kings of the Shilluk* (iv, " Report of the Wellcome Tropical Research Laboratories), 1911, p. 222.   [3] Frazer, loc. cit., p. 27.
[4] Seligman, loc. cit. Frazer, *Dying God*, p. 21.

to the royal corpse [1] but we are not told that she had to become a
corpse herself. At any rate, however, we recognize this African
queen as a sister of Ishtar the virgin-harlot, who follows her lord
the king to his grave, and with the power vested in her naked body
effects his happy resurrection.

And this is why men fail to procreate their kind when Tammuz
and Ishtar are absent : they have substituted a mythical penis and
vagina-ideal for the real ones. For if death itself is viewed by the
unconscious as coitus, the moment of the king's death must be the
supreme " Osirification " of royalty. If every corpse is a penis
the king who was a penis in his lifetime must become a penis indeed
at death.

Romulus was cut to pieces and the pieces buried in the ground
on the seventh of July and the festival that commemorates this event
is connected with the fertilization of the fig. The several limbs of
the phallic corn-god Osiris were put on a sieve by Isis and the kings
sacrificed red-haired men at the graves of Osiris. Red was also the
colour of the royal corpse of the Baja and in the fertilizing sacrifice
of the red goat we discovered a repetition of regicide. The body of
Halfdan, King of Norway, was cut up and buried in different parts
of his kingdom for the sake of ensuring the fruitfulness of the earth.
This Halfdan belonged to the family of the Ynglings who traced their
descent from Frey the god who reigned as king in Upsala and whose
body was kept after his death as an embodiment of fertility.[2] And
well it might be ; for he is a phallic god, and it was an omen of a good
harvest if the priestess who carried the phallic image in a waggon
became pregnant while performing her holy duty.[3]

The dying kings of Egypt, Africa and Western Asia descend into
the womb of Mother Earth. They fertilize the earth by their death
because their death appears under the mask of coitus. Now an African
ruler is usually sown up in a bull's hide at his death.[4]

There is no doubt that in these rites there is, as Rank suggests, a
hint of returning into the womb, but if this was all surely a cow's
hide would be more suited to the occasion. The corpse in the bull's
hide means that the dead king is identified with the bull, he is completely transformed into a bull, he is all penis. For the ideas of death
and coitus are so remarkably involved in each other in the unconscious
that whereas coitus is fraught with the anxiety of death, death appears
under the mythical mask of a coitus. This organic tendency found

---

[1] Meyer, loc. cit., p. 115.   [2] Frazer, *Adonis*, 330–9.
[3] W. Mannhardt, *Wald und Feldkulte*, 1904, i, pp. 588–90.
[4] L. Frobenius, loc. cit., iii, pp. 85, 86. Tremearne, loc. cit., pp. 33, 438.

a super-organic repetition in the Primal Horde where the death of the Jealous Sire appears to have been the necessary preliminary to cohabitation. Royalty represents a return of this form of society and the king ascends the throne by killing his father. Like the leader of old a king is a phallic being and his coronation a coitus ceremony with others who act as scapegoats for the death-aspect of the life-giving act. And when his day comes to act this tragic part in the drama of life and death his decease appears in the guise of the supreme life-giving act to his worshippers. The king as the Phallus of Society ascends the throne by coitus and descends to the shades by the same means.

6   Cecrops and other Serpents

Cecrops, the first king of Athens, had a serpent's tail and he was succeeded by another snake king, Erichtonius. Of both we know little ; they seem to belong to a phase of Greek religion that had gone out of fashion before the ascendency of the Olympians. He had a wife called Agraulos and many daughters. One of them is also called Agraulos ; a very suspicious coincidence for a king. At any rate Immisch regards the daughters as " doubles " of the town goddess Athena, and as the serpent king's cult was closely connected with that of the goddess this seems a probable conjecture. If the reading of an inscription found on the Acropolis is correct Athena was called " Kekropeia ", the consort of Cecrops. At any rate he gave his verdict in her favour in her strife with Poseidon.[1] The relations between his successor Erichtonius and the town goddess are equally intimate. Hephaestus desired the love of the virgin goddess but he was frustrated in his aim by her resistance. The semen, however, dropped to the earth and the earth gave birth to an infant. Athena was the foster-mother of this child, and the child Erichtonius became the second king of Athens.[2] She put him in a cista and gave it to the daughters of Cecrops to take care of. They ought not to have opened it ; it was taboo. But such is the curiosity of women— or the nature of taboos in general ?—open it they did and were frightened to death by the serpent that emerged from the box.[3] Serpent the myth calls it but the actual object, the symbol of King Erichtonius, that was contained in the cista in the days of Pausanias

---

[1] *Roschers Lexikon*, ii, pp. 1014–23.
[2] Ibid., p. 1303.
[3] Frazer, *Pausanias*, i, p. 182.

was no serpent—it was a wooden phallus.[1]   It is therefore more than
a hint at their phallic nature if we establish the fact that the rulers of
early Athens were serpents.[2]   And their successors retained or
revived their serpent nature.

" Nero as Neos Agathos Daimon, as a snake, claims to be the
fertility *daimon* of the whole world, while Kekrops is content to
bring fertility to the Kekropidae." [3]

The serpent-kings seem to represent a very ancient phase of
royalty, as everywhere we find them before the existence of bull-
kings, perhaps even before the invention of agriculture.   The Baja
king's snake fertilizes the women, and in the Sumerian phase of
Babylonian culture we find Tammuz and Ishtar as ophidian deities.[4]
In Athens this transition is represented by Theseus, the hero of the
town and fourth king of the Ionians.

Theseus was a son of Aegeus or a son of Poseidon.   The reason
why he seems to have two fathers is simply that the two were one and
the same person,[5] that Aegeus was another Poseidon.[5]   Mythically,
however, the tradition of two fathers was explained by asserting
that both had connection with his mother Aethra in the same night.
While his father Aegeus was a grandson of Erechtheus, his mother
Aethra was a granddaughter of Pelops.[6]   Theseus appears to be a
sort of focus for various myths connected with the cult of royalty.
Another version tells us that Aethra had connection with Poseidon
in the temple and at the inducement of Athena Apatouria or Phratria
or Meter, so that she herself appears to be the heroic counterpart
of the town goddess.[7]   As the common cult of Athena with Poseidon
by a whole series of Greek towns is testified to,[8] it seems that Theseus
is connected with a very old phase of Greek religion.

Aegeus hid his sword under a rock upon which there was an altar
of Zeus Stenios.   Not very far from this altar there was a temple
devoted to the bridal Aphrodite and a river called Taureios, a
name that is certainly derived from Poseidon Taureios, the Bull
Poseidon.   Poseidon seems also to have been the original divinity
who was supplanted by Zeus Stenios,[9] and there was a temple of

---

[1] E. Küster, *Die Schlange in der griechischen Kunst und Religion*, 1913,
p. 149. Frickenhans, *Ath. Mitt.*, xxxiii, 1908, p. 172.

[2] J. E. Harrison, *Themis*, 1912, p. 263.

[3] Harrison, loc. cit., p. 277.   [4] Langdon, op. cit., pp. 114, 115.

[5] Servius, *ad Aen.*, vi, 445, 7, 761. *Myth Vat.*, i, 46, 2, 128.

[6] Plutarch, *Theseus*, 3. Pausanias, i, 11, 5, 510, 8.

[7] Jahn, *Aufsätze*, vi, p. 75.   [8] G. Wide, *Lakonische Kulte*, p. 56.

[9] Höfer, *Beilage d. Jahresberichtes des Wettiner Gymnasiums in Dresden*,
1910, p. 34.

Poseidon Phytalmios quite near.[1] He was to be brought up by competent teachers of youth and to return to Athens when he could lift the rock under which his father's sword was concealed.

As a youngster his hair was shorn in honour of the Delian or Delphian Apollo and thereafter a peculiar style of hairdressing, short on the forehead and long at the back, was called Théséis. After his return to Athens, he conquered a whole group of monsters on the Isthmus so that he had to be cleansed from the disastrous effects of murder by the Phytalids, a fig-clan who reverenced Poseidon Phytalmios as the source of fertility in plant life.[2] Figs seem to have been prominent in these ceremonial lustrations.[3]

But he was soon the victorious hero in another battle. His father Poseidon had sent a bull to Marathon. The bull destroyed all the fields,[4] so it became incumbent on the king to protect his subjects. It happened that Androgeus, son of Minos and Pasiphaë, had just arrived at Athens. Aegeus evidently thought that the son of a bull-god, if anybody, would be a fit champion to deal with a bull and this encounter proved fatal to the prince of Crete.[5] According to another version he was killed when participating in the games held in honour of Laius, who, as we know very well, was a king of Thebes who had been killed by his son Oedipus.[6] A third version regards Aegeus himself as the murderer of the bull-prince,[7] and Mommsen [8] connects the ritual of the Pharmakoi at the Thargelia with the death of Androgeos.

For the present, however, we shall regard this death as highly significant for other reasons. If the son of the bull-king, Minos, was killed either by Aegeus or a bull we must regard Aegeus and the bull as one and the same person. This implies that Theseus really kills his father when he kills the bull, a guess that is confirmed by evidence from other sources. For the third occasion alleged for the death of Androgeus connects this event with Oedipus who killed Laius and the bull is sent by Poseidon, the bull-shaped father of Theseus.

This bull-fight reappears in the career of our hero in connection with the Mino-taur, a brother of the above-mentioned Androgeus. Now Apollodorus and others [9] allege that the annual tribute of seven

[1] Pausanias, ii, 38, 8 ; i, 27, 8. Plutarch, *Theseus*, 3.
[2] Plut., *Thes.*, 12, 23. Paus., i, 37, 4.
[3] Toepffer, *Att. Geneal.*, pp. 135, 249.
[4] Plut., *Thes.*, 14, Diodor, 4, 59.   [5] Paus., i, 27, 10.
[6] Apollodorus, 3, 15, 7.   [7] Diodor., iv, 60.
[8] *Heort*, 417.   [9] *Roschers Lexikon*, i, p. 343.

youths and maidens sent from Athens to Crete was an atonement for the death of Androgeus, whereas some authors [1] identify the bull of Marathon with the Cretan bull.

Seven maidens and seven youths had to be sent to Minos, but two of the maidens were youths in girls' clothes, and this scene is still repeated at the festival called Oschophoria. [2]

The Oschophoria was celebrated on the first day of the harvest festival called Pyanepsion. It was a procession of youths with vine-stalks, two of them clad as maidens. It seems that a race of the ephebi with vine-stalks decided who was to take part in the procession. The procession was headed by a herald with a crowned staff and probably ended at the temple of Dionysus. At the same time, however, another procession took place with the olive-branch, the *eiresione*, in honour of Apollo. [3]

Theseus seems to be connected with both ceremonies. For if the youths in the procession called Oschophoria are the same that were sent to satiate the hunger of the Minotaur, we must recognize Theseus in the herald who leads this sacrificial *pompe*. On the other hand, however, our hero either dedicated an olive branch to Apollo before he went on his perilous expedition or promised the god the olive-branch as a token of his victory. [4]

Minos himself came to fetch his victims. [5] Theseus had volunteered to become one of them, not with the intention of being devoured by the gluttonous man-bull, but to put an end to this shameful tribute. Troubles began on the journey. Minos, like a real bull, wished to cohabit with Eriboia, one of the sacrificial victims. Theseus rescued the girl and married her himself. [6] Minos doubted the descent of Theseus from the ocean-god Poseidon. To prove his divine origin Theseus paid a visit to his father. It seems to have been worth his while to perform this act of filial piety for his father granted him the fulfilment of three wishes. One of these wishes saved his life when he came back from the labyrinth, the second helped him to return from the nether world, and by the aid of the third, he killed his son Hippolytus. [7]

[1] Apollodor., ii, 5, 7, 4. Diodor., 4, 59. Hygin., f. 38. Paus., i, 27, 20.

[2] Plut., *Thes.*, 23.

[3] Mannhardt, *Wald und Feldkulte*, 1904, ii, pp. 214–17.

[4] Theseus in *Roschers Lexikon*, pp. 692, 693. Mannhardt, loc. cit., ii, pp. 692, 693.

[5] Paus., i, 17, 3. Diodor., 4, 61.

[6] Plutarch, *Thes.*, 29. Athen., 13, 4, 557.

[7] "Theseus," *Roschers Lexikon*, p. 695.

Having followed the career of our hero up to this point we shall break off to obtain some information with regard to his antagonists Minos and the Minotaur.

Minos was a king of Cnossus in Crete, or rather the typical representative of Cretan kings in general. He is said to have been of exceedingly amorous disposition, even for a mythical hero, so that his wife Pasiphaë laid the curse on him that all women with whom he had intercourse should die of his embraces.[1] He held office for eight years and at the end of that period he retired to the oracular cave on Mount Ida and there communed with his divine father Zeus, giving him an account of his kingship and receiving instructions for the period that was to follow. " This tradition plainly implies "— as Frazer says—" that at the end of every eight years the king's sacred powers needed to be renewed by intercourse with the godhead and that without such a renewal he would have forfeited his right to the throne." [2] At such a momentous crisis in his life, when throne and life were at stake, Minos prayed to the gods to vouchsafe him a portent as proof of his divinity and royal rights. A white bull of surpassing beauty arose from the sea, sent by the sea-god Poseidon. The bull was so beautiful that Minos spared its life and substituted another animal for the sacrifice. Poseidon punished him by inspiring his wife with an invincible love for the bull.

" In order to gratify this passion the artist Daedalus constructed a hollow wooden cow in which the lovesick queen was hidden when the bull mounted it. The result of their union was the Minotaur— a monster with the body of a man and the head of a bull whom the king shut up in the labyrinth." [3] The legend seems not only to reflect the marriage of a divine bull and cow, enacted periodically by the king and queen in bovine masks,[4] but also seems to show that this marriage was connected with some great danger that threatened the life of the king. If the bull is Minos, we may conjecture that he appeared in bull's shape at the end of the octennial period to prove by his ability to procreate his kind that the day for killing him had not yet come.

The labyrinth was a real palace and its windings represented human intestines.[5] It indicates the influence of Oriental royalty, while Minos himself has many features in common with the pharaoh.

---

[1] Apoll., 3, 15, 1.   [2] Frazer, *The Dying God*, pp. 70, 71.

[3] *Roschers Lexikon*, p. 2993. Frazer, *The Dying God*, p. 71.

[4] Frazer, loc. cit.

[5] E. F. Weidner, " Zur babylonischen Eingeweideschau," *Orient. Stud., Fritz Hommel.*, 1917, p. 191.

The ceremony held every eight years for the renewal of his power and life may be compared to the Sed festival, involving both the death and sacred marriage of the king, while his appearance in a bovine mask may be regarded as a sign of his " Osirification ". There may be a ceremonial reason that explains the alleged fatal consequence of his love ; for we remember that the cows that had intercourse with Apis were instantly killed after the act. Is it a mere coincidence that Minos like Osiris-Apis is represented as a judge of the dead ?

We resume the narrative of our hero's adventures. When he arrived at his destination, Ariadne, the daughter of King Minos, at once became enamoured of the beautiful hero. Indeed she must have inherited this love from her mother who had also been irresistibly attracted by the bull of Poseidon. This young hero was the same thing : for was he not the son of Poseidon and the conqueror of the bull ?

According to Pherecydes, Ariadne told our hero that he would find the Minotaur sleeping in the centre of the labyrinth. All he had to do was to cut his locks from his forehead and then he could kill him as a sacrifice to Poseidon. After that he returned by the aid of the well-known thread.[1] He was well rewarded for his victory by the love of Ariadne. On returning home, however, a misfortune befell our hero. His father told him to return home with a white or red sail so that he should see from far off that his beloved son was safe and sound. But Theseus was forgetful, indeed, fatally so. He had approached the coast and still had not given orders to exchange the black sail for one of more hopeful aspect. His father had been on the look out from a rock and when he caught sight of the black sail he concluded that his son was dead. In his grief he jumped into the sea from the rock. Aegeus was dead, and his son Theseus became king of Athens and the real organizer of the democratic state.[2]

But on his return he does something else. After burying his father he establishes, on the 7th of Pyanepsion, a harvest festival to Apollo and the Oschophoria to Dionysus. He also entrusts the Fig-clan with celebrating a festival in his honour on the 8th of Pyanepsion.[3]

The victor in the battle has brought home the olive-branch to Apollo. What sort of a contest is this in which Theseus was victorious ? He killed a bull. The bull was dedicated to Poseidon ; Poseidon is his father. But he killed his father in a more direct

[1] *Roschers Lexikon*, loc. cit., p. 698.
[2] *Roschers Lexikon*, vol. i, 146 (Aigeus) and " Theseus," p. 113.
[3] Plut., *Thes.*, 712.

manner ; the result of his victory is that Aegeus " the Wave Man ",[1] another Poseidon, perishes in his native element.

In the Sudan it is initiation that kills the king and there are traces of an initiation ceremony in the ritual of Oschophoria.

The ceremony is connected with the youths, the ephebi, of the town. Moreover, the Deipnophoroi, or food-bearers, who took part in the ceremony supplied the chosen ephebi with provisions and then " played the part of the mothers of the youths on whom the lot fell ".[2] But the most remarkable coincidence is that Theseus cuts the hair of the bull-monster before he kills him in just the same manner as his own is cut at initiation. Moreover, his son Hippolytus is the typical " hero of the Shorn Hair ", the *daimon* of initiation ceremonies.[3] He kills his son because he thinks that Hippolytus has attempted to commit incest with his mother, and again it is the bull of Poseidon that appears as the instrument of death.[4]

Perhaps the death of the ancient kings of Athens was connected with initiation. When a king died, the hair of the youths was shorn and they effected the transition from puberty to manhood. The connection between the two rites is given by the Oedipus complex ; it was the death of the Paternal Tyrant that made it possible for the youths to become men in the sexual sense of the word.

They atoned for the deed by a symbolic death and castration ; the locks were dedicated to a dead god. After having taken the strength of the bull-monster by clipping his hair it is quite easy for Theseus to kill him. The only peculiar circumstance in this connection is the scene of the contest. If the windings of the labyrinth are, as testified by Babylonian inscriptions, the intestines it would seem that the labyrinth itself represents the womb.[5] Thus we should find our hero castrating and killing a bull while he has intercourse with Ariadne and the fact that the bull's hair is shorn like his own shows that this descent into the womb is closely connected with the idea of his own castration. Having killed the totemic representative of his father in a heroic battle and his real father, the king, " by accident," and having descended into the nether world, or been castrated or married Ariadne (which all mean the same thing), the ruler of Athenian democracy ascends the throne. He is the winner of the race at the Oschophoria and as king a triumphant

---

[1] " Aigeus," in *Roscher*, vol. i, p. 146.
[2] J. E. Harrison, *Themis*, p. 323.
[3] Harrison, ibid., p. 336.
[4] " Hippolytos," in *Roscher*, p. 2682.
[5] O. Rank, *Das Trauma der Geburt*, 1924, p. 147.

victor in all the sexual contests mentioned above, the bearer of the herald's staff and the *eiresione*. Yet at this juncture of the ritual he betrays his descent from serpent kings, for the herald crowns his staff with two snakes entwined.[1]

Erechtheus or Erichtonius, the phallic serpent king, is said to have been the originator of the ritual procession with the branch or twig,[2] and Cecrops, the first of the serpent race, is connected by myth with Egypt.[3]

Perhaps, however, this latter feature is projected back from the bull kings to their serpent predecessors. At any rate we know that Cretan culture represents a link between Oriental and Greek civilizations and the fact that the royal bull-fight of the Athenian king takes place at Cnossus may be regarded as a sure sign that Greek royalty was profoundly influenced by the Orient. Whereas Cecrops and Erichtonius were more closely connected with the serpent and the bough, the bull is prominent in the myths of their successor Theseus, though the snake-entwined staff still represents an earlier development of the same ideas.

The fundamental concept is always the same but the cultural setting differs from age to age. Originally the king and queen were two snakes. The female snake became exalted into the goddess Athena ; the male may have had something to do with Poseidon. When the kings of Athens began to imitate Oriental rulers, the bovine was the correct mask of royalty and Theseus, the man who killed the bull and wedded Ariadne, the ideal of a king. Theseus is protected by the town goddess but the olive-branch, the symbol of the victor, is due to another king-god, Apollo. But Apollo scarcely appears on the scene —he is already replaced by Dionysus. It is to the temple of Dionysus that the Oschophoria march with the vine-stalk, and when Athens had long become a republic the ceremony of the *hieros gamos*, the marriage of the " queen " to the representative of the bull Dionysus, was still enacted on the 12th of Anthesterion. The marriage took place in the old official residence of the king called the Cattle-Stall.[4]

But the typical sacred marriage of Greece was the wedding of Zeus and Hera enacted, as shown by the researches of Frazer, as a fertility charm. In this fertility rite it seems that Zeus and Hera, or the Lord and Lady of May, were represented by a divine king and queen. As, in an early phase of the development of Greek religion,

---

[1] Harrison, loc. cit., p. 323.
[2] *Roschers Lexikon*, loc. cit., p. 1304.
[3] *Roschers Lexikon*, ii, p. 1016 (Kekrops).
[4] Frazer, *Magic Art*, ii, p. 137.

the king was Zeus on earth (or Cronos or Dionysus) it will be significant for our general hypothesis if we can show that the annually returning ceremonies of these gods were survivals of a pre-human pairing season.   Indeed this is anticipated halfway by Jane Harrison, for in her brilliant book on Greek religion she regards the king as identical with the Olympian victor, the holder of the green-branch or may-pole, the *Eniautos-daimon* of the year.[1]   On the other hand she positively asserts that the serpent king was a phallic being and that the original shape of the *Eniautos-daimon* was the phallus.

Moreover, as the season of rut was also the season of battle between the Old Males and Youth, the novices of the horde, these ceremonial survivals of the pairing season are often closely connected with puberty ceremonies, or, what amounts to the same thing, with the tragic ascent of the young king to his father's throne and harem.

7   THE MAY-KING

We take the Hymn of the Curetes found at Palaikastro as our starting point and thus follow Miss Harrison, who has given us an admirable book on the subject.

The translation given by her runs as follows :

> " Io, Kouros most Great, I give thee hail, Kronian, Lord of all that is wet and gleaming, thou art come at the head of thy Daimones. To Dikte for the Year, Oh, march, and rejoice in the dance and song, That we make to thee with harps and pipes mingled together, and sing as we come to a stand at thy well-fenced altar, Io, etc.
> " For here the shielded Nurturers took thee, a child immortal, from Rhea and with noise of beating feet, hid thee away. Io, etc.
> " And the Horai began to be fruitful year by year (?) and Dikè to possess mankind and all wild-living things were held about by Wealth-loving Peace. Io, etc.
> " To us also leap for full jars and for fleecy flocks, and leap for fields of fruit and for hives to bring increase. Io, etc. Leap for our cities and leap for our sea-borne ships and leap for our young citizens and for goodly Themis." [2]

Leaping seems to be a feature of fundamental importance in a periodic, or, to use Jane Harrison's expressions, in an *eniautos* festival. The worshippers or chorus " leap " and they try to induce a god,

---

[1] The sin of Salmoneus ; he aspired to the dignity of a second Zeus. On a fifth century crater he wears the emblems of an Olympian victor. (Harrison, *Themis*, pp. 79, 80.)

[2] Harrison, *Themis*, 7.

the principal actor, evidently a projection of their own personality or rather of their specific emotion for the time being, to do the same. They attribute special importance to this " leaping " of the *Eniautos-daimon* ; it induces luck and especially fertility. Why should this be the case ? What is the connection between this periodic " leaping " and the results which are supposed to follow ?

In many parts of Europe dancing or leaping high in the air are approved homeopathic modes of making the crops grow high. The homeopathic element as well as the projection to the crops are secondary features and the original connection between jumping, dancing, muscular activity in general and fecundity must be explained on other lines. In Voigtland, the leaping takes place at midnight on the night before Shrove Tuesday and the higher the woman leaps from the table the better for the flax. She must be completely naked when she jumps. The same rite was observed in Silesia (district of Goldberg and Strigau) ; the housewife who jumped for the benefit of the flax had to be naked. Another variant of the same thing was the dance of naked girls at Sallfeld in the fields to make the flax grow.[1] " Girls with bunches of the three or nine different kinds of flowers would take the offered hands of boys . . . and jump together over the midsummer fire." [2] This jumping was for a plentiful harvest.[3] The identity of the Shrove Tuesday and Midsummer leaping is proved by the custom as observed in Baden. Boys and girls would jump in couples over the midsummer flame, believing that the flax would grow as high as they jumped over the fire.[4] In the county of Hont (Hungary), youths and maidens jump over the Midsummer fire together and if they manage to jump skilfully this is regarded as a favourable omen for their married life.[5] At Menyhe in Northern Hungary a girl who jumps over the fire will be married within a year. The fire is made by young lads in the graveyard.[6] In the Muraki district (Hungarian-Croatian boundary) it is the office of an old maid to call out the names of a boy and a girl who are to jump through the flames together. They are henceforth regarded as a

[1] Mannhardt, *Wald und Feldkulte*, 1904, i, p. 484, quoting *Journal von und für Deutschland*, 1790.

[2] M. Trevelyan, *Folk-Lore and Folk-Stories of Wales*, 1909, p. 27.

[3] Idem, loc. cit., p. 23.

[4] E. H. Meyer, *Badisches Volksleben*, 1900, pp. 103, 225. Quoted by Frazer, *Balder the Beautiful*, 1913, i, p. 168. Cf. in Little Russia, Ralston, *Songs of the Russian People*, p. 280.

[5] A. Ipolyi, *Magyar Mythologia*, 1854, p. 193.

[6] F. Atovich, " Zobor-vidéki Szent-Ivánnapi Szokások," (Midsummer Customs in the Zobor District), *Ethnographia*, 1900, xi, p. 226.

" pair ", exchange presents and usually become a married couple.[1] Again we find that the way a girl jumps through the flames is regarded as a foreshadowing of how she will fare in married life at Kolon.[2] In the neighbourhood of Bühl and Achern only unmarried lads brought the fuel used for the fire, only the unmarried young men and women sprang through the flames, and an invitation to jump together over the bonfire was regarded as tantamount to a public betrothal. Moreover, as in the cases mentioned above the spectators drew omens of their married life from the height to which each of them bounded,[3] we shall therefore be justified in assuming that leaping or jumping in all these cases is a mitigated form, a survival, of the sexual act, a conclusion which can also be proved in another and more direct manner. A Baganda chief either jumped over his wife or had sexual connection with her in order to secure a successful termination of a war, and indeed we are told that in every case when jumping over a wife or stepping over her legs is mentioned it is regarded by the Baganda as equivalent to or instead of having sexual connection with her.[4] We assume that jumping became a symbol of coition because it had once been associated with the sexual functions in a specific manner and we shall now proceed to inquire into the nature and origin of other seemingly meaningless motor elements which form a conspicuous part of these periodic festivals.

In England we find " The game at best, the girls May rould must bee, Where Croydon and Mopsa he and she, Each happy pair making one hermaphrodite, And tumbling, bounce together, black and white." It was the custom for young married couples to roll down a slope together on May Day, and in some parts of Russia the priest is rolled by women over the sprouting corn in the belief that this will promote the growth of the crops.[5] People roll naked in the dew the night before Easter Sunday in Bohemia.[6] In Posen we find only a survival of the original nakedness in the custom of getting the benefit of the

---

[1] S. Résö-Ensel, *Magyarországi Népszokások* (Folk-Customs in Hungary), 1867, pp. 269, 270.

[2] Ibid., 185. For further Hungarian data see Bellosics, " Magyarországi adatok a nyári napforduló ünnepéhez," *Ethnographia*, xiii, 1902, p. 25. Róheim, *Magyar Néphit és Népszokások*, 1928, p. 309.

[3] Schulenburg, *Z. f. E.*, xxix, 1897, 494 (Verhandlungen) quoted by Frazer, *Balder*, i, p. 168.

[4] J. Roscoe, *The Baganda*, 1911, pp. 357, 365.

[5] Frazer, *Magic Art*, ii, p. 103.

[6] A. John, *Sitte, Brauch und Volksglaube im deutschen Westböhmen*, 1905, p. 65.

Midsummer dew by going into the fields with bare feet.[1] Witches go out naked to gather the dew and thus steal the fertilizing power from their neighbours' fields.[2]

Frazer well reminds us that rolling together in the fields is "probably a mitigation of an older and ruder custom," i.e. of the sacred marriage celebrated in the fields for the benefit of the crops.[3] After leaping and rolling, we may pass on to consider sliding and dancing in this connection. In Belgian Wallonia every year on the 25th of March the rock called " Ride Cul " was the object of a pilgrimage. Boys and girls seated themselves on the top of the stone on little faggots of wood and then they let themselves slide down the rapid decline and from the incidents of the descent they drew omens which all referred to their future married life.[4] At Carnac, the young girls who wanted a husband undressed completely and rubbed their navels against a menhir especially devoted to this usage.[5] People who had been married for many years and were childless went at the time of the full moon to a menhir, took off their clothes, and the women ran around the menhir endeavouring to escape the pursuit of their husbands, which they ended, however, by allowing themselves to be caught. On the 15th August the women of Croisic left their houses before sunrise and danced round the Pierre Longue.[6]

Dances are periodically performed all over the world with the avowed intention of promoting the growth of the crops, fertilizing animals and plants. At the beginning of January dancers with peculiar head-dresses called " *die schönen Perchten* " dance through the streets of Salzburg. Their appearance means that the harvest will be a good one. In the Tirol it is generally believed that the more " *Perchten* " " run " (the technical name of the ceremony) the better the harvest will be. At Gastein one of them has got a doll called " Fatschkind " attached to a string which he throws at the women who are standing about to witness the performance. And they are fully conscious of the meaning of the ceremony, for if desirous of offspring they catch the " child " in their arms but try to evade it if otherwise inclined.[7] The paramount importance of dancing and

---

[1] O. Knoop, " Der Tau im Glauben und in der Sage der Provinz Posen," *Z. d. V. f. Vk.*, 1912, p. 91.

[2] Knoop, loc. cit., p. 95.

[3] Frazer, *Magic Art*, ii, p. 104.

[4] P. Sebillot, " The Worship of Stones in France," *American Anthropologist*, iv, 1902, p. 80.

[5] Sebillot, loc. cit., p. 82.   [6] Sebillot, loc. cit., p. 91.

[7] M. Andree Eysn, *Volkskundliches aus dem bayrisch-österreichischen Alpengebiet*, 1910, pp. 165-83.

kindred forms of savage ritual has perhaps not yet received the consideration it deserves. If you wish to ascertain the totem clan of a Bakuena
the proper question to ask is " What do you dance ? " [1] Animals
play a prominent part in these periodic dances of primitive man ;
either the dance is totemic, an imitation of the doings of the eponymous
animal ancestor, or, as the Tarahumares assert, the dance has been
taught by the animals. In spring, the singing of the birds, the cooing
of the dove, the croaking of the frog, the chirping of the cricket,
all the sounds uttered by the denizens of the greensward are the
Indians' appeals to the deities for rain. " And as the gods grant
the prayers of the deer expressed in its antics or dances and of the
turkey in its curious playing by sending the rain, they easily infer
that to please the gods they, too, must dance as the deer and play
as the turkey." [2] This dancing is a serious affair and there is a
purpose in it, for the word for dancing means literally " to work ".[3]
The deer-hunt and the ceremonial race of the Huichol may be
compared to these ceremonial dances of the Tarahumare. In the
opinion of the Huichol, the deer-hunt ensures good luck for the
coming year. The deer is the emblem of sustenance and fertility
and his blood is sprinkled over the corn seed that it may become
equally sustaining. He is the sacrifice most valued by the gods and
without him rain and good crops, health and life cannot be obtained. [4]
There can hardly be a doubt that the energies devoted to these dances,
hunts and races, which last from the beginning of April to the end of
August, [5] are derived from a sublimation of the libido, for there is
a converse ratio between success in love and in the deer-hunt ; good
luck in love means bad luck in deer-hunting. [6] This is no mere
conjecture : it can be demonstrated by comparing the ritual of these
Indians to the rites and beliefs of their pre-Columbian ancestors.
Preuss tells us that the gods of ancient Mexico were supposed to
dance at their own festivals and he shows the phallic nature of these
dances. [7] Indeed, he goes so far as to declare that a study of Mexican
hieroglyphs shows that *coitus was regarded as the principal activity
of the gods.*[8] Dancing was also the principal activity of the young
men in the *telpochcalli*, the *Männerhaus*, and the god Tezcatlipoca

[1] G. W. Stow, *The Native Races of South Africa*, 1905, p. 408.
[2] C. Lumholtz, *Unknown Mexico*, 1903, i, p. 331.
[3] Ibid., ii, p. 332.   [4] Lumholtz, loc. cit., ii, pp. 40, 43.
[5] Lumholtz, loc. cit., ii, pp. 10, 41.   [6] Lumholtz, ii, pp. 40, 41.
[7] K. Th. Preuss, " Phallische Fruchbarkeits-Dämonen als Träger des
altmexikanischen Dramas," *Archiv für Anthropologie*, xxix, 1903, pp. 163,
164, 154.
[8] Preuss, ibid., loc. cit., p. 149.

was regarded as the *Megistos Kouros* of the Curetes.[1] The Kobéua tell us that all the masks are demons or that the demons are the " masters " of the masks. The appearance of these dancers is connected with funeral ceremonies, partly because in the Primal Horde the death of the father was the sign for the beginning of coitus, and then also because the separation of the soul from the body was reinterpreted as coitus by primitive mankind. They mostly represent animals in a state of sexual excitement and commence a dance which is evidently an imitation of coition. They stroke their artificial phalli and show how the seminal fluid spreads into every corner of the house, into the plantations and the forest. They leap at the women and girls who fly from them with screams and laughter. The intention of the dance is to bring fertility to the whole village, women, animals and plants at the same time.[2] So far we have succeeded in showing the prevalence of a phallic element in periodic (*eniautos*) festivals and the close connection between this element and various forms of motor discharge, such as leaping, rolling, sliding and dancing, that occur in the same connection.

The Curetes who ask Zeus the King and Father of Men and Gods—their *Megistos Kouros*—to leap for full jars, fleecy flocks, etc., and leap themselves to encourage him were our starting point and it is to them that we now return. We have so far found analogies, now we are going to find the Curetes themselves in the actual folk-customs of Eastern Europe.

" Leap for full jars and leap for fleecy flocks and leap for fields of fruit and for hives to bring increase . . . for our cities, our sea-borne ships, for our young citizens, and for goodly Themis "—all this sounds most familiar to a Hungarian ear. For we find the same formulae with slight local variation still in use among Hungarians, Slavs, and Roumanians at the present time.[3]

In certain districts of Western Hungary at new year (*eis eniauton !*) masked dancers called *regösök* (i.e. " men who perform an incantation," formerly, perhaps, " who fall into a trance ") appear at the house of every well-to-do peasant and chant the following spell : " Rise, farmer ! God hath descended to thy house, to the spread table. I am conjuring (*regö rejtem*) by permission of the great God, for this farmer, hundredfold of corn on one acre, hundredfold of wine on one

[1] Preuss, pp. 164, 165.
[2] Koch-Grünberg, *Zwei Jahre unter den Indianern*, 1910, i, pp. 138, 174, 195.
[3] Cf. Róheim, " Hungarian Calendar Customs," *Journ. Royal Anthropological Institute*, 1926.

acre, hundred chickens under a hen, hundred geese under one goose-mother !

" I conjure, I conjure. At the end of the village in a house there lives N.N. (name of a girl) here we have N.N. (name of a boy or vice versa) I conjure them together, and they shall roll together like a cat's tail if I let it into my shoe." [1]

Our *regősök* do not leap, but they dance about and make a tremendous din with their drums, kettles, and rattles. One of the dancers should regularly be a bull and a second personates a stag. But it is two circumstances that interest us here ; the enumeration of all conceivable forms of plenty just as in the hymn of the Curetes, and the fact that this seems to be only the introduction to what is the real purpose of the incantation : to unite by their magical power a particular girl to a particular boy and to finish the song by a slightly veiled allusion (the tail in the shoe) to the act of coitus.

Let us see a second sample of the same species. In Pankasz, the County of Vas, Western Hungary,[2] god is said to be descending upon the farmer's house and specially upon his table where a meal is pre-pared, in the same way as above, and then the performers wish a hundredfold of corn, a hundredfold of hay, lard up to the height of the door, milk as much as there is water in the well, hundredfold of poultry, etc. Then they name the boy and the girl who are to be wedded and say : " Let him twist and twirl, as a fox turns his tail in a hole or even better than that." At Milej (Göcsej district) they go through all the cattle and crops and other forms of earthly goods that are actually in the possession of the particular farmer on whom they have called, and then pronounce the same blessing for each animal or plant, concluding as usual with the marriage incantation and wishing " to roll the girl and twist her like a little hare twisting its tail ". One of them represents a cat, the other a pig, the third a bull. Here they appear at Christmas—the first day of the year in bygone centuries.[3]

The sexual element is still more emphasized in the incantations performed by another group of lads who call on St Lucy's day, the 13th of December, a day of special importance in Hungarian folklore. They are called *palázolók*,[4] a word which explains the origin of these customs and the reason why customs that are found in connection with Christmas and New Year in other countries should

[1] Sebestyén, *Regősénekek*, 1902, pp. 88, 89.
[2] Sebestyén, loc. cit., pp. 114, 115.
[3] Gönczi, *Göcsej*, 1914, pp. 272, 276.
[4] Sebestyén, " Dunántuli Gyüjtés," *M.N.Gy.*, viii, 1906.

be displaced to the 13th of December in Western Hungary. The
word is derived from the Southern Slav *polazar*, *polaznik*, the "lucky
bird" of New Year (Christmas) in the Balkans. Now in the
nineteenth century the day that was Christmas for the
Magyars was the 13th December for the Southern Slavs, who
reckoned according to the Old Style. The *polaznik*, therefore, who
came from his own people on a friendly call to his Hungarian neighbour arrived there on St Lucy's Day, so that the Hungarians themselves received and adopted the Christmas (New Year) ritual as
something that ought to be performed on the 13th of December.[1]

A young lad appears as the Leader ; his followers are half a dozen
school children. They bring some straw with them and begin to
strew it over the whole room. Then they sit down or kneel on
the straw to imitate the hen sitting on her eggs and begin to murmur
their incantation. The refrain after each stanza is "*kitty, kotty*" ;
the whole performance is called *kotyolni*, a slightly modified form of
the verb *kotlani*, i.e. to cackle. The verses either refer to plenty
in general or contain particular wishes of a coarsely sexual nature,
for instance, that the girl's buttocks should be the size of the oven-door,
her breasts as big as a large jar, and especially that the man's penis
should stand as firm in its place as the axe in its handle.[2] At Niczk,
in the county of Vas, the ceremony is performed by lads between
15 and 20, and when they have finished their incantation they roll
up and down in the straw.[3] In Bosnia the Christmas *polaznik*,
i.e. visitor, goes straight to the hearth and taking a piece of the
badnjak, he strikes the rest of the log with it till the sparks fly about.
"As many sparks, as many calves, goats, lambs, as much luck, wealth
and blessing," is his saying [4]; in Serbia, "As many lambs, calves,
male children as sparks." That the act of producing sparks originally
stands for engendering children can be proved by the sexual meaning

[1] Sebestyén, *A regösök*, 1902, p. 416.
[2] Róheim, *Adalékok a magyar néphithez*, 1920, p. 157. "*Battre de son
marteau l'enclume*"—"*den Penis in die Vagina treiben*." K. Amrein, "Beiträge
zu einem Französischen erotischen Idiotikon," *Anthropophyteia*, vi, 1909,
p. 34. "Eine Axt ohne Stiel ist ein Mann ohne Weib," H. von Wlislocki,
Volksdichtungen der siebenbürgischen und südungarischen Zigeuner, 1890,
p. 174. "The union of the blade with haft might well be taken to symbolize
the physical union of male with female." A. B. Cook, "Cretan Axe-Cult
outside Crete," *Transactions of the Third International Congress for the
History of Religions*, 1908, ii, p. 194.
[3] Sebestyén, *Dunántuli gyüjtés*, p. 154.
[4] Lilek, "Volksglaube und volkstümlicher Cultus in Bosnien und der
Hercegovina," *Wiss. Mitt. aus Bosnien*, iv, p. 453.

given to this act in various countries. For instance, in Mecklenburg the saying goes that a man who cannot strike a spark with the steel has no hope to beget children.[1] The next step would be the projection of the magical coition from the multiplication of the human species to the fertility of domestic animals ; hens playing a conspicuous part as " eggs " are one of the most universal symbolic equivalents of children, while the flight of the bird frequently represents the sexual act. In Macedonia the " first foot " arrives on the 2nd of January. He lays a stone and a green twig on the hearth. He casts some salt on the flames and squatting by the fireside he wishes his hosts " a prosperous year, a plentiful crop, and many blessings ". As the grains of salt burst in the fire he says : " As I am sitting, even so may the hen sit and warm the eggs. As this salt splits even so may the eggs of the clucking hen split and the chickens come forth." In Pravi, the visitor wishes that " as many sparks fly from the splitting salt so many chickens may be hatched by the brooding hen." [2] All these good wishes are evidently closely related to the formulae of the Kolyadki, the incantation originally recited at the Kalends of January : " The ears shall be plentiful as blades of grass. The sheaves shall be in number like the stars ! the stacks shall be like hills, The loads shall be gathered together like black clouds ! " [3] In the colinda pitiereilor lads of about 14 years go round the village on Christmas Eve. They stir the embers in the hearth and " wish " all sorts of wealth to their hosts " as many sheep as he has hairs on his head," etc.[4]

The Curetes, as we know, are the followers of the *Megistos Kouros*. He comes to Dikte for the year at the head of his *daimones* ; they dance and leap, and by this action the Horai, female genii of nature, become fruitful and everything in nature from the flocks to the young citizens commences to increase. Similarly we find a band of masked dancers headed by a *Megistos Kouros*, the " visitor ", appearing at the commencement of the year in Europe and elsewhere and inducing fertility by various forms of motor *détente*, by striking fire, rolling, dancing, and leaping.[5] The connection between the

---

[1] S. Troyanowitch, " Manners and Customs," in Stead, *Servia by the Servians*, 1909, p. 183.

[2] D. F. Abbott, *Macedonian Folklore*, 1903, p. 84.

[3] W. R. S. Ralston, *The Songs of the Russian People*, 1872, p. 194.

[4] T. Schmidt, *A hazai oláhság kolinda-költészete* (The Colinda of the Roumanians in Hungary), 1913, p. 10.

[5] For the custom of " leaping " in the New Year cf. John, *Erzgebirge*, p. 183. Strackerjan, *Aberglaube und Sage aus dem Herzogtum Oldenburg*, 1909, ii, p. 42. Startori, *Sitte und Brauch*, 1914, iii, p. 54.

ancient Cretan and the modern European custom becomes yet more evident if we pause a moment to consider who the Curetes really are. Miss Harrison tells us that the ritual commemorated in the Palaikastro hymn is the ritual of tribal initiation. "The Kouretes are young men who have been initiated themselves and will initiate others." [1] We shall therefore turn back again to our Hungarian *regösök* for an analogy. "Hail, Kronian ... thou art come to Dikte for the year," the Curetes say, and at Hegyfalu in the county of Vas we find that the young lads of the village form various groups on New Year's Eve with a leader for each. At every house where they arrive they begin with the following incantation : "Farmer, farmer, farmer ! May God descend on your house, With six oxen, six horses and with a little golden plough." These formulae are slightly modified at every village as the real meaning is only half understood. We find God descending "With his host (at the head of his *daimones* !) with a table spread, a full cup," or "with his host, his guardian angel, table spread, full cup, roast chicken".[2] But that the *regösök* are the Curetes, i.e. those who have been initiated, acquired magical powers and now initiate others, is conclusively proved by the sequel of their usual Christmas performance at Vámos-Család. They hold a meeting at the village inn to perform the ceremony of "baptizing the lads", i.e. of initiating them into the age-grade of adult men. All those who desire to be initiated choose a godfather among the men, and he, after accepting the glass of wine offered by the novice and laying his left hand on the boy's shoulder, receives him into his own age-grade.[3] At Niczk the initiator squirts a mouthful of wine into the face of the novice.[4] It is only after having undergone this ceremony that the boy is allowed to call on girls and to dance with the young men. The fact that the New Year visitors are divided into various age-grades among the Roumanians,[5] that the unmarried girls "dance the New Year in" at Westerlandföhr,[6] that in Northumberland the first person who calls

---

[1] Harrison, *Themis*, 1912, 19, 3. In the Roumanian custom of the *plugusori*, this miniature plough appears not only in the song, but in reality as a New Year fertility rite, Schmidt, *A hazai Oláhság kolindaköltészete*, 1913, p. 36. Moldván, *A Magyarországi románok*, 1913, p. 220.

[2] Sebestyén, *Regös énekek*, pp. 177, 189.

[3] *Idem*, loc. cit., p. 71.

[4] *Idem*, loc. cit., pp. 76, 77.

[5] Cf. Schmidt, loc. cit.

[6] Müllenhoff, *Schleswig-Holsteins Sagen*, xxi. Sartori, loc. cit., iii, pp. 54, 55.

at the New Year ought to be an unmarried lad,[1] that the first-comer in Wales must be a boy,[2] as in Holderness, Silesia, and the Lower Engadine,[3]—all this acquires a new and unexpected meaning. It is the young *kouros*, the penis, performing fertility magic for the year (*eis eniauton*).

The Curetes leap, dance, and sing, inducing their *Megistos Kouros*, Zeus, to do the same for the purpose of general welfare and fertility. If the Cretan rites of the Curetes and the Thracian religion of Dionysus are essentially one and the same,[4] perhaps A. B. Cook is right in explaining the *du-thor-ambos* as Zeus-leap-song, sung by a *thiasos* of those who leap and dance rhythmically together, a spring song of fertility-magic for the New Year, the song that makes Zeus leap or beget.[5]

In lower Austria the ceremonial crowning of the King of New Year has degenerated into a mere farce. The most ridiculous and stupid lad is crowned with a crown and given a sceptre of straw and is then chased out of the room with insult and injury. He must wait at the door till the youngest girl goes and fetches him. She becomes queen for the following year and receives the good wishes of her mock subjects.[6] In Polish villages of Silesia the boys run towards a pole with a hat on it on New Year's Day and the winner of this race is " king " like the victor at Olympia.[7]

Though degenerated into a mere game these New Year customs with their elements of contest and marriage and their mock kings clearly show their real meaning. The fertility daimon of the rutting season was chased by the horde and held his office by main force.

---

[1] Henderson, *Northern Counties*, 1879, p. 73.

[2] J. Rhys, *Celtic Folklore, Welsh and Manx*, 1901, i, p. 338. According to Manx custom, " a company of young lads and men generally went in old times on what they termed the *qualtagh* at Christmas or New Year's Day." Rhys, loc. cit., i, pp. 336, 337. The presents received are called *calenning*, ibid., p. 338. Cf. the Kolyadki, etc., in Eastern Europe. For New Year's wishes similar to the Russian, Hungarian, Roumanian, etc., formulae, cf. " A pocket full of money, And a cellar full of beer, A good fat pig, etc.," E. M. Leather, *The Folklore of Herefordshire*, 1912, p. 90.

[3] Gutch, *East Riding*, 1912, p. 86. Drechsler, *Sitte Brauch und Volksglaube in Schlesien*, i, p. 48. Hoffman Krayer, *Feste und Bräuche des Schweizervolkes*, 1913.

[4] Harrison, loc. cit., p. 30.

[5] Harrison, loc. cit., p. 203.

[6] Th. Vernaleken, *Mythen und Bräuche des Volkes in Österreich*, 1859, p. 291.

[7] Sartori, *Sitte und Brauch*, 1914, iii, p. 76.

" Kings " of this type play a considerable part in the summer and spring ceremonies of Central Europe. In Hungary there was a time when the Whitsuntide king actually represented the authorities.[1] He acceded to his throne by means of a horse-race and an isolated tradition regards him as having been deprived of his royal power after a year. This was done by the nobles of the country in his sleep. From ancient Babylon to modern folklore the traditional chain is unbroken, for Tammuz the King is said to be asleep when he has really been killed by his loving subjects. One of these tree spirits whose death is mourned for and whose revival is expected is the Russian Yarilo. In the district of Kostroma the burial of Yarilo was celebrated on the 29th or 30th of June. An old man carried the coffin containing a Priapus-like figure. This was Yarilo. In Little Russia this image was surrounded by drunken women who wailed for the death of the phallus like the women of Jerusalem for the death of Tammuz.[2]

In Hungary it is true that we find no phallus in the hands of the Whitsuntide ruler, but instead of this he is the bearer of the *eiresione*, the Maypole.

A branch, usually oak or birch, that is set before the door of the beloved girl is called *maio* in Italy. Therefore the proverb " to put a maypole before the door " is equivalent to saying to fall in love with somebody. It is the same in Spain—*majo* = " tree of lovers ".[3] The birch-tree must be stolen in Jászó (Abauj Torna, Hungary) and the girl before whose door it is placed gives the ribbons to decorate the tree. If she refuses her suitor she must overthrow his pole, otherwise it means that she accepts his courtship.[4] Until about fifty years ago the young men of the parish used to deck a large bunch of rosemary with white ribbons in Wales and place it at the bedroom windows of the maidens they admired. In some places people who wished to insult or annoy an enemy took a horse's head and fastened it to the latch of the door.[5] At the Côte d'Or or Nivernais the ox's or horse's head is hung at the door of the faithless girl's house [6] and perhaps the horse's head has something to do with a peculiar Hungarian tradition that survives in a folk-tale, according to which the bridal couple used to stand on a horse's head. Kálmány

[1] Róheim, " Hungarian Calendar Customs," *J.R.A.I.*, 1926, p. 377.
[2] W. R. S. Ralston, *Songs of the Russian People*, 1872, p. 245.
[3] Mannhardt, *W.U.F.K.*, i, p. 163.
[4] *Anzeiger. Ethn. Ung. N. Mus.*, v, 1910, 126, 67.
[5] M. Trevelyan, *Folk-Lore and Folk-Stories of Wales*, 1909, p. 25.
[6] Mannhardt, *W.U.F.K.*, i, p. 167.

regards this as a pre-Christian marriage ceremony ; at present, however, people who live in clandestine love are spoken of as having married " at the horse's head ".[1]

The Bulgarians in the counties of Temes and Torontál (formerly Southern Hungary, at present Roumania) bring green garlands to their lady-loves at Whitsuntide and by placing the same garlands under their pillows they will dream of their future lovers.[2]

As we can show the close connection existing between these branches, love, and procreation, there cannot be much doubt as to their real meaning. In the Inn valley the may-tree is planted at the door of the last married couple and it is not removed till they have a child.[3] After that the symbolic phallus is superfluous ; it has done its duty.

In Leipzig the young girls present a decorated tree to a young woman after her nuptials ; it is called a " may " and the playthings hanging from it contain unmistakable allusions to the expected result of the marriage. We can therefore understand why the bride covers her face with a gesture of shame when the fir-tree is brought in at the marriage ceremony in Volhynia.[4]

It is hardly possible to mistake the real meaning of the maypole and this has frequently been acknowledged by authors without any bias in favour of psycho-analysis.[5] But we have hitherto had no attempt to make use of this knowledge in explaining the details of the ceremony. For instance, we are told that the tree has to be stolen,[6] just as stealing material objects will appear in dreams, neurosis and otherwise, as a symbolic equivalent of prohibited inter- course. Anxiety is represented by the prohibitions of the period ; it is regarded as dangerous to hand anything out of the house on May Eve, whereas everybody attempts to steal something, as this will bring prosperity to the family. Rake handles and forks ought to be stolen on this day if they are to keep for some time,[7] and we shall probably be justified in regarding these objects as more practical equivalents of the stolen maypole. If we remember that the male loses something in coitus whereas the female receives something,

---

[1] Kálmány, " Vérint való testvérek," *Ethnographia*, 1912, 43, 102.

[2] Czirbusz, *A temes és torontálmegyei bolgárok*, 1913, 101, 102.

[3] M. Andree-Eysn, *Volkskundliches aus dem bayrisch-österreichischen Alpengebiet*, 1910, 190.

[4] Mannhardt, *Wald und Feldkulte*, i, p. 222.

[5] Buschan, " Das Sexuelle in der Völkerkunde," in *Moll, Handbuch der Sexualwissenschaften*, 1912, p. 290.

[6] A. Wrede, *Rheinische Volkskunde*, 1919, p. 187.

[7] Sartori, *Sitte und Brauch*, 1914, iii, p. 172.

and that the act is accompanied by the unconscious dread (wish) of castration we shall understand the loss of the maypole and fights connected with this symbol.

It is important to notice that the return of the libido represented in its phallic shape is no mere individual affair, there is usually one big maypole for the whole community. The objects that decorate the maypole are either re-statements of its symbolic meaning, as for instance, eggs (testicles), sausages, or the cock at the end of the Swedish and Wendish midsummer-pole,[1] or they are garlands, wreaths put on the top of the pole by the girls and doubtless symbolizing their person in the particular aspect that corresponds to the symbolism of male objects. After having danced round the pole we find the boys climbing to the top, and what climbing up a penis means is evident to everybody who is even superficially acquainted with dream-symbolism.

We shall end this chapter by another group of May customs. In Switzerland (Sarganserland) it is the duty of the young men as a body of the *Knabenschaft* to "ring in May" by running through the fields with the church bells. The sound of the bells brings heaven's blessing to the fields.[2]

There are other connecting links between the ways of initiated savages as a class, the Curetes and European spring festivals. A general feature of primitive secret societies is their reign of terror against the uninitiated. Licence for themselves and great severity with regard to the morals of other people are the characteristic features of their behaviour. On May Eve they have the privilege of taking anything they can lay hands on and they usually abuse this privilege in a very lawless manner. On the other hand the initiated youth represent the moral tendencies of the community. Their dreaded witticisms remind us of the *aischrologia* of Greek phallic processions.

But youth has to fight for mastery, and the fight between Summer and Winter formed an intrinsic part of May festivities. Two companies of men and youths were formed. One had for its captain a man dressed in a long coat much trimmed with fur, with a stout stick of blackthorn and a kind of shield on which were studded tufts of wool to represent snow. This was Winter with his followers, who eventually had to give way to the other party, having Summer

---

[1] Mannhardt, *Wald und Feldkulte*, i, pp. 169–83. Dreschler, *Sitte Brauch in Schlesien*, 1903, i, p. 114.

[2] W. Manz, *Volksbrauch und Volksglaube des Sarganserlandes*, 1916, p. 34.

as their leader, decorated with flowers and ribbons.¹ These spring fights are sometimes between lads and lasses, and in the cantons of Freiburg and Waadt the young men storm the so-called " Chateaux d'Amour " protected by the maids of the village.² Perhaps if we combine the two pictures we shall get nearer to the original—the " Chateaux d'Amour " protected by old Winter and victoriously stormed by the young men. If we remember that this takes place on May Day, the period when the " pole " comes back, we shall be reminded of the fact that the Season of Love is for the higher mammals the Season of Battle, and that the Battle between the Old Male (Winter), who selfishly retained all the females of the Horde in his castle, and the brother-horde was the starting point of human society. Now a May Day tradition of Wales tells us about the pirate O'Neil who was a greater danger to the virtue of the women than to the prosperity of the men. On a May Day, however, he was captured and burnt at the stake by the men of Llantwit and to commemorate this event an effigy is still annually set up on May Day in Colhugh meadows and burnt.³

The maypole itself, or a demon-image, is frequently burnt or thrown into water ; the act is connected both with the idea of fertility and with the more complicated, because exclusively human, concept of sin and virtue.

In this chapter we believe we have shown that the periodic re-appearance of the object-symbol (pole) or personal representations of the sex-impulse and the periodic repetition of certain play-activities (climbing, leaping, etc.) are conclusive proof of the former periodicity of the libidinal impulse in mankind. The *eniautos daimon* is a phallus.⁴ But he has to conquer another, older demon of his kind before he can take possession of his kingdom, and in the captain of Winter we recognize the Old Male of the pre-human horde. The Season of Rut was the Season of Battle.

What we have hitherto shown is :—

(*a*) that the female personification of a season, the May Queen, etc., is the survival of a pre-human rutting-season ;

(*b*) that the god with the laurel-branch (*eiresione*, maypole) is the Young Male, the phallus, victorious in the struggle for love and life against the representative of a previous generation.

We shall now resume the study of pairing seasons in European

---

¹ Trevelyan, *Folk-Lore and Folk-Stories of Wales*, 1909, pp. 25, 26.
² Hoffman-Krayer, *Feste und Bräuche des Schweizervolkes*, 1913, p. 157.
³ Trevelyan, loc. cit., p. 26.
⁴ Cf. J. E. Harrison, *Themis*, 1912.

folk-custom. The significance of these rites for our present purpose lies in their intimate connection with Celtic royalty. Now if we can show the same latent content in Celtic as in African royalty the theory of a polygenetic origin of this institution gains in force, though of course it does not preclude the possibility of a one-origin theory.

Among the Letts, the songs sung on Midsummer Eve relate how John searches for his lost wife and finds her again. The lady-love of John is represented as carrying water, and we find once the bride, then again the bridegroom, identified with the sun or other natural phenomena.[1] Bielenstein has found the only possible explanation of these songs. He regards John as collectively representing the men and his wife or lady-love as standing for the women who celebrate the festival.[2] The story of their love is a projection of the emotions which quickened the hearts of human men and women at this period, and the periodic *hieros gamos* of superhuman beings a proof of the former periodicity of human libido.

At Nalbach, boys take a girl by force, with whom they dance the whole year round after the vespers on Midsummer Night.[3] In Poland, at Bilez, they dance round the fire and call upon St John to choose a wife but in the sequel they substitute the names of one lad after another for that of St John and one lass after another poses in the part of "white John's" bride.[4] This mythical bride of the summer solstice reappears in the Roumanian fairy queen Ileana Cosinzana—"Helen with St John",[5] the prototype of feminine beauty. Boys and girls go round the village on St John's Eve singing obscene songs,[6] and in other songs the lads are warned against sleeping on this night lest they should not be able to find a wife.[7] Perhaps this *hieros gamos* at Midsummer was supposed to induce fertility. This might be the meaning of a song sung by the peasants in White Russia at sunrise "Iván and Márya bathed on the hill ; where Iván bathed, The bank shook ; Where Márya bathed, The grass sprouted." [8]

---

[1] Cf. Mannhardt, *Wald und Feldkulte*, i, p. 468. *Idem*, "Die lettischen Sonnenmythen," *Z.f.E.*, vii, 1875. K. Krohn, "Die Freierei der Himmelslichter," *F.U. Forschungen*, 1903. Schroeder, *Arische Religion*, ii, 328, 192. *Idem*, "Lihgo," *Mitt. d. anthr. Ges. in Wien*, xxiii, p. 238.

[2] Bielenstein, *Baltische Monatsschrift*, 1874, H. 1–2.

[3] N. Hocker, "Gebräuche aus den Harzgegenden," *Z.f.D.M.*, i, 89.

[4] Mannhardt, *Wald und Feldkulte*, i, p. 467.

[5] Vulcanu, *Román népdalok*, xiii.

[6] Usener, *Götternamen*, 107.

[7] Schroeder, *Arische Religion*, ii, p. 320.

[8] W. R. S. Ralston, *Songs of the Russian People*, 1872, pp. 241, 242.

Ileana Cosinzana is the " Fairy Helen " of Hungarian folklore and it is therefore significant to find her name under the guise of " Hungarian Helen " in the Midsummer Night's songs. In other variants, however, just as in the Polish parallels, we find St John replaced by a real lad and " Fairy Helen " by a real girl.[1] Among the Croatians of the Muhr Island it was at the Midsummer Night's fire that girls and lads were allotted to each other by an old maid and many of these pairs married later.[2] In Upper Jentz, every lad received a girl allotted to him at the Midsummer fire.[3]

The exact date can only have been fixed at a relatively high stage of culture, but the custom itself of lads finding girls for themselves at the beginning of the warm season is immeasurably older, and proves that these festivals are the survivals of a human pairing season. The custom of re-allotting lads and girls to each other year by year may be regarded as a typical survival of the original marriage " lasting beyond the mere act of propagation till after the birth of the offspring ",[4] that is from one rutting season to the next. " *Maio mense religio est nubere et item Martio* " the Romans thought.[5] " In May when every lusty heart flourisheth and burgeoneth, for as the season is lusty to behold and comfortable, so man and woman rejoice and gladden of summer coming with his fresh flowers : for winter with his rough winds and blasts causeth a lusty man and woman to cower and sit fast by the fire." [6]

A game of the German peasants in the Harz mountains is called " searching for the May bride ". The custom is observed on Monday at Whitsuntide by the inhabitants of Ellrich. They all go out into the hills and every girl carries a may-bush, while the boys are blindfolded and try to catch the bush. Anybody who succeeds in doing so gets the girl who holds the bush as his " may-bride ". He dances round the maypole or may-tree with her, plants the bush before her door, and is regarded as her knight for a year [7] or for

[1] Ipolyi, *Magyar Mythologia*, p. 193. Réső Ensel, *Magyarországi Népszokások*, p. 185. Atovich, " Zobor-vidéki szentiváni szokások," *Ethnographia*, 1900, p. 220.

[2] Réső Ensel, loc. cit., pp. 269, 270.

[3] Sartori, loc. cit., iii, p. 229.

[4] Cf. Westermarck, *The History of Human Marriage*, 1901, pp. 19, 20.

[5] Porphyrion, *ad Horat. Ep.*, ii, 2, 209.

[6] Malory, *Le Morte D'Arthur*, Bk. xx, chap. i (Everyman's Library, vol. ii, p. 336).

[7] E. Kück und H. Sohnrey, *Feste und Spiele des deutschen Landvolks*, 1911, p. 122.

the month of May. The girl who fetches the highest price at the auction is the " Queen of May ", and the lad who " buys " her is the May King.¹ A protocol of the year 1683 describes the custom as practised at Speier in Baden. " *Abusus in juventute mit dem lahntgerufen (Lehnchen rufen).*

Quod fit hoc modo : Convenit iuventus utraque una cum civibus et tot quot possunt domo abesse ad ingressum in sylvam ubi duo designati duas ascendunt arbores sibi invicem respondentes, aliis sub illis haerentibus, fitque hoc loco pridie. S. Georgij quando horum unus altissima voce incipit in hunc modum :

Höret ihr burger überall,
Was gebeutet Euch des Königs hochwürdiger marschall
Was er gebeut und dass soll sein.

Exempli causa : Hans Claussen soll Margreten loos (Drei schritt ins Korn) und buhler sein (drei wieder zurück). Über ein jahr gebet es ein braut herauss."

Probably the nature of the intimacy between the knight and his bride does not amount to more than what townsfolk would call a flirtation, but there may be exceptions to this rule and the exceptions may have been the rule in less sophisticated ages. It is interesting to note the close connection between the girl and the green bush. In the Palatinate, a regular auction is conducted and the auctioneer speaks of the girls as if they were so many fir-trees, but is careful to indicate whom he means by giving the age and other personal characteristics of the girl as if he was speaking of a tree.² At Hohenstein, in Northern Thuringia, we have the " Whitsuntide dance " followed by the call of the " Whitsuntide lad " on the parents of his lady-love, formally asking them to give him their daughter as his " Whitsuntide girl ". If the parents and the girl accept him, he plants a " Whitsuntide may " before her door, and she gives him a cake in return. On Monday each pair walks round an ash-tree and as circumambulation is a prominent feature of all Indo-Aryan marriage ceremonies,³ this shows that the relation between the two

¹ A. Wrede, *Rheinische Volkskunde*, 1919, pp. 187, 188. Cf. R. Reichhardt, *Die deutschen Feste in Sitte und Brauch*, 1911, p. 138. Schell, " Bergische Hochzeitsgebräuche," *Z. d. V. f. Vk.*, x, 1900, p. 40. Schmitz, *Volkstümliches aus dem Siebengebirge*, 1901, pp. 24, 25.

² E. Fehrle, *Deutsche Feste und Volksbräuche*, 1916, p. 67. A. Becker, " Frauenrechtliches in Brauch und Sitte," *Beiträge zur Heimatkunde der Pfalz*, iv, p. 10.

³ A mother of a child born out of wedlock runs round an elder bush three times instead of going to church. Schmitz, *Volkstümliches aus dem Seibengebirge*, 1901, p. 26.

was originally not so chaste as Usener supposes,[1] but was rather regarded as a form of marriage or mating.[2]

Among the Báwariyas the bride and bridegroom go outside the village to a Jand-tree, move round it seven times and then cut off a branch with an axe. In a Bhil marriage the pair walk round a Salyara-tree, which is placed in the marriage booth, twelve times.[3] The custom is still observed in some parts of the Rhineland, although it is gradually dying out. In medieval documents the custom is called *Mailien*, *Mädchenlehn*, or *Maidchen*, the easy transition from the word May to Maid making it possible to indicate both the time and the object of this distribution. The lad buys the girl for a year or only for the time "till the beans are in blossom". At Kirchhain and Ziegenhain, the girl was always mentioned in connection with a lad with whom she was known to be on terms of intimacy and her love was then compelled to offer a greater sum for her than the other lads.[4] At Frankfort the children went from house to house singing, "*Heute zum Lehen, Morgen zur Ehe, Übers Jahr zu einem Paar.*"[5]

In this way they go through the whole population ; every widow and maiden is assigned to a swain and this frequently gives rise to quarrels and slander.[6] The last lines seem to show that this pairing is regarded in the light of a marriage on trial and that the custom is connected with the idea of fertilizing the corn. In the valley of the Isar we find the dance round the maypole and the allotment of a lad and a girl to each other for the day.[7] In Holland the custom of holding a girl-market in May was observed at Lochem, Schagen, and Schermerhorn, and it seems that the couples allotted to each other by this method lived together as husband and wife for some time before they found it necessary to ask the blessing of the church.[8] Similar maiden markets are still in existence, or at least they were

---

[1] H. Usener, *Über vergleichende Sitten und Rechtsgeschichte*, 1902, p. 55.

[2] H. Schurtz, *Altersklassen und Männerbünde*, 1902, p. 113. A thirteenth century poem alludes to the knight sleeping with his may-bride " das wil ich disen summer lanc, in slafgeselle sin ", Mannhardt, loc. cit., i, p. 754.

[3] Crooke, *Popular Religion*, ii, p. 119.

[4] Mannhardt, *Wald und Feldkulte*, 1904, i, p. 450.

[5] Ibid., i, p. 452.

[6] O. Heilig, " Badische Volksbräuche des 17. Jahrhunderts," *Z. d. V. f. Vk.*, xvii, p. 97.

[7] Cf. *Östr. Volksk.*, xiii, p. 160. M. Andree-Eysn, *Volkskundliches aus dem bayrisch-österreichischen Alpengebiet*, 1910, p. 191.

[8] W. Zuidema, " Zu den Mailehen," *Z. d. V. f. Vk.*, xviii, p. 102. J. Schrijnen, *Nederlandsche Volkskunde*, i, p. 242.

recently observed, in some villages of Hungary and Transylvania, most of them being held in spring or summer.[1] We merely allude to the well-known English custom of " Valentines ",[2] to the ball-play of newly-wedded couples or lovers at Easter,[3] to the redistribution of lovers at the New Year in Venezuela. Easter customs, and especially Easter eggs, seem both to symbolize and to promote love-making. Among the Serbians it is the custom for the girl and the lad to exchange eggs and kiss each other through wreaths on the Sunday after Easter, and naturally this is a welcome occasion for love-sick lads to obtain the coveted privilege of kissing the lady of their choice.[4] They roll their eggs against each other and if the girl loves the boy she will indicate this by letting him break her egg,[5] evidently a symbolical, i.e. unconscious, intimation of the fact that she desires him to break through her hymen (the egg-shell) on his way to her ovary. At Sargans the egg is a present from the girl to the lad she loves,[6] or the means by which she obtains a lover.[7] All these and many other customs point to a human mating period at spring and we shall therefore explain the May-Bride and the King of May, as well as other divine pairs, as projections of the feelings of their *thiasos*, of humanity in general, rather than supposing with Mannhardt that mankind pairs in spring in imitation of the vegetation spirit.

To begin with, in many cases the May Queen is one of many, the girl who has fetched the highest price at the auction, and he who buys her is the Lord of May.[8] The earliest date at which this May or Spring Bride reappears is the first or perhaps the second of February. In England the second of February used to be called " Wives' Feast Day ".[9] In the Hebrides the mistress and servants of each family take a sheaf of oats and dress it up in women's apparel. They put it in a large basket and lay a club by it and this they call " Briid's

---

[1] Moldován, *A magyarországi románok*, 1913, p. 416.

[2] Mannhardt, loc. cit., p. 455.   [3] Mannhardt, loc. cit., p. 471.

[4] V. Juga, *A magyar szent korona országaiban élő szerbek*, 1913, p. 99.

[5] E. Szöke, "Vonások a volt Temesi bánság népéletéből," *Fehértemplomi m. kir. áll. Fögm. értesitője*, 1889–90, p. 20.

[6] W. Manz, *Volksbrauch und Volksglaube des Sarganserlandes*, 1916, p. 38.

[7] I. Blau, " Huhn und Ei in Sprache, Brauch und Glauben des Volkes im oberen Angellthale," *Zeitschrift für österreichische Volkskunde*, 1901, p. 232.

[8] A. Wrede, *Rheinische Volkskunde*, 1919, p. 188. Reichhardt, *Die deutschen Feste*, 1911, p. 138.

[9] Hazlitt, *Dictionary*, ii, p. 663.

bed "; servants and mistress cry three times : " Briid is come, Briid is welcome." In the morning they expect to see the impression of Briid's club in the ash and this is regarded as presaging a good crop and a prosperous year. The sheaf used in making Briid's bed seems to have been the last sheaf cut at harvest.[1] The name appears as Breed, Bride, Briid, and Bridget and seems to have been the name of a Celtic goddess Brigit, a sort of Minerva or Vesta connected with a perpetual-fire cult[2] and thus easily assimilated into a Christian Candlemas festival. The name lent itself to various interpretations which must, however, have been in accordance with the fundamental meaning of the festival : either the idea of returning "light" (" bright "-ness)[3] or of a returning " bride ".[4] At the same date Dame God is invited in at Iceland and the lady of the house goes out of doors, clad as lightly as possible, to meet her.[5] At any rate we can discern the fundamental idea of a returning female genius, bringing warmth and fecundity by her approach. The idea of a returning bride is very well brought out in the following little scene enacted on the first of May at Briançon in the Dauphiné. They dress a boy, who has been jilted by his love, all in green and he pretends to be asleep on the earth. A girl who loves him wakes him by giving him her arm and a flag. After this the whole party goes to the village inn and the boy dances with his love. But they must marry within a year on pain of being expelled from the age-grade of the young people and accounted as bachelor and old maid. The lad is called " le fiancé du mois de Mai ". In the inn he discards his green mantle and the girl makes a bunch of the flowers which she wears when they dance together.[6] The bride who has left the lad is of course the winter, but also a real person, and the magic game with the spring bride leads to a real marriage.

Man could hardly represent the seasons in a play taken from human love if that love had not once been conditioned by them, and thus the bride of spring means the return of the love impulse with the genial warmth of the spring sun. In the Government of Nerechta, on

---

[1] M. Martin, *Description of the Western Isles of Scotland*, 1673 (1703), p. 119. J. G. Campbell, *Witchcraft and Second Sight in the Highlands*, p. 274. Macdonald, *Religion and Myth*, p. 141, quoted by Frazer, *Magic Art*, ii, pp. 94, 95, with other Scottish and Manx parallels.

[2] J. G. Frazer, loc. cit., ii, p. 240.

[3] M. Höfler, " Lichtmessgebäcke," *Z. d. V. f. Vk.*, xv, 1905, p. 313.

[4] Mannhardt, *Wald und Feldkulte*, i, p. 426.

[5] Höfler, loc. cit., Olrik, " Wettermachen und Neujahrsmond im Norden," *Z. d. V. f. Vk.*, xx, 1910, p. 58.

[6] Mannhardt, loc. cit., i, p. 434.

the Thursday before Whitsuntide, a girl wakes another, who plays the part of a man, with a kiss [1] ; a distorted but recognizable parallel to the French custom. In some parts of the Swedish province of Blekinge they still choose a Midsummer's Bride and she selects for herself a bridegroom, the two being then regarded as man and wife. Moreover, the custom is again brought into close connection with the general re-distribution of pairs at spring or summer, for the youths follow the example of their " *Megistos Kouros* " and each of them chooses a bride.[2] In Sardinia we have a parallel in the youth and the girl who call each other " Sweethearts of St John ", and evidently influence the growth of vegetation by making wheat and barley sprout in a pot.[3] In Germany, Hansel and Gretel may stand for the spring pair as they appear at Whitsuntide and declare that they come from the real paradise, the country where wheat, corn, and oats are in plenty.[4] For other cases of May Queens and Lords of May or Whitsuntide we refer the reader to the well-known collection of facts supplied by Frazer and Mannhardt and pass on to the mythological equivalents of these personifications of the returning sex impulse. Arthur's fickle lady [5] Gwenhwyvar is the " white ghost ",[6] and this seems to forbid an interpretation which connects her with the May Bride. But what happens among the Saxons in Transylvania ? The girls carry an image called " death " round the village on the 25th of March. The boys attack the girls, rob the " death " of her festive splendour and attire one of the girls with it, who is now called " the queen " and paraded round the village in her clothes.[7] Thus the " white ghost " or " winter " or " death " may become a " spring queen ". And Malory tells us : " So it befell in the *month of May*, Queen Guenever called unto her knights of the Table Round ; and she gave them warning that early upon the morrow she would ride on Maying into woods and fields beside Westminster. And I warn you that there be none of you but he be well horsed and that you be all clad in green." [8] This is no mere courtly fashion, for in the Myvyrian we find her saying,

---

[1] Mannhardt, loc. cit., i, p. 435. [2] Frazer, *Magic Art*, ii, p. 92.

[3] Frazer, *Adonis*, p. 202. [4] Mannhardt, loc. cit., i, p. 430.

[5] The name is still applied in Wales to a girl of doubtful character. J. Rhys, *Studies in Arthurian Legend*, 1891, p. 49.

[6] Rhys, loc. cit., p. 38.

[7] Wlislocki, *Volksglaube und Volksbrauch der Siebenbürger Sachsen*, 1893, p. 63. J. K. Schuller, *Das Todaustragen und der Muorlef*, 1861, p. 4.

[8] Malory, *Morte D'Arthur*, bk. xix, ch. i.

" *Green is my steed of the tint of the leaves* ".[1]   She thus appears to belong to the same family of vegetation spirits as Jack in the Green and his leaf-clad female counterparts.   We have found reason to assume that once there existed a custom of youths obtaining wives in spring by capture, and this is just what happens to our May Queen, Guenever.   The name of the man who accomplishes this deed is significant ;   it is Mael-was or prince-youth [2]—our familiar friend, the Megistos Kouros !   The *Vita Gildae* tells us that this Mael-was carried her away *violatam et raptam*, and that he had been looking out for her *per unius anni circulum*.[3]   Just what we should expect. Moreover, he is called king of the *Aestiva Regio*, Somerset, of course, but perhaps also a mythical Land of Summer.   And then Melwas also has a green cloak and carries his prize to a leafy bower.[4]   Moreover, there seem reasons to assume that Gwalchmai, the king's nephew, was the original hero who rescued her ;   in a still earlier version he may have been the Young Prince who ravished the queen.[5] And who is Gwalchmai ?   The name means the Falcon of May.[6]

His adventures with the Green Knight suggest one of those New Year or Whitsuntide Kings in popular custom who represent vegetation, are clad in a green bush, die by having a false head chopped off, and revive immediately after their death.

" On a New Year's Day, while Arthur is keeping his Christmas feast at Camelot, a gigantic knight, clad in green, mounted on a green horse and carrying in one hand a holly bough and in the other a Danish axe, enters the hall and challenges one of Arthur's knights to stand him ' one stroke for another '.   If he accepts the challenge he may strike the first blow, but must take oath to seek the Green Knight at twelvemonth's end and receive the return stroke.   Finally Gawain accepts the challenge and taking the axe smites the Green Knight's head from the body.   To the dismay of all present the trunk rises up, takes the head, and repeating the challenge to Gawain to meet him on the next New Year's morning at the Green Chapel, rides from the hall." [7]

Holly and mistletoe symbolize Christmas and the right given to the men to kiss any girl or woman.   Now, another adversary

---

[1] Rhys, loc. cit., p. 57.   [2] Rhys, loc. cit., p. 51.

[3] Rhys, loc. cit., p. 52.   [4] Rhys, loc. cit., pp. 66, 77.

[5] J. L. Weston, *The Legend of Sir Gawain* (Grimm Library, vii), pp. 75, 76.

[6] I. Pokorny, " Der Ursprung der Arthursage," *Mitt. Anthr. Ges. in Wien*, xxxix, 1909, p. 111.

[7] Weston, loc. cit., p. 86.   Madden, *Sir Gawayne*, p. 299.   Ballantyne Club.

of Gawain is King Gramoflanz, or rather Guiromelans, a "king who defended a tree against all comers and was himself called *a Mistletoe branch man*".[1] And a third person who plays the part of the beheaded giant is Curoi, son of the Oak, whom Cuchulain conquers, thus obtaining the sovereignty of Erin's heroes.[2]

If, as Frazer has given abundant reasons for assuming, ancient Aryan kings were connected with the oak and had the mistletoe for their external soul we must regard the Green Knight with his bough of holly, the Mistletoe King, and Curoi the Son of the Oak, as originally one and the same person. Evidently if it were not the tree king whom he beheads, Cuchulain could never obtain sovereignty as the reward of his valour.

In Herefordshire, holly and ivy are used for decoration at Christmas,[3] and all three, holly, mistletoe, and ivy, seem to be connected with ideas of fertility and death. In Kent, a carnival custom used to be observed that reminds us very much of the sex-totems of the Kurnai. The boys stole a wooden image of a girl from the girls and this image was called an Ivy Girl. The girls did the same to the boys and the doll they got hold of was a Holly Boy. Both parties finished by burning the image that represented the other sex.[4] Among the Kurnai the killing of the animal that represented the other sex is a preliminary to a fight between the sexes and then to marriage,[5] and it is well known that carnival is the time for arranging marriages. Holly and mistletoe seem both to be male sex symbols, but whereas mistletoe inclines more toward the fertility side of the concept, holly is connected with the idea of death.

In Wales a sprig of mistletoe which had been used for Christmas decoration brought luck to its possessor for the next year. If an unmarried woman placed a sprig of mistletoe under her pillow she would dream of her future husband. Welsh farmers used to say when mistletoe was scarce : "No mistletoe no luck." It gave "luck", that is, fertility, especially to the dairy. To ensure this a branch of mistletoe was placed beside the first cow that gave birth to a calf after the first hour of the New Year.

On the other hand, if you pluck a sprig of holly berries, there will be death in the family. If you bring holly berries into

---

[1] Cook, "The European Sky God," *Folk-Lore*, xvii, p. 347.
[2] Cook, loc. cit., p. 334.
[3] E. M. Leather, *The Folk-Lore of Herefordshire*, 1912, p. 20.
[4] Mannhardt, loc. cit., i, p. 422. Brand, *Popular antiquities*, i, p. 68.
[5] Róheim, *Australian Totemism*, 1925, p. 60.

your house there will be a death on the premises within a year and a day. The person who severs the holly flowers from the bush will meet with misfortune, accident, or death.[1] It seems that death is especially connected with plucking or cutting the plant. If the holly with its red berries were a symbol of the penis, we should understand how it came to be connected with marriage, to represent the boys, and finally why plucking it, that is castration, should bring death. Holly brought into the room means death within a year and a day in Wales, and when the Green Knight brings the Holly Bough into Arthur's court it is exactly in a year and a day that Gawain must suffer the mortal blow.

" Faithful to his compact, Gawain, as the year draws to an end, sets forth amid the lamentations of the court to abide his doom which all look upon as inevitable. On Christmas Eve he comes to a castle where the host receives him kindly and bids him remain over the feast as his guest. The three last days of the year the host rides forth on a hunting expedition, leaving Gawain to the care of his wife and making a bargain that on his return they shall mutually exchange whatever they have won during the day. His hostess is very kind to him. Gawain being the maidens' knight she does all she can to obtain him as her lover. But for once the hero of many amorous adventures is not inclined, only a kiss passes between them which he in fulfilment of the compact passes on to the husband on his return. The second day it is two kisses, and the third day three. But besides the kisses she gives him a green lace which if bound round the body has the property of preserving its owner from harm. Here for the first time Gawain prefers safety to honour. He keeps the green lace, hoping that it will save him from the axe.

" The following morning he rides forth at daybreak and comes to the Green Chapel, a cave in a desolate part of the country. The Green Knight appears and as the axe descends, Gawain flinches instinctively. He is rebuked for this ' cowardice ' by the knight who tells him that he cannot be Gawain. The second time he remains steady but the axe does not touch him. The third time the knight strikes, inflicting a slight cut on the neck. Now the Green Knight reveals himself as his host. He knew about his wife's dealings with Gawain *and the three strokes equalled the three trials of his guest's fidelity.* Had Gawain not proved partially faithless by concealing the gift of the lace he would have escaped unharmed." [2]

The knights of Arthur's Table Round were quite justified in

[1] Trevelyan, *Folk-Lore and Folk-Stories of Wales,* 1909, pp. 88, 89.
[2] Weston, loc. cit., pp. 86–8.

believing that Gawain was riding to his last adventure. For if we regard his first meeting with the Green Knight as the ascent of an *eniautos daimon*, of the King of the Year to the throne, it is evident that the return stroke, the anniversary of his deed, must be his death-day.

The Mule-sans-Frein [1] is a record of a voyage to the Other World and here again there is the same giant who likes to have his head cut off, with Gawain as the hero of the adventure.[2] Moreover, in the *Diu Krone* of Heinrich von dem Türlin, the castle visited by Gawain is *Der Meide Land*—the Celtic other-world. The fairy queen of this country offers him the choice between becoming her consort and receiving the balsam of eternal youth.[3]

Originally, as we have seen, there is no choice at all about the matter, for the hero of the Irish other-world tales enjoys eternal youth by becoming the consort of Queen Morgan le Fay. Now it is Queen Morgan le Fay who, the Green Knight avows, has induced him to tempt Gawain to this adventure, and in certain forms of this [4] visit, called the "invitation" forms, the visit is regularly preceded by a lady asking the knight to follow her. A comparison with the stories of Bran, Oisin, etc., shows that what came to be regarded as a mere "adventure" in romantic literature, originally and mythologically was the supreme adventure of death, but of the departure of the soul viewed as an eternal marriage to a goddess.

The same softening down which has transformed Gawain's death into a dangerous adventure has modified what originally must have been his marriage into a test of chastity. It is a very good rule to go by in interpreting myths not to believe in the alleged sexual continence of the hero, and a poor sort of hero he would be, to be sure, if we were to take his reluctance in love affairs seriously. Fortunately we have not far to seek for proofs.

In the *Diu Krone*, Gawain arrives at a Turning castle where he is hospitably received. Only his host has again the strange craving for the head-chopping trick, and he gives Gawain the alternative of either smiting off his host's head then and there and having the same thing done to him on the morrow or of starting the game by having his own head smitten off instantly.

This host reveals himself as the magician Gansguoter with whom Arthur's mother had eloped and the uncle of Gawain's lady-love,

---

[1] Madden, loc. cit., 306. *Hist. Litt.*, xxx, p. 76.
[2] Weston, loc. cit., p. 91.   [3] Weston, loc. cit., p. 37.
[4] Weston, loc. cit., p. 87.

Amurfina.[1] But it is in the Carle of Carlisle [2] that we at last find the open statement that our hero weds the daughter of the Carle whose head he has struck off.[3] Still perhaps somebody will object that the daughter is not the wife. But we know that Cuchulain is the Irish equivalent of Gawain and Curoi, the Son of the Oak, is the Green Knight. An Irish romance tells us how, one November eve, Cuchulain slew Curoi and carried his wife Blathnath off to Ulster.[4]

These variants taken together, we get the picture of an Oak King challenged by means of Holly or Mistletoe. In the encounter the Young King [5] kills his predecessor and marries his predecessor's wife. Year by year the tragic scene is repeated and it is the anxiety of retributions that makes the combatants change sides, alternately playing the part of father and son. " In fact Curoi and Cuchulain contended with alternate success for the hand of Blathnath—a trait which recalls their alternate decapitation." [6] It is significant that while Cuchulain openly fights and kills his son there are traces of this encounter where the victory goes to the son in the legend of Gawain. For the only knight who originally overcame Gawain was Perceval. Now Perceval is the hero of the Fair Unknown story and the Fair Unknown is Gawain's son.[7] Moreover, it is important to observe that the fight with his son (Perceval) takes place instead of the fight with the King of the Mistletoe,[8] in other words the fight for royalty is originally the fight between father and son.

Gawain himself is King of Galloway and it is in Galloway that the Chateau Merveil is situated.[9] This is the magic castle of the other world, the Land of Maidens, and Gawain as consort of its Queen is naturally the King of the Castle.

There are three queens in this castle of wonders. Arthur's mother is one, Gawain's mother the second, and his sister the third,[10] and the adventure of this castle is connected with his plucking a bough of the tree of which King Mistletoe is the guardian. It seems, therefore, that Celtic, like Oriental, royalty, was a revival of

---

[1] Weston, loc. cit., p. 90.   [2] Madden, loc. cit., p. 270.
[3] Weston, loc. cit., p. 51.
[4] Rhys, *Hibbert Lectures*, 973. Cook, *Folk-Lore*, xvii, p. 336.
[5] On Gawain as King see A. B. Cook, " The European Sky God," *Folk-Lore*, xvii, p. 346.
[6] Cook, loc. cit., p. 336. On Cuchulain, see Róheim, " Cu-chulain and the Origin of Totemism," *Man*, p. 1925.
[7] Weston, loc. cit., p. 63.   [8] Cook, loc. cit., p. 345.
[9] Cook, loc. cit., p. 348.   [10] Weston, loc. cit., p. 22.

a state of things in which parricide and incest were the leading features of life.

Celtic heroes of old were reconciled to their death by wedding the Fairy Queen. The mistress of Avalon has a bough in her hands, a bough broken from the tree of life. Myth can accomplish the impossible, make up for castration by coitus. Gramoflanz too is reconciled to the loss of his bough by wedding Itonje, Gawain's sister [1] ; very naturally, for the wedding shows that his bough is not lost after all. It is here that we arrive at the second meaning of the decapitation episode. The three strokes are equivalent to the three nights spent with the wife of the Green Knight, and we have shown that these were originally anything but nights of chastity. Moreover, the slight wound received by Gawain is due to the same reason ; for everywhere the receipt of a lady's girdle means having had intercourse with her. If we regard the amorous Gawain, the maiden's knight, as a phallic hero we shall understand why the night of his *hieros gamos* is also the night of his decapitation. For the head cut off is a substitute for the penis and the leafy mask worn by the demon of vegetation a survival of the secondary sex characters of the rutting season. Because coitus is archaically regarded as castration or fission, the scenes of marriage and decapitation are inseparable.

But Gawain is not really beheaded after all. He is saved by the magic girdle, that is, by the love of woman. In Wreshow, a village near Königgrätz in Bohemia, the May King's decapitation occurs in the following manner. King and Queen are marched round the village in a bridal procession and then the King is sentenced to death. But the Queen has power to redeem him for a certain sum. First she refuses but when the sword has been thrice swung (the three strokes) she rescues her husband and they march off a happy pair.[2]

This is the function of woman, the function of the other world in myth belief and real life. If it were not for object-love, the expenditure of the semen would seem to be castration, but the woman's magic girdle changes what seemed to be decapitation into a marriage ceremony.

There is little else to be said on this topic except simply to quote a fragmentary poem called *The Marriage of Sir Gawaine* with its Irish equivalent.[3]

---

[1] Wolfram, *Parcival*, xiv, p. 359.
[2] Reinsberg Düringsfeld, *Böhmischer Festkalender*, pp. 265-7. Mannhardt, *Wald und Feldkulte*, i, p. 422.
[3] Madden, loc. cit., p. 288.

One Christmas, King Arthur came to Tearnewadling in Cumberland. A baron with a great club on his back challenged him to fight, returning for the purpose on *New Year's Day*. The dates are significant but still more significant the part played by oak and holly in what follows. When he rode out to keep his appointment he met a hideous hag sitting " Betwixt an oak and a greene hollen ". The hag makes love to Arthur who can only extricate himself by promising that Gawain should wed her. He goes on to fight the baron who claims to be a king and the brother of the hag. Gawain must fulfil what Arthur promised. He finds the woman underneath a green holly tree. On the marriage night she becomes as beautiful as she was previously repulsive. She asks Gawain to choose : would he prefer her to be beautiful by night or by day. Gawain leaves it for her to decide, she says now she will always be beautiful having found a knight who gives her " her will ". There is an Irish parallel to the tale. Nutt points out that in the English version the original question was : " What do women most desire " and the answer is " Sovereignty ", i.e. their will, while in the Irish, the woman is sovereignty.[1]

It had been foretold that one of the sons of Daire Dountech would be king of Ireland and that his name would be Lugaid. But all five were called Lugaid. At an assembly held by Daire a fawn appeared and was pursued by Daire's sons, till a magical mist separated them from the men of Erin. They were overtaken by a snowstorm and found a great house with fire and abundance of food in it. It was kept by a horrible hag who bade the first of the Lugaids share her couch. When he refused to do so, she declared : " Thou hast severed from thee sovranty and kingship." After this the other brothers arrived in turn and in turn they refused her embrace. Last of all came Lugaid Laigde who had caught and devoured the fawn. " Then Lugaid of the Fawn goes with her into the house for the sake of food and ale. Howbeit the hag went into the couch of bronze and he followed her, and it seemed to him that the radiance of her face was the sun rising in the month of May and her fragrance was likened by him to an odorous herb garden. And after that he mingled in love to her she said to him : " Good is thy journey, for I am the Sovranty, and thou shalt obtain the sovranty of Erin." [2]

And this is what we have been trying to show—coitus successfully performed is sovereignty and the king is the penis.

[1] Weston, loc. cit., p. 50. Academy, 1892, Nos. 1042, 1043.
[2] Weston, loc. cit., pp. 49, 50. Cook, *Folk-Lore*, xvii, p. 342.

Having concluded this chapter on these Kings and Queens of May we are now in a position to do justice to other theories besides our own. For although we have been too much preoccupied with our own views to lay stress on these facts we may regard it as generally known that the gods and rulers we have been investigating are regularly associated with the sun and with vegetation. "But Sir Gawaine from it passed nine of the clock waxed ever stronger and stronger, for then it came the hour of noon and thrice his might was increased. And then when it was past noon and it drew towards evensong, Sir Gawaine's strength feebled and waxed passing faint that unethes he might dure any longer." [1] So we find a bond of sympathy between Gawain and the sun, still more perhaps in its yearly than in its daily course. For Gawain, as we have mentioned before, is the Falcon of May and his bride, who is Sovereignty, sits under a green bush of holly in fragrance like a garden of herbs and with a face like sunshine in May.[2] They are our old friends the King and Queen of the Year, the personification of a periodic libidinal impulse.

King and queen, the ego ideals of the male and the female, phallus and vagina, performed their *hieros gamos* at a festival that was the survival of a pre-human rutting season, and their connection with fertility in nature bears witness to a time when man, in greater harmony with nature than at present, like the beasts and plants of the field performed the act of procreation at a definite season.

8 Apollo and Cadmus

It is not so difficult to find the bridge that connects the King of May with the kings of Athens or Thebes.

Plutarch mentions three festivals that were celebrated every nine years at Delphi : the Stepterion, the Charila, and the Herois.[3] Perhaps there is an original connection between these rites, at any rate between the first two as they both remind us in certain details of the Daidala. The doll called Charila—"The people's joy "— was buried at the end of each Enneateris at Delphi. Charila was a poor girl who committed suicide because she did not receive any

---

[1] Malory, *Le Morte d'Arthur*, iv, 18.

[2] The hag is the Loathly Messenger of the Grail. In Wolfram besides the hideous Kundry we find Kundry la Belle and she is Gawain's sister. Weston, *Gawaine*, p. 50.

[3] Plutarch, *Quaest. gr.*, 12, p. 293.

of the food distributed by the king during a famine. The oracle
gave the counsel that her ghost must be placated if the famine was
to cease and this is what is repeated at the end of each eighth year.
The king distributes food among the people and strikes the doll
Charila with his shoe. The doll is then buried at the very place
where Charila committed suicide.[1] As Nilsson remarks, the myth
seems to indicate that the doll was buried not only to mark the end of
an enneateric period but also as a harvest charm for plentiful crops
and that there was an element of lustrative or placative character
in the ritual. The Charila is buried, the Daidala burnt, and the
false bride burnt at the Bulgarian nine-yearly festival of St George.
Both the burning and the dragon-slaying (the latter the outstanding
feature of St George) are prominent in another enneateric festival
of Delphi. Just as the Charila indicated the end of the old period,
it was the Stepterion which opened the New Year. A wooden
building like a royal palace was erected and a group of men led by
a young boy approached the palace stealthily. They carried burning
torches and penetrated into the building. Inside they overturned
the table, set the palace alight, and then beat a hasty retreat. After
this the boy had to do strict penance till he was purged of his guilt
by sacrifices offered at Tempe and he returned as a Daphnephoros,
bearing the laurel of Apollo.[2] Strabo calls the building " Python's
hut ". Plutarch speaks of a royal palace. We shall see the solution
of this apparent contradiction, but at any rate there is no reason to
doubt that the general opinion of scholars is correct and that the
young lad represents the god himself, the whole performance being
a dramatized version of the myth of Apollo slaying the serpent
Python.

Python was the son of the Earth or Gaia. Either Python himself
or his mother was said to have been the original possessor of the
oracle at Delphi. All our authorities agree in relating that the
serpent was killed by Apollo but the reasons for which the god is
said to have fought the serpent are varied. The Homeric Hymn
says that the dragon, or rather she-dragon, was becoming a pest to
mankind. Euripides and Apollodorus regard the god as fighting
for a selfish aim, to become the possessor of the oracle, while many
others tell us that Apollo, while yet a babe in arms, had to protect
his mother Leto with his powerful arrow from the attacks of the

[1] H. Usener, *Kleine Schriften*, iv, p. 116. M. P. Nilsson, *Griechische Feste*, 1906, p. 467.

[2] Th. Schreiber, *Apollon Pythoktonos*, 1879, pp. 9–16. Nilsson, loc. cit., p. 150.

serpent who had been pursuing her when she was with child.[1] The reason alleged for the enmity of the serpent is the usual and therefore meaningless formula of Greek mythology ; the jealousy of Hera against Leto who had been, of course, made pregnant by Zeus. We shall search for a better reason and call attention to the fact that a peculiar relation is supposed to exist between pregnant women and serpents and that these beliefs may be regarded as world-wide. Some people believe that menstruation is due to the bite of a serpent.[2] The Orinoco Indians do not allow menstruating women to go into the forest, believing that by this action they would expose themselves to the amorous attacks of serpents.[3] In Sussex " there is a vulgar notion among the peasantry that if twenty persons were present at the time an adder is irritated and one of the twenty only was in a pregnant state, that that one alone would be bitten by the reptile ".[4] But the quantity of serpents in various parts of the world who promote birth or grant the wishes of sterile women for children prove that the serpent in this case is the generative principle, the male penis, and biting a euphemism for coition. Hence " to dream of being bitten by a serpent portends success in a love affair ",[5] and in the Polynesian story of Ina and the eel, the animal who bites her becomes her lover.[6] We shall therefore regard the version which attributes the enmity of the Python towards Leto to the jealousy of Hera as a late one, and rather interpret the nature of the persecution she suffers as sexual aggression. In an original version of the story which had not been subjected to the secondary elaboration of centuries the Python must have been the lover or rather the husband of Leto. This interpretation is confirmed by a parallel version of the story in which Apollo's adversary is the giant Tityus instead of the serpent Python. Beside the more familiar Apollo Pythoktonos we have an Apollo Tityoktonos. Tityus attempted to have intercourse with Leto and was killed by the infant Apollo for his temerity. Both the name and character of this giant warrant our interpretation and the identification of the myth with the story of the death of the phallic serpent. The word is derived from the root " to swell ",[7] and as he was generally regarded as a personification of unbridled

[1] Schreiber, loc. cit., pp. 1–9.
[2] Ploss-Bartels, *Das Weib*, 1908, i, p. 391. Reinach, *Cultes, Mythes et Religions*, ii, p. 398. Crawley, *The Mystic Rose*, 1902, p. 192.
[3] F. S. Gilij, *Saggio di Storia Americana*, ii, pp. 132, 133.
[4] E. Peacock, " Adders swallowing their young," *Folk-Lore*, xix, p. 474.
[5] W. W. Skeat, *Malay Magic*, 1900. p. 305.
[6] Róheim, " Psychoanalysis és ethnologia," *Ethnographia*, 1918, p. 210.
[7] P. Kretschmer, *Griechische Vaseninschriften*, p. 204.

lust [1] there can be no doubt that the name indicates the penis in erection.[2] After his death his liver is continually devoured by vultures or a serpent, because, as the ancients well knew, punishment conforms to the Law of Talion, or, as we can add in the light of psycho-analysis, because it is an exaggerated repetition of the vice itself. Now the ancients regarded the liver as the seat of the amorous passion, and the ever-growing liver would be an eternally re-erected penis associated with the serpent, that well-known personification of the phallic principle. Both Python and Tityus are sons of Gaea, the latter sometimes of a heroine who is a hypostasis of the great earth goddess.[3] There is a certain amount of unconscious truth in the conjecture which identifies Leto with Gaia and regards Apollo and the serpent as brothers.[4] At any rate they are near relations, in our opinion originally father and son. " *Apollo apud Delon vero formam habet draconinam,*" [5] we are told. Apollo Pythoktonos is, of course, Apollo the Python-slayer, but Apollo Pythios is simply the Python Apollo. Porphyrius has a peculiar inversion of the usual myth, for according to him it is Python who killed Apollo and buried him in the tripod [6]—showing that the two protagonists of the drama were regarded as mutually convertible. Serpents were sacred to the god. They were kept in his grave at Epirus and regarded as the progeny of his famous antagonist. A naked virgin did service as the priestess of these serpents, and if the creatures deigned to receive the food from her hands this was a sure sign of plenty in the following year.

The serpent is one of the god's attributes ; the Pillar Apollo, Apollo Aguieus especially, is associated with a serpent rising out of the pillar or coiling itself round the tree-trunk.[7] Medieval and

---

[1] " *Sane de his omnibus rebus mire reddit rationem Lucretius* (iii, 991) *et confirmat, in nostra vita esse omnia que finguntur de inferis. Dicit enim Tytyon amorem esse, hoc est libidinem quae secundum Physicos et Medicos in iecore est . . . Unde etiam exesum a vulture dicitur in poenam renasci : etenim libidini non satisfit re semel peracta, sec recrudescit semper,*" Servius, *ad Verg. Aen.*, vii.

[2] Cf. G. Kaibel, *Göttinger gelehrte Nachrichten*, 1901, pp. 490, 595.

[3] Waser, " Tityos," *Roschers Lexikon*, 1922, pp. 1033–55.

[4] Schreiber, loc. cit., p. 58. De Witte, *Elite des monuments céramographiques*, ii, p. 164. [5] *Myth. vat.*, iii, 8, 16.

[6] Porphyr., *Vit. Pyth.*, 16. Heliodorus, a poet of the Roman epoch, ascribes the same amorous intentions to Python as others do to Tityus, Schreiber, loc. cit., p. 56. Heliodorus, b. Tzetzes *ad Lycophr.*, 208.

[7] E. Küster, *Die Schlange in der griechischen Kunst und Religion*, 1913, pp. 123, 124. Visser, *Die nicht menschengestaltigen Götter der Griechen*, 1891, pp. 146, 147.

modern Greek and other European folklore holds that the young
adder or serpent is an animal that kills its father,[1] and if our assumption
is correct this is exactly what the legend of Apollo Pythoktonos
contains. In the hero Cadmus we find another dragon-slayer
who is a dragon himself. Cadmus is a local Theban hero who built
the Cadmea, the stronghold of the town, with the aid of the Sparti.
His chief adventure is the slaying of the dragon and there seems to
be a close connection between this dragon and the father of his bride,
the war-god Ares. According to the scholium to Eurip. *Phæn.*, vii,
p. 248, the dragon is the son of Ares and the father of Harmonia.[2]
This would make Cadmus obtain his bride by killing her father—
a plausible conjecture if we only remember that the dragon is normally
represented as the son of Ares and therefore Harmonia's brother,
that Ares is regularly inimical to his son-in-law and, as Crusius
concludes, that the conquest of the dragon was one of the tasks
which Cadmus had to accomplish to obtain the hand of Harmonia.[3]
Harmonia seems to be a double of Aphrodite, the wife of Ares,
and some scholia mention a marriage between Ares and Harmonia,
so that the inimical attitude of the war-god with regard to Cadmus
may be attributed to a jealousy which was both parental and sexual
in origin.[4] We must not forget that Cadmus is a king of the same
town in which Oedipus ruled ; in the Oedipus legend we have
the old king killed by his son who marries the queen his mother,
and in the Cadmus myth, incest between a father and a daughter
and the father killed by a hero who in some versions appears as a
foreigner but who originally undoubtedly was one of the Sparti,
the snake-clan,[5] himself. The dragon-slayer becomes a dragon
himself, and when he dies both he and his wife Harmonia are turned
into serpents. Their child has a serpent for its foster-mother,
and this helpful totem-animal aids the boy in attaining the dignity
of royalty.[6] The metamorphosis into dragon's shape is regarded
as the expiation of the murder committed by killing the dragon ;
and possibly the alternative version of the petrifaction of Cadmus
and Harmonia is also connected with the original weapon used by

---

[1] B. Heller, " Népies és folklorisztikus elemek Zrinyi müveiben,"
Ethnographia, xxx, p. 38. E. Legrand, *Collection de monuments pour servir
a l'étude de la langue néohellénique*, No. 16, 1873, pp. 10, 66.

[2] *Roschers Lexikon*, article " Kadmos ", p. 836.

[3] Crasius, " Kadmos," *Roschers Lexikon*, ii, p. 836.

[4] Jason is another dragon-slayer and conqueror of the Sparti (cf. the article
on Jason). See also F. Schwenn, " Ares," *A.R.W.*, xxii, p. 229.

[5] On the serpent as blazon of the Sparti, *Pausanias*, viii, 11, 8.

[6] " Kadmos," loc. cit., p. 832.

Cadmus who kills the beast by throwing a stone at him.[1] He is king of Thebes because he has killed the old snake, the old king, and wedded the snake-maiden. This wedding seems to have been regarded as a ritual coition, a *hieros gamos* perhaps akin to the rite performed at the spring festival of Dionysus at Athens where the ἄρχων βασιλεύς as representative of the god had intercourse with the βασιλισσα.[2] This is somewhat more than mere guesswork, for Pausanias describes the bridal chambers of Harmonia and Semele on the Acropolis. These are tabooed places which nobody has ever set foot in, they are called both ἄβατον and ἐνηλύσια—" places of coming ". A " place of coming " means a place where a bolt fell from heaven dedicated to Zeus the Descender. " In the *abaton* at Thebes, along with the thunderbolt which was hurled on the bridal chamber of Semele there fell a log from heaven and they say that Polydorus adorned this log with bronze and called it Dionysos Kadmos." [3] It would be tempting to follow the path of which we have caught a glimpse but we must not forget that the hero we are after is not Cadmus at all but rather Apollo. Cadmus only serves as a parallel to point out the probability of our conjecture that Apollo the serpent-slayer is a serpent himself. If we can trace a historical connection between Apollo and Cadmus it is evident that our argument gains additional force. Apollodorus relates how Cadmus, after the murder of the dragon, had to purify himself by serving Ares for a period of eight years,[4] and both the custom and the period reminds us of Apollo. Nonnus seems to have conserved a trace of a myth which represented Cadmus as competing with Apollo in the musical art,[5] and his marriage with Harmonia (Harmony) points in the same direction. Apollo appears as the chariot-driver of the bridal pair,[6] which in the language of the unconscious is equivalent to regarding Apollo as sharing the conjugal functions of Cadmus. All these might be mere analogies but the decisive part played by the oracle at Delphi in the Cadmus legend justifies the view of Crusius who regards the myth as originally composed of a Theban and a Delphic element.[7]

[1] Crusius, " Kadmos," in *Roschers Lexikon*, 835, 878.

[2] E. Fehrle, " Die kultische Keuschheit im Altertum," *Religion-geschichtliche Versuche und Vorarbeiten*, vi, 1910, p. 90.

[3] Pausanias, ix, 12, 3. Harrison, loc. cit., 91. Cf. " Pollux," *Etymologicum magnum*.

[4] Apollodorus, iii, 4, 2. K. O. Müller, *Prol.*, p. 304. Schreiber, loc. cit., p. 16.

[5] " Kadmos," in *Roschers Lexikon*, p. 847.

[6] " Kadmos," ibid., p. 842.   [7] Op. cit., p. 883.

If we therefore believe that Apollo, the young dragon, slew the old one as Cadmus did, we shall naturally have to put the question : Where is Harmonia, the dragon-wife ? And we shall not have very far to search to discover her in the She-Python, the prophetess Pythia. She becomes ἔνθεος by receiving the divine spirit of the god through her vagina, i.e. by intercourse with Apollo.[1] If we remember the frequently incestuous character of these *hieroi gamoi*, perhaps the existence of an Artemis Pythia at the Didymaion [2] may gain a new significance. Another prophetess of the god is Cassandra, "she who has her brother for her husband." [3] And who is this brother-husband ? Apollo, the god whose love gives her prophetic inspiration.[4] According to a parallel version she gains prophetic insight when a serpent licks her ears in the grove of the god.[5] There can be no doubt that the two myths relate the same event in a modified form, the serpent is Apollo himself and the ear a substitute for the vagina. A wax figure in the Naples Museum [6] represents the snake slain by Cadmus as a *genius loci*, surrounded by emblems of fecundity.[7]

After having found some possible survivals of an original pairing season in myth and ritual we shall become interested in the question, when did this battle between two phallic serpents and the *hieros gamos* of the victor, the young serpent, with the old serpent's daughter, presumably his own sister, take place ?

Plutarch's IXth Greek question is : "Who is the Hosioter among the Delphians and why do they call one of their months Bysios ? " Jane Harrison's answer to this question throws light on the path we are about to travel along. The month Bysios was, as Plutarch tells us, at the beginning of spring, the time of the blossoming of many plants. The 8th of Bysios was the birthday of the god and in olden times on this day only did the oracle give answers. At Magnesia the new daemon comes in at the time of sowing ; at Delphi the Thyiades "wake up" their infant god Liknites at the time when the Hosioi offer their secret sacrifice presumably of, and then to, the Hosioter, the Bull. The death of the old-year daemon may be followed immediately by his

---

[1] Cf. Origen, *c. Cels.*, vii, 3. Chrysostom, *Hom. XX in Cor.*, 22. Schol. Aristophanes, *Ploutos*, 39, all quoted by Fehrle, loc. cit., 7.

[2] Gruppe, *Griechische Mythologie*, 1906, i, p. 287.

[3] E. Siecke, *Mythologische Briefe*, 1901, p. 69.

[4] E. Siecke, *Mythologische Briefe*, 1901, p. 69.

[5] Fehrle, loc. cit., p. 87. *Roschers Lexikon*, article "Kassandra", pp. 975, 978.

[6] Apollodorus, iii, 12, 5.   [7] *Cat.*, 3226.

resurrection as the spirit of the new year.[1] In the winter the god—
a word for which we may substitute the idea of a fertility daemon—
is absent and this is the period of his ἀποδημία. On the 7th of
Bysios, the day which for Delphi was the beginning of the spring and
the year, he reappears and this day was probably also the day of his
dragon-slaying and marriage. At the beginning of the winter farewell
hymns are sung and in spring he is welcomed back again.[2] For
us the absence of the phallic daemon in winter and his reappearance,
birth, and marriage, in spring are easily comprehensible as late
reflections of the physical conditions under which mankind once
propagated the human species. When this feature had become
obscured, many phallic daemons, whose reappearance coincided
with the reappearance of the warm season, became projected into
nature and acquired what have been called " solar " attributes. As
mankind lost the periodicity which remained immutable in nature,
the *eniautos* demon ceased to be what he originally was, a human
phallus,[3] and became closely connected with the manifestations
of periodicity in natural environment.

But why is the idea of death associated with that of a new life ?
Why must the old serpent die before the young one can be mated ?
The question is only asked here to show the reader whither we are
going, without the intention of giving an immediate answer. We
shall first add another question and then solve both at the same stroke.
This second question is : why are periodic phallic festivals regularly
associated with puberty rites ? For the Curetes who " leap "
for the year are youth newly initiated and the spring fertility god
is the ideal and representative of the ephebi. He is usually represented as a young hero, an ephebos himself.[4] Born on the 7th of
Bysios, that is, about February, we may imagine him as attaining
maturity in his own month Apellaios. Now according to Hesychius,
the ἀπελλάζειν is Laconian for ἐκκλησιάζειν " to hold " or
" summon ", to be the member of an assembly, and therefore Apollo
would be the god of the human fold or assembly.[5]

At first this does not seem to explain much, but we shall see how

---

[1] Harrison, *Themis*, 1912, p. 155.

[2] Roscher, " Apollon " article in the *Lexikon*. Schreiber, *Apollo Pythoktonos*, 47, 65. (Verg., *Aen.*, iv, 144 ; Dion., *Perieg.*, 527.) Roscher, *Studien*, i, pp. 37, 57. Müller, *Dorier*, i, p. 332.

[3] Cf. Harrison, *Themis*, p. 268. " The form taken by the traditional hero and the king is unquestionably that of a snake, and the snake is used in phallic ceremonies for the promotion of fertility."

[4] " Apollon," in *Roschers Lexikon*, i, p. 442.

[5] Harrison, loc. cit., p. 439.

new light arises from the shrine of Phoebus. More information on the ἀπελλαῖα is forthcoming from the regulations of the phratria of the Labyadae found at Delphi. The ἀπελλαῖα were probably the offerings made at puberty initiation and the ἀπέλλαι the assembly convened for the occasion.[1] " Apollon is the projection of these rites : he, like Dionysos, like Herakles, is the arch-ephebos, the Megistos Kouros. Apollo Phoibos of the unshorn-hair [2] is youth just about to be initiated." [3] It was the custom for those who were passing from childhood to manhood to go to Delphi and offer there the first fruits of their hair to the god. Theseus went there, and a place at Delphi is called Theseion after him. He only shaved the forepart of his head, as Homer says was the practice of the Abantes, and this sort of tonsure was called Theseis after him.[4] Hair cutting was therefore the regular puberty rite in ancient Hellas,[5] or at least one of the puberty rites for, as we shall see immediately, there may have been others. The rite is familiar among primitive tribes all over the world. The Omaha call their puberty ceremony *We bashna*, "to cut the hair." "The severing of the lock was an act that implied the consecration of the life of the boy to Thunder, the symbol of the power that controlled the life and death of the warrior, for every man had to be a warrior in order to defend the home and the tribe. The ritual song which followed the cutting of the lock indicated the acceptance of the offering made, that is, the life of the warrior henceforth was under the control of the Thunder to prolong or cut short at will." [6] Having found one of the typical puberty rites in Greece we shall not be surprised at finding traces of others. The Wonghibon, who knock a tooth out at puberty, say that Thurmulun takes the youth to a distance, kills him, cuts him up, and then restores him to life again but knocks out a tooth.[7] In some tribes they say Daramulun swallowed the boy and after a time vomited him up again as a young man possessing all the tribal knowledge

---

[1] Homolle, " Inscriptions de Delphes," *Bull de Corr. Hell.*, xix, 1895. Nilsson, loc. cit., p. 465.

[2] *Il.*, xx, 39.

[3] Harrison, *Themis*, p. 440.

[4] Harrison, loc. cit., p. 440, quoting Plutarch, *Vit. Thes.* Cf. ibid., Eur. *Bacchae*, 493.

[5] Cf. Apollo as κουροτρόος to whom the first locks are dedicated, *Od.*, T. 86. Hesiod, *Theog.*, 347. Kallim, *Ap.*, 12, quoted by Roscher, " Apollon," p. 442 (loc. cit.). Harrison, loc. cit., 336, 379. Nilsson, loc. cit., 460.

[6] Fletcher and la Flesche, *The Omaha Tribe* (xxvii Annual Report), 1911, 122.

[7] Howitt, *Native Tribes*, 587.

but minus a tooth. Or again, Daramulun "pretended" to Baiamai that he always killed the boys, cut them up and burnt them to ashes. Then he formed the ashes into human beings and restored them to life with a tooth missing.[1] As Miss Hárrison has pointed out, the rebirth from teeth in the myth of the Sparti is the record of an initiation originally told for the uninitiated.[2] The original myth must have been that the young men of the serpent and lance totems (these are the emblems of the Sparti [3]) are swallowed by a serpent who vomits them up again minus a tooth.[4] The knocked-out teeth of the novices are often hidden in an ant-hill, near a water-pool or under the bark of a tree, in this case they may have been buried and this would give rise to a myth according to which the novices (" the serpents " represented by a single dragon in the myth) were killed and afterwards resuscitated from the buried teeth. According to our myth, Ares or Athene prevail upon Cadmus to sow the dragon's teeth after his victory and to plough the earth. Armed men arise and either immediately begin to fight each other or they do so when Cadmus cunningly throws a stone between them.[5] The word *Sparti* is usually connected with *speirein*, " to sow," but perhaps Usener is right in regarding this as a secondary folk-etymology derived from the myth. He interprets the Sparti from a root *spar* or *skar* as the " dancers " and thus brings them on a level with the Curetes (Corybantes) with whom they are sometimes associated.[6] This would both agree very well with the puberty-ceremony interpretation of their myth and explain the fact that they arise fully armed, like the Corybantes and other " sword dancers " who represent the young warriors of the tribe. In the light of initiation rites the incomprehensible episode of the Sparti fighting against each other becomes very easy to understand. " The skill of the *eeramoun*, or uninitiated boys, would be tried in sham fights too. They were given bark shields and their attackers had bark boomerangs ; great was the applause when the boys ably defended themselves." [7] The novices are covered with bushes and led to another and smaller cleared circular space, where they are

---

[1] R. H. Mathews, " The Bŭrbŭng of the Wiradthuri Tribes," *Journ. Roy. Anthr. Inst.*, xxv, 295.

[2] Harrison, loc. cit., p. 434. [3] Paus., viii, 11, 8.

[4] Cf. the vase of the Vatican collection which represents Jason, the hero of the Sparti adventure, as swallowed by or born from a dragon. Harrison, loc. cit., p. 435.

[5] Crusius, " Kadmos," *Roschers Lexikon*, pp. 827, 828.

[6] Usener, *Kleine Schriften*, iv, p. 182. Pasparios.

[7] K. L. Parker, *The Euahlayi People*, 1905, pp. 68, 69.

hidden under a heap of bushes and where the wrestling contests take place in the presence of the women. So as to prevent any quarrelling, brothers as a rule are made to wrestle with each other, though the participants may have to be separated by relatives intervening with raised hands.[1] " A snake dance is performed . . . followed by the wrestling matches." [2] The Kippurs, newly initiated young men, commenced the fight by attacking each other with spears and clubs, the older men looking on. The Kippurs would then retreat and the seasoned fighting men step into the ring. " The former had been fighting in solemn earnest, burning to distinguish themselves ; but the older men too had many an ancient feud to satisfy." [3] And as there is frequently a close connection between festivals of an agrarian character and rites of initiation [4] the idea of sowing the *teeth* and of ploughing fits very well into this connection. Crusius explains the fight of the Sparti by referring to similar contests in agrarian ritual.[5] These contests represent and promote the victory of the summer over the winter, they might therefore very well have taken place simultaneously with ploughing and sowing, that is, in spring.

We must pause to look back at the ground we have covered. Apollo or Cadmus, the young serpent, killed the old serpent at springtime and married the old serpent's daughter. This periodic re-marriage as a survival of a period when mankind had their season of rut every spring meant the beginning of a new year, i.e. a new rutting season. But the god who accomplishes the double feat of dragon-slaying and the fecundating nuptials is closely connected with initiation rites, is, in fact, the *Megistos Kouros*, the representative or projection of these rites, the personification of youth at the age of initiation.

If we inquire into the question of Greek initiation rites we shall find them closely connected with the spring, with the idea of fertility in nature. Demades, the orator, quoted by Athenæus,[6] says that " the ephebi are the spring of the demos ", and hence the festival of Korythalia or " Youth-Bloom " included the celebration of youth in nature and mankind. The *korythale* is Dorian for the Ionian

---

[1] W. E. Roth, " On Certain Initiation Ceremonies," *N.Q.E. Bulletin*, No. 12, 1909, p. 175.

[2] Roth, ibid., p. 177. First the dragon, then the Sparti.

[3] Howitt, *Native Tribes of S.E. Australia*, pp. 598, 599.

[4] Cf. Róheim, *Dying Gods and Puberty Ceremonies* (unpublished).

[5] See Crusius, " Kadmos," loc. cit., 888, and his *Beiträge zur griechischen Mythologie*, p. 19.

[6] iii, 55, 99.

eiresione.[1]   But the *eiresione* is the may-branch carried about in procession at spring and again after the harvest and representing fecundity in vegetation.[2]   It is therefore important to notice the close connection between this may-branch, puberty, and marriage. " And others when their sons and daughters come to maturity place laurel-boughs before the doors in ceremonies of puberty and marriage.[3] Moreover, the Korythalia was a festival of Artemis Korythalia, a goddess who corresponds to Artemis Daphnaia and Artemis Orthia. The latter is the goddess who is " erect ", i.e. who makes the phallus erect.   At her altar the ephebi were scourged, probably with branches intended to convey fertility.   But the may-branch, the *eiresione* or *koruthale*, is said to be either a branch of the oil-tree or a laurel. The laurel in Greek is Daphne and this is the name of the girl beloved by Apollo and changed into a laurel-tree to escape from the overtures of the amorous deity.   Why should she wish to escape ? Because she is Artemis Daphnaia, the god's sister.   Apollo had also a nurse called Koruthale and the *koruthale* is the laurel-branch.   When Apollo returns purified in the person of a young boy who has killed the dragon Python we see a laurel branch in his hand.   Frazer conjectures that the festival of Daphnephoria at Thebes was celebrated in honour of Cadmus as dragon-slayer.   Perhaps these dragons are near relations of the serpent who guards the apples of the Hesperides and succumbs to the force of Heracles.   Moreover, we see that the idea of carrying or breaking a bough is brought into close connection with that of illicit love and that the bough represents both a maiden and the phallus.   The god who conquers the monster, Adam, Heracles, Cadmus or Apollo, and obtains the illicit fruit or forbidden branch is the Megistos Kouros, a personification of human desire at puberty, and therefore we find it appropriate that shoots should be planted before the door when the boy attains to puberty or the girl to the marriageable age.

The bearer of the laurel branch is the god who killed the serpent Python.   Now the serpent stands for the phallus and the hut of Python is a royal palace.   Apollo, his successor, like Python himself, is a god of procreation [4] and the ego-ideal of the ephebi.   Cadmus is king of Thebes, the old royal castle was the Cadmea and in it there was a pole, a *kadmos*.   This *kadmos*—the maypole of European

[1] Harrison, loc. cit., p. 503.
[2] Nilsson, *Griechische Feste*, 1906, p. 184.
[3] Harrison, loc. cit., p. 503.
[4] Gruppe, *Griechische Mythologie*, 1906, p. 853.

folklore—is the husband of Harmonia who is merely another name for the goddess of love, Aphrodite.[1]

Thebes was also the town ruled by King Oedipus, and Boeotia in general the Greeks regarded as the home of snake cults. It is significant that the greater part of the mythical material in which we find an open or nearly open statement of the Oedipus situation should be connected with divine rulers. Of course we do not follow Frazer in interpreting these incest myths as proofs of matrilinear descent and a tendency to keep the power in the family in royal dynasties.[2] No such matter-of-fact considerations could ever have influenced the savage, with his intense horror and repression of incest, to commit it as a matter of policy. It is by applying the analogy of the individual to the social organism that we can understand what has been taking place.

A process that is always going on in every individual organism is the genitopetal and the genitofugal migration, the flux and reflux of the libido. The penis, Ferenczi tells us, is the instrument that relieves the organs of the body of the superfluous libido and thus makes it possible for them to adapt themselves to reality. From time to time society is compelled to develop a penis of this sort. It did so in the dim beginnings of mankind ; the penis was the Jealous Sire who had all the pleasure and procreation for himself and represented the pleasure-principle in the Primal Horde. The other members of the Horde had to take him as their ideal, find pleasure in his pleasure just as the cells of the body participate in the action of the penis. But soon the strain became unendurable. They wanted more, they desired to become procreators themselves. A sudden reflux of the libido from the penis to the body takes place, accompanied by the self-castration of society, the autotomy of the penis. The next phase of social development may be regarded as a parallel to hysteria. In this disease we find a regenitalization of the auto-erotic zones, in savage society a gerontocratic rule, a tribe with many fathers or phalli. The animal phobia is a typical feature of infantile hysteria, an attempt to project the embodiment of the libido outside the organism, to have an imaginary non-human penis. In society this form of settling difficulties is represented by *totemism*, a society of equals with a mythical father-equivalent.

However the main characteristics of totemic society are repression and anxiety. The strain of repression becomes too great and in the

---

[1] Schwenn, " Ares," *A.R.W.*, xxii, p. 224.

[2] Frazer, *The Dying God*, 1911, p. 193. Cf. the explanation of Oedipus as a myth of nature. C. Robert, *Oedipus*, 1915, i, p. 58.

course of evolution society again grew a penis. The king appears on the scene as a revival of the old ideal and ascends the throne by ceremonial or real coitus. This is Oedipus, and Reik [1] in his paper on Oedipus and the Sphinx has shown that the myth of Oedipus contains a totemistic equivalent to the incest and parricide in the fight of Oedipus with the Sphinx. The tragedy of Oedipus, Jocasta and Laius he regards as the return of repressed elements and it is significant both that the more archaic form of the myth of Oedipus (Sphinx) is connected with Egypt and that the return of the repressed incest-attitude is connected with a king. Oedipus means a "swollen foot", a penis in erection, and we find him on a vase standing opposite a naked Sphinx with the mask of a goat and an erected penis.[2] Naturally the new attitude could only be the revival of the old one, just as the object-love and the genital primacy attained at puberty represent the revivals of the phallic organization with its Oedipus complex. It is well known that the erotic reality-principle, that is, the attainment of genital primacy, is closely connected with, and is the condition of, the attainment of the general reality-principle, and in the historic case we are investigating the genitopetal current of the libido led not only to the development of a second social penis in the person of the king but also to a repetition of incest. And this second incest meant perhaps the most important progress in reality man had made ; it was Agriculture.

However there was another great difference between the new and the old Oedipus situation. In the Primeval Horde, incest was the only possible form of libidinal satisfaction. Though repressed, it still remained an object of desire ; but the libido of humanity could never again flow freely in the old channels. Yet what might be quite impossible for the commoner became for this very reason the only possible thing for the beings whom, as a supernatural ideal, he projected from the depths of his longings into reality. But this new social organization was not the Primal Horde, it was merely an unconscious, imitation of the first pattern. It was possible to realize desire and keep in harmony with reality in the shape of non-incestuous intercourse, while the infantile, or archaic, libido might find gratification in the phantasy-identification with the Primal Father or Divine Phallus.[3] Relieved of this burden in reality the commoner could work and the king could suffer. For he was not only the idol but also the divine scapegoat of his people.

[1] Reik, " Oedipus und die Sphinx," *Imago*, vi.

[2] *Roschers Lexikon*, iii, p. 738.

[3] Cf. however the summary for the relation between a genital character in the individual and the phallic type in the structure of society.

V THE SCAPEGOAT

1 THE KING AS SCAPEGOAT

IN Babylonian texts we find the king doing penance for the people.[1] A Chinese father is responsible for the behaviour of his son and a Chinese official for anything that happens in his district. The local officials—nay, viceroys of provinces and even the emperor himself—are regarded by their subordinates or subjects, or profess to regard themselves, as personally responsible for such occurrences as disastrous earthquakes, epidemics, and inundations.[2] King Süan prays for rain in the eighth century B.C. and asks what he has done to merit the dire calamity of such a drought.[3] As representative of the sky, the emperor is responsible not only for himself but for the whole people. And thus the Emperor Tang in the eighteenth century B.C. prays : " If I have sinned my sin shall not be visited on the people of the ten thousand districts but if the people of the ten thousand districts have sinned let me be responsible for their guilt.[4] The king who is killed for famine or drought may be called a scapegoat himself and in some cases, for instance in Uganda, we find a regular scapegoat ceremony as a mitigation or equivalent of regicide. " At first," Frazer says, " the substitute for the divine father was the divine son, but afterwards this rule was no longer insisted on and still later the growth of a humane feeling demanded that the victim should be a condemned criminal. Yet the downward career of fallen deity does not stop here ; even a criminal comes to be thought too good to personate a god on the gallows or in the fire and then there is nothing left but to make up a more or less grotesque effigy and so to hang, burn or otherwise destroy the god in the person of this sorry

---

[1] A. Jeremias, *Handbuch der altorientalischen Geisteskulture*, 1913, p. 100.
[2] R. F. Johnston, *Lion and Dragon in Northern China*, 1910, p. 345.
[3] A. Bertholet, *Religionsgeschichtliches Lesebuch*, 1908, p. 6. Legge, *Chinese Classics*, iv, p. 520.
[4] W. Grube, *Religion und Kultus der Chinesen*, 1910, p. 29.

representative.[1]   We shall now proceed to investigate some prominent scapegoat ceremonies.   If our interpretation of royalty has not been a mistake we shall expect it to be equally valid for the scapegoat.

2   Cock and Wren

(a)   Killing the Cock

We propose to consider certain customs connected with periodical animal processions.   In most of these we find some feature of an ambiguous nature and the veneration paid to the animal does not prevent its being killed or chased with scorn and derision.   In European folklore there seems to be a certain parallelism between the vernal appearance of the phytomorph and zoomorph representatives of re-awakening life.

The oak brought into the village by the Wends on the 2nd of July must certainly be regarded as a sort of maypole.   The head of each family gives it a stroke when it is felled in the wood.   They dance round it when brought into the village and every young married woman who had come from another village had to dance round the tree and put some money into it.   The tree was called a cross-tree because of the cross at the top but a still more essential element was the cock by which it was surmounted.[2]   In Sweden the pole, although called a maypole, is brought in at Midsummer and we find a red cock on the top of the pole.   Finn Magnussen mentions it in his mythological work :   " *Gallum illum, qui ad recentiora usque tempora apud Suecos misticos in culmine majalis arboris collocari soluit.*" [3]

What is the cock at the top of the pole ?   We should not be surprised if we found that it was the same thing as the pole itself.

In certain villages of Masovia, on Easter Monday the girls walk round with a cock and the boys with a green bush.[4]

In Polish Upper Silesia the boys on Easter Monday march round " with the cock ".   On a small two-wheeled carriage a cock with gorgeous plumage moves his head up and down as if he were crowing and a pair of dolls perform a dance for joy at the resurrection of the Saviour.[5]   The same procession with the *Kokotek* (little cock) also appears at Christmas in Upper Silesia.   They have a revolving

---

[1] J. G. Frazer, *The Scapegoat*, 1913, p. 400 (*Golden Bough*, part vi).
[2] W. Mannhardt, *Wald und Feldkulte*, 1904, i, p. 174.
[3] Ibid., p. 160.   [4] *Ur-Quell*, ii, p. 36.
[5] Drechsler, *Sitte, Brauch und Volksglaube in Schlesien*, 1903, i, p. 104.

disc on the carriage, dolls dancing on the disc, and the image of a cock in the middle.[1]

In some cases, however, the cock relinquishes the reserve manifested in these rites. He does not content himself with merely putting in an appearance but he does something, or rather something is done to him. The ceremony called "striking the cock" (*Hahnschlag*) occurs on Ash Wednesday, at harvest-time, at country wakes and weddings. At the country wakes the ceremony is probably enacted merely for the sake of fun, at any rate it has lost its original meaning and must have been transferred from another ceremonial complex. As for the meaning of the ceremony as a harvest-rite we shall defer considering this question till we know the origin of agriculture. If we can find a theory that will explain the meaning of the *Hahnenschlag* both as a feature of Carnival and of wedding-ceremonies we shall be as near the solution of the problem as we are likely to get.

In German and Austrian Silesia the following ceremony usually takes place on Shrove Tuesday, though in some districts it is put off till the harvest. A carriage drawn by eight horses proceeds at a slow pace, carrying a fine cock that is regarded as a great criminal and is fettered accordingly. The procession makes for the common ; it is headed by a " clown "—a rider in a medieval Frank costume. The sinister figure of the hangman standing upright on the carriage accompanies the poor sinner. At last they arrive at the common. The lord of the poultry yard is put into a pot with a hole in it, his head sticking out of the hole. It is for the hangman to read out the death warrant passed on the cock for his sins. Now the young men of the village take their chance. They are blindfolded and have to strike at the pot with a flail or stick. Anybody who misses it has to pay a fine and is laughed at into the bargain, but if he manages to strike the pot he is proclaimed as *Hahnkönig*. A festive meal at the inn, where the cock is disposed of, ends the amusement.[2] The details of the ceremony vary ; the cock may be attached to a pole and the onlookers sprinkled with his blood (Bohemia).[3] In the district of Vechta the cock was put into a beehive with its head peeping out at a hole. The young men of the village formed a circle round the basket, they were blindfolded and then they slashed at

[1] *Mitt. d. schl. Ges. f. Vk.*, iv, 1902, p. 78. A. Dieterich, *Kleine Schriften*, 1911, p. 335.
[2] P. Drechsler, *Sitte, Brauch und Volksglaube in Schlesien*, 1903, i, pp. 58, 59.
[3] Wuttke, *Der deutsche Volksaberglaube*, 1900, p. 291.

the cock's head with their swords. He who succeeded was proclaimed Carnival King. The young girls crowned him as such with their flowers and ribbons and all had to submit to his orders.[1]

At Carnival the young men form a humorous procession of maskers and go round collecting eggs and sausages for their Carnival feast. They do not ask for these articles, they take them, and the cock king is the head of this lawless gang. When they are ready it is time to choose a new king who, of course, will be in office till the next year. The cock's legs are bound together and the poor bird hangs down on a rope from the garret. They all jump as high as they can to tear the cock's head off and the victor in this sport is " cock-king " for the year to come.[2]

In Forbes (Budweis District) the cock is killed for the first wedding in Carnival. The cock has a frock, a pair of trousers, and a nice red cap. Sentence is passed, the cock is bewailed, and its head slashed off by the hangman who is dressed in red.[3] At Königinhof the ceremony is performed every five years. A girl is elected as " cock's bride ". She plays the part in which we usually see a young man, or the young men in general. She is blindfolded and has to hit the cock's head off with a flail. If she cannot do this at the first stroke, it is clear proof that she has lost her virginity. But if she manages, the procession goes round the village with the dead cock and his bride. She has the first piece of cock and the first dance of the evening.[4]

It is evident that our informants regarded the custom as a piece of merrymaking, and did not attribute sufficient importance to the details, for we have hardly any information as to the sin for which the cock is condemned to death. At Grez-Doicen, and very generally in France, we find a goose playing the sad part elsewhere allotted to the cock. All the calamities that occurred in the community during the past year were enumerated and the goose held responsible for all of them. Drawings of an impolite nature represented the evil deeds and practical jokes for which the goose was to be blamed and finally the animal was sentenced to death. Then the young men rode for the goose, which was hanging from a rope, and he who could shoot the bird's head off with his pistol had won the day.[5]

---

[1] L. Strackerjan, *Aberglaube und Sagen im Herzogtum Oldenburg*, 1909, ii, p. 57.   [2] Ibid., ii, pp. 55, 56.

[3] Th. Vernaleken, *Mythen und Bräuche des Volkes in Österreich*, 1859, p. 304.

[4] Th. Vernaleken, *Mythen und Bräuche des Volkes in Oesterreich*, 1859, pp. 305, 206.

[5] G. I. Schepers, *Wallonia*, ii, pp. 169–71. Sebillot, *Le Folk-Lore de France*, 1906, iii, p. 247.

It is hardly more than a guess if we suggest that the rude drawings were also obscene and that the mischief for which the cock (goose) has to suffer belongs principally to the sphere of sexual activity. At least, however, we are in accordance with ecclesiastical authority in giving this interpretation. The pious Benedict of St Peter's Church in Rome has given us a description of the Carnival observed in the year 1142 in the capital of Christendom. Roman knights held a tournament at Monte Testaccio and the apotropaic character of these rites seems to be revealed by our author's explanation " *ut nulla lis inter eos oriatur* ". The three animals sacrificed at this ceremony were a bull, a bear, and a cock, and our author explains the cock as " *luxuria lumborum nostrorum* ".[1] Now, somebody might object that if we are not prepared to follow ecclesiastical opinion and identify the bull with pride and the bear with temptation we have no right to refer to it when it coincides with the view we intend to put forward on the part played by the cock in these ceremonies. But this view is supported by the well-nigh universal testimony of European folklore. " Cock and hen are symbols of married life." [2] According to the Talmud, cock and hen were carried in procession before the bridal pair as " symbols of fecundity ".[3] Fehrle's opinion deserves to be quoted. " It is easily comprehensible that the cock should be brought into connection with fecundity-rites and regarded as a personification of the harvest on account of its strong sexual impulse." [4] Moreover, we must not forget that the beheading of the cock frequently occurs on Ash Wednesday, thus marking off Carnival from Lent. Now Carnival was and still is the season for marriages in the country, whereas all carnal desires are forbidden in Lent. Therefore from a late and allegorical point of view (which, nevertheless, has its roots in the origins of these customs) beheading the cock may be regarded as a farewell to sexual gratification, just as the burial simply means the end of Carnival.

All this is in perfect harmony with the view put forward by Clement who regards Carnival as a festival of fecundity [5] ; and with the part played by the cock in marriage rites.

[1] F. Schneider, " Ueber Kalendae Januariae und Martiae im Mittelalter," *Ar. f. Rel. W.*, xx, 1921, pp. 391–3.

[2] H. von Wlislocki, *Volksglaube und religiöser Brauch d. Zigeuner*, 1891, p. 135.

[3] I. Scheftelowitz, *Das stellvertretende Huhnopfer*, 1914, p. 105. Talmud, *Gittin*, 57a, *Berakot*, 57a.

[4] E. Fehrle, *Deutsche Feste und Volksbräuche*, 1916, p. 77. *Id.*, " Der Hahn im Aberglauben," *Schweizerisches Archiv f. Volkskunde*, xvi, p. 65.

[5] K. Clement, " Der Ursprung des Karnevals," *Archiv für Religionswissenschaft*, 1918.

In the village of Walkenstein (Lower Austria) it was the custom to form a circle round the bride. The wings of the " family cock " (*Haushahn*) had been clipped and it was led into the middle of the circle. The bride had to chase the animal till it died from sheer exhaustion.[1] In Polesia the cock is bound to a ladder and a fire lighted below. It is thus roasted alive before they cook it for the wedding feast.[2] In Hungary the wedding procession is headed by a cock guarded by two men with drawn swords. As soon as the ceremony is over a mock trial is held and the poor bird, having been found guilty of bigamy, is solemnly sentenced to death and executed by the two men with swords.[3] In Thuringia the cock is killed on the third day of the festival and the girls race for a cake, the boys for a kerchief.[4] In Göcsej (Hungary) a live cock or " running cock " is an important feature of the wedding ceremony.[5] Among the White Russians the cock is finally given to the priest or rather to his wife.[6] In Poland they go round with the cock, killing the poultry of the wedding guests and thus collecting the materials for another meal.[7] A Slovak bridegroom must cut the cock's head off with a flail ; if he cannot manage to do so in three strokes he is fined.[8] The ceremony is observed by the Czechs in an elaborate manner. In the district of Beraun it takes place on the third day of the feast as follows.

One of the guests brings a black cock from the bride's parents and the best man, taking the cock, declares that he must be beheaded and the marriage sealed with his blood. The cock is bound to a pole and the best man, acting as judge, hangman and priest at the same time, sentences him to death. Then he walks round the cock three times, stops opposite the poor criminal and slashes twice with his sword in the air, once to the right, once to the left. At the third stroke he cuts the cock's head off and then all the guests attack it with brooms and flails. If he cannot manage to cut the head off at the third stroke he must run away and he has to bear the mockery of the company. The best woman now takes his place and shows the bride how to pluck the cock.

---

[1] Vernaleken, loc. cit., p. 304.

[2] I. Piprek, *Slawische Brautwerbungs und Hochzeitgebräuche*, 1919, p. 40.

[3] H. N. Hutchinson, *Marriage Customs in many Lands*, 1897, pp. 251, 252.

[4] Kunzer, " Volkskundliches vom Thüringer Walde," *Z.d.V.f. Volksk.*, vi, p. 181.

[5] Gönczi, *Göcsej*, 1914, p. 329.   [6] Piprek, loc. cit., p. 50.

[7] Piprek, loc. cit., p. 69.

[8] Piprek, *Slawische Brautwerbungs und Hochzeitgebräuche*, 1914, p. 40.

The Walacks also treat the cock as a criminal. His crimes are enumerated to the guests and his head cut off.[1] In the Creuse district it is a black hen ; they make it dance, then cut its head off. Sometimes it is killed together with a cat ; both are cooked together and eaten by the young married couple in the hope that the bride will bear many children and have plenty of milk for them. In some parts of Berry a hen decked with ribbons is brought to the church ; this is done in order that the couple should have many children.[2] In all these cases, or for instance in Poland, where the bride receives a hen that lays eggs,[3] there can be no doubt that cock and hen are symbols of sexual activity.

Not satisfied, however, with this too general explanation, we shall go further and ask : who is the cock, and who is the hen ? When the young woman among the Wends arrives at her new yard, she lets a hen fly from her carriage. If the hen flies away the young woman will not remain long in the new house, she will fly away like the hen.[4] At d'Eguzon a white hen was carried before the bride. They made the fowl cry out by pulling its feathers till at last it was killed. The same ceremony took place in the Vosges mountains ; and here we are told that the cries of the fowl represented the regret of the bride at losing her virginity. [5] Among the Garos in Assam the priest sacrifices a cock and a hen, holding them close together, and if, on falling, the birds' beaks are turned toward each other, this is a good omen for the married couple.[6]

All this points to a simple conclusion : *cock and hen mean groom and bride.*

In social anthropology, a science which, whether based on psychoanalysis or not, makes use of inferences, a theory is valid if it can explain otherwise meaningless features of a custom. Now we know that there is a group of rites in which the aggressivity of a whole class is manifested against an individual, who has been raised to a position that, from an infantile point of view, or in reality, is higher than their own. An instance of what we mean are certain rites of coronation,[7] certain features of couvade [8] and especially signs of an

---

[1] Piprek, loc. cit., pp. 97–9.   [2] Sebillot, *Folk-Lore,* iii, p. 246.

[3] Scheftelowitz, loc. cit., p. 11.

[4] W. von Schulenburg, *Wendisches Volksthum,* 1882, p. 122.

[5] P. Sebillot, *Folk-Lore de France,* iii, p. 246.

[6] Playfair, *The Garos,* 1909, p. 101.

[7] Róheim, " A kazár nagyfejedelem és a turulmonda," *Ethnographia,* p. 1917.

[8] Th. Reik, " Die Couvade und die Psychogenese der Vergeltungsfurcht," *Imago,* iii.

aggressive conduct of the young men and girls towards the newly married couple.[1]

At Hétfalu (Transylvania) the girls kill a hen and the boys a cock[2]; the same distinction is made at Niort.[3] In certain customs of various Slavic people, a prominent feature is that the groom receives a hen from the bride's parents and in the speeches made by these people for the nuptials the bride is frequently identified with some female animal.[4] In Russia proper a hen is caught by the girls and dressed like a woman. This is called the " ceremonial hen " and regarded as a symbol of the bride's domestic qualities and her fertility. [5]

If the cock and hen mean groom and bride, how are we to interpret the ceremony itself? We notice that in the French ceremony quoted above the squeaks of the hen are regarded as proceeding from the bride who is bewailing her virginity. In Morocco the lack of virginity is made up for by spilling the blood of a fowl.[6] Perhaps we may see the same connection in European customs ; spilling the hen's blood, or the death of the hen means the defloration of the bride.

There is a form of our custom in which the cock, hen, or frequently a goose, is suspended from a rope and dangles in mid-air, and the gallant young men gallop away under it on horseback and try a thrust with some instrument or try to tear the animal off the cord with their hands.[7] In some cases, however, a doll dressed up like a woman is suspended from the rope and the custom is then called *Jungferstechen*,[8] " pricking a virgin," about as bold a statement of coitus as we may well expect.

It is doubtful, however, whether all this is entirely sufficient to explain the origin of what we may call a symbol in the psycho-analytic sense of the word. There is nothing unconscious about the fact that coitus is the aim of marriage and we should therefore

---

[1] For instance they are pulled up by their arms. Strackerjan, *Abergl. u. Sagen aus dem Herzogtum Oldenburg*, ii, pp. 38, 305.

[2] Réső Ensel, *Magyarországi népszokások*, 1867, p. 148.

[3] Sebillot, *Folk-Lore*, iii, p. 246.

[4] A. John, *Sitte, Brauch und Volksglaube im deutschen Westböhmen*, 1905, p. 153.

[5] Piprek, loc. cit., p. 10.

[6] E. Westermarck, *Marriage Ceremonies in Morocco*, 1914, pp. 229, 241, 246, 248.

[7] Sebillot, loc. cit., iii, p. 247. Drechsler, loc. cit., ii, p. 73. The game was played with a duck at Eaux Bonnes. H. Taine, *Eine Reise in den Pyrenäen*, N.D., p. 96 (with illustrations). Kück und Sohnrey, *Feste und Spiele des deutschen Landvolks*, 1911, p. 174.

[8] Drechsler, loc. cit., ii, p. 73. F. Tetzner, *Die Slawen in Deutschland*, 1902, p. 334.

expect that if coitus between the married couple were all that was
meant by the custom this meaning would hardly have become
unconscious, i.e. lost.

Now we have reserved a curious performance with the bridal
hen as found among the Ruthenians for this part of our argument.
The bride carries a black hen along with her, puts it under the oven,
and if she asks : " Is the hole under the oven deep and will my
mother-in-law die in a year ? "[1] the mother-in-law is bound to do
so within this period. The hen under the oven is evidently the
husband's mother in her grave. If the hen is an old woman we must
suppose that the cock represents an old man. Among the Saxons
of Transylvania if there is something the matter with a child a small
human image is made to represent the disease. It is bound to a
cock's neck and the following rhymes are spoken :

> " *Alter Mann, alter Mann*
> *Meines Kindes Gebrech mitnehm.* "[2]

That is, the danger is transferred from the child to the " old
man ". Or we may compare the custom of the Jews in Barcelona
in the thirteenth century of killing an old cock as vicarious sacrifice
for a new-born child.[3]

In Bohemia, when the family cock dies it means the death of the
head of the family[4] ; and therefore it would be only logical to
conclude that by striking off the cock's head the bridegroom, now
about to become a head of a family himself, means to kill his predecessor—the head of a family. If the hen is the old woman, the
mother-in-law, the cock must be the father-in-law, the old man.
At this phase of its evolution the custom, like many myths and tales,
would represent the contest between the father and the suitor for
the girl. But if we go back to what was before exogamy, we shall
see that just as cock and hen are substitutes for the father- and mother-
in-law, these again are substitutes for the father and mother. This
is why the cock-killer becomes a cock, or a cock-king[5] himself
and why the bride is the cock's bride.[6] The man who strikes the

---

[1] Piprek, loc. cit., p. 41.
[2] H. v. Wlislocki, *Volksglaube und Volksbrauch der siebenbürger Sachsen*,
1893, p. 95.
[3] Scheftelowitz, *Huhnopfer*, p. 32.
[4] Wuttke, *Volksaberglaube*, p. 203.
[5] Strackerjan, loc. cit., ii, pp. 55, 56. W. Mannhardt, *Die Korndämonen*,
1868, p. 15. U. Jahn, *Die deutschen Opfergebräuche*, 1884, pp. 187, 189.
Drechsler, *Sitte, Brauch und Volksglaube in Schlesien*, i, 1903, p. 58. Kück
und Sohnrey, *Feste und Spiele*, 1911, p. 60.
[6] Verlaken, *Mythen und Bräuche*, p. 305.

cock is blindfolded because, like the blind Hother killing the god Balder, his moral responsibility is reduced ; he dare not see the evil he is about to perpetrate.[1] Oedipus suffers the talion punishment of losing his eyesight after, our cock-killer before, the fatal deed. A seemingly unimportant German nursery rhyme fully bears out this interpretation. An animal must be slaughtered and eaten on Shrove Tuesday and frequently the animal is a calf. In Plauen children sing the following rhymes weeks before :—

> *" Neue, neue Fasenacht,*
> *Der Vater hat e Kalb geschlacht,*
> *Hat er sich in'n Finger gehackt,*
> *Hammer uns halb tot gelacht."* [2]

The wounded finger, like the lost eyesight, is a substitute for the wounded penis. The animal sacrifice is a totemistic repetition of parricide and the father has punished himself unintentionally, i.e. unconsciously, for what he unconsciously meant to do by killing the animal. The children seem to feel the same aggressive impulses towards their own father that he shows by killing the animal since they are evidently pleased with the notion that he has to cut into his finger. At the same time, their laughter shows that they are seeking a form of abreaction for the tension of the Oedipus complex. It is probable enough that the interpretation given for the slaughter of the calf will also be valid for the ceremonial slaughter of the cock that takes place at the same date. A repetition of the crime of Oedipus, projecting, however, the idea of crime to the representative of the father, seems therefore to be an essential preliminary of marriage and a feature of Carnival among European people. The cock is, of course, a comparatively late [3] but on account of its combativeness and polygamous habits a fairly well-chosen symbol of the Jealous Sire. Probably the classical case of individual totemism described by Ferenczi under the name of little Árpád is not an isolated freak of circumstance but shows that many country children in Europe acquire the first elements of sexual knowledge by watching the life of the poultry yard. For little Árpád, eating the cock meant eating the father, and a cooked hen was " a cooked mother ".[4]

We know, moreover, that the oral element formed an important factor in the series of pre-human tragedies that ultimately led to

[1] The cock-killer has to run away if he cannot manage to hit the head off at the third stroke. Piprek, loc. cit., p. 90.

[2] R. Reichhardt, *Die deutschen Feste in Sitte und Brauch*, 1911, p. 85.

[3] Fifth century B.C. See V. Hehn, *Kultur pflanzen und Haustiere*, 1911, p. 320.

[4] S. Ferenczi, " Ein kleiner Hahnemann," *Zeitschrift für Psa*, i, p. 1913.

the formation of totemism and although a historical, direct, derivation of a late ceremony like cock-killing from these pre-human events or even from totemism [1] seems improbable, we find, as in the case of individual neurosis, the same permanent elements welding themselves into a unity and reflecting the features of the original scene that seems to have served as a starting-point for so many essential features of our mental life.

Now it happens that the ceremonial eating of the cock which has been killed by the bridegroom or best man forms an important part of the marriage ceremony.[2] In the district of Vitebsk the best man carries the roasted hen that has been brought along with the bride into the nuptial chamber. He tries to give everybody a piece but it is torn from his hands and thrown to the floor. In other cases it is the married couple that eat the roasted hen in the nuptial chamber.[3] The ceremonial nature of this cock and hen eating becomes evident when the wedding cake receives the shape of a cock or hen and is consumed at the marriage. In Mecklenburg the bride received a cock made of butter and the groom a hen of the same stuff. A particular cake made of sugar was also called a *Brauthahn*.[4] In the Borisov district, the groom's wedding cake is ornamented by a drake and the bride's by a duck. There seems to be an unconscious concept of oral conception connected with these ceremonies ; at least this is what the peculiar dough-images that decorate a wedding cake in Grodno point to. One of them represents the bride kneeling and holding up her chemise to her knees. Opposite to her stands the bridegroom with a turnip in his hand. The turnip is suspicious, and what follows shows plainly that it is meant for the penis. The other images represent domestic animals arranged all in pairs. A boar on sow, a gander on a goose, a stallion on a mare, and a cock on a hen.[5]

If we believe that the cock-killing is a symbolical repetition of the Oedipus tragedy, we must regard the cock-eating as the oral-identification that is regularly found as the closing act of the great human drama. This last scene is enacted when the bridegroom learns to act like a cock by eating his cock-father and overcomes the feeling of sexual guilt by becoming a cock himself. It seems,

---

[1] However, we find the possibly totemistic prohibition of eating poultry in India and Britain, Hehn, loc. cit., p. 337.

[2] Cf. N. W. Thomas, " The Scapegoat in European Folklore," *Folk-Lore*, xvii, 282.

[3] Piprek, loc. cit., 66.   [4] Bartsch, loc. cit., ii, 66, 67.

[5] Piprek, loc. cit., pp. 58, 59.

however, that notwithstanding our previous remarks there is an element in the sexual act itself that is unbearable for the conscious ego and therefore calls for symbolic representation.

If thrusting at the hen or goose in the games (*Jungfernstechen*) means ceremonial defloration, what does the cock's cut-off head represent ? The cock is the penis ; cutting the head off stands for castration. In certain Southern Slav ceremonies the cock's head is cut off by the best man the moment he reaches the threshold.[1] In the department of Indre, a young man takes the cock to the house of his intended but stops at the door to pluck it.[2] The door or threshold of the intended are her vagina and the ritual a projection of what the man dreads for his " cock " to a real cock. Fear of the vagina makes him stop at the door ; what he really dreads is that the door should cut off his cock's head. The cock in these rites is therefore a real *scapegoat* not only for the sins but also for the anxieties of the community. Are sin and anxiety really the same, and how can the same symbolic act mean both the father's death and the punishment suffered for parricide by the murderer, coitus and the loss of the virile power ?

We suspect that the answer to all these riddles must be sought for in the physiological nature of the sexual act.

(b) Hunting the Wren

Having set out to study the ceremonies which involve the periodical death or periodical expulsion of an animal, we shall continue our investigation by considering the hunting of the wren.

In the Isle of Man the custom was observed on Christmas Eve or morning. The servants and boys would go to hunt the wren. The boys had poles decked with ivy and the custom was to stone the bird to death with the object of distributing the feathers for luck. The wren seems not always to have been stoned ; we hear that it was fastened to a pole with extended wings and carried round in procession to every house. At every house the following rhyme was chanted :—

> " We hunted the wren for Robin the Bobbin
> We hunted the wren for Jack of the Can
> We hunted the wren for Robin the Bobbin
> We hunted the wren for every one."

[1] Piprek, loc. cit., p. 132.
[2] N. W. Thomas, " The Scapegoat in European Folklore," *Folk-Lore*, xvii, 1906, p. 282.

There seems to be an indication of a vicarious sacrifice for the whole community. The rhymes also contained reference to boiling and eating the bird. The feathers were distributed to all who would give a coin for them and the general belief was that these feathers preserved their owners from shipwreck for a year.[1]

Frazer does not mention another version and explanation of the Manx custom. No doubt some of the details of this account look as if they were a bit coloured to suit the taste of the romantic reader, but on the whole I think we cannot well neglect this version in attempting to explain the custom.

" The ceremony of hunting the wren is founded on this ancient tradition. A fairy of uncommon beauty once exerted such undue influence over the male population that she seduced numbers, at various times, to follow her footsteps till by degrees she led them into the sea where they perished. This barbarous exercise of power had continued so long that it was feared the island would be exhausted of its defenders. A knight errant sprung up, who discovered some means of countermining the charms used by the siren and even laid a plot for her destruction which she only escaped at the moment of extreme hazard by assuming the form of a wren. But though she evaded punishment at that time, a spell was cast upon her, by which she was condemned to reanimate the same form on every succeeding New Year's Day, until she should perish by a human hand. In consequence of this legend every man and boy in the island devotes the hours from the rising to the setting of the sun on each returning anniversary to the hope of extirpating the fairy. Woe to the wrens which show themselves on that fatal day, they are pursued, pelted, fired at and destroyed without mercy ; for it is believed that every one of the relics gathered in the pursuit is an effectual preservation from shipwreck for the ensuing year." [2]

Is the wren hunt an annual cathartic rite and the anxiety it intends to dispel somehow connected with the fear of drowning ? Can we regard the hunt for the wren as a repetition of the perilous seaward rush of the amorous knights ? We must work our way through the various " meanings " superposed on each other in this custom to be able to answer these questions.

To begin with it is evident that, as Frazer remarks, the custom

---

[1] G. Waldron, *Description of the Isle of Man*, 1865, p. 49. J. Frain, *Account of the Isle of Man*, 1845, ii, pp. 124, 141. Letter in *Morning Post*, 27th December, 1911, quoted by Frazer, *Spirits of the Corn*, 1912, ii, p. 318.

[2] *Mirror*, vol. iv. Kuhn, *Die Herabkunft des Feuers und des Göttertranks*, 1886, p. 97.

is one of those in which the " worshipful animal is killed once a year with much solemnity ",[1] although it is otherwise taboo to kill the representatives of this species. In Wales it is said that " a robin and a wren must never be killed ", and " if you kill a wren your house will be burned down ".[2] Anyone who kills a wren or harries its nest will break a bone or meet with some misfortune within a year.[3] At Saint Donan, in Brittany, the belief goes that children will suffer from the St Lawrence fire in their face if they touch the wren in its nest. In other parts of France the punishment for this offence is that the person will be struck by lightning, or that the fingers with which he did the deed will shrivel up and drop off, be maimed, or that the cattle will suffer in their feet.[4]

A prohibition against killing connected with an annual ceremonial slaughter undoubtedly looks like totemism.[5] Moreover, the killers of the wren are called " wren boys ",[6] which might perhaps be interpreted as the youths of the wren totem. If, however, we search for an explanation that explains not only taboo and killing but the particular features of both we shall have to go far beyond and below totemism.

To begin with, the custom, with evident show of reason, has been connected with regicide.

At Carcassonne the young people went about beating the bushes for the wren on the first Sunday of December. The first to strike down one of these birds was proclaimed king. On the evening of the last day of the year the king and all who had hunted the wren marched through the streets. The ceremony was repeated on the morning of Twelfth Day, the king wearing a crown and adorned with a blue mantle and a sceptre. The wren was borne in front of him fastened to a pole which was adorned with a verdant wreath of olive, oak, and mistletoe.[7]

It is truly astonishing to find that the author of *The Golden Bough* refrains from connecting these customs with regicide, notwithstanding the fact that here we find the " mistletoe ", that is, the " golden

---

[1] Frazer, *Spirits of the Corn*, ii, p. 322.

[2] M. Trevelyan, *Folk-Lore and Folk Stories of Wales*, 1909, p. 113.

[3] J. Brand, *Popular Antiquities*, iii, p. 194.

[4] Frazer, loc. cit., ii, p. 318. P. Sebillot, *Traditions et Superstitions de la Haute-Bretagne*, 1882, ii, p. 214.

[5] Ch. S. Burne, " Presidential Address," *Folk-Lore*, 1910, p. 30. N. W. Thomas, " Animal Superstitions and Totemism," *Folk-Lore*, xi, p. 242.

[6] L. Eckstein, *Comparative Studies in Nursery Rhymes,* 1906, p. 172.

[7] Frazer, *Spirits*, ii, p. 321. I. W. Wolf, *Beiträge zur deutschen Mythologie*, ii, 1857, p. 437.

bough " itself, in the hands of the man, who, be it in sport, is king by right of having killed his predecessor. For in Pembrokeshire it is the wren that is called king,[1] and generally it is recognized as the King of the Birds.

The tale that accounts for this royal dignity seems to contain the clue to the custom. Once upon a time when the birds spoke and everybody understood their language, it was decided that they must have a king. He who flew highest was to be king. The eagle, of course, soared above all the rest and when he was so high up that he could have scratched the sun's eyes out, he thought it was no use flying any higher and began to descend. But the wren had been hidden in the eagle's breast all the while and as he was not at all tired he flew upwards till he saw God sitting on his throne. Then he came down and claimed forthwith to be king of the birds.

The other birds felt that he must have won by a ruse, and they proposed a second trial. Not the one who could fly highest but he who could penetrate deeper than the others into the earth should be king. But again it was the small wren, and this time quite fairly, who won the match by crawling into the hole of a mouse.[2]

If we found this tale of " flying highest " as a dream-text our experience would tell us that flying regularly meant coitus. Let us try this as a working hypothesis and see where it will lead us. In a variant of Central Asia, the prize of the contest is the daughter of the Sky God [3] and not the mere title of royalty. Moreover, we have in Brittany the variant that the birds all meet for the wedding of the wren :—

> " *Aux noces du Roitelet*
> *L'epoux est tout petit.*" [4]

Who can this little king be who flies highest, penetrates deepest into the earth, wins the sky-girl as the prize of his flight, and is hidden in the eagle's breast ? Flight is coitus, then the penis is the small part of the body that penetrates deeper into Mother Earth (reversal, the daughter of the sky-god) than any other part of the body. The contest between the eagle and the wren, the Rex and the Regulus, is that between the powerful body with all its muscles and the seemingly insignificant, yet all-important, member of generation.

---

[1] H. J. Bryne, " All Hallows' Eve and other Festivals in Connaught," *Folk-Lore*, xviii, p. 439. D. H. Mountray Read, " Some Characteristics of Irish Folklore," *Folk-Lore*, xxvii, p. 259.

[2] Grimm, No. 171. Bolte-Polivka, *Anmerkungen*, iii, pp. 278–83.

[3] Dähnhardt, *Natursagen*, iv, p. 169.

[4] Dähnhardt, *Natursagen*, iv, 1912, p. 164.

This is why the birds all assemble to the " marriage feast " of this zoomorphous Tom Thumb. The diminutive stature is an essential feature ; in Wales he is kin to the robin, on the Faroes he is the mouse's brother.[1]

In Denmark the bird is called *gjertrud smutte*, for *smutte=schlüpfen*,[2] and we really find it gliding into a mouse-hole. At La Ciotat, near Marseilles, a large body of men used to hunt the wren about the end of December. The wren was hung on the middle of a pole which two men carried as if it was a heavy burden. They paraded round the town and finished by weighing the bird in a pair of scales.[3]

The king and the little king, eagle and wren, body and penis, are two aspects of a whole. Therefore we believe that the Ascension Day custom observed at Liepe near Eberswald of setting a couple of eagles free not only resembles [4] but is probably another aspect of the customs we have been investigating. For in certain French variants of our custom the wren is not killed but is set free, let loose like a scapegoat. At Entraigues it was presented to the priest on Christmas Eve and he set it free in the church after the midnight mass.[5]

The race between the eagle and the wren is regression into the uterus, a race in which the penis must always be slightly in advance of the body. At Laguenne near Limousin the inhabitants elected a person who bore the name of *Roi de la Tire-vessie*. He had to strip before a crowd of spectators and throw himself into the water, then he had to pass underneath the bridge with his head under the water. This done he proceeded to the town, but before doing so he mounted a wagon, holding on his wrist a wren, its head covered with a hood and silk-tassels on its feet. To one side of the wagon were assigned the people who had married within seven years of the ceremony ; to the other side those who hoped to enter the bonds of matrimony ; and the two parties then struggled till one pulled the wagon over to its side. Then the king entered the town with his wren and seated himself on a large stone ; three times in succession he called upon the Seigneur de Laroche or his representative to receive his homage. Then he plucked feathers from the wren and flew them in the air. In the early part of the seventeenth century a wooden wren was made fast to a pole after the homage had been rendered and each inhabitant of the town had to shoot an

---

[1] *Folk-Lore*, xvi, p. 488.   [2] Dähnhardt, loc. cit., ii, p. 125.

[3] Frazer, *Spirits*, ii, p. 321.

[4] N. W. Thomas, " The Scape-Goat in European Folklore," *Folk-Lore*, xvii, p. 271.   [5] Frazer, ibid.

arrow at it ; if it was not hit, they had to give the Seigneur a silver bow of the value of sixty livres.[1]

If we regard the man who holds a wren in his hands as a representative of the phallus, as the *Eniautos daimon* of the returning impulse of procreation, we shall understand his sub-aquatic swimming as a wish-fulfilment representing coitus with a complete return into the amniotic fluid. The contest between the newly married and those who wish to take their place is a struggle for the phallus and hence also the wren is carried into the houses of the newly-married. In all these ceremonies, however, there seems to be an ambiguous attitude with regard to the organ of generation. Its representative, the wren-killer, becomes king, but only after having killed the wren, i.e. the phallus, and the wren in his hand is shot at by the whole population. By doing so the wren becomes a scape-goat ; they disclaim their part in his sin. The small bird is the true emblem of royalty, the phallus is king of birds and men.

3 MARS AND THE SALII

On the Ides of March or on the day before this festival the *sacrum Mamurio* was enacted. This ritual shows a rather singular fashion of honouring a divinity. A man who was clad in hides appeared and was thrashed with long white staves ; he was called Mamurius and there is an ironical proverb " to play Mamurius with somebody " —meaning to beat him.[2] In ancient times, when Numa was king in Rome, a shield fell from heaven and the oracle declared that the town in which the shield was kept would keep also the mastery or imperium.

" *Quod ne (aliquando) posset auferri vel ab hoste cognosci, per Mamurium fabrum multa similia fecerunt, cui et diem consecrarunt quo pellem virgis feriunt ad artes similitudinem.* "[3]

We must say that there is a singular lack of coherence between the ritual and the myth. The smith Mamurius, or rather Mamurius veturius,[4] helped his native city in a very important matter, and it

---

[1] N. W. Thomas, " The Scape-Goat in European Folklore," *Folk-Lore*, xvii, p. 273.

[2] H. Usener, *Kleine Schriften*, iv, 1913, p. 122, quoting Joannes Lydus, *Demens*, 4, 36, 71. Bonn (105, 15).

[3] Servius *ad Aen. Lib.* vii, 188.

[4] Varro, loc. cit., 6, 45, p. 226 (vi, 49, G. Schr.) *itaque Salii quod cantant Mamuri Veturi, significant veterem memoriam.* Plutarch, *Numa*, 13, quoted by Usener, loc. cit., p. 126.

is difficult to understand why he should get his fee in the form of a beating. We have some vague hints of a misfortune that sprang from this attempt to dupe fate itself but these hints are hardly sufficient to explain the ritual. In this predicament we may rely on etymology as showing a short cut to explain the ritual. *Mamurius Veturius* means the old Mars.[1] And who is Mars ? The father of Romulus and Remus, the Primal Father or ancestor of the Roman nation.[2]

Now this Primal Father of the Romans is a typical scapegoat who bears the burden of all evil away from Rome to the land of the Oscans.[3] The ceremony took place on the eve or on the day of the Ides of March and the Ides of March is the marriage festival of Mars and Nerio. In the traditional version of the myth we find that Mars figures as the rejected or duped suitor of the goddess Nerio, but there can be no doubt that we have here a secondary elaboration of the original version.[4] Varro quotes the expression *Nerienem Martis*, and other authorities also regard Nerio "the Strong One" or "Strength" (*virtus*) as the spouse of the mighty war-god.[5] But Usener has also shown that the marriage of Mars and Nerio was originally regarded as the prototype of all human marriages,[6] and in this case it is hardly possible to regard the marriage as originally not consummated.

Why, then, we must ask, does myth represent Nerio as a virgin and deny her union with the young war-god ? Perhaps the myth represented on a cista of Praeneste contains the key that unlocks this secret. We see Minerva (Nerio) holding a child called Mars above a pot that contains fire or boiling water and applying an ointment, probably ambrosia, to his mouth.[7] A mirror of Clusinum shows Minerva in the act of bathing a child who is described as *maris*

---

[1] It makes no difference whether we derive *Veturius* from *vetus* = Ϝετος = year (Pott, *Etymologische Forschungen*, i, pp. 108, 208 ; Corssen, *Ausspr.*, i, p. 408), or follow the Romans and Usener (loc. cit., p. 126) in connecting the name with *vetus* (old). There is no doubt about the fact that Mamurius is one of the many reduplications of Mars.

[2] Cf. the authorities quoted by J. B. Carter in *Roschers Lexikon*, Lieferung, 160, pp. 174, 175.

[3] Usener, loc. cit., pp. 122, 123, quoting Prop., v, 2, 61.

[4] *Maio mense religio est nubere et item Martio in quo de nuptiis habito certamine a Minerva Mars victus est ; obtenta virginitate Minerva Nerine est appellata*, Porph. *ad Hor. ep.*, ii, 2, 209, and Ovid, *Fasti*, ii, 690.

[5] See Usener, loc. cit., p. 135. Wissowa, *Religion und Kultus der Römer*, p. 134.

[6] See Usener, loc. cit., pp. 137, 141.

[7] Marx, "Ein neuer Ares-Mythus," *Archeologische Zeitung*, xliii, 1885.

husrnana, while the god of the shades is preparing another jug of water for another Mars child—*maris halma*.[1] Luckily we have other variants of this myth and in these the goddess who holds the boy above the flames in order to endow him with immortality is always a mother-substitute, the nurse. Thus Isis tries to make the son of Malkandros one of the immortals[2] and Demeter, the Earth Mother, does the same to Demophoon.[3] The scene is always interrupted by an alarmed outcry of the mother who, according to her own view of the situation, comes just in time to prevent the goddess from killing her child.[4] The ambiguity of the scene is the ambiguity of motherhood and indeed of all human relations ; the human mother protects the child and projects her own aggressivity to a supernatural representative of the mother imago. Thetis, who holds Achilles above the flames and anoints him with ambrosia to raise him into the ranks of the immortals, is his real mother.[5] It is therefore a legitimate conjecture to assume that Nerio (Minerva) may have been originally both the mother and the wife of Mars. This would explain the tendency of our myth to represent this incestuous marriage as one that had never been consummated, and also why the God of War had to be baulked in his desire and Strength, the Goddess, had to remain a virgin.[6] The young god is defeated by the incest-taboo. We shall find a confirmation of our view in the myth of Anna Perenna. A facetious story was related in Rome about Anna Perenna, " the yeared-through year " (past), who is smuggled into the nuptial chamber of the young god in her bridal attire and adds insult to injury by jeering at him when he finds an old woman instead of the beautiful bride.[7] But as Mars was born on New Year's Day, that is, the 1st of March,[8] the goddess of the year that had passed away must certainly have been his mother. In a local legend of Bovillae, Anna is represented as a kind old woman who provides bread for the hungry people in a famine and thus rescues them from starvation,[9] as the mother feeds her infant child.

The goddess who is the original spouse of the young god is both the old woman and the young virgin ; the year that is past and the year

[1] Deecke, " Maris," *Roschers Lexikon*, ii, p. 2376. Ibid., p. 1935.

[2] Apollodorus, i, 5, 4.   [3] Plutarch, *De Iside*, 16.

[4] L. Laistner, *Das Räthsel der Sphinx*, 1889, ii, p. 309.

[5] Cf. Apollodorus, iii, 13, 5, 6. Ovid, *Metam.*, xiv, 600.

[6] Myth represents Mars as born from the virgin Juno. Ovid, *Fasti*, v, 256.

[7] Ovid, *Fasti*, iii, 690.

[8] Natalis Martis, Calend. Philocali und Constantini Feriae Marti. Cal. Praen, *C.I.L.*, i, p. 387, quoted in *Roschers Lexikon*, ii, p. 2399.

[9] Ovid, *Fasti*, iii, 657. Cf. Preller, *Römische Mythologie*, 1858, p. 305.

to come are the mother of our childhood and the eternally rejuvenated mother we find in each new love. The lady who is wedded to the god on the first full moon of the year is properly speaking not Anna Perenna—veiled as Nerio—but Anna Perenna the mother in the aspect of Nerio the young bride. Now we can understand why the old Mars, i.e. Mars the Father, must be driven out of the country before his son the young Mars can celebrate his nuptials with the mother-goddess. As Usener puts it : " The young god must grow in strength and age in order to be able to conquer, expel or kill the old god," and as soon as he has accomplished this deed he thinks of getting a wife.[1] For the ritual itself shows the identity of the victor, and tells us who is responsible for the ignominious retreat of the old god. Minucius Felix has the following remark about the ceremony : " alii (or Salii) incedunt pileati, scuta vetera circumferunt, pelles caedunt." [2] Now whether alii or Salii is the correct reading makes no difference, for the reference to the peaked hats and the shields makes it certain that the old god was driven out by the priests called Salii, especially as we know that the refrain of their song was Mamuri Veturi,[3] which has been compared by Roscher to the 'Ιήπαιάν [4] and must therefore be regarded as an exclamation of triumph breaking forth in the moment when the "Jumpers" (Salii : ab salitando) have managed to expel the old god.

In his historical times the " Jumpers " are the dancing and jumping priests of Mars, the ancestor of the Roman nation and the old god of war and fertility.[5] Their dance is a war dance or sword dance and their garb shows distinct traces of its military origin.[6] In March the " Jumpers' " procession brings forth the shields of the war god : this was called ancilia movere. In October the shields are stored for the winter : this is the ancilia condere.[7] If the chief performance of a priesthood consists in jumping with shields we must come to the conclusion that the shields in question are objects of specific importance. The calendars call the first of March the old New Year's Day, either Natalis Martis or Caesus ancilis.[8] The sequel of the story we have heard is that Mamurius Veturius makes twelve

---

[1] Usener, loc. cit., pp. 127, 135. [2] Minuc. Fel., Octav., 243.
[3] Varro, loc. cit., vi, 45, p. 226 (vi, 49, Götz, Schöll). Ovid, Fasti, iii, 389.
[4] Roscher, Apollo und Mars, pp. 32, 35.
[5] On Mars as god of fertility see L. Preller, Römische Mythologie, 1858, p. 297. E. Bickel, Der altrömische Gottesbegriff, 1921, p. 81.
[6] G. Wissowa, Religion und Kultus der Römer, 1902, pp. 480, 481.
[7] Roschers Lexikon, ii, p. 2406.
[8] Preller, Römische Mythologie, p. 319, note 5.

shields (the twelve months) all completely similar to the first one.[1]
But if the old Mars is the father of the war god he is truly the right
person to " make ", i.e. to procreate the twelve copies of his own son.
(Thus, for instance, a patient who suffered equally from incapacity to
work for any length of time in the same job and from sexual impotence,
dreamed that he was kicked out of a factory on account of his ignorance
of the " secret of manufacturing ".   The associations showed that he
had heard a joke in a foreign language which he only half understood,
and which turned on the identity of the words " manufacturing "
and " coitus " in the language in question.)   The shields made by
the god are his sons.   It is therefore evident that the shield must fall
from heaven on the same day that they are born, as both things,
shield and god, mean exactly the same.   The moment he is born
Hephaestus is hurled from the sky : he falls into the sea and stays
there for nine years with Eurynome or Thetis.[2]   Mythical birth
is repetition of real birth ; a child falls from his mother's womb,
a god from the sky.   A child lives for nine months in the amniotic
fluid, a god for nine years in the ocean.   In Mexico, Tamoanchen
is the " House of the Coming Down or the Being Born ",[3] and in
North America we have the myth of the pregnant woman falling
from the sky and being delivered of the hero.[4]   Children usually
believe that human beings are born from the anus and unconsciously
identify the child with the excrement.   On the other hand glittering
objects usually symbolize the fæces and the bright shield falling
from heaven might be a specific case of this infantile sex-theory.
In the shape of the shield the " Jumpers " bring forth their god,
but the god himself is a " jumper " or " dancer ",[5] the leader of the
community of dancers, received by a host of young men, the patrician
dancers, who must be *patrimi* and *matrimi*.[6]   Two days after the
day when the young " Jumper ", the leader of the other " Jumpers "
has expelled Old Age from the city and married the ever desirable
mother of infancy we have the Liberalia, a festival dedicated to
Liber " *pro eventibus seminum* ".   The young men who had come of

[1] Ovid, *Fasti*, iii, 370. Preller, loc. cit., p. 314.
[2] *Iliad Σ*, 360. Pausanias, i, 20, 3.
[3] Ed. Seler, *Gesammelte Abhandlungen*, ii, 1032, 1065.   *Idem*, " Die
achzehn Jahresfeste der Mexicaner," *Veröff. d. kngl. M. für V.*, vi, 1899,
pp. 138, 139. Reitzenstein, "Kausalzusammenhang," *Z. f. E.*, 1909, p. 652.
[4] D. G. Brinton, *American Hero Myths*, 1882, p. 52. H. R. Schoolcraft,
The Myth of Hiawatha, 1856, p. 15.   [5] *Salisubsulus*, Catullus, 17, 6.
[6] Usener, " Pasparios," *Kleine Schriften*, iv, 1913, p. 193.   Wissowa
(loc. cit., 382) mentions the Lusus Troiae, enacted by young men of noble
origin, as a parallel to the Salii.

age received the *toga virilis* in honour of Liber and a festive procession carried a huge phallus round the city and the country. A Roman matron honoured the symbol of procreation by a garland.[1]

We shall be able to show that there is an intrinsic link between puberty-rites and the ceremonial expulsion of scape-goats. The nature of this link is very easy to guess if we remember that in the ritual of initiation we have the reversal of the same father-son conflict that is represented also in the scapegoat ceremony. In the case of the shield-bearing priests of the Roman war-god, we must suppose a further development. On the one hand the puberty-initiation ritual is also an initiation into the age-grade of warriors and the ritual connected with war, and on the other hand we know that the universal ritual of puberty initiation branches off into the initiation rites of the various secret societies just as the age-grade of adult men or warriors becomes differentiated into the members of these secret societies or if we wish to express the same thing in Latin, *sodalitates*. Among the Blackfeet the warriors are organized in the " Society of Mosquitoes " as lower and the " Dogs " as higher age-grades.[2] The Hidatsa have the societies of " big swords ", who perform a sword-dance, the bow-lances, etc. The Arapaho have a general organization of adults called the " warrior " society and special societies like the " club-men ", " spear-men ", etc.[3] Dionysus of Halicarnassus equates the Salii with the Curetes, and if this equation has any foundation [4] our interpretation of the former may be regarded as beyond a doubt. They are simply the armed young men of the tribe after the ritual of puberty initiation, and their name is even used in this sense by Homer.[5] Their prominent feature is dancing and their dance, the *Pyrrhichos* or *Prylis*, is the sword-dance of Germanic tribes.[6]

Now death and revival, the characteristic features of puberty and initiation rites, are also the nucleus of sword-dances and other popular

---

[1] Varro in Augustine, *De civitate dei*, vii, 21, vi, 9. Ovidius, *Fasti*, iii, 771. Wissowa, loc. cit., p. 244. Preller, loc. cit., p. 444.

[2] Maximilian Prinz zu Wied, *Reise in das Innere Nord-Amerika*. Coblenz, 1839–41, ii, pp. 138–43.

[3] J. Mooney, " The Ghost Dance Religion," *xixth Annual Report of the Bureau of Ethnology*, pp. 986–9.

[4] Dionysus of Halicarnassus, *Ant. Rom.*, ii, 70a.

[5] Cf. J. E. Harrison, *Themis*, 1912, p. 194, on the Salii, Usener, *Kleine Schriften*, iv, p. 190.

[6] L. von Schroeder, *Mysterium und Mimus im Rigveda*, 1908, 126. K. Müllenhoff, " Über den Schwerttanz," *Festgaben für Gustav‛Homeyer*, 1871.

seasonal acting. In the Clausthal the central figure of the sword-dance is the *Schnortison* who is killed and immediately afterwards revived in order to take part in the dance.[1] The German sword-dance is the English Morris-dance with St George the Dragon-killer who kills all his adversaries only to see them all revived by the Fancy-doctor or Doctor Iron-beard, as the Germans call this humorous survival of the old tribal medicine-man who killed and revived the boys at initiation.[2] Among the Csángós (Hungarians) of Transylvania, the " Boritza Dancers " appear on the 28th of December. In their left hand they used to carry a wooden sword, but now it is a peculiar axe, which characterizes them as an eastern branch of the sword-dancers or Morris-dancers. There are four young lads wearing masks and a peculiar costume. Three of them attack the fourth and enact the following drama. The masked man is cut into four pieces with the wooden swords, he is skinned like an ox and then revived by a comical ceremony, i.e. by having the breath of life blown into him through his mouth, ears, and anus.[3]

We see, therefore, that what are called Salii in ancient Italy is the same thing as the Curetes-Corybantes in Crete and Phrygia, the sword-dancers in Germany, the Morris-dancers in England and the " Boritza " (pine-tree) dancers in Transylvania. In India the family is represented by the Maruts " the frolicking (jumping) sons of a good mother ". They are a united group of dancing armed youths of the same age.[4] Their leader is, of course, not St. George but Indra the Dragon-slayer, which amounts to the same thing. His official title is *Indra marutvant* [5]—Indra with the Maruts. It is true that he performs all the great deeds of a hero alone. It is he, and he alone, who has killed the dragon Ahi-Vritra and liberated the waters, but behind him we discern the chorus of Maruts, the brother-horde who claim their share of the glory and the sacrifice. It is hardly too bold to assume that all the heroic adventures of the god are but repetitions of his first great adventure, for, hardly born, he kills his father.[6]

---

[1] Müllenhoff, loc. cit., pp. 33–5.

[2] Cf. E. K. Chambers, *The Medieval Stage*, 1903, i, ch. ix, x. C. A. Miles, *Christmas*, 1912, p. 300. E. M. Leather, *The Folk Lore of Herefordshire*, 1912, p. 145. Mannhardt, *Waldkulte*, i, pp. 325, 350, 352, 358.

[3] A. Horger, " A hétfalusi csángók borica tánca," *Ethnographia*, x, p. 112.

[4] L. von Schroeder, *Mysterium und Mimus im Rigveda*, 1908, pp. 49, 50.

[5] Schroeder, loc. cit., 92. A. Hillebrandt, *Vedische Mythologie*, 1902, iii, p. 323.

[6] Hillebrandt, loc. cit., ii, p. 517; iii, p. 162. Oldenberg, *Die Religion des Veda*, 1894, p. 134. Schroeder, loc. cit., pp. 329, 330.

And the mythical consequence of this deed was evidently also its real cause "and then the falcon brought me Soma", the text says.[1] Knowing as we do that Soma means the seminal fluid,[2] we can easily interpret this myth. Indra must use force to obtain what his heart desires—the free outlet for the "waters", i.e. his seminal fluid or *soma*. What he really possesses after the deed of parricide is his mother, but in the myth the stress is carried over from the object (mother) to the means by which the libidinal object can be conquered (seminal fluid). And who is Indra's father? He is Tvashtar the divine smith,[3] known in Rome as Mamurius Veturius.

4 THE GOAT OF AZAZEL

Scapegoats there may be in many lands, but the original scapegoat is a citizen of Jerusalem. The details and origin of the ceremony are explained in *Lev.* xvi, 1, as follows :—

"And the Lord spake unto Moses after the death of the two sons of Aaron, when they drew near before the Lord, and died ; and the Lord said unto Moses, Speak unto Aaron thy brother, that he come not all times before the holy place within the veil before the mercy seat which is upon the ark ; that he die not : for I will appear in the cloud upon the mercy seat. Herewith shall Aaron come into the holy place : with a young bullock for a sin offering, and a ram for a burnt offering. He shall put on the holy linen coat, and he shall have the linen breeches upon his flesh, and shall be girded with the linen girdle, and with the linen mitre shall he be attired ; they are holy garments ; and he shall bathe his flesh in water, and put them on. And he shall take of the congregation of the children of Israel two he-goats for a sin offering, and one ram for a burnt offering. And Aaron shall present the bullock of the sin offering, which is for himself, and make atonement for himself, and his house. And he shall take the two goats, and set them before the Lord at the door of the tent of meeting. And Aaron shall cast lots upon the two goats, one lot for the Lord and the other lot for Azazel. And Aaron shall present the goat upon which the lot fell for the Lord, and offer him for a sin offering. But the goat upon which the lot

---

[1] Schroeder, loc. cit., p. 335.

[2] Cf. for the proofs of this view A. Hillebrandt, *Vedische Mythologie*, 1891, i, p. 359, and the whole argument in Ad. Kuhn, *Die Herabkunft des Feuers und des Göttertranks*, 1886.

[3] Cf. Oldenburg, *Die Religion des Veda*, 1894, p. 233.

fell for Azazel shall be set alive before the Lord, to make atonement for him, to send him away for Azazel in the wilderness." . . . After having performed the necessary ceremonies for the atonement of the holy place " Aaron shall lay both his hands upon the head of the live goat and confess over him all the iniquities of the children of Israel, and all their transgressions even all their sins, and he shall put them upon the head of the goat and shall send him away by the hand of a man that is in readiness into the wilderness and the goat shall bear upon him all their iniquities unto a solitary land and he shall let go the goat in the wilderness." [1]

We may as well separate the ritual introduction from the scapegoat ceremony and prepare the way for the analysis of the latter by analysing the former. The ritual prescription of linen clothes for the priest is very general in antiquity. The priests of Heracles observed it in Gades ; it is a well-known Phoenician custom and especially prominent in Egypt. Plutarch and Herodotus tell us that the aim of linen clothes is to avoid everything that is unclean. As parallels to this custom Plutarch mentions hair-cutting, while Herodotus characteristically refers to circumcision.[2] In lustration rites Plutarch says that as we shave all the hairs of our own body and make it quite smooth, would it not be ridiculous therefore to don garments made of the hair of animals, i.e. wool ? [3] By purity both authors mean avoiding the excretions and secretions of the body or in other words : repression. The linen breeches covering the " flesh " (Scham in the German translation) and the reference to hair-cutting and circumcision, i.e. castration rites, all point in the same direction—the priest can only enter the holy of holies as a desexualized, i.e. castrated, male.

The latent meaning of the " purity " observed by the priests of the ancient Orient may well be illustrated by the case of a modern spiritualist and misogynist. He regards himself as the great prophet in the struggle of humanity against sexuality and specializes this struggle into a propaganda for the depilation of the whole body. Eroticism, he says, is the great evil or weakness of the soul and coitus its most horrible manifestation. By depilation he means especially the genitals and he gets into a perfect fit of rage when the subject is mentioned. He declares that he never loved his mother, never kissed her, but always adored his father and was extremely religious even as an infant in arms. His hatred of pubic hairs is connected with a scene of his fourth year when he saw his mother undressed

---

[1] Lev., xvi, 1–24.   [2] Herodot., ii, 37.
[3] Plutarch, De Iside et Osiride, 4, 5.

and was terribly frightened at the sight of her hairy vagina. He does not hate women, only the hair on their genitalia. How should he hate them since he would very much prefer to be a woman than a man and does all he can to effect the transformation. The horrible thing in coitus is that it reminds him of what his father and mother did when they slept together, so that all intercourse is just a sort of incest. His dreams have the latent content of losing the penis and obtaining a compensation for this loss from the father who should do to him what he did to his mother.[1]

Why should castration be the condition on which the priest can enter the tabernacle ? Eisler has penetrated to the depths of Semitic religion in a paper that explains the meaning of the tabernacle. Originally—he says—the empty tent, the common house of the tribe, was the real object of veneration, the portable temple, the body of the national deity. Year by year the festival of " opening " (*tasrit*) by the introitus of the high priest into the sanctuary was held as a symbolic act of hierogamy.[2] In *Bab. Joma*, 54, we are told that on the great festivals the curtain of the sanctuary was shown to the people and on the curtain the image of cherubim entwined in each other's arms. And the priests said : " See, God loves his people as a man loves a woman." Rashi says in his commentary : " The cherubim embraced each other like man and woman." Characteristic features of the whole attitude are the ritual purity and the anxiety felt by laymen and clergy on entering the sanctuary ; there was always a chance of being killed by a jealous god.[3] But Eisler makes a mistake in equating Jahve with the tabernacle or in regarding the tabernacle as the body of the divinity. Jahve is the god who dwells in the tent but is not the tent itself. The tent is a symbol of the Mother-Goddess ($A\gamma\tau\alpha\varsigma$ $T\eta$ = Asirtu = House = Temple = Dwelling)[4] while Jahve corresponds to the horns of the ram (ram = Jabal = Abel) in the Kaaba, to the phallus in the vagina.[5] Entering the body of the Great Mother means incest, and danger threatens the son from the father, the paternal phallus as owner of the vagina.[6]

---

[1] Szilágyi, " Der junge Spiritist," *Zeitschrift für Psa*, ix, p. 402. What his father and mother did is horrible because of the repressed desire for intercourse with the mother.

[2] R. Eisler, " Kuba-Kybele," *Philologus*, lxviii, 1909, 164.

[3] Eisler, loc. cit. [4] Eisler, loc. cit., p. 161. [5] Eisler, loc. cit., p. 133.

[6] Cf. on the symbolism of the threshold and the passage into a house, Róheim, " The Significance of Stepping Over," *Journal of Psycho-analysis*, iii, pp. 320–6.

However, the object of our curiosity is not so much the punishment itself as the means employed for averting this punishment. One of these is ritual purity as a symbolic castration ; this is a prophylactic measure to avoid castration by carrying it through in a symbolic equivalent. Then we have the burnt sacrifice of bull and ram. It seems that the priest of the Bull- and Ram-God is a bull himself, and as for his identity with the ram we have the ingenious suggestion of K. Abraham who regards the blessing performed by the Kohanim with fingers spread out as an imitation of the cloven-footed ram.[1] Killing a bull and a ram would therefore mean both the crime itself and the talion punishment for the crime. The priest can enter the tabernacle after having killed the murderous Father-God and after having suffered the punishment for parricide by dying himself in the guise of bull and ram.

So much for the introduction. We shall now attempt to explain the ceremony itself as well as the meaning of the Day of Atonement.

The fat of the sin-offering had to be burnt upon the altar and the man who let the goat go to Azazel had to wash his clothes and bathe before he came back into the camp.

" And it shall be a statute for ever unto you : in the seventh month, on the tenth day of the month, ye shall afflict your souls and do no manner of work, the home-born, or the stranger that sojourneth among you : for on this day shall atonement be made for you to cleanse you, from all your sins shall ye be clean before the Lord. It is a sabbath of solemn rest unto you, and ye shall afflict your souls, it is a statute for ever. And the priest, who shall be anointed and who shall be consecrated to be priest in his father's stead, shall make the atonement, and shall put on the linen garments, even the holy garments ; and he shall make atonement for the holy sanctuary, and he shall make atonement for the tent of meeting, and for the altar and he shall make atonement for the priests, and for all the people of the assembly." [2]

The date of the festival or rather festive period must shed a ray of light on its significance. Wellhausen has put forward the hypothesis that the Day of Atonement is really the day of the New Year since the Yobel year still begins on the tenth of the seventh month.[3]

From New Year to the Day of Atonement we have a period of

[1] K. Abraham, " Der Versöhnungstag," *Imago*, vi, p. 88. Cf. on the bull and the ram, Th. Reik, *Probleme der Religionspsychologie*, 1919.
[2] *Leviticus*, xvi, 29–33.
[3] Wellhausen, *Prolegomena*, p. 105.

uniform character in the ten penitential days.[1] The period, like the Twelve Days of European folklore,[2] like the five additional days of the Egyptian [3] and Mexican calendar,[4] is due to an effort to reconcile the lunar with the solar year.[5] This view gains additional force if we consider that New Year's Day was also regarded as a day of penance and for some time also as a day of fasting.[6] Moreover, the Babylonians had a New Year's period of eleven days and of a penitential character including probably a Day of Atonement, that is, a Day of Calming the Heart, meaning the heart of the enraged gods.[7] Perhaps the whole series of celebrations from New Year to the Feast of Tabernacles ought to be regarded as one festive period commencing with the penitence, the expulsion of evil, and ending in a joyous harvest festival.[8] The Ho of Northern India celebrate this orgiastic Saturnalia in January after having sacrificed a cock and a hen and expelled the spirit of evil.[9] A genuine scapegoat ceremony is performed by the Baja at the beginning of the harvesting season. Two red he-goats and one white she-goat are killed. The first red goat is sacrificed in order to avert all disease and calamity. "All that is evil may alight on this," they say and the curse sticks to the goat.[10] Then they kill the second he-goat and the she-goat and pray for a good harvest and for fertile women. But as soon as the

---

[1] J. Elbogen, *Der jüdische Gottesdienst in seiner geschichtlichen Entwicklung*, 1913, p. 118.

[2] Cf. for instance, P. Sartori, *Sitte und Brauch*, 1914, p. 5, and for further literature, Róheim, *Adalékok a magyar néphithez*, 1920. O. Weinreich, *Triskaidekadische Studien*, 1916.

[3] Cf. Plutarch, *De Iside*, 12.

[4] K. Haebler, *Die Religion des Mittleren Amerika*, 1899, p. 148.

[5] H. Grimme, "Das Altar des israelitischen Versöhnungstages," *Archiv für Religionswissenschaft*, xiv, p. 138.

[6] Elbogen, loc. cit., p. 148. "Abgesehen vom Bekenntnisse trägt die Tefilla denselben Charakter wie die des Neujahrstages," loc. cit., p. 151.

[7] M. Jastrow, *Die Religion Babyloniens und Assyriens*, 1912, ii, p. 123.

[8] This view is taken by Pfleiderer, *Die Religion ihr Wesen und ihre Geschichte*, ii, pp. 297, 298, and Mannhardt, *Mythologische Forschungen*, 1884, p. 131.

[9] E. T. Dalton, *Descriptive Ethnology of Bengal*, 1872, p. 196. Frazer, *Scapegoat*, 1913, p. 136.

[10] Only the old people eat the meat and it does not matter what happens to them. According to the Baja, young and esteemed persons will not touch the food fraught with evil. Frobenius, *Und Afrika sprach*, 1913, iii, p. 179. Cf. the idea that it is doing the poor people a dishonour to give them the *kapparah* fowl; they ought rather to receive money instead as it is like sending them all the sins that cling to the fowl. J. Schefterlowitz, *Das stellvertretende Huhnopfer*, 1914, p. 35.

sacrifice is made the Baja must abstain from sorghum and from women till the sorghum is completely ripe. The period of abstinence comes to an end by sacrificing beer on the grave of the ancestors.[1]

The assumption of an inverted Carnival period at the beginning of the year, a period commencing with melancholia and ending in an orgiastic mania, is supported by diverse minor circumstances. The Festival of Tabernacles must once have partaken of the usual features of these festivals among primitive races. There was the performance of a torch dance at night, the ceremony of pouring water into a cup on the altar, probably in order to promote fertility.

Eisler's interpretation of the ninth day as "Joy of the Dove-Goddess", meaning by "joy" marriage, is not quite reliable, especially as this part of the festival seems to be of late origin. But the symbolic meaning of the *Lulab* (palm-stalk) and the *Ethrog* (in German *Paradiesapfel* or *Liebesapfel*) still survives in popular custom when the pregnant woman has to bite off the stalk of the *ethrog* to facilitate parturition.[2] A festive period of this type gives us certain hints regarding the probable interpretation of the scapegoat ceremony. The goat itself affords at least a strong presumption of an interpretation based on sex-symbols. If a Lango man is accused of adultery or seduction he may undergo the test known as consecrating the goat. He produces two he-goats and two she-goats and the party of the accuser and the accused stand in line opposite each other. The girl whom he is alleged to have seduced stands in the centre and the accused brings forth a he-goat which he causes to pass round the girl. Having done this he spits in his hand and says : " Pu ! Behold goat whether I have seduced this person ! If thou wishest, urinate, if thou wishest, defecate." He then rubs the head, back, and stomach of the goat with the hand on which he spat. Should the goat make water while it stands he is convicted, as the urine of the goat typifies the man's semen.[3]

If a serious epidemic breaks out among the Kikuyu they take a ram, a he-goat or a ewe-lamb and slaughter it at the village. Pieces of the meat are impaled on wooden skewers ; then everybody takes a piece and throws it with the disease into the bush.[4] In Kitui, if a village is afflicted by some serious sickness the headman calls in

---

[1] Frobenius, *Und Afrika sprach*, iii, 1913, pp. 179, 180.
[2] Mannhardt, *Wald und Feldkulte*, i, p. 284. Cf. Nowack, *Lehrbuch der hebräischen Archäologie*, 1894, ii, p. 182, and the tract *Sukka* in the *Talmud*.
[3] J. H. Driberg, *The Lango*, 1923, p. 214.
[4] C. W. Hobley, *Bantu Belief and Magic*, 1927, p. 34.

a medicine-man who concocts some medicine by grinding up a number of plants. A small boy and girl are then chosen, The villagers form a group and they lead a goat twice round this group, followed by the little girl and the medicine-man. Then the medicine-man makes an incision in the right ear of the goat and the blood drips into a half-gourd containing the magical concoction. Then they run into the bush and the medicine-man throws the blood in front of him. The same night the village headman must cohabit with his wife, and this is considered of such importance that the elder must take an oath that it has been done.[1]

This is clear enough ; throwing the blood of the goat into the bush is a rite that is made complete, i.e. explained, by the cohabitation that follows. The he-goat of Mendes in Egypt was a god whose principal function consisted in fecundating the women. The word *ba* means ram, goat, and soul, and the Mendes texts attribute to the ram-god both the fecundating function of the penis and of the soul.[2]

In the case of the Hebrew rite, both the name of the demon and Jewish tradition help us to comprehend the latent meaning of the scapegoat ceremony. One of the two goats is sacrificed to Jahve and the other driven to the demon Azazel in the desert. Commentators originally believed that Azazel and the goat meant the same thing and translated Azazel as *caper eminarius* (Vulg.) or *der ledige Bock* (Luther).[3] Although this view is based on a false etymology there is nevertheless a grain of truth in it if we consider the fundamental identity of the sacrifice and the recipient of the sacrifice (Robertson Smith). The correct etymology is probably the one given by Grimm, who translates Azazel as " the little hairy one ". This might very well be the name given to the goat or to the usual zoomorphic demon—inhabitant of the Semite deserts. In *Lev.*, xvii, 7 we have the prohibition of sacrificing to the *seirim* or he-goats, " after whom they go a-whoring." [4] In the *Song of Songs* we have the roes and the hinds of the field, certainly not ordinary beasts but demons of love and lust :—

> " I adjure you, O daughters of Jerusalem
> By the roes and by the hinds of the field
> That ye stir not up or awaken love
> Until it please.[5]

---

[1] Hobley, loc. cit., p. 95.
[2] Lefébure, " Le Bouc des Lupercales," *Revue de l'Histoire des Religions*, lix, 1909, pp. 71, 75.
[3] Nowack, *Hebräische Archeologie*, ii, p. 186.
[4] Whoring is the technical term for a pagan sacrifice.
[5] *Song of Songs*, ii, 7 ; iii, 5.

Or we may compare the song of a Hausa *bori*, i.e. disease-demon :

> " If death comes
> I shall get inside a cave, a vagina,
> I and my goats." [1]

Babylonian demons are composite beings with human and bestial attributes.[2] The hairy bull-shaped Eabani who lives with the herd and copulates with the sacred harlots,[3] is one of these beings, just as the hairy animal-shaped Jinn of the modern Arab are beings whose prominent function seems to be coitus with mortal woman.[4] Considering all these analogies I think we are justified in giving a quite concrete interpretation to the demon Azazel : " the little hairy one " is the penis. This interpretation is completely borne out by all we learn from Jewish tradition about the demon. In the book of Henoch (xiii) we find Azazel as the leader of the fallen angels. He instructs men in the arts of magic and war and women in the arts of seduction. And because Azazel still seduces men by these arts the sins of Israel are laid upon a ram on the Day of Atonement and sent to Azazel in the desert, says the Midrash Abkhir.[5] Here we find an open statement of what is meant by " sin " and what sins the goat typifies and bears into the desert. The sin is desire, libido, coitus, the sin of the fallen angels who coveted the women of mankind. Israel is cleansed of this sin in the eyes of the God-Father by means of projecting it, throwing it out in the literal sense of the word and also in the metaphorical, for the sins are projected to Azazel and he is made responsible for them. " The Azazel-goat is instituted to expiate the sins of Uzza and Azazel, i.e. the sin of celestial revolt (Tanna d. b. R. Yishmael)." The goat is sacrificed to expiate sexual sins (Yoma, vi, 4, Rashi and Yoma, 39*a*).[6]

If a patient relates an episode of everyday life and then goes on to a dream, then perhaps to some novel he has been reading, it is nearly certain that the *post hoc* is also a *propter hoc* and that sequence in order of time indicates a common latent meaning. The compilers of the Bible must have been subject to the same laws that govern the human mind in general and it is probable that there must be something in common between the latent meaning of the scapegoat

[1] Tremearne, *The Ban of the Bori*, 1914, p. 350.
[2] C. Fossey, *La Magie Assyrienne*, 1902, p. 30.
[3] Jensen, *Das Gilgamesch Epos*, 1906, p. 6.
[4] R. C. Thompson, *Semitic Magic*, 1908, p. 88.
[5] B. Heller, " La Chute des Anges," *Revue des Etudes Juives*, 1910, lix, p. 205.
[6] *Jewish Encyclopedia*, 1902, pp. 366, 369, " Azazel."

ceremony and of the chapters that precede or those that follow this rite. The whole preceding chapter (xv) is about ritual impurity in consequence of pollution, i.e. an outflow of the seminal fluid or menstruation. Now this, according to our view, is the dramatized contents of chapter xvi, i.e. the scapegoat ceremony. The next chapter contains a new variation of the same theme. Anybody who spills blood is unclean " for the life of the flesh is in the blood " (xvii, 11). Finally, chapter xviii contains the list of sexual taboos of defilement due to incest, homosexuality, and bestiality.

" None of you shall approach to any that is near of kin to him to uncover their nakedness. I am the Lord. The nakedness of thy father, even the nakedness of thy mother, thou shalt not uncover : she is thy mother, thou shalt not uncover her nakedness " (xviii, 6, 7).

Ancient Israel was far from being the only nation for which sin essentially meant coitus and coitus was fraught with the burden of feelings of guilt. K. Th. Preuss says in his introduction to Cora ritual : " It is really difficult to understand what the Cora means by sin. I have searched in vain for an explanation. The data contained in the texts confirm the view that the deed in question, a sexual act, is regarded as sin only because of the belief of these tribes, the Cora, Huichol, and Mexicano, that chastity enhances magical power and it is therefore necessary in case of great ceremonies or enterprises." [1] The sin committed by mythical heroes is called " culling flowers " (euphemism for coitus) and is followed by the loss of something the texts call " life " which Preuss interprets as magical power. Among the Sulka, Parkinson says, we find the remarkable view that both man and woman, married and unmarried, are defiled by sexual intercourse.[2]

In Israel the attitude survives under the guise of many symbols. A red thread is attached to the horn of the goat, red being the colour of sin,[3] especially of sexual debauchery. The custom and the corresponding attitude must have deep roots in the soul of the Jewish people, for it is the only rudiment of the sacrificial cult that has survived to the present day, although in a slightly modified form, I mean, of course, the custom of the *kapparah* (atonement) fowl. The *kapparah* fowl may be a modern variant of the scapegoat or perhaps it existed in its present form in ancient Israel as a parallel and the goat was the sacrificial animal connected with a public confession, while each family may have had its own private scapegoat

---

[1] Cf. Preuss, *Die Nayarit Expedition*, 1912, i. Cf. ibid., " Die Sünde in der mexikanischen Religion," *Globus*, lxxxiii, pp. 253, 268.

[2] Parkinson, *Dreissig Jahre*, p. 179. [3] *Isa.*, i, 18.

in the shape of an animal representing a smaller value, as a fowl or pigeon.[1] At any rate we find that in the thirteenth century at Nuremberg rich Jews were not content with sacrificing a cock but they added rams, ewes, and goats. Some families and rabbis observed the custom not only on the Day of Atonement but also at the New Year. Jacob ben Ascher [2] writes in his book *Tur Ōrāḥ Hajjim* (§ 605) : " In some districts fowls are sacrificed the day before the Day of Atonement as an expiatory sacrifice. The cock is an excellent substitute, for the word *geber* means in Hebrew both cock and man." The head of the congregation lays his hand on the head of the person for whom the sacrifice is offered and says : " This one instead of this one, as substitute for this one." Before killing the animal he presses his hand on the head of the cock doing exactly what the priest in Jerusalem did with the goat. It is, of course, not merely a matter of chance that the scapegoat was replaced by a "scape-cock "; for the cock means the male as procreator, and we find the animal as a well-known symbol of the libido in Greece and India. Jews in Palestine used to carry a cock and hen before the bridal pair as symbols of fertility,[3] and in Posen the Jews have a cock and hen flying above the bridal canopy.[4]

Luckily the ceremony itself occurs in the dream of an obsessional neurotic published some years ago in the *Zeitschrift für Psychoanalyse*. He dreamt that N., his teacher of religion, was performing the ceremony *kapores schlagen*. He had a very big cock as big as a dog. There was also a little cock, and he asked the teacher why they did not have the little cock for the ceremony since if it was good enough for his father it ought to be good enough for him too. But the teacher said : " It is wrong what father does, the little cock is the son of the big cock and we must sacrifice the big one." He did not understand this answer, and when he saw him stroking the big fat cock he was shocked at the sight. How can a religious man do such a thing ? he thought. Next day he added the following detail : Beside the cock there was seminal fluid, in fact the seminal fluid came out of the cock. When the teacher stroked the cock he said : " The Hebrew word for cock is *raue*." The association to this meaningless word is *roué* [5] and Reue.[6] Then there was a French governess who used to touch his penis and call it " little bird ". As a child of three the sight of fowls being killed was his greatest delight. After

---

[1] Cf. *Lev.*, xiv, 4. *Zach.*, v. *Lev.*, iv, 1–17.

[2] Fourteenth Century, Spain.

[3] Talmud, *Gittin*, 57a.   [4] Scheftelowitz, *Huhnopfer*, pp. 34, 35.

[5] A frivolous person (French).   [6] Contrition (German).

his dream he woke every morning with the obsession "my father is dead", and then he had to repeat the following formula : "The cock is not my father because the cock had a beard and my father has no beard."

It is evident that in the dream, the dreamer, as represented by the teacher, realizes a deeply repressed wish: he kills his father instead of sacrificing his own little cock, i.e. his penis and the incestuous desires regarding his mother. For when speaking about the fat cock he is reminded of his mother and how he was sometimes very pushing in his caresses. In reality the father paid no attention to his little cock when he showed it and would not let him stroke the big cock.[1] Thus the two aspects of the Oedipus complex, i.e. his rejected love to his father and the father as a rival with the mother, are welded into the desire to sacrifice the father's big cock, i.e. to castrate the father.

Old ritual survives in modern folklore and haunts the dreams of the patient in the consulting room. But although the goat may have been transformed into a cock on his way from Jerusalem to Vienna, he still remains what he originally was, i.e. the penis. On the Day of Atonement, Israel the Firstborn of the Nations, effects its reconciliation with God, the Father of Mankind. The reason for the estrangement between father and son must be explained by the ritual and the rite itself is a periodic expulsion of the penis, a periodic discharge of the seminal fluid, and at the same time a periodic castration. Morality in general is based on castration anxiety and the moral equilibrium is restored by a symbolic imitation of the dreaded punishment. In Babylon we find the word *shi-ir-tu* meaning something that is torn to pieces and therefore "evil", while *taknu* means the opposite : "put together ; regular." In Hebrew we have *terefa*, "torn to pieces," and therefore forbidden, bad, and *kashar*, "whole" and "holy".[2] By tearing itself to pieces voluntarily in the scapegoat ritual the community alleviates the permanent anxiety of being "torn to pieces" in reality.

In this connection we may perhaps mention the oath of Mati-ilu of Arpad taken by him when he acknowledges the sovereign rights of Assurnirari of Ashur (755). The oath is a conditioned curse and represents everything that shall happen to Mati-ilu if he breaks the oath as done to a goat that is sacrificed for the purpose. This is the same principle as in the scapegoat ceremony ; the goat is a

---

[1] E. Weiss, "Totem material in einem Traume," *Zeitschrift für Psa*, ii, p. 163.

[2] M. Jastrow, *Die Religion Babyloniens und Assyriens*, 1912, ii, p. 164.

substitute for man.   Now the goat of Mati-ilu was first beheaded
and then, if Weber's conjecture is correct, castrated.[1]   This analogy
supports our view of the scapegoat as a sort of self-castration of the
community.

5   THARGELIA

The Thargelia were celebrated at Athens on the 6th and 7th of
the month Thargelion.   On the first day the community was
purified of all sins and evil by the expulsion of the two *pharmakoi*
and on the second the firstfruits were brought in and dedicated to
the new-born god of expiation, of atonement, to Apollo.

The human scapegoats of this festival are called *pharmakoi*, that
is, "sorcerers."   Mythologists seem hardly to understand how the
place should be cleansed of evil by the expulsion of sorcerers and
therefore they translate the word " those who serve magical purposes,
magic incarnate in human shape ".[2]   But is it not necessary to
explain the simple meaning away, as we get a completely coherent
version if we translate the word as sorcerers.   It is a universal
feature of primitive life in all countries and periods that diseases,
deaths, blight of crops and in general, calamities of every kind are
attributed to the activity of the magician and we might therefore
regard the ritual as an attempt to get rid of evil by expelling the
author of evil.   Supposing that such a view really existed among the
ancestors of the Greeks, we might easily understand why they
expelled, stoned, or burned a male and a female magician as representatives of wizards and witches in general.   The *pharmakos*
would then have to be a monstrous, idiotic, or misshaped person
as these were generally regarded as sorcerers, as embodiments of
black magic.

Various forms of the custom are mentioned in Athens.   Besides
the Thargelia, the custom occurred also when plague, drought,
or famine befell the city.   One of the victims was sacrificed for
the men and the other for the women.   Both wore strings of figs
round their neck, the male scapegoat having a string of white and
the female a string of black figs.   After being marched round the
city they were stoned to death outside.

[1] J. Pedersen, *Der Eid bei den Semiten*, 1914, p. 110. Ploss, *Das Kind*,
ii, p. 145.

[2] Fr. Schwenn, *Die Menschenopfer bei den Griechen und Römer*, 1915,
p. 38, quoting Fick and Osthoff in *Bezzenbergers Beiträge*, xxiii, p. 189;
xxiv, p. 144.

The Ionians in Ephesus and Clazomenae had a somewhat different variant of the custom. When a city suffered from plague, famine, or other public calamity an ugly or deformed person was chosen to take upon himself all the evils of the community. First they made him fast for some time and then they fed him with figs, a barley loaf and cheese. After this meal they threw him to the ground and gave him seven strokes on his penis with branches of the wild fig and other wild plants. The branches of the wild fig were not despoiled of their leaves and the tune sung at this ceremony was called a fig-song, the hero of the tragedy being a Fig-Man. Finally he was burnt on a pyre made of the wood of forest-trees and the ashes were cast into the sea.[1]

Ritual can be analysed directly or through the medium of its explanatory myth, for most rites are alleged repetitions of a certain mythical precedent and latent contents of the myth exist sometimes in a less veiled form. In this case we shall use both methods and start by analysing the myth.

The discovery of the mythical first *pharmakos* of the Thargelia is due to Usener's genius. It is he who pointed out the common root word of Thargelia and Thersites, although in opposition to the view of Pausanias who regards *thér*, animal, as the root of the whole complex. Usener is inclined to go back to an Indo-germanic root ; *dharsh*, courage, strength.[2] In the brilliant army of Achaians gathered to besiege the fortress of Troy there is only one unheroic hero. " He was the ugliest man in the Greek army, bald and hump-backed, with one leg longer than the other." [3] This is quite wrong for a hero but just the right shape for a *pharmakos*.

It is a significant fact that Thersites is killed by Achilles when he laughs at him because the hero falls in love with the Amazon-queen whom he has killed. For Achilles is also the avenger, who kills the first *pharmakos* for having stolen the sacrificial vessels of Apollo, or rather it is Achilles who catches him red-handed and the people who stone him to death afterwards.[4] According to another version this Thersites was hurled from a rock because of cowardice at the Calydonian boar hunt ; throwing from a rock is one of the typical ways of killing a *pharmakos*.

So far the results of this inquiry may be very illuminating from

---

[1] Frazer, *Scapegoat*, pp. 253–5. Schwenn, *Menschenopfer*, pp. 36–40. Nilsson, *Griechische Feste*, pp. 105–15. Usener, *Kleine Schriften*, iv, p. 255.

[2] Gilbert Murray, *The Rise of the Greek Epic*, 1911, p. 225.

[3] H. Usener, *Kleine Schriften*, iv, 239–54.

[4] Usener, loc. cit., pp. 242, 243.

the point of view of understanding the epic figure of Thersites,
but they have scarcely any bearing on the nature of the scapegoat
ceremony. However, things appear in a different light when we
are told that the Dorian form of the name would be Theritas and
that Theritas was a god and had a temple in Lacedaemon.

According to Hesychios, Thereitas is another name of Enyalius,
but Pausanias thinks that Ares was called Thereitas by the Spartans,
either because the god of war must have the indomitable courage
of a wild animal ($\theta\eta\rho$), a lion, or on account of his mythical nurse
Thero. It makes little difference which equation we accept, for
Enyalos was another war-god, the son of Ares, or another Ares.[1]

The ephebi or Spartan youths fought an annual battle with their
fists and feet in a grove, and like the *pharmakos* the defeated were
hurled into the water. But before this annual battle the ephebi
performed a sacrifice to Enyalius at a place called the Phoibeion
and a sacrifice to Achilles at his temple on the road to Arcadia.[2]
If Enyalius is Theritas we have here the ritual form of the old battle
of Achilles and Thersites.[3] And if Achilles kills or expels the war-
god in the shape of the ugly *pharmakos* Thersites at the death of
Penthesilea, we can understand the other form of the same myth
in which Ares himself tries to attack Achilles at the very same
moment, for was not Penthesilea his daughter?[4] Thus the
inappropriate scoffing of the ugly clown seems to be but a degenerate
survival of a father's just wrath. But if, as there seems no reason to
doubt, these conclusions are correct we have established a rather
striking parallel between Italy and Greece, between Rome and
Athens or Thebes. For, in both cases, it is the war-god, Mamurius
Veturius or Ares, who is cast out of the city at the festival of the
New Year.

Ares is the great ancestral deity of Thebes or rather of the royal
family of Thebes. Various explanations are offered for this as
he is not directly regarded as the father of Cadmus. One of these
explanations refers to his daughter Harmonia, offspring of his marriage
with Aphrodite the clan ancestress ($\pi\rho o\mu\acute{a}\tau\omega\rho$ $\gamma\acute{e}\nu o\nu s$) and wife
of Cadmus.[5] The other genealogical version is connected with

[1] Cf. the articles " Enyalos " and " Enyo " in *Roschers Lexikon*. Pueblo
war-gods are intrinsically connected with the idea of fertilization. H. K.
Haeberlin, " The idea of fertilization in the Culture of the Pueblo Indians,"
(*Mem. Am. Anthr. Assoc.*, iii), 1916, p. 34.
[2] Pausanias, iii, 19, 7, 20, 2, 20, 8. *Battle of Ephebi*, 14, 8.
[3] Murray, loc. cit., p. 227.
[4] Quint. Smyrn., i, 675. *Roschers Lexikon*, i, p. 480.
[5] *Roschers Lexikon*, i, p. 483.

the dragon-slayer Cadmus. Dragons are usually the guardians of springs and Cadmus kills the dragon at a spring. We should expect the spring in question to be called serpent's or dragon's spring or something of the kind, and it is with some surprise that we learn its name : 'Αρεία χρήνη, i.e. Spring of Ares. However, as we are told that the dragon killed by Cadmus was called δράκων Ἄρεος and originally regarded as the son of the war-god we begin to suspect the original identity of the deity and the serpent.[1]

It would be quite in keeping with traditions to assume that just as Cecrops, the ancestor of the Cecropidae and Erechtheus, the ancestor of the Erechtheidae, is a serpent, Ares, the god of the Theban Acropolis should manifest himself in the same zoomorphic shape. Ares has a daughter Harmonia who with her husband Cadmus survives in dragon shape on the Cadmea, for dragon-slayers in Greece are frequently, we might even say normally, dragons.[2]

However, Ares, being a sort of sublimated serpent, survives the death of his animal alter-ego and orders Cadmus to sow the dragon's teeth in the earth. The result is a new host of antagonists for the hero. Iron-clad men, procreated by the dragon's teeth, rise in arms against him and these are the ancestors of the Thebans. Names such as Echion, the Son of a Serpent, Udaius and Chtonius the Earth-men clearly indicate the origin of these beings. "They are ritual or poetic ἐπικλήσεις of the serpent god."[3] The Thebans descend from these earth-born serpents ; they are the race of Cadmus, the sons of the war-god, and at the same time the serpent people.

In a typical dragon-slaying myth the sequence of events would be somewhat as follows. The hero conquers the dragon and then weds the princess. In our case we should of course expect the marriage of Cadmus and Harmonia as the sequel of the great victory. This is in fact what actually happens, only in a symbolic form. For "to sow" is merely a euphemism for coitus, procreation.[4] Instead of Harmonia we have Mother Earth as the spouse of our hero. But is that really a great difference ? For we are told by Pausanias that at Thebes on the Acropolis there was the bridal chamber of Harmonia and Semele and that in the *abaton*, along with the thunderbolt which was hurled on the bridal chamber of Semele, there fell

---

[1] F. Schwenn, " Der Krieg in der griechischen Religion," *A.R.W.*, xxii, p. 225.

[2] Cf. *Roschers Lexikon*, " Kadmos," pp. 889, 890.

[3] Schwenn, loc. cit., p. 227.

[4] Schwenn, loc. cit., p. 227. Usener, loc. cit., iv, p. 191. Dieterich, *Mutter Erde*, 1913, p. 92.

a log from heaven, and they say that Polydorus adorned this log with bronze and called it Dionysus Cadmus.[1]

In the Theban version of the myth Semele is the daughter of Harmonia, which is another way of saying that the two goddesses mean the same divine being. But Semele is the Slavic Zemlja. Lat. *humus*, the Earth,[2] and the children of the Dragon's Teeth, the Sparti, are thus really the children and enemies of the Dragon Cadmus. The struggle between the two serpents is for Harmonia the daughter-wife of the old dragon.[3]

We thus find the same relation between Cadmus and the Greek war-god as between the young and the old Mars. In both cases the scapegoat or vanquished god is the Old Male of the Primal Horde. But in Thebes, where serpent fights against serpent, we can go a step further than this. For that the snake is the phallus is abundantly proved by many details of Greek religion. Miss Harrison says : " The form taken by the traditional hero and the king is unquestionably that of a snake and the snake is used in phallic ceremonies for the promotion of fertility." [4]

The war-god is incarnate in a spear ; high officials of Thebes bore the δόρυ (= spear, beam, or tree) as symbol of their office,[5] Cadmus is a καδμος, a pole or pillar in the temple [6] and both of them are serpents, that is phalli.

For who but a phallic demon could be the proper husband of the goddess of love, the beautiful Aphrodite ? The festival of Hybristika with men in female and women in male attire, celebrated in honour of Ares, seems to have been a marriage ceremony. In Troezen we again find that the god whose temple is in the immediate vicinity of a *temenos* dedicated to the demons of birth is closely associated with the sexual sphere. At Tegea we have an image of Ares Gynaikothoinas, Ares who feasts with the women.[7] And the other spear god Mars ?

" The original root of the word seems to have been *mar* or *mas*, meaning the virile power of a procreating deity." [8]

We should have arrived at the same conclusion if we had not

---

[1] Pausanias, ix, 12, 3. Harrison, loc. cit., p. 91.
[2] Hehn, *Kulturpflanzen und Haustiere*, p. 465. Roscher, article on " Semele ".
[3] Schwenn, loc. cit., p. 229.   [4] Harrison, loc. cit., p. 268.
[5] F. Schwenn, " Der Krieg in der griechischen Religion," *A.R.W.*, xx, p. 299.
[6] *Idem*, *A.R.W.*, xxii, p. 228.
[7] Schwenn, " Der Krieg," *A.R.W.*, xxii, pp. 234, 235.
[8] L. Preller, *Römische Mythologie*, 1858, p. 296.

followed Usener in connecting Thersites with the festival and gone beyond him in finding the martial god, the true male, in the unworthy guise of the hunchback. The string of figs worn by both scapegoats must have a definite significance. Figs were sacred to Dionysos meilichios,[1] and especially holy to Priapus whose image was always made of the fig-tree.[2] The fig was also closely associated with the phallic Hermes and Cybele and the phallus of the Dionysiac festivals was made of the fig-tree.[3] It is with the branches of the fig-tree that they beat the Fig-Man's genitalia and his very name of Fig-Man shows that he is a living embodiment or personification of the phallus. At this point two very interesting parallels have been indicated by Paton and Frazer.[4]

On the one hand we have Adam and Eve, the original scapegoats and ancestors of the human race, whose sin is evidently the act of coition,[5] and who after the fall cover their nakedness with the leaves of the fig. According to Paton's interpretation, the male and the female *pharmakos* represented a married couple who like Adam and Eve had incorporated the fig-demon of fertility by eating the fruit and wearing a mask of fig-leaves, the aim of the ceremony being a fertilization of the fig-tree by means of imitative magic. The process of caprification, that is, the artificial fertilization of the cultivated fig-trees by hanging strings of wild figs on the boughs, takes place in Greece and Asia Minor in June, that is, about the month after the Thargelia. We should be inclined to accept and yet to reject these conclusions regarding the practical aim of the ritual as accidental or secondary and to interpret the whole rather as a ceremony of the fig-totem. Adam who has eaten the fig that belongs to the serpent, i.e. had intercourse with the woman belonging to the God-Father, would be the ancestor of the fig-totem. As such he appears on the scene clad in the leaves of the fig as his mask, has intercourse with a female masked representative of the fig-totem, and is chased from the scene as a punishment for this act of totemic incest.

In New Guinea the coco-palm and the sago are the staple food of the natives just as the fig was in Asia Minor. The essential

[1] *Athen.*, iii, p. 78c.   [2] Horatius, *Sat.*, i, 8.

[3] I. Murr, *Die Pflanzenwelt in der griechischen Mythologie*, 1890, pp. 32, 33.

[4] W. R. Paton, "The φαρμακοι and the Story of the Fall," *Revue Archéologique*, iv Serie, ix, 1907, p. 57.

[5] Cf. L. Levy, " Sexualsymbolik in der biblischen Paradiesgeschichte," *Imago*, v, p. 16.

thing in the totemic ritual of the Marind in connection with these plants is that they have intercourse with young girls whom they kill and devour afterwards in order to promote the fertility of the plant. The typical myth tells us how the uninitiated (Adam) attempted to take part in these orgies and were driven off by the initiated (God-Father).[1]

Similar ritual prototypes may have been the starting point of the Adam myth, of the ritual of Thargelia[2] and of the Nonae Caprotinae.

On the 7th of July the Nonae Caprotinae were celebrated in Rome. This was the Saturnalia of slave women. They dressed in the attire of free women and left the town. "They feasted under a wild fig-tree, cut a rod from the tree, beat each other, and offered the milky juice of the tree to the goddess Juno Caprotina, whose surname seems to point her out as a goddess of the wild fig-tree (*caprificus*). Here the rites performed in July by women under the wild fig-tree, which the ancients rightly regarded as a male and employed to fertilize the cultivated female fig-tree, can hardly be dissociated from the caprification or artificial marriage of fig-trees which according to Columella was best performed in July ; and if the blows which the women gave each other on this occasion were administered, as seems highly probable, by the rod which they cut from the wild fig-tree the parallel between the Roman and Greek ceremony would be still closer, since the Greeks, as we saw, beat the genitals of human victims with branches of wild fig-trees.[3]

Frazer also points out the traces of the scapegoat ritual associated with the festival. The disappearance of Romulus took place at the Goats' Marsh (*ad Caprae paludem*), a name which suggests that the place was not very far from the goat-fig (*caprificus*) where the slave women performed their ceremonies. The patricians bury the pieces of his body in the earth, thus fertilizing the earth, while his successors may have fertilized the women with the rod made of the fig-tree.

"Can the king have played at Rome the same fatal part in the fertilization of fig-trees which, if Mr Paton is right, was played in Greece by the male victim ? " Sir James Frazer asks.[4]

Romulus having been nursed under the *Ficus ruminalis* and killed near a fig-tree, we can hardly avoid the conclusion that Romulus

[1] Wirz, *Die Marind-anim von Holländisch-Süd-Neu-Guinea*, ii, p. 60.
[2] At the Thargelia the scapegoat is expelled and then the firstfruits are offered to Apollo. In the Bible, Adam, the scapegoat, is expelled for having eaten the firstfruits belonging to a supernatural being.
[3] Frazer, *Scapegoat*, p. 258.   [4] Frazer, *Scapegoat*, p. 259.

is the Fig-Man and Rome the Fig-Town.[1] It is curious how these two symbols, the fig and the goat, are continually associated with each other and with fertility or lustration ritual. The Akikuya believe that women conceive through the milky juice of the wild fig. A goat is sacrificed and the women bound to the tree by ropes made of the goat's intestines. According to the Akamba the wild fig is inhabited by the spirits of the dead. The Baganda perform a ceremony in which husband and wife eat the genital organ of a he-goat under a wild fig-tree.[2]

Another ceremony in which we have the conjunction of fig and goat was performed at the Lupercalia.

On the 15th of February, that is two weeks before the expulsion of the old Mars, Rome witnessed the ceremonial procession of the Luperci. " As a day of atonement the festival was called *februatus* from *februare* in the meaning of lustration and expiation, whence also the name of the whole month of February was derived. From ancient times there had been two colleges of Luperci, the Fabiani and Quinctiliani, consisting each of young men.[3] A cave with a spring in it dedicated to Faunus was called Lupercal and was in closest proximity to the *temenos* of the diva Rumina (*ruma* = breast) with the famous *Ficus ruminalis*. This was the place where the ancestral twins Romulus and Remus had landed and where the she-wolf became their second mother by giving them a mother's breast.[4]

But who is Faunus the genius of the place whose image stood in the Lupercal " *nudum caprina pelle amictum, sicut Romae Lupercalibus discurritur* " ?[5] As his garb indicates the close connection with the ritual it may be assumed that his mythological function bears a close relation to the latent content of the rite. In the list of the first kings of Latium we find Faunus as son and successor of Picus. But Picus, the woodpecker, is " picus Martius " the bird of the war-god.[6] In myth as in pseudo-history Faunus is hidden under the guise of the shepherd Faustulus[7] and both are offshoots of Father Mars. For while Mars is the physical father of a shepherd tribe we find beside Amulius, as representing the hostile aspect of the father-image, the

---

[1] Cf. Frazer, loc. cit., and *Magic Art*, ii, pp. 313–19.

[2] Frazer, *Magic*, pp. 316–18.

[3] Preller, loc. cit., p. 343.

[4] Cf. Mannhardt, *Mythologische Forschungen*, pp. 73, 74.

[5] G. Wissowa, " Faunus," in *Roschers Lexikon*, i, p. 1485, quoting Justin, 43, 1, 7.

[6] Cf. Preller, *Römische Mythologie*, p. 298.

[7] Faunus and Faustulus both derived from *faveo*.

shepherd Faunus-Faustulus as foster-father of our fig hero.[1]   He
represents a shepherd stage of existence and as herds of sheep and goats
on the hills are frequently led by a he-goat we find Faunus in the
shape of this animal.   Ovid calls him *bicornis*,[2] *cornipes*,[3] and *semicaper*.[4]
Is this simply due to a confusion of the Latin Faunus with the Greek
Pan ?[5]   Ritual shows that this view is not justified, for the whole rite
has one slogan, one aim, and that is " *Italidas matres, sacer hircus
inito* ".[6]   And who could doubt that the sacred goat, the husband and
fertilizer of all mothers in Italy, is the same Faunus whose function
is to multiply the herd and who, as the god of copulation, especially
in the realm of animal life, is called Inuus[7] " *ab inuendo passim cum
omnibus animalibus* " ?[8]   Here again he is a true son of the woodpecker.   For Picus under the name of Picumnus with his brother and
double Pilumnus (*pilum* = peaked hat) are the patron divinities of
children and fertility.[9]

The proper sacrifice for a he-goat is a young she-goat[10] and the
festival of the Lupercalia begins with this sacrifice " *cornipedi Fauno
caesa de more capella* ".[11]   Although in the ritual we find that the
animal sacrifice is a she-goat the legend refers to the sacrifice of a
he-goat[12] that is for the god Faunus.

We have already mentioned the *collegia* and *sodalitates* of ancient
Rome and compared them to the secret societies of primitive tribes.
The Kwakiutl organizations are " killer-whales ", " rock-cods ",
" sea-lions ".[13]   In Rome we have the *hirpi Sorani*[14] and at the Lupercalia the " wolf-goats ",[15] perhaps a fusion of the two groups[16] with
two separate ceremonies.   The theory of an original duality of
the festival is supported by the reference to the gentes[17] and the
sacrifice of a goat and a dog[18] at the commencement of the
ceremony.[19]

The behaviour of the young wolves and goats is similar to that of

[1] Wissowa, loc. cit., p. 1464.
[2] *Fastorum*, ii, 268.
[3] Wissowa, ibid., p. 361.
[4] Ibid., ii, p. 101.
[5] Wissowa, loc. cit., p. 1454.
[6] Ovid, *Fasti*, ii, 441.
[7] Wissowa, op. cit., p. 1455.
[8] *Serv. and Verg. Aen.*, vi, 776.
[9] Preller, loc. cit., p. 332.
[10] Horatius, *Carm.*, i, 4, 12. Ovid, *Fasti*, ii, 361.
[11] Ovid, *Fasti*, ii, 34.
[12] Ovid, *Fasti*, ii, 445.
[13] F. Boas, " The Social Organization and the Secret Societies of the
Kwakiutl Indians," *Report of the U.S.A. National Museum*, 1897, p. 419.
[14] " Wolves of the Sun-God."
[15] *Luperci* = *lupi et herci*.
[16] Fabii and Quinctii.
[17] Fabii and Quinctii.
[18] Substitute for a wolf.
[19] Mannhardt, *Mythologische Forschungen*, 73–101.   Idem, *Wald und
Feldkulte*, ii, p. 318.

initiates in all countries. They were free to talk scandal about well-known personages, to insult people ; they could be witty and especially obscene, beat people and especially the women, with whips made of the hide of the sacrificed goats. Women received the strokes or *februatio* on their backs or hands. The ceremony survived into the Christian period, for the people believed that the celebration of the Lupercalia averted the pest and other diseases.[1]

After all these analogies with the puberty and secret society ritual of primitive tribes we may perhaps attempt to explain a peculiar feature of the ritual. The foreheads of two young noblemen, probably representing the two original groups, were touched with knives dipped in goat's-blood. Then the blood was wiped from the knives with wool that had been soaked in milk and the youths had to laugh out aloud.[2] In the ritual of initiation the novices are killed (the bloody knife) and then reborn, that is, they are again infants with milk as their food. We might call the ritual an extremely abbreviated recapitulation of the essential features of an initiation ceremony containing in the knife (or blood) and the milk the symbols of death and rebirth.[3]

In Australian initiation ceremonies we find all sorts of obscene pantomines and ludicrous scenes, the essential thing being that the boys must not laugh on any account.[4] After initiation comes the release of all restraints, laughter, buffoonery,[5] and sexual freedom. The two youths probably represent the two halves of the tribe or the two tribal heroes Remus as leader of the Fabii and Romulus as leader of the Quinctii.[6] But the twins fighting against the paternal tyrant stand for the brother-horde of the primeval epoch ; they repeat their struggle by killing the Jealous Sire, the Goat or Phallic Being, Faunus in the ritual, and they suffer the punishment for his death by being killed themselves with the knife, identifying themselves with the Sire in the blood-communion and being reborn as goats (*fauni, creppi*) who are entitled to fertilize the women.

But in doing this they give back to the dead what they have taken from him, for the whip is a part of the sacrificed *sacer hircus* who thus remains even after his death the ultimate agent of fertilization. But

---

[1] Mannhardt, *Mythologische Forschungen*, pp. 81–3.

[2] Mannhardt, *Mythologische Forschungen*, pp. 74–5.

[3] Cf. Mannhardt, loc. cit., p. 99.

[4] K. L. Parker, *The Euahlayi Tribe*, 1905, p. 72.

[5] R. H. Mathews, *Ethnological Notes on the Aboriginal Tribes of New South Wales and Victoria*, 1905, p. 125.

[6] Mannhardt, loc. cit., p. 76.

this ritual whipping or scourging is really a *februatio*, i.e. a cathartic ceremony, and aims at the expulsion of evil, be it disease, death or sin.

We believe we have fully established the identity of the two goats, the one which, on the 15th of February, fertilized the mothers of Italy in Rome, and the bearer of the sins of Israel who, or which, carried these sins away to the desert on the 10th of Tisri in Jerusalem.

6 SCAPEGOATS AND INITIATION

Masked dances in Europe are usually connected with the expulsion of a hostile being, death, disease or a scapegoat. We shall now try to prove that this feature of the ritual is based on initiation ceremonies.

The division of the people into age-grades is an archaic feature of society in Europe, surviving, however, especially in mountainous regions such as Switzerland or Transylvania. The May ceremonies at Ragaz and Valens now performed by youngsters were previously part and parcel of the ritual of the organized *Knabenschaft*. A leaf-clad mummer called the May-bear parades the streets followed by young men with sticks. Finally they throw the May-bear into the Tamina from the bridge.[1] In the Lucerne canton we have on the second Thursday before Christmas the ceremony called *Posterli-Jagen*. The young men drive the Posterli, a masked figure representing an old woman, a donkey or a goat, and leave it in an out-of-the-way corner of the village. In various parts of Switzerland we have processions with other masked beings who are all pelted and driven out of the village. In Uri, Winter is represented as a bear, in Wallis as a " Wild-Man " clad in the hide of a goat.[2]

In Silesia the Sunday after Laetare is called Dead Sunday or Summer Sunday and it is on this day that " Death " is carried. " Death " is a doll and the ceremony is accompanied by the following song :—

> *Nun treiben wir den Tod hinaus*
> *Den alten Weibern in ihr Haus*
> *Den Reichen in den Kasten*
> *Heute ist Mittfasten.*[3]

On the last day of the year Satan is driven out of each Votjak village by the unmarried lads and lasses.[4]

[1] W. Manz, *Volksbrauch und Volksglaube des Sarganserlandes*, 1916, p. 39.
[2] E. Hoffman-Krayer, " Fruchtbarkeitsriten im schweizerischen Volksbrauch," *Schweizerisches Archiv für Volkskunde*, xi, 1917, p. 240.
[3] P. Drechsler, *Sitte, Brauch und Volksglaube in Schlesien*, 1903, i, p. 66.
[4] M. Buch, *Die Wotjäken*, 1882, p. 153.

The Basoga conclude their puberty ceremony by a purification rite at which a goat and a fowl are killed [1] and we think that Satan driven out of the village must be the " goat " again in a new form. According to J. T. Sun, the Sumerian concept of a " demon " was represented by the pictogram for " seed ", and meant also " to be full ", i.e. full of sexual power, " to grow large," and the phallus.[2]

The identification of the devil with the penis is a frequent feature in the obscene stories of the Southern Slavs. A girl runs away from home to avoid the sin of being married. She meets an anchorite and the man shows her his penis and tells her it is the devil and that his devil gives him a lot of trouble. She has the right sort of hell for this devil and so they exorcise the demon in the natural way.[2] In other variants of the same story coitus is described as " sending the Pope to Rome " instead of sending the devil to hell.[3] A priest cohabits with a girl after her confession that she has had intercourse with a Moslem, and calls the act of coition " driving the Moslem out ".[4]

If we regard society as the body and the expelled spirit, be it god or devil, as the phallus, we cannot fail to see that our ritual is both a super-organic coitus and a super-organic castration. Indeed, as analysis has shown the fundamental part played by the dread of castration in all forms of psychic disease, we shall hardly be surprised to find the dreaded punishment of sins in a ritual of self-abasement that professes to be a substitute for an adequate punishment.

Every year in spring when the willows burst into leaf on the banks of the river a magical ceremony for the multiplication of buffaloes was performed by the Mandams. The actors were disguised as buffaloes ; they wore the entire skins of the animals with horns and tails complete, the heads of the buffaloes were thrown over their heads, their eyes peered through the eye-holes of the animals and they imitated the motions of the buffaloes. The scene they acted was the leap of the buffalo bull on the buffalo cow. When that scene had been publicly acted in the presence of the whole population wound up to the greatest excitement, the actor who personated the buffalo bull was mocked by the women and children, bespattered with filth and ignominiously *driven away from the village into the prairie*. In another account we are told that the personator of the buffalo bull was

---

[1] J. Roscoe, *The Northern Bantu*, 1915, p. 187.

[2] F. S. Krauss, " Südslavische Volksüberlieferungen," *Anthropophyteia*, ii, p. 382. J. T. Sun, " Symbolism in the Sumerian Written Language," *The Psychoanalytic Review*, 1914, p. 271.

[3] Ibid., pp. 383–7.

[4] Ibid., p. 272.

" painted black to represent the devil ".   The O-kee-pa was celebrated for three purposes.   Firstly it commemorated the subsiding
of the waters after the Deluge.   Then it was the occasion for the buffalo
dance, and finally for the initiation of young men.   The first ordeal
the young men had to go through was that of the " hiding man ",
that is, drawing the foreskin over the glans and hiding it with a sinew.
The black representative of the Owl or Evil Spirit appeared on the
fourth day, holding a wand with a red ball at the end.   At the screams
of the women the conductor of the ceremonies came with his medicine
pipe for their protection.   He thrust the medicine pipe before the
monster, making him motionless and then he let him loose again.
At last the Evil Spirit, retreating, swaggered up against one of
the men disguised under the buffalo hide.   Then he placed himself
in the attitude of a buffalo bull and imitated the bull leaping on the
cow with various actors.   This performance was accompanied by
shouts of approval from the multitude, as they believed that the supply
of buffaloes depended on this ceremony.   It was after this performance
that he was thoroughly exhausted and became the laughing-stock and
butt of the women.   They gathered round him and pelted him with
dirt.   He began to cry and one of them caught his wand from his hand
and broke it across her knee.   The woman who deprived him of this
symbol of virility was escorted by two matrons on each side.   She was
then lifted by her attendants over the door of the medicine lodge
where she harangued the multitude, saying that " she held the power
of creation and also of life and death over them, that she was the
father of all buffaloes and could make them come or stay as she
pleased ".

This was followed by the initiation of young men.[1]   The prelude
to the ceremony is hiding the glans in the foreskin and it is followed
by initiation.   As for the ceremony itself, it evidently refers to the
" castration " suffered by the male in the act of coition.   First the
representative of the Evil Spirit fertilizes the buffalo cows, then he is
exhausted and the wand, as a no more erected penis, is torn from him
and broken to pieces by a woman, who thus becomes the " father "
of buffaloes.   It is exactly analogous to a case of obsessional neurosis
that I had in analysis, where I found that the notion of the " Mother
with the Penis " was derived from the idea that in coitus the father was
castrated by the mother so that she retained his penis in her vagina.

[1] G. Catlin, *Illustrations of the Manners, Customs, and Condition of the
North American Indian Tribes*, 1876, i, p. 167.   *Idem, O-keep-pa, a religious
ceremony, and other customs of Mandans*, 1867, pp. 9–24.   Quoted by
Frazer, *Totemism and Exogamy*, iii, pp. 139, 140.   *Scapegoat*, p. 171.

The buffalo bull or devil is both the penis and the Jealous Sire of the Cyclopean Horde. The derision expressed by the women is but a disguise for the fact that he engenders the new generation with them. With regard to this meaning, if there was any doubt left after the rite it would be removed by a feature that accompanies the ceremony. The men offered the use of their wives to the older men and the offer was generally accepted. The same feature characterized the bull-dance of the Hidatsas.[1] For the present our interest is mainly centred on the fact that there we have the demon-chasing as part of a fecundity-rite and that this symbolic representation of autotomy-castration-coitus is followed by a more realistic repetition. First the bull is wrenched from the social body and then the penis from the bull's body : in both cases by women.

Now we are reminded of the fact that the high priest, when he enters the Holy of Holies to perform the scapegoat ceremony, is symbolically " castrated " and that circumcision itself is brought into close connection with the Day of Atonement. According to the *Pirke R. Eliezer*, xxix, the circumcision of Abraham took place on the Day of Atonement and the blood that dropped down on the very spot where the altar afterwards stood in the temple on the Moriah is still before the eyes of God to serve as a means of atonement. If Reik is right in regarding the Sinai episode and the Day of Atonement as a puberty ceremony [2] the ritual of the Mandan and of the Suk would afford the closest analogy to this supposed combination of scapegoat and puberty (circumcision) ceremony.

" On the third day of the third month a man known as the Sosion appears with an attendant, cursing the candidates and their parents and generally making themselves a nuisance. The female relatives of the candidates assemble afar off and stone the Sosion for his conduct. He vows vengeance and shoots an arrow at the hut containing the candidates. A mock battle ensues, the Sosion is overpowered by the youths, he admits defeat and consents to perform his function. The Sosion takes the hot iron and as each youth emerges from the door sears his shrivelled skin. The youths retire to the hut and their mothers are told that the Kipsigutwa, a ferocious animal, is killing them."

By a not infrequent reversal of facts, circumcision (castration)

---

[1] The buffalo dance of the Blackfeet represented the mating of buffalo by women choosing their men. " Gives-to-the-Sun and Natokema danced, imitating the capers of mating buffalo." W. McClintock, *The Old North Trail*, 1910, p. 99.

[2] Th. Reik, *Probleme der Religionspsychologie*, 1919, p. 240.

is here represented as the victory of the brother-clan over the representative of the father-imago. The fact that he is stoned by the women brings the Sosion into close relation to our scapegoats while his exoteric equivalent, the Kipsigutwa, throws some further light on the intimate details of his nature. This Kipsigutwa is a dog-like animal from Mount Mutelo with one horn and one eye which stabs people with its horn. All Suk are buried on their side facing Mount Mutelo so as to maintain the direction of the umbilical cord.[1] May we interpret the animal with the horn as the penis ? And the one eye and one horn as the representation of castration either on the penis, or by reversal, on the father as castrator ? This penis-symbol comes from Mount Mutelo and the above-quoted rite of burial shows that this is equivalent to deriving it from the uterus.

Any severed part of the body may serve as scapegoat, as the bearer of sin and uncleanness. Thus, for instance, in the Kilimanjaro district when clitoridectomy is performed they say : " We wash you of all the uncleanness of heretofore, we cleanse you of all uncleanness of childhood, that you may follow a new path to your death." [2] At the boys' initiation ceremony the trophies of the hunt are smeared with the excreta of the novices, whereby the sin and uncleanness of the whole proceeding are conveyed to these articles.[3]

But to return to the circumcision of Abraham and the Day of Atonement. The priest enters the Holy of Holies after the death of his two sons, with his penis carefully covered, and sacrifices a young bull and a ram. The festival is also connected with another episode in the life of Abraham ; the sacrifice of his son Isaac. The close connection of circumcision with the father-son conflict is quite plain, and expressed in one of the explanatory myths that are made to account for the origin of this institution in the Bible.

Moses is on his way back to Egypt with his wife and child and the sceptre of the Lord in his hand. Jahve has just assured him of his protection, as Moses seems continually to be wavering between desire and reluctance to follow the Voice of the Lord. Miracles were needed to convince him of his vocation, for thus, believing himself, he will make others believe. "What is that in your hand ? " asks the Lord. " A stick," says Moses. He is told to throw it away; it is transformed into a serpent and he is afraid of the serpent. Then he is told to lay his hand on the serpent and lo ! as soon as he has

[1] I. Barton, "Notes on the Suk Tribe of Kenya Colony," *J.R.A.I.*, 1921, pp. 92–5.

[2] Ch. Dundas, *Kilimanjaro and its People*, 1924, p. 211.

[3] Ibid., p. 219.

mustered courage the serpent is re-transformed into a stick. His hand then becomes snow-white and afterwards again like normal flesh. Water taken from the Nile and changing to blood is the third miracle he performs with success.[1]

The third miracle gives the setting of the whole scene. We have various reports on drawing water from the Nile as an Egyptian rite. We are told by Diodorus that at Acanthus priests pour the water of the Nile every day from 360 urns into a cask which, like that of the Danaides, has a hole at the bottom.[2] Epiphanius compares the transformation of water into wine at the Cana wedding to the custom of the Egyptians who used to draw water from the Nile on the 11th of Tybi and believed that the water was magically transformed into wine or that special healing power, magical virtue, was to be attributed to it.[3] The account given by Plutarch throws unexpected light on the meaning of this miracle. He tells us that Osiris is born on the 361st day [4] of the Egyptian year. This is the festival of drawing water and when performing this act a certain Pamyles of Thebes heard a voice, ordering him to proclaim " the birth of the great king, Osiris " and in memory of this event the festival of Pamylia, which is similar to that of the Phallephoria, is celebrated.[5] Osiris being frequently and continually identified with the water of the Nile, there can be no doubt that Holl is right in identifying the water drawn from the river with the god himself. It is the birth of Osiris, who like Moses (The Child) [6] comes from the water. The Greek equivalent of Osiris is Dionysus. The water-miracle is equally performed by Dionysus, and what is more, exactly at the same date (5/6th of January = 11th Tybi) as in Egypt. Elis, Naxos, Eleusis, and Teos all claim to be the birthplace of the wine-god and Teos had a special sign to prove this claim : the water in the spring became wine. They put three empty urns in the temple and by the morning they were full of wine.[7] If we remember that wine, according to the Egyptians, sprang from the blood of fallen giants,[8] the connecting links between Osiris-Dionysus and Moses become very close indeed.

The phallic feature is disclosed in the cult of the Egyptian and the

---

[1] *Exodus*, iv.   [2] Diodorus, i, 97.

[3] K. Holl, " Der Ursprung des Epiphanienfestes," *Sitzungsber. d. Kngl. Preuss. Ak-d-Wiss.*, 1917, p. 431.

[4] Cf. the water poured from 360 urns the preceding day.

[5] Plutarch, *Is. et Os.*, 12.

[6] D. Völter, *Aegypten und die Bibel*, 1909, p. 97, quoting Brugsch, *Aegyptologie*, p. 118.

[7] A. Meyer, *Das Weihnachtsfest,* 1913, p. 15.

[8] Plutarch, loc. cit., 6.

Greek god ; and in the case of their Hebrew brother the other two cardinal miracles are rapid transformations of the wand into serpent (and back again) and of his own hand into the hand of a corpse ; transitions of the same symbol from courage to anxiety.

Now Moses goes on his way with the sceptre of the Lord in his hand, followed by his wife and child. The fatherless child has found a supernatural father in the Lord of Hosts and is at last induced by him to head the rebellion of his people against the father of the country, the Pharaoh. Throughout the narrative that follows the acute ambivalency of the father-son relation is marked by doubling the original pair. If the Pharaoh will not let Israel perform the sacrifice at Mount Sinai, the King of Heaven will strike the firstborn of Egypt, for is not Israel the firstborn of the Lord ? And now comes the peculiarly archaic episode that explains the origin of circumcision. Although intending to kill the son (the firstborn) Jahve attacks the father, Moses, and tries to kill him. His wife Zippora comes to the rescue ; with a sharp stone she cuts the prepuce of her son and with it she touches the feet (or the penis ?) of Jahve (or of Moses ?) and says, "Thou art a blood bridegroom to me ! " And then he desisted.[1]

The uncertainty of the translation offers almost insurmountable difficulties to any attempt at explanation. If, however, we remember that circumcision is originally a puberty ceremony we shall regard Moses and his son as originally one and the same person, while the subsequent decomposition is the symptom of an ambivalent situation. Then Jahve would correspond to the initiation-demons of primitive tribes who intend to kill the novice but at last are satisfied with the prepuce as a substitute. It would then be the newly circumcised who was originally called " blood-spouse " and circumcision would be the preparatory act of marriage. The ceremony takes place at the moment when Moses is about to commence his career as a hero ; the fit time for initiation. It is significant that Moses, the hero of this initiation-myth, should be connected with Osiris in whose myth castration plays such a prominent part and that, nevertheless, the circumcised is regarded as a bridegroom. And then the other explanatory myth : Abraham is the first to be circumcised and this is his covenant with the Lord. As supreme reward for his fidelity he is promised the birth of a son, and in general, innumerable progeny.[2]

Now there is what seems a contradiction between the psycho-analytical explanation of circumcision and the alleged intention of this

---

[1] *Exodus*, iv, 24.　　　[2] Moses, i, 17.

rite. Those who practise the rite regard it as an introduction to sexual intercourse and this explanation has been accepted by various ethnologists.

The Central Australian custom of burying the foreskin in trees or throwing it into a water-pool where it makes the water-lilies (child-symbol) grow has led Frazer to a similar hypothesis.[1] He reminds us of the fact that in Unmatjera traditions, the Alcheringa ancestors put their foreskins in their Nanja-trees [2] and it is from the Nanja-tree that reincarnation takes place.

But we have been able to show that the Nanja-tree is simply a substitute for the mother just as reincarnation is a veiled representation of incestuous intercourse.[3] The foreskin in the Nanja-tree would therefore be equivalent to the penis in the mother and the central ritual of initiation would mean both renouncing and symbolically realizing the incest-wish. In the Chad basin it is the custom to bury the foreskin in the same sort of hole that receives the sacrifices sent to Mother-Earth.[4]

Is there no possibility of reconciling these contradictory hypotheses?

We remember that circumcision is really not an equivalent but a mitigation of castration. In this case the mitigation must be due to some dynamic agency acting in the elder generation and this can be no other than the protecting aspect of fatherhood, the tendencies of love and identification with the younger generation. This identification is effected by means of the penis as common ego-ideal. What happens is this. The elder generation starts to castrate the younger and what they really do is to make the penis appear as if it were in a *perpetual state of erection*. Erection itself has been described by Ferenczi [5] as the coming out, the birth of the glans penis from the foreskin, and this might be the unconscious reason why our primitive tribes regard the circumcised as born a second time, born for sexual life. But the fundamental explanation of the part played by castration and castration-rites in the evolution of humanity lies deeper. The equivalence of punishment and gratification in the unconscious has long been noticed by psycho-analysis. What even if castration itself, the punishment for incest, be determined by some deeply latent causal relation? We again refer to Ferenczi's interpretation of the

---

[1] Cf. Frazer, " The Origin of Circumcision," *Independent Review*, 1904, pp. 204–18. *Totemism and Exogamy*, iv, p. 181.

[2] Spencer and Gillen, *Northern Tribes of C. A.*, p. 341.

[3] Róheim, *Australian Totemism*, p. 1925.

[4] L. Frobenius, *Und Afrika sprach*, 1913, iii, p. 139.

[5] S. Ferenczi, *Versuch einer Genitaltheorie*, 1924.

sexual act as an attempt at autotomy, self-castration, as an attempt to get rid of the pain-engrams left by the traumata of the phylogenetic past. In this case we should have a double explanation of our ritual ; initiation (symbolic castration, circumcision) *is both an archaic introduction, a prelude to sexual life, and a punishment for incestuous desire ; the scapegoat ritual, as social castration, is both the expiation of sin and the repetition of the sinful deed.*

There are two sides to every medal, two scapegoats in Athens and Jerusalem. One of them for Azazel, the phallic demon, the rebellious son, for the being who represents sin. The other for Jahve, another phallic demon, the imperious father, the being who represents virtue. Among the Mandan we have the Medicine Pipe [1] and the phallic evil being. The fate of the two goats is different—the one for Jahve is sacrificed at the altar, the other driven into the desert. Can we lay any stress on this difference ? I think it points to the close connection and differentiation of the ego-ideal from the repressed. By inhibiting détente, deflecting the libidinal strivings from their original aim and maintaining them at a certain equilibrium, the cementing forces of society are formed. Here we have identification instead of object-eroticism and the ego with its conflicts bulks prominent in the social structure. There are two features of the primal conflict represented in the initiation rites, death at the hands of the Father-God and castration by him. It is evident that in fighting, killing, there is a relatively greater admixture of the death-impulses than in castration, and thus the goat is sacrificed to Jahve the super-ego but chased into the desert for Azazel. A " goat " leads both to the ego-ideal and the repressed, through the goat Israel acknowledges and disclaims its sins. Moreover, as fission is the fundamental phenomenon represented in our ceremony, since the expulsion of the goat is itself a sort of social fission, it would be natural to assume that there was a functional element in the ritual, that duality represented fission itself.[2]

But a functional explanation alone is no explanation. There must be some tendency in this doubling and we have not far to seek for it. One goat is killed, the other saved : it seems as if after having formed a substitute for the body in the scapegoat another substitute for the scapegoat was introduced to cancel the effect of the rite. The scapegoat dies for the community : but identification with the penis-substitute produces a second substitute who is not killed but turned

---

[1] For the phallic interpretation of the pipe cf. above.
[2] Cf. I. Hermann, *Psychoanalyse und Logik*, 1925.

loose. That is : if castration is inevitable there had better be two phalli so that one, at any rate, remains. Perhaps these two phalli are then identified with the nipples : for in Athens one of the *pharmakoi* represents the female sex.

The circumcision of Abraham atones for, as it contains, all sins, and as Isaac was rescued by the substitution of a ram, Israel, the firstborn of god, is saved by the substitution of a goat.

7 CATHARTIC RITUAL

Having this far sought for the physiological equivalent of our rite we should not like to neglect the psychic phenomena that are either the corollaries of these life-processes or derived from them. In the ritual of confession we have a frequent corollary (Jerusalem, Eskimo) of the scapegoat ceremony and a primitive prototype of psycho-analysis itself. It is well known that psycho-analysis was developed from cathartic therapy and this again was a sort of confession. True, there is an essential difference between even the simplest forms of the cathartic method and confession pure and simple. In analysis, it is the repressed which is got rid of by verbal repetition ; in confession, it is only the conscious. How do we lift repressed concepts into the higher psychic systems ? By a new libidinal cathexis they become connected in the fore-conscious with word-concepts and thence find their way into consciousness. Undoubtedly something similar takes place when we get rid of a conscious secret ; the outspoken word means an approach to reality and another step away from the unconscious. By confession another person or persons become cognizant of the secret and share in the weight of guilt which is thus partly projected to them. A confession of sins is a repetition of them and the person to whom they are confessed is a new partner in committing them. We might also say that they are projected to this second person, at least, the analogy with this psychical process is suggested by certain forms of the ritual. It looks like projection when the priest confesses the sins of the people and lays his hands on the head of the goat. Projection is still more evident in the forms of the rite where we have actual throwing ; the god is stoned, the sins of the people transferred to him by means of these stones. The fundamental feature of the whole rite is that something is thrown out of the social body, and we have explained this fundamental feature as a super-organic repetition of cohabitation. But if a ritual that is certainly a typical case of projection can be traced back to coitus, may this contention not be valid for projection itself ? Or if somebody resents the materialistic point of view, may we not at least call projection the psychic analogy to cohabitation ? [1] In cohabitation substances of a traumatic nature are " thrown out " of the body of the male into that of the female and at the same time the male forces his psychical and physical rhythm on the female. Something similar takes place in projection ; a psychical content, " substance " is treated as if it did not belong to the subject but to another person, i.e. " thrown out ". Psycho-analytic experience shows that there is frequently a fundamental truth, a " Dialogue of the Unconscious ", a unity at the bottom of this projection, and it is certain that the greatest degree of unity between two living beings is attained at the moment of orgasm. If it could be shown that projection was the characteristic psychic attitude of the male and introjection of the female the hypothetical analogy with coitus would decidedly gain force.

Two other fundamental features of the Day of Atonement are fasting and the confession of sins. According to Jewish ideas, anyone who assumes a high public office after confession of his sins in the past is " made a new creature free from sin like a child ".[2] The scholar, the bridegroom, the Nasi, and the proselyte, they all must fast, confess their sins and are born anew.[3] The cathartic ritual of the Luperci is performed at a cave at the very place where the ancestral twins, Romulus and Remus landed, and Rank has shown that the hero coming out of the water is the child coming forth from the womb.[4]

We shall gain further insight into the inter-relation of these phenomena by studying the Japanese ritual of *Oho-harahi*, " the great Purification," and its mythical prototypes. We have to deal with two ceremonies, the *Oniyarahi* or demon-expelling and the *Oho-harahi* or great purification, both performed on the last day of the year. The demons expelled are personified wintry influences with the diseases they bring with them, while the *Oho-harahi* purifies people from sin and disease. Four bands of twenty youths, each wearing a four-eyed mask, march simultaneously from the four gates of the palace driving the devils before them. A man is disguised as a demon of pestilence and driven off with peach-wood bows and arrows of reed. It used to be the custom at Asakusa in Tokio for

[1] Cf. the chapter on projection in *Psychoanalysis and Social Anthropology*.
[2] *Sanh.*, 14, a *Midr. Sam.*, xvii.
[3] *Yer. Bik.*, iii, 65, c. d. *Midr. Sam.*, loc. cit. [1] and [2] quoted from the article on " Atonement ", *Jewish Encyclopedia*, p. 280.
[4] O. Rank, *Der Mythus von der Geburt des Helden*, 1922.

a man got up as a devil to be chased round by another wearing a mask on the last day of the year. 3,000 tickets were scrambled for by spectators and pasted up over the doors as a charm against pestilence. Parched beans are scattered over the city and the saying is : " Out with the devils and in with luck." [1] In the Shogun's palace a specially appointed *toshi-otoko* (" year-man "), a substitute for the head of the family (that is, for the Shogun) sprinkled parched beans in all the rooms. The women would pick them up in a number equal to the years of their age and fling them backwards to fling away ill-luck. At the same time the *Oho-harahi*, a ceremony to " purge offences and rectify transgressions ", is performed. It consists of a preliminary lustration, expiatory offerings, and the recital of a formula. [2] These expiatory offerings, the *harahitsumono*, were regarded in the same light as the scapegoat, as material vehicles by which the transgressions of the people were conveyed away. [3]

The notion of expiating ritual guilt by giving ransom is familiar to the Japanese. The more intimately the objects offered are connected with the person of the offender the more effectual is the sacrifice. Among objects of ransom presented by the Mikado at purification ceremonies, clothing is by far the most important. The clothing was put in a vase, the Mikado breathed on it three times, and then returned it to be taken away by the diviners and thrown into a stream. [4]

The parallelism between the spirits of disease on the one hand and the sins of the people on the other, between the man who is expelled as a personification of disease and the parts of the body severed from man as material vehicles of impurity, is very instructive. But the real *ex Oriente lux* will be thrown on our subject when we examine the two mythical prototypes of our purification ceremonies.

At the beginning there was the divine couple, brother and sister, Izana-gi-oho-m-kami and Izanami-oho-mi-kami. After walking round the " Jewel-Spear " or pillar of Heaven, correctly explained by Hirata and others as a phallic symbol, they begin to procreate an endless array of gods. The last deity they produced was the Fire-God and in giving birth to him Izanami's vagina was burnt so that she sickened and died. During her illness she vomited the deities of metals, she defecated the earth-gods, and her urine was transformed into the deities of water.

But the grief of her lord and brother knew no bounds. He killed his son who had lost him his sister-wife and followed her to

---

[1] Aston, *Shinto*, 1905, pp. 308, 309.
[2] Aston, loc. cit., p. 294.
[3] Aston, loc. cit., p. 302.
[4] Aston, loc. cit., p. 262.

the Nether World. She is touched by the appearance of her lord and although she has tasted the food of Hades she attempts to obtain her release from the Dark Powers and return with her lord to the Land of Light. But there is one condition to be observed. He may not look round to see what she is doing. But " Izanagi did not give ear to her, he secretly took his many-toothed comb, and breaking off its end-tooth made of it a torch and looked at her ". Her body was already putrid, maggots swarmed over it, and the eight thunder gods had been generated in her various members.[1]

Now these two episodes are so important that we are tempted to explain them before going on with our narrative. The end-tooth of the comb is the famous *wo-bashira*. " The *wo-bashira* (male pillar) is doubtless only a modified phallus (*kunado*). This term is applied to the end post of a railing of a bridge or of the balustrade of a staircase and is so called from its obviously phallic shape and function." [2]

Making a torch of the " male-pillar " by which to penetrate into darkness would therefore be more than looking, it would mean an attempt of the male to penetrate into the female by means of the " male-pillar ". But what he sees changes his desire to anxiety, his lust into a precipitated, headlong flight. The exact translation given by Florenz, helps us to comprehend the meaning of this sight :
" *Da es von Maden schwärmte und sie in Fäulnis zergangen war, und in ihrem Kopfe befand sich der Grosse Donner, in ihrer Brust befand sich der Feuer Donner, in ihrem Bauche befand sich der schwarze Donner, in ihrer Scheide befand sich der Spalt-Donner, in ihrer linken Hand befand sich der Junge Donner in ihrem rechten Hand befand sich der Erd-Donner, in ihrem linken Fuss befand sich der rollende Donner in ihrem rechten Fuss befand sich der liegende Donner,—insgesamt waren acht Donner-gottheiten entstanden und vorhanden.*" [3]

But she says :
" Thou my beloved Sovran-Husband ! If thou dost this, I will kill 1,000 of the human-grass of your country day by day."

And Izanagi answered :
" Thou my beloved Sovran Younger Sister ! If thou dost this I will raise 1,500 birth-huts day by day. Then certainly a thousand men will die a day but 1,500 will be born ! " [4]

Again we pause. This is an account of the origin of death.

[1] Aston, loc. cit., pp. 86–93. K. Florenz, *Die historischen Quellen der Shinto Religion*, 1919, pp. 13–23.

[2] Aston, loc. cit., p. 190.

[3] Florenz, loc. cit., 23.   [4] Florenz, loc. cit., p. 21.

Death is due to the revenge of Izanami for the separation of her brother and lord ; *but this separation is his birth.*

Had Izanagi not been born (separated) from his sister, i.e. mother, we should not die. Izanagi concludes the episode by having 1,500 birth-huts erected a day.

It is evident that all these thunders are only mythical exaggerations of the one thunder, " the cleaving thunder " in woman's vagina, i.e. the child who cleaves the vagina in twain by being born. This points to an important conclusion : the " male-pillar " desiring to penetrate into woman is stopped by something, by an anxiety. This anxiety is represented by a woman who is about to give birth to " a thunder ", i.e. it is derived from the birth-shock.

To make assurance doubly sure we will now refer to a parallel version of this episode in the myth of Hohodemi. In the Nihongi version of this myth, Hohodemi transforms the *Wo-bashira* of his comb into a torch and by its light he, although forbidden by her, espies his wife, transformed into a sea-monster, in the very act of giving birth. As in the myth of Izanagi, a separation of the lovers is the consequence of the transgression.[1]

Now for the sequel of the myth of Izanagi. " What a hideous and polluted land I have come to unawares," he exclaims, thus identifying the polluted woman with the polluted land. In fact it would seem that his flight upward from the " polluted " nether world is nothing but the child's escape from the " polluted " vagina. He is pursued by the Ugly Females of Yomi and escapes, throwing various objects behind him on his way. The last object thrown backwards by him are peaches, generally used in exorcism and recognized by Aston [2] as the symbol of the vagina. It would not be the first case in which exorcism follows the principle of *idem per idem.* Izanagi blocks up the passage of the underworld by a great rock and pronounces the divorce formula against the pursuing Izanami.

However, if we continue to analyse the myth, at this point we must ask who is the hero of the story. The answer is, the August Male who invites, i.e. the Phallus. And then : what is the dire result of coitus, of breaking through the taboo ? Answer : the separation of male from female after coitus. For in the moment of supreme orgasm male and female are a unity and when the seminal fluid is separated from the penis this unity is dissolved. Having found that the great resistance is directed against the loss of the seminal

[1] Florenz, loc. cit., p. 210.　　　　[2] Aston, loc. cit., p. 109.

fluid, we may regard the unity attained in coitus as a device of nature to conquer this resistance. The loss of semen becomes possible since there is no loss at all if the vital fluid has been projected into an environment that has been identified with the ego. Identification is the means of overcoming the anxiety and it is by identification with the seminal fluid that the male regresses to the birth shock, while the female probably does the same by identifying herself with her child. The fundamental anxiety is at the loss of a part of the body and hence the consolation consists in regressing to an original archaic scene when something was severed yet nothing was lost, for the part that was cut off was identical with the whole. It is evidently true that Izanagi's ascent from the shades is his birth ; but this flight is not the reason for death and purification. The reason is the torch made out of the male pillar, and the only possible consolation for him after coitus is birth, i.e. the identification with the seminal fluid.[1]

Then Izanagi declares that he has been in a polluted, dirty land and that a *purification* of his august body is absolutely necessary. This is the first prototype of the present purificatory ceremonies and demands our careful attention. The ritual is simple enough ; it consists in throwing things away. The conclusion is unavoidable that what we call a " sense of guilt " goes back to a more primitive attitude, that it is the equivalent of anxiety and represents it in a more integrated psychic system. Anxiety again is tension and the method to get rid of it is an autotomic reaction. But as he throws the objects away they give rise to new deities, just as primitive organisms give rise to new individuals by splitting and just as the spermatozoön ejected in the cathartic act of coitus gives rise to new beings.

" From the august staff thrown away by him originated the deity called " Standing erect pass not here ". The name of the deity who sprang up from the girdle was " the long path of the way ". From his skirt sprang up the deity " Untie put down ", from his jacket the deity " Master of Disease ", from his trousers the god of crossways.[2] Now these gods of the way, like the hermae of Greece, are phallic images, thus confirming the conclusion we came to above that the " material vehicle " of sins, the object that is ejected, is the bearer of life.

[1] This view presupposes the fundamental anxiety of the whole, not of the severed part ; for the male in coitus, for the woman in giving birth. Now it is Izanami (not the child) who dies when she gives birth.

[2] Florenz, loc. cit., pp. 26, 27.

Izanagi, after having thrown away his clothing, dives into the middle current and washes his body. Further deities arise as a result of this purification. These are " the Wonderful God of the Eighty Evils " (or Dirts), " the Wonderful God Who Heals," " the Great God Who Heals," " the Powerful Woman." When he dived to the bottom to continue his ablutions the divinities that sprang up were " the Lord of the Sea Bottom ", the venerable " Old Man of the Sea Bottom ", and so on.

Thus the ritual purification after the coitus myth of the nether world voyage consists in a series of life-giving acts and the gods of disease, i.e. of anxiety from disease, spring up from these repetitions of coitus followed by the healing agencies. Then we have the beings of the sea-bottom, the meaning of which will be discussed in connection with Dionysus.

The myth of Susanowo containing the second purification episode in mythology is a slightly modified repetition of the incestuous love-myth of Izanagi.

Susanowo was ordered by his father Izanagi to become Prince of the Sea. But he howled continually, as he wanted to go to the Land of the Hereafter, to his mother Izanami. His father thereupon banished him to the shades, that is, told him to do the very thing he wanted to do. But before departing he wished to take leave of his sister, the Sun Goddess Ama-terasu-oho-mi-kami. But the Sun Goddess was far from pleased at his arrival. She confronted her brother in manly garb, wearing her royal necklace of jewels and armed with sword and bow. The pair stood face to face, but Susanowo assured his sister that he had not come to rob her of her lands. To prove the purity of his intentions he proposed that they should produce children by biting off and crunching bits of the jewels they wore and blowing away the fragments. Susanowo considered himself justified and waxed insolent. He broke up the divisions between his sister's ricefields, stopped up the ditches of water between the fields, sowed them over again, and let the piebald colt of heaven loose in the fields. A still more heinous offence was his defecating in the hall of the new palace where the Sun Goddess and her court were celebrating the festival of the new rice, a ceremony that demanded special attention to religious purity.[1] All this would have been forgiven by his sister had he not flayed the piebald colt of heaven backwards and then made a hole in the sacred weaving hall where the Sun Goddess and her ladies were engaged in weaving

---

[1] Florenz, loc. cit., p. 37. Aston, loc. cit., p. 277.

the garments of the gods. They were so frightened that they pricked their own vaginas with their spindles and died. The Sun Goddess herself was so indignant that she retired into the rock-cave of Heaven and left the world to darkness.[1]

The great purification ceremony is ordered at present for heavenly and earthly transgressions. The offences of Heaven are those committed by Susanowo in Heaven, to wit : the breaking down of divisions between ricefields, filling up of irrigation channels, removing water pipes, sowing seed over again, planting skewers, flaying alive, flaying backwards. The earthly offences seem somehow to form a corresponding group. Here, mischief done to the human body is the centre of attention, there mischief done to the ricefield. The earthly offences are : Cutting of living bodies, cutting of dead bodies, leprosy, incest of a man with his mother or daughter, bestiality, killing animals, bewitchments, etc.[2]

We suspect that the mischief done to his sister's ricefield is merely the " heavenly ", i.e. symbolical equivalent of what appears in the second list as incest. The salient feature of the myth is that the weaving goddesses die when they prick their vagina with the spindles, and it is evident that these goddesses are only a series of repetitions of Amaterasu herself. Izanami dies because the fire-child burns her vagina,[3] and the vaginal wound precedes the retreat of the Sun Goddess into the rock cave. The nether world, whither Izanami goes, and this rock cave, are both equivalents of the one goddess, and it is not she but rather the male, the torch, the spindle, who penetrates into the realm of darkness. The seeming lack of logic in the construction of the Susanowo myth is a proof of these conjectures. For the myth begins by the " Imperious Quick Turbulent Male " crying with desire to go to the nether land to see, like his father before him, his divine mother. Izanagi's wrath at hearing this request and his ordering his son to do the very thing (as a punishment) that he most desired to do are both characteristic and speak for themselves.[4] But then the Imperious Male turns to Heaven instead of Hell, seeks his sister instead of his mother, procreates children with her (as his father did with *his* sister) and then repeats this incest in a symbolical manner. The fact that the goddesses are weaving, and the hole in the weaving hall all have their easily

[1] Aston, loc. cit., pp. 97, 100. Florenz, loc. cit., pp. 37, 38.
[2] Aston, loc. cit., pp. 299, 300.
[3] Cf. the phallus of her husband appearing in the same myth as a torch.
[4] Florenz, loc. cit., p. 30.

comprehensible symbolic meaning, while the colt flayed backwards seems to be the penis in erection.[1]

After the reappearance of the Sun Goddess from her dark cave, which corresponds in the Izanagi myth to the reappearance of that divinity from the world below, we have, just as in the first case, the purification of the Male God.

Then Susanowo is condemned to the sacrifice of the "thousand tables"; his hair, finger, and toenails are cut. From the nails of his fingers they made "the good things to be thrown away", from those of his toes, the "bad things to be thrown away". There is still much superstitious anxiety in Japan connected with the cutting of finger-nails and they are usually buried in the earth.

This cutting of finger-nails (castration) represents one aspect of the process, the other is contained in the descent of the Imperious Male to the nether world (coitus). But the sufferings of the "thousand tables" containing the sins of Susanowo were thrown into the sea by the gods, thus carrying all the sins to the nether world as their place of origin. We shall follow them to their destiny in studying the cult of Dionysus.

There are connecting links between the ideas of the Dionysiac cult and the myth of Izanami. Izanami dies when giving birth to a child of fire; Semele is consumed by the heavenly fire of her lover Zeus, the house is set on fire and the unborn babe rescued from the flames by his omnipotent father.[2] Indeed, the central feature of Dionysiac myth and religion is the idea of the dismembered child, or if we put the same thing in a more general fashion, of the dangers to which the new-born is subjected. From these dangers he is sometimes rescued, or he may succumb to them, and in this latter case the infanticide committed is the sin that is expiated and repeated in ritual.

Zagreus, the son of Zeus by his daughter Persephone, was dismembered and eaten by the Titans when engaged in childish play (Hyginus) or in the shape of a bull, and according to Firmicus Maternus a bull was always torn to pieces to commemorate the event. They ate everything but the heart; this was swallowed by his father Zeus or given to Semele who drank it and gave birth to Dionysus.[3]

The nature of a god is revealed by his enemies. Now the Titans

---

[1] Pulling back the foreskin.

[2] Nonn. Dionys., 8, 193. Apoll. Rhod., 4, 1137. Höfer, "Semele," in *Roschers Lexikon*, iv, p. 671.

[3] F. Voigt, "Dionysos," *Roschers Lexikon*, i, p. 1056.

who attacked Dionysus painted themselves white all over with gypsum.[1] In commenting on Demosthenes, Harpocration tells us that the initiates into the mysteries were painted in memory of these Titans, whereas the latter were painted white lest they should be recognized as the murderers of the young deity.[2] There can be no doubt about the meaning of this scene, the boy who is killed and resuscitated by initiates in the white guise of ghosts is the novice at the puberty ceremony. To make assurance doubly sure we have the casual remark of Clement, that Dionysus was playing with the *bull-roarer* when surprised by the Titans.[3] The Titans devoured the morsels, but the heart was rescued by Zeus. Lightning strikes the rebels, and from their ashes humanity originates, fraught with the heritage of the sin of the Titans. Refuge from this sin is sought in Orphic initiation.[4]

The Titans represent a former generation of gods, they are led by Cronos the father of Zeus in their insurrection against Uranus and Gaea. They divide the parents, Heaven and Earth, lying in close embrace, and castrate their father Uranus. It is perhaps not superfluous to re-learn what we already know, and here we are told in so many words that the demons who castrated their father are those who initiate youth.

Heaven and Earth in close embrace, the unborn gods in their mother's dark womb from which they are released only after their great deed ; does this not look as if the separation of Uranus from Gaea meant the birth-shock also ?

We must pause for a moment to reconsider the myth of Dionysus. Zeus and the Titans seem to take opposite sides in the battle yet they both equally devour the flesh of the young god. Now we have a single version of the myth,[5] according to which Dionysus was attacked by the Titans when viewing his own image, this being his attempt to gain mastery over the world. Had he succeeded he would have done to his father Zeus just what he before him had done to Cronos, his sire. There was a prophecy according to which the goddess Metis would first bear to Zeus a daughter, Athene Tritogenia, equal in wisdom to her father, and then a son, who would in his turn be king of gods and men. To prevent this, Metis

---

[1] Weniger, " Feralis exercitus," *A.R.W.*, ix, p. 232.
[2] Weniger, loc. cit., p. 242. Harrison, *Themis*, pp. 14–16.
[3] Harrison, op. cit., p. 14.
[4] S. Reinach, *Cultes, Mythes et Religions*, 1909, ii, p. 59.
[5] E. Rohde, *Psyche*, 1907, ii, p. 117.

is swallowed by Zeus when *enceinte* with Athene, and it is thus that the goddess of wisdom is born from the head of Zeus.[1]

Instead of Zeus we see a mother goddess in action at this second birth, his mother Demeter, who pieced his mangled limbs together and made him young again.[2]

In our myth Athena plays a part in rescuing the heart of Dionysus; does this not indicate a link between the two myths in which Zeus gives birth instead of procreating? For after being killed by the Titans, it is Zeus who becomes second mother to the Babe-God.

> " Achelöus' roaming daughter,
> Holy Dirce, virgin water,
> Bathed he not of old in thee,
> The Babe of God, the Mystery?
> When from out the fire immortal
> To himself his God did take him,
> To his own flesh, and bespake him:
> ' Enter now life's second portal,
> Motherless Mystery; lo, I break
> Mine own body for thy sake,
> Thou of the Twofold Door, and seal thee
> Mine, O Bromiso '—thus he spake—
> 'And to this thy land reveal thee'." [3]

The god appears as the babe's second mother for the ritual of initiation, i.e. rebirth from a male being is an attempt to eliminate the mother-fixation and also the danger threatening the father from the Oedipus complex. But perhaps it is more than this, for Zeus has swallowed Metis: he is a condensation of father and mother. He forms a unity with the Titans: they represent the dangers of the birth-act, he actually gives birth to the god. Is not initiation a repetition of birth?

There is more than one way to prove this view. The Titans and Zeus are male beings, true; but the reason why they prosecute the god is the jealousy of Hera against Semele. More important still is it that this tearing to pieces is re-acted in the cult by women, the Maenads or Bacchae, and the mythical prototypes of these women are the nurses, i.e. the mothers, of Dionysus.

The calf of the roe and kids were rent asunder by the raving women.[4] In Potniai a kid was sacrificed to Dionysus Aigobolus as a substitute for a beautiful boy.[5] In Chios a man was torn to

---

[1] *Roschers Lexikon*, iii, p. 2939. [2] *Diodorus Siculus*, iii, 62.

[3] Euripides, *Bacchae*, 518. Translation quoted from J. E. Harrison, *Themis*, 1912, p. 33.

[4] Voigt, " Dionysos," in *R.L.*, p. 1037. [5] Voigt, loc. cit., p. 1038.

pieces and sacrificed to Dionysus Ὀμάδιος. The Maenads tear one of their own children to pieces, the Proetids of Sicyon and the women of Argos devour infants, and Nonnus attributes the same cannibalistic appetite to the first nurses of Dionysus.[1] Pentheus, " the man of sorrows," is changed into an animal by the god and in this shape he is torn to pieces by his own mother.[2]

Now there is no doubt that whatever that the Bacchic processions were intended to promote the fertility of the country. We shall only note one case ; Aristotle tells us that the God was expected to appear in a column of fire to the community in the country of the Bisaltae ; and this apparition meant a plentiful year.[3] It is in fire that he is born and in fecundity rites he is rent to pieces by the women : what could be more in accordance with the avowed aim of the ritual than a mimetic representation of the birth of the god of fertility ? To quote Jane Harrison : " *The Dithyramb, as we have seen, is a birth song,*" a δρώμενον, giving rise to the divine figures of Mother, Full-grown Son and Child ; it is a spring song of magical fertility for the new year, it is a group song, a κύκλιος χόρος, sung by a thiasos of those who leap and dance rhythmically together. *Di-thur-ambos* is really " Zeus-leap-song ", the song that makes Zeus leap or beget,[4] and in the centre of his thiasos he appears as Dionysus Liknites, " He of the Winnowing Fan." For it is said that at birth he was placed in a winnowing fan as a cradle, and it was the general practice in Greece and elsewhere to place infants in winnowing fans as an omen of wealth and fertility.[5]

Now that we know what the dismembered child means we shall perhaps be able to understand the events that take place at the festival of the Agrionia. The daughters of Minyas were overwhelmed by their lust for human flesh and one of the infants they devoured was the son of Leucippus. Ever since this horrible deed the men of this clan have been called the " Mourners " on account of their grief and the women " the Destroyers ". At Orchomenus the women of the clan had annually to expiate this ancient sin at the spring festival of the Agrionia. They were chased by the priest of Dionysus and if he caught one of them, he had the right to kill her.[6]

It seems that the spring festival of souls, the Anthesteria in Athens, is the equivalent of the Agrionia. At this festival the queen was married to the representative of the god whose *sparagmos* (dismemberment) was probably performed as a prelude to his marriage.

[1] Voigt, loc. cit., p. 1038.   [2] Voigt, loc. cit., p. 1054.
[3] Voigt, loc. cit., p. 1031.   [4] Harrison, *Themis*, p. 203.
[5] Frazer, *Spirits*, i, p. 6.   [6] Schwenn, *Menschenopfer*, p. 55.

Moreover, we know that the reappearance of the god at this festival was symbolized by a boat on wheels ; that is, he came from beyond the sea.[1] The latter detail is significant because at the Agrionia, as performed at Chaeronea, we have the reversal of this situation, the women in search of Dionysus but not finding him, for he has escaped to the Muses.[2] Now the Muses are originally goddesses of water and Dionysus, nurtured by the nymphs, must find the new company familiar to him from his infancy.

If we rely on the parallel with the *hieros gamos* at the Anthesteria we may well expect that the ritual in question has something to do with fecundity. A parallel case of female φάρμακοι is the Locrian custom of sending two noble girls to the temple of Athena at Ilium. They were φάρμακοι, chased and killed by the Trojans, their ashes were thrown into the sea. The event was said to commemorate the cohabitation of Ajax with the chaste Cassandra in the temple of the goddess.[3] Thus, perhaps, the women chased and killed for their sins may in both cases represent coitus, and then the whole ritual would become easy to comprehend. It is because the child has been dismembered, i.e. as a consequence of the birth-shock, that the priest must always chase the women, i.e. the male must renew his attempt to regain the prenatal situation.

At Tenedos we have the same ritual. A pregnant cow is treated as if it were a woman. The calf is killed by a priest with a double axe, and the murderer chased to the sea by throwing stones at him.[4] As luck would have it the double axe is mentioned in a very similar myth.

The god who appears at the head of his nurses is confronted by his heroic double Lycurgus, and driven into the sea with the double axe. In his terror he rushes headlong into the waves till at the bottom of the sea he finds protection in the lap of Thetis.[5]

The necessity of condensing the two actors into one in both cases is no serious obstacle in identifying the myth with the ritual. The human calf, killed with the double axe, is of course the god himself, whom Lycurgus with the double axe, called ox-driver, drives into the lap of Thetis. In another variant, it is Perseus who has killed the god and thrown his corpse into the sea at Lerna.[6] As for Lycurgus, he is a heroic double and a priest of Dionysus. We have interpreted

---

[1] Nilsson, *Griechische Feste*, 1906, pp. 269, 270. Frazer, *Spirits*, i, pp. 31, 32.

[2] Nilsson, loc. cit., p. 274.   [3] Schwenn, op. cit., p. 47.

[4] Voigt, in *Roschers Lexikon*, vol. i, p. 1056.

[5] *Idem*, ibid., p. 1050.   [6] *Idem*, ibid., p. 1057.

the scapegoat ritual in terms of the relation between the body and the penis or germ-plasm. In the ritual we might say that the body is represented by the multitude and the phallus by the priest driven into the sea : in the myth, Lycurgus is the relentless body and Dionysus, driven into the lap of a goddess, represents the phallus or germ-plasm.

For identifying Dionysus with the phallus, there happens to be abundant evidence, especially in connection with the submarine and nether-world aspects of his cult. In the country Dionysiac festivals, the phallus is personified as the friend and drinking companion of Dionysus. This personification may be due to the poetic liberty taken by Aristophanes : according to Athenagoras it is the god himself who is carried in the ithyphallic procession, that is, the god is the phallus. Priapus, the local deity of Lampsacus, was either identical with or a son of Dionysus.[1]

According to the legend of Argos as told by Pausanias, Polymnos showed the god the way through the depths of the sea at Lerna when Dionysus descended to the nether world to fetch his mother Semele. According to other variants of the myth, there was an obscene but mythologically very significant condition connected with this service done to the god : " si sibi gereret morem atque uxorias voluptates pateretur ex se carpi." According to one version the god did as he was bidden and descended to the other world with his guide. But where the god could triumph the mortal succumbed, and Polymnos died during the journey.[2]

Mythologists seem to agree in one detail : that Polymnos or Prosymnos was originally one of the names of Dionysus. Buttman's explanation, who reads Pros-limnos, " He who is adored at the *limné*, i.e. sea of Lerna," is not generally accepted but Polumnos, " He of the many songs " is Dionysus himself. Dionysus flies to the Muses when sought for by the women at Chaeronea, and one of his nurses is called Polymno. Philamnos, who established the mysteries of the god at Lerna, is called a son of Polyhymnia.[3] But Poluhumnos was also a name given in antiquity to the phallus.[4]

Myth hints at many things. At Tenedos and in the myth of Lycurgus we had two representatives of the Dionysiac idea *chasing and killing each other*. Here we find them in intercourse with each other, and one of them is the penis. The penis " *dies* " in going down to the *nether world* in search of his mother, but who then is the

---

[1] *Idem*, ibid., pp. 1062, 1063.
[2] *Roschers Lexikon*, article " Polymnos ", p. 2659.
[3] Ibid., 2659.   [4] Ibid., 2660.

Dionysus who triumphantly reappears and with his rescued mother ascends to Olympic honours ? We know him well as the god in the cradle (Liknites)—" his Majesty the Baby ! " For the penis is the child and the child is the penis, the corpse of the god thrown into the sea at Lerna by Perseus and reappearing among the women of Elis as the bovine spirit of fertility.

We might thus come to the conclusion that birth is the original sin of the Dionysiac cult and Orphic mystery. This event would be re-enacted in the *sparagmos*, whereas the scapegoat ceremonies, chasing the god to the underworld below the sea, are dramatic representations of coitus as an attempt to regain the prenatal and thalassal environment.

However, according to a popular epigram,[1] the goat dies as an expiatory sacrifice for having attacked the vine. What does this condensed statement mean ? That the god dies for a sin committed by him. What is meant by the attack on the vine we can gather from the myth of Lycurgus. This second Dionysus, who drives the god into the sea, dies for his temerity and his sin is an attack upon the vine. Blinded by Dionysiac fury, he kills his father or son Dryas, commits incest with his mother, and in doing so he thinks he is attacking the plant of the god.[2]

Moreover, we should expect to find a babe in the cradle, yet frequently find the male organ of generation. The Titans who dismember Dionysus are the same who castrate their father Uranus, and whose leader Cronos is in his turn castrated by his son Zeus. If this is so, we can interpret the ritual of the dismembered child as representing the castrated penis, and the chasing of the scapegoat into the sea as a repetition of the same event.

But if this is possible we must consider whether we have not made a slight mistake. What we have shown is that dismemberment is represented in myth as birth. This does not prove that it actually means birth. If we consider the whole mythological situation we have first Cronos and the Titans castrating Uranus, then Zeus doing the same to Cronos and finally the prophecy uttered predicting the same fate in the future for Zeus. To escape from his doom he reverses the situation and turns the tables against the child-god. Dionysus, however, is not castrated but only cut to pieces and even this is mitigated into a second birth. We have shown that the scene is derived from an initiation ritual and initiation is a mitigated form of castration.

---

[1] Voigt, loc. cit., p. 1058.　　　　[2] Ibid., p. 1051.

If dismemberment is already a substitute for castration we shall regard the whole fertility cult with the women raving round the phallus as an over-compensation of the dread of castration. We have a whole series with decreasing intensity ; first castration, then dismemberment, then birth, and finally driving a scapegoat into the sea.

For we must not forget that ritual is a means of dispelling anxiety, of substituting something analogous for the object of real dread. *Instead of castration we are told it is birth or thalassal regression.* The audience of the drama sees the god of fertility rushing headlong into the thalassal or uterine environment and this allays their dread of castration. It is possible to return into the uterus as a whole, castration is evaded, immortality is gained.

In certain cases the expulsion of the scapegoat merges into the ritual of carrying out or destroying death. In Spachendorf a human figure of straw and rags is carried out of the village and burnt in a ditch. Everybody tries to catch one of the burning rags and by rushing home with it and burying it in his own land to fertilize the garden or field.[1] In Haller, a boy dressed as a bridegroom receives fire from the bride and lights the " castle ".[2] In Eifel we have a straw figure burnt on Shrove Tuesday. But first he is accused of every theft that has been committed in the district, and then the verdict of guilty is pronounced. Like the other dolls of his kind he is burnt on a pyre and the youngest married woman jumps over the flames.[3] In Erlangen they throw these dolls into the river for the fertility of the year.[4] In Leipzig the prostitutes carry an image of death through all the streets, show it to the young married women and then throw it into the river.[5]

The doll in the ditch, the equivalent of the " bridegroom ", the one who has committed all the sins and fertilized the fields and women, is evidently the principle of life, the penis. Yet we find him called " death " and we find the ceremony " carrying out death ". Now this is what actually happens in every repetition of the sexual act, pain and anxiety-producing substances are expelled from the body and the result is fertility.

It has often been observed by ethnologists, though hardly explained,

[1] Vernaleken, *Mythen und Bräuche des Volkes in Oesterreich*, 1859, p. 29.
[2] Sartori, *Sitte und Brauch*, 1914, iii, p. 108.
[3] Mannhardt, *Wald und Feldkulte*, 1904, i, p. 499.
[4] Frazer, *Dying God*, p. 234.
[5] Kauffmann, *Blader*, 1902, p. 284.

that cathartic and fertility rites are frequently connected.[1] Indeed it would be difficult to mention any ritual that was not either cathartic or fertilizing and frequently we have both together. In the intichiuma ceremonies as well as in harvest or first-fruit rites, the idea of removing the taboo is always connected with that of fertility. It is the cathartic theory of coitus given by Dr Ferenczi which solves this riddle by showing how from the point of view of the Ego the life-giving act means a release of tension, i.e. catharsis.

[1] Cf. also in my book *Magyar Néphit és Népszokások*, 1920.

VI SUMMARY

IN the original cells that contained life there must have been a tendency to repeat the primal catastrophe to which life owes its existence. There was a tendency for fission and there was a resistance against the repetition of fission. In animals with more specialized functions and organs we have the ejection of gametic cells as a substitute for fission. Probably there was a phase of transition represented by a segregation of the genital organ from the body, and Ferenczi describes the genital act as an attempted self-castration which finally results in separating not the penis but the seminal fluid as its symbol or substitute from the body.[1] This is the dread of castration inherited from our remote ancestors, a complex that plays a central part both in neurosis and in the primitive forms of magic and religion. The great dread of the savage is connected with the idea of hair-cutting, nail-paring, etc., the loss of any part of the body. These parts symbolize the penis and are believed to contain the soul. At the moment of death a serpent or bird leaves the body ; the final act of life is represented as the very thing that the savage has always been afraid of. But the unconscious is at work to cover the unbearable in a more pleasing garb. As the soul, the bearer of immortality, has been developed from the germ-plasm, so the bearer of biological immortality, death, appears as a coitus, a nuptial ceremony. In cohabitation the expenditure of the semen is made bearable by the fact that it is put into another introjected organism, the seminal fluid that enters the womb.

This is the origin of the world beyond the grave. The soul enters heaven as the sperm enters the ovum, and for the same reason. The idea of the loss of the semen or of death would not be bearable without this consolation. There are certain individuals in savage society in whom this castration complex is particularly strong and who manage to get rid of it by castrating others instead of being castrated

[1] Ferenczi, *Genitaltheorie*, p. 40.

381

themselves. These are the wizards, the ancestors of savage medicine-men. It is because coitus is a sort of self-castration that the savage needs a castrator, and projects the image of the castrator into space. The black magician is the man who consents to play this part. The tension connected with coitus produces a feeling of compulsion, of being always castrated, and develops into the persecution mania of the savage, into his dread of the black art. In the magician narcissistic resistance results in projection. He will not lose the semen, he avoids woman, he prefers the fore-pleasure of tension to orgasm. This tension he maintains always on the same high level, it is materialized in his staff, it is projected into environment, it is the substratum of his magical power. Myth tells us that the magician prefers power to woman ; it would be still nearer the truth if we said that he prefers his staff, his penis, to woman. He lays stress on the impulse, not on the object. For fear of losing the genital substance he completely identifies himself with it, he becomes a penis. Naturally the penis, the castrator, is made responsible for death. Death is always due to the black art and somebody must die as a scapegoat for the whole community. Our study of love-magic pointed to the pregenital phases of libido, and in the case of the medicine-man we followed his career from the oral to the anal and genital or, we ought rather to say, to the phallic phase. He sucks disease out of the patient whom he also " eats " and cuts to pieces. But the substance he extracts is not only a symbolic equivalent of milk, it is also the anal symbol of a shining crystal and the phallic object, a serpent. The specific feature in the constitution of the magician or medicine-man, the trait that is carried over from one phase of libido-development to the other, is sadism. According to Hungarian belief, a wizard is born with a tooth, that is, he has no pre-ambivalent phase of development, and therefore probably can never have a post-ambivalent one. Like the oral organization, his anal attitude is of the destructive type and the penis appears as a magic weapon in his hand. Yet it is evident that in his own environment he has managed to attain a certain degree of social reality principle. A magician, a man who owns mana, is somebody who is in touch with reality, whose words " come true ". Identification with the father is an important factor in attaining the ego— and libido—reality,[1] and it is from a representative of the father-imago that mana is derived. This identification was oral and sadistic in its nature and it seems that the essential thing was the oral

---

[1] *Realitätsprincip, erotische Realität.*

ingestation of the penis.   When the spirits cut an Australian medicine-man into pieces they put a serpent into him, that is, the serpent was put into him when he cut the father into pieces and ate him.   This is the same serpent that gives him the right to tamper with women and the same serpent which he projects into the patient.   But the brothers eating the paternal corpse were reviving an infantile sucking period, so that their oral father-identification was also the revival of a previous mother-identification.   If they were eating the father's penis we must say that they were playing the mother's part also from a libidinal point of view, although this penis, like their pipe, was both a penis and a nipple.   The subject of this serpent, ghost, or penis in the medicine man led us on to a study of possession ; a being, be it man or woman, who has the Holy Ghost within him is pregnant or full of semen and in ejaculating words of prophecy the wizard either ejaculates semen or gives birth to a child.   Thus we see that nearly all libidinal possibilities are represented and condensed in the medicine-man.   In his relations to the supernatural world he is the defeated part in coitus, the mother, while in his dealing with the laity he is the threatening father, the protecting mother and the sucking child.   In connection with his three phases of libido development he represents three types of psycho-neurosis.   Ceremonial cannibalism is connected with maniac raving and fits of melancholiac depression.   In his professional activity, shooting the anal quartz crystal into the patient, he is under compulsions that remind us of obsessional neurosis, and his trance is a hysterical reproduction of coitus.   As the medicine-man represents all the phases of fixation and all the actors in the Oedipus drama, he is the fit lightning conductor for all the libidinal and psychic factors concerned in producing disease.   In dealing with the patient his original sadism is sublimated by identification, from the point of view of the ego, and by the fact that his cure is essentially a symbolic coitus from the point of view of the libido.   And so is disease itself.   We have two animistic disease theories.   In one case the patient is possessed by a soul, by seminal substance in the wrong place, by the father's penis.   He has been turned into a woman, castrated.   The cure is a repetition of castration, the penis is taken away, or we may also call it the expenditure of seminal fluid, the relief obtained from the discharge. The second animistic theory that the soul has left the patient corresponds to what happens to the male in coitus.   He has lost his seminal fluid, he is castrated.   Here the female attitude manifests itself in the cure ; he wants the medicine-man to put a soul, i.e. seminal fluid, into his body.   Thus we find disease always closely connected with the tendency towards, and dread of, castration. It is a reflux of the libido from the genital organ to the body and the medicine-man, the person who reverts this genitofugal into a genitopetal current, obtains relief for tension, is a symbol of the penis. Just as the genital act summarizes, condenses all pre-genital organizations, the medicine-man with his numerous pre-genital fixations is still from the patient's point of view a second super-organic and supernatural penis.

With some hesitation we have also suggested that the whole coitus-symbolism of death is merely a device of the unconscious, a genitalization of the death-impulse. Now the medicine-man begins his career by dying and continues to be fatally addicted to patients and corpses. Moreover, Freud has shown that the same feature which plays such an important part in the make-up of the medicine-man, the attitude we call sadism, is derived from the death-impulse. We therefore suggested the possibility that all this life-giving coitus activity of the medicine-man is merely a genitalization of his own death-impulse and his healing an effort of the libido to counteract a more than usually strong tendency to die. It is evident that the same theory applies to disease equally well. For who can doubt that disease is an inroad made by death into life? It is a defence mechanism of the unconscious to make it appear as if it were life itself.

The successive chapters of these lectures represent the same fundamental attitude on an ever-extending scale. First, in magic and animism we had the individual, in the medical art a group formed of patient and healer, and lastly in royalty we have society itself. This growth from the organic to the super-organic is clearly demonstrated by the fact that primitive societies are governed by medicine-men, therefore the forces at work in group-formation must be the same libidinal attitudes we have discovered in discussing disease and healing. In the case of the Divine King, phallic symbolism is still more prominent than with his predecessor the medicine-man. He has left the traces of pre-genital organizations behind; in becoming a king he appears completely as a phallus, the lightning conductor, or scapegoat of society. Sovereignty is a woman and the man who attains to it is Sir Gawaine, the maiden's knight. In the life of the individual the object-love of puberty is a revival of the infantile Oedipus situation, in the evolution of humanity the phase represented by royalty is a revival of the Primal Horde. The king is the man who commits incest and is killed, but as he is also the penis he shows that his predecessor, the Jealous Sire of the Primal Horde, must also have been the phallus of the group. From this point of view the Primal Horde appears as a super-organic attempt to imitate the process of specialization that led to the development of the gametic cells, and this process itself may perhaps have been a centralization of libidinal substances. A succession of genitopetal and genitofugal currents of the libido is the history and tragedy of humanity. The first genitopetal phase is represented by the Primal Horde, but it is followed by a society on a democratic or at least gerontocratic basis, that is, a social body without phallic centralization. Again, the genitopetal current is at work till a revival of the original organization, a society with one penis, is the result.

It must be understood quite clearly, however, that in calling such a society genital or phallic we are far from implying that the individuals who lived under the rule of Divine Kings in Sumer or Egypt had attained anything like the genital phase of character development. That such a tendency is at work in the origins of civilization and that the love for the Mother City is based on a real sublimation of incestuous trends in the individual cannot be denied. But even in the relation of the king, the phallic element in this social organization, to the other sex we see the non-attainment of erotic reality, of object love. The king is the spouse of Ishtar, the mother-imago—he marries his sister and has intercourse with numerous wives and concubines. How closely the castration phobia follows this unlimited type of wish-fulfilment we have seen in discussing the taboos of royalty. The king is a person who has numerous " mothers " but may never see his real mother,[1] the father of the whole people who never sees his sons except on his death-bed.[2] It is the problem of the father that is dealt with in a quite inadequate manner by setting up a dummy in the person of the king. We might indeed rather regard this society as organized on the basis of a castration phobia and its dramatization, although this castration phobia is at least a genital and not a displaced, i.e. an anal, castration.[3] It is instead of developing a genital character themselves that these forerunners of our civilization project the Phallic Ruler into space. The genital type of society is evolved at the expense of genitality, in individual character formation. By a genital character, we mean a free output of both the aggressive and the libidinal trends, a certain ease in bearing the limits imposed on these strivings by the interests and desires of our fellow-beings. A genitofugal trend in the social

[1] Cf., for instance, J. Roscoe, *The Bakitara or Banyaro*, 1923, p. 118.
[2] J. Roscoe, *The Banyankole*, 1923, p. 51.
[3] Cf. *Psycho-analysis and Social Anthropology*, the chapter on " Racial Psychology and Evolution ".

organization means and is conditioned by a genitopetal trend in the individual, therefore in democratic Athens the Holy Monarch dwindles to a mere survival and instead of the tyrant-ridden subject of the East we have the free citizen of the Demos. But Liberty has always been more a fiction than a reality, and the history of mankind appears to be a series of hardly successful attempts to attain genital primacy.

INDEX